Applied Financial Accounting and Reporting

Applied Financial Accounting and Reporting

GEOFF BLACK

UNIVERSITY PRESS

OXFORD
UNIVERSITY PRESS

Great Clarendon Street, Oxford OX2 6DP

Oxford University Press is a department of the University of Oxford.
It furthers the University's objective of excellence in research, scholarship,
and education by publishing worldwide in

Oxford New York

Auckland Bangkok Buenos Aires Cape Town Chennai
Dar es Salaam Delhi Hong Kong Istanbul Karachi Kolkata
Kuala Lumpur Madrid Melbourne Mexico City Mumbai Nairobi
São Paulo Shanghai Taipei Tokyo Toronto

Oxford is a registered trade mark of Oxford University Press
in the UK and in certain other countries

Published in the United States
by Oxford University Press Inc., New York

British Library Cataloguing in Publication Data
Data available

Library of Congress Cataloging in Publication Data
Data available

ISBN 0-19-926471-6

1 3 5 7 9 10 8 6 4 2

Typeset by Newgen Imaging Systems (P) Ltd., Chennai, India
Printed in Great Britain
on acid free paper by
Ashford Color Press Limited, Gosport, Hampshire

■ PREFACE

In calling this book '*Applied* Financial Accounting and Reporting', my aim is to show how often extremely complex rules and regulations have practical impact on the way businesses, large or small, present their financial results. In many ways, there could not have been a better time to write such a book. Major financial scandals in recent years have led to a severe loss of trust in corporate governance and the auditing and accounting professions, but those charged with creating a strong and reliable regulatory framework have made great efforts to restore confidence. Moves towards an internationally accepted raft of standards have gained pace, and specific countries, notably the USA, have introduced tough new laws to curb financial abuse.

I have used extracts from many companies' actual reported results (see Acknowledgements) as illustration. I have also referred to one specific company, Domino's Pizza (UK & IRL) plc, throughout the book so that readers can look at *all* aspects of an actual company's reported results—including some areas such as pensions, stock options, share buy-backs, and joint ventures, which tend to be omitted from many texts, despite being of growing importance and relevance.

Each chapter commences with a statement of objectives, and, after the core content, there is a brief chapter summary (reproduced at the end of the book as a revision aid), a glossary of terms found within the chapter, and many different questions and case studies (over twenty per chapter). A running case study charts the progress of a fictional company, MinnieMax Ltd. Most questions are answered within the book, others have suggested answers or discussion areas available on the companion website. Finally, a list of web references is given, and also further reading suggestions for those who want other interpretations of a specific topic. The companion website gives a range of useful additional materials for lecturers and students.

I am always interested in getting feedback from students and lecturers, whether they like the book, dislike it, find errors in it, or simply want to give suggestions for improving it.

G.B.

■ ACKNOWLEDGEMENTS

I am especially grateful to Andrew Mallows of Domino's Pizza (UK & IRL) plc for allowing me not only to reproduce that company's annual report, but also to use selective extracts from it for illustration throughout the book. I would also like to thank Tim Page of Oxford University Press for his constant enthusiasm and encouragement during the writing period, and those (anonymous) university lecturers who reviewed the manuscript and made many constructive suggestions for its improvement.

In addition, I am indebted to the following companies and organizations for material reproduced to illustrate specific aspects of company reporting, or to use as case study materials:

The Accounting Standards Board
Alvis plc
Avon Rubber plc
British Airways plc
Brixton plc
H.P. Bulmer Holdings plc
Hugo Boss AG
Carpetright plc
Constellation Corporation plc
Courts plc
Daily Telegraph
Financial Times
Heart of Midlothian plc
Kingfisher plc
Majestic Wine plc
Manchester United plc
Marconi plc
Northern Foods plc
H. R. Owen plc
Pace Micro Technology plc
Pendragon plc
Pizza Express plc
Renishaw plc
The Roche Group
Scapa Group plc
Scoot.com plc
Severn Valley Railway (Holdings) plc
Somerfield plc
Tate & Lyle plc
Tesco plc

■ CONTENTS

LIST OF FIGURES

■ LIST OF TABLES

1

Principles and practices

OBJECTIVES

By the end of this chapter you will be able to:

- Understand what is meant by 'financial accounting'.
- Contrast financial accounting with management accounting.
- Identify the 'user groups' of accounting information.
- Understand the underlying principles and concepts of financial accounting.
- Appreciate the role of standard setting in a national and international context.
- Consider the application of principles and policies to published annual reports.

1.1 Introduction

It is rare for accountancy to be worldwide news, talked about nightly on TV discussion shows and written about by editors of both serious and tabloid newspapers. Accountancy and scandal are words which are rarely seen in the same sentence—but in recent years, journalists throughout the world have been writing articles on what they perceived to be a meltdown in accounting procedures and reliability. The collapse of a major US energy supply group, Enron Corporation, was blamed on dubious accounting rules, whilst in the UK many employees were finding that their pension benefits were being downgraded by companies citing as justification a new 'accounting standard'. In the courts, previously well-respected company directors were being charged with 'false accounting', and governments of several countries decided to order inquiries into the role of the accountancy profession. New accounting rules in the USA were cited as being responsible for the writing off of $60bn of assets by two telecoms groups, whilst the body responsible for devising global accounting rules was itself accused of being part funded by the same companies it was trying to regulate.

Accountants would claim that their role is not to portray a financial picture which is unique in its perfection, honesty, and reliability. What they do attempt is to present often highly complex data that can be relied upon as a reasonably truthful and fair summary of financial events. There has, historically, been considerable scope for different interpretation of similar transactions according to the discretion of company directors. Over time, various restraints have been imposed and sanctions applied to try and ensure uniformity of treatment, a process which is continuing and evolving.

In calling this book *Applied Financial Accounting and Reporting*, the intention is to link theory with practice and give readers the opportunity to consider how specific accounting procedures relate to actual companies, and to consider the legal and professional restraints imposed on corporate reporting. For this purpose, the annual report of Domino's Pizza UK & IRL plc, a pizza delivery company listed on the London Stock Market, is reproduced on pp. 307–45, and many topics referred to within chapters are linked to that company's financial statements. If you want your own copy of the Domino's Pizza annual report, go to **www.dominos. co.uk**, click on 'The Business' then 'Investor relations'. You will be able to download it in a 'read-only' format.

You will see the 🔍 symbol to prompt you to look at a particular section of the report. Domino's Pizza has been chosen for a number of reasons, including:

- it is a well-known high street brand;
- it is an expanding and profitable company (sales and profit more than doubling in four years);
- it publishes a clearly set-out annual report complying with best practice;
- it is not a complex multinational with highly intricate and specialized financial aspects which may confuse rather than enlighten.

As well as Domino's Pizza plc, extracts from many other companies will be used to show the variety of ways in which information might be presented. Look for the symbol 🔍 These companies are listed in the Acknowledgements on p. vi.

There is a significant degree of change happening regarding the scope, quality, and content of accountancy's procedures, rules, and regulations (known as GAAP—Generally Accepted Accounting Principles, or 'regulatory framework'). In particular, a move from national to international rules, a process which has been gaining pace for several years, is accelerating. This means that countries which previously set their own rules for financial reporting are rapidly harmonizing them with their international equivalents. However, new legislation—national and international—is regularly introduced or updated, with new standards issued or old ones rewritten. This book is based on the regulations existing in mid-2003.

1.2 The background to accounting

1.2.1 What is accounting?

There have been numerous attempts to develop an all-embracing definition of accounting. One which is often quoted was published by the American Accounting Association in 1966:

[Accounting is] The process of identifying, measuring and communicating economic information about an organisation or other entity, in order to permit informed judgements by users of the information.

The key aspects of accounting are, it suggests, *identifying, measuring, and communicating*:

- *identifying* the key financial components of an organization, such as assets, liabilities, capital, income, expenses, and cash flow;
- *measuring* the monetary values of the key financial components in a way which represents a true and fair view of the organization;
- *communicating* the financial information in a way that is useful to the users of that information.

The systematic recording of financial data is universally based on *double-entry bookkeeping principles* (see pp. 25–38), which have been in use by businesses for many centuries. However, there is no global agreement regarding the way in which accounting information should be summarized and communicated. Analysis and appraisal can be distorted by national differences in accounting procedures and there is a growing movement to harmonize the accounting treatment for specific areas of difficulty. Regulatory frameworks have been developed within national and international contexts to help ensure commonality of approach, and large organizations are expected or required to observe accounting standards. These standards impose common procedures for coping with specific accounting difficulties with the aim of avoiding inconsistencies between companies and encouraging the improvement of the quality and usefulness of accounting statements.

1.2.2 Branches of accounting

Accounting is split into two key areas:

1. *Financial accounting*, which is that part of accounting which records and summarizes financial transactions to satisfy the information needs of the various 'user groups' such as investors, lenders, creditors, and employees. It is sometimes referred to as meeting the *external* accounting needs of the organization.

2. *Management accounting*, which is sometimes referred to as meeting the *internal* accounting needs of the organization. It is designed to help managers with decision making, planning, and control. As such it often involves estimates and forecasts, and is not subject to the same regulatory framework as financial accounting. A leading professional body, the Chartered Institute of Management Accountants (CIMA), has defined management accounting as:

An integral part of management concerned with identifying, presenting and interpreting information used for:

- formulating strategy
- planning and controlling activities
- decision taking
- optimising the use of resources
- disclosure to shareholders and others external to the entity
- disclosure to employees
- safeguarding assets

The above involves participation in management to ensure that there is effective:

- formulation of plans to meet objectives: (strategic planning)
- formulation of short term operation plans: (budget/profit planning)
- acquisition and use of finance (financial management) and recording of transactions (financial accounting and cost accounting)
- communication of financial and operational information
- corrective action to bring plans and results into line (financial control)
- reviewing and reporting on systems and operations (internal audit, management audit).[1]

The CIMA definition is deliberately all embracing, and there are some obvious infringements on what financial accountants might see as their 'territory'. It reinforces the notion that there are overlaps between financial and management accounting, particularly in the recording, interpreting, and communicating aspects. However, if you look at most (if not all) textbooks devoted to management accounting, there are unlikely to be any references to 'disclosure to shareholders and others external to the entity', and in practice this is usually seen as a financial accounting function.

1.3 A statement of principles

In the United Kingdom, an Accounting Standards Board (ASB) was set up in 1990 with the aim of improving standards of financial accounting and reporting. In 1999 the ASB produced a statement of principles[2] which sets out certain fundamental principles for the preparation and presentation of financial statements. The Statement of Principles also identifies the following seven groups of users of financial information, together with the information which they need from the financial statements:

User group	Information needs
Investors	Investors need to assess the financial performance of the organization they have invested in to consider the risk inherent in, and return provided by, their investments. For example, they would want to know if the company made a profit and what part of that profit was being paid to shareholders as a dividend. Other areas of interest would be to find out if the company had more assets than liabilities, and if its cash inflow was greater than its outflow. 'Earnings per share' is a key indicator of performance. For example, see Domino's Pizza's earnings per share shown at the foot of the group profit and loss account on p. 320.
Lenders	Lenders need to be aware of the ability of the organization to repay loans and interest. Potential lenders need to decide whether to lend, and on what terms. For example, to what extent is the company's profit before interest payments greater than those interest payments?
Suppliers and other trade creditors	Suppliers need to take commercial decisions as to whether or not they should sell to the organization and, if they do, whether they will be paid. They will be interested in such aspects as how well the company is funded and how quickly it pays its creditors' bills. For example, see Domino's Pizza's creditor payment policy on p. 317.

(Continued)

---

[1] *Management Accounting: Official Terminology* (CIMA, London, 2000).
[2] Accounting Standards Board, *Statement of Principles for Financial Reporting* (London, 1999).

Employees	People will be interested in their employer's stability and profitability, in particular that part of the organization (such as a branch) in which they work. They will also be interested in the ability of their employer to pay their wages and pensions.
Customers	Customers who are dependent on a particular supplier or are considering placing a long-term contract will need to know if the organization is likely to continue in business for the foreseeable future. Do the directors consider that the company is a 'going concern'? For example, see Domino's Pizza's director's report on p. 317—the fourth bullet point under the heading 'Corporate Governance'.
Government and their agencies	Reliable financial data helps governments to assemble national economic statistics which are used for a variety of purposes in controlling the economy. Specific financial information from an organization also enables tax to be assessed.
The public	Financial statements often include information relevant to local communities and pressure groups such as attitudes to environmental matters, plans to expand or shut down factories, policies on employment of disabled persons, etc. For example, see Domino's Pizza's policy on the employment of disabled people on p. 318.

We could also add an eighth group—*the management of the organization*—as they are the 'stewards' of the business and need to have reliable financial information on which to base their decisions.

1.3.1 Concepts, principles, and policies

As well as identifying the user groups, the Statement of Principles sets out the concepts that underlie the preparation of financial statements for external users. The Statement will be referred to several times within this text as it contains important guidance on such matters as definitions of key elements found within financial statements and how they should be recognized, measured, and presented. Overall, the Statement contains eight chapters, but the first three are worthy of consideration at this early stage.

The objective of financial statements (chapter 1)

The objective of financial statements is to provide information about the financial performance and financial position of an enterprise that is useful to a wide range of users for assessing the stewardship of management and for making economic decisions. That objective can usually be met by focusing exclusively on the information needs of present and potential investors, the defining class of user.

Present and potential investors need information about financial performance and position that is useful to them in evaluating the entity's ability to generate cash (including the timing and certainty of generation) and in assessing the entity's financial adaptability.

The reporting entity (chapter 2)

This sets out the conditions that determine the principle whether companies should prepare general purpose financial statements, both as individual companies or within groups of companies. It also focuses on situations where one business 'controls' another or where there is a significant investment in another company but not 'control'. This is considered in more detail on pp. 231–45. In essence, a business should prepare and publish financial statements if there is a legitimate demand for the information that its financial statements would provide.

The qualitative characteristics of financial information (chapter 3)

For financial information to have value, it must first be *material*. It is material if its misstatement or omission might reasonably be expected to influence the economic decisions of users. Materiality is considered a 'threshold quality', i.e. without it the information is insignificant. Assuming that the information *is* material, it must have:

- Content which is *relevant*. It is relevant if it has the ability to influence the economic decisions of users and is provided in time to influence those decisions.
- Content which is *reliable*. It is reliable if it can be depended upon by users to represent faithfully what it either purports to represent or could reasonably be expected to represent and therefore reflects the substance of transactions and other events that have taken place; it is free from deliberate or systematic bias and material error and is complete; and if prepared under conditions of uncertainty, a degree of caution has been applied in exercising the necessary judgements.
- *Comparability*. It has comparability if users can discern and evaluate similarities or differences over time and between different companies.
- *Understandability*. It has understandability if its significance can be perceived by users who have a reasonable knowledge of business and economic activities and accounting and a willingness to study with reasonable diligence the information provided.

The Statement contains a diagrammatic representation of its chapter 3, which is shown in Figure 1.1.

1.3.2 Accounting policies

Accounting policies determine *which* facts about a business are to be presented in the financial statements, and *how* those facts are to be presented. Policies should be adopted that enable a business's financial statements to show a *true and fair view*. Indeed, one of the responsibilities of a company's auditors is to report on whether the financial statements give a true and fair view.

Look at Domino's Pizza's audit report (p. 319). What does the 'Opinion' say about the report's truth and fairness?

A UK accounting standard, FRS 18, was published in December 2000 which requires businesses to adopt accounting policies which are 'most appropriate' to their particular circumstances for giving a true and fair view. The policies must be reviewed regularly and changed if others are more appropriate. Sufficient information must be disclosed in financial statements to enable users to understand the policies adopted and how they have been implemented.

Two concepts, *going concern* and *accruals*, are considered to have a pervasive role in selecting policies. Both are referred to in the UK's 1985 Companies Act as 'fundamental principles'.

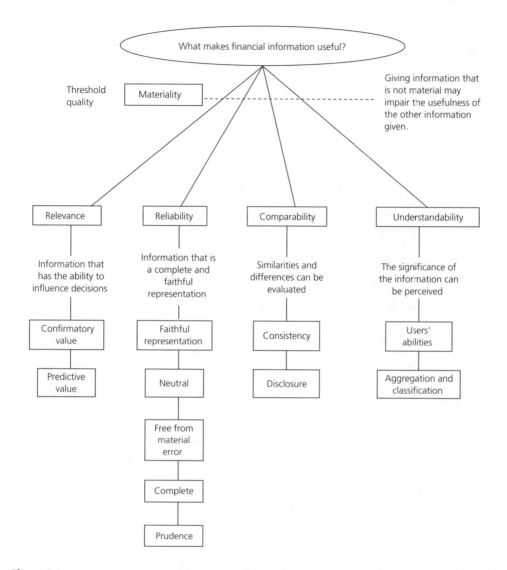

Figure 1.1 The qualitative characteristics of financial information

Source: Reproduced by kind permission of the Accounting Standards Board.

Going concern concept

Financial statements are drawn up on the basis that the business can continue in operational existence for the foreseeable future. In other words, the business is assumed to be a 'going concern' (i.e. it can 'keep going') unless there is information to the contrary. This is extremely important, as investors, lenders, and suppliers may otherwise consider the company a suitable business to invest in, to lend money to, or provide goods and services to. If the business is *not* a going concern, the value of its assets (e.g. commercial premises, machinery, and stock) may need to be revalued to a much lower level than if the business was a viable, healthy organization.

> Look at Domino's Pizza's 'Corporate Governance' Statement (p. 317). Has the 'going concern concept' been adopted?

Look at the following extract from the annual report of Scoot.com plc:

Going concern

Scoot.com plc is in the development stage of its business and its strategy to develop a branded infomediary service. In the 15 month period to 31 December 2000, the Group incurred operating losses before exceptional items and goodwill amortisation of £37.5m (1999: £16.4m loss); the net cash outflow from operating activities was £37.3m (1999: £15.6m outflow).

In order to trade profitably with positive cash flow from operations, the Group must continue to identify new subscribers to achieve the critical mass customer base necessary to generate sales levels that meet its operating costs. The directors are pleased with the progress that has been made in developing a profitable business. To achieve this fully, the Group intends to increase the focus on operating efficiencies and raise additional lines of finance where necessary.

The directors have prepared detailed forecasts for at least a year from the date of this statement that reflect their plans, including aggressive marketing campaigns, close management of individual businesses and benefits expected from the continued integration of Loot in the UK. They expect Scoot (UK) to become cash flow positive in the fourth quarter of 2001 and they expect the current operations of the Group as a whole, including its Benelux and France joint ventures, to become cash flow positive in the fourth quarter of 2002. In the meantime, Scoot's continuation as a going concern is dependent upon its ability to generate sufficient cash flows from other sources to meet its obligations as they fall due in the foreseeable future.

As the Group's businesses continue to develop rapidly, this makes their future cash flows more difficult to predict than that of a more mature business. As a result, the directors will need to raise funds of potentially up to £20m from non-operating sources. To this end, an additional facility has already been secured in the form of an equity line of credit (the facility enables the directors to issue up to 60m ordinary shares). This facility is subject to shareholder approval. If required, the directors intend to draw upon this facility at key points during the implementation of the Group's plan . . . The directors have a range of other funding options under consideration including the disposal of non-core assets and additional debt or equity fundraising from either existing or new investors, The directors expect that the final funding arrangements will comprise a combination of these alternative sources.

On the basis of the combination of potential fund raising options above, the directors are confident that they can secure adequate resources to fund the development of the business. Accordingly, they consider that it is appropriate to prepare these financial statements on a going concern basis, therefore no adjustments that would otherwise be required have been made.

Comment

Unlike Domino's Pizza, this loss-making company has had to justify in considerable detail its use of the going concern. Note particularly the last sentence, 'therefore no adjustments that would otherwise be required have been made'. This refers to the fact that if the going concern concept was *not* applicable, various values contained within the financial statements would have to be reassessed, particularly those of assets such as cars, computers, equipment, and stocks. If the business were to fail, the amounts realized on such assets would often be a tiny fraction of their 'going concern' valuation.

Accruals concept

With the exception of cash flow information (see pp. 207–19), financial statements should be prepared on the *accrual basis* of accounting. This requires the non-cash effects of transactions and other events to be reflected, as far as possible, in the financial statements for the accounting period in which they occur, and not, for example, in the period in which any cash involved is received or paid. Revenue and profits dealt with when calculating profits or losses are matched with associated costs incurred in earning them, so when calculating profit, *all* income and expenditure, whether or not 'paid for', must be included. The accruals concept is sometimes referred to as the 'matching' concept.

In basic terms, the concept means that if you are told that a company made a profit of £10m in the year ended 31 December 2004, this has not been calculated by simply adding all the cash received in the year, and then deducting the cash paid! *Every* relevant transaction, regardless of whether cash is paid or received in the period, must be included when arriving at the profit figure. Numerical examples of this are shown in Chapter 3.

 Look at n. 15 on p. 334 of Domino's Pizza's annual report. Identify 'Accruals and deferred income'. This represents unpaid, not yet invoiced liabilities.

1.4 **Published accounts**

Large corporations will publish financial information, usually as a requirement of a specific stock exchange or due to national legislation. For example, in the UK, Acts of Parliament require that *all* of the approximately one million limited companies must publish financial statements. Although there is no equivalent in the USA of the UK's Companies Acts, major US companies will be registered with the Securities and Exchange Commission (SEC), which sets out detailed requirements for audit and the rules of financial reporting. For smaller UK companies, only a brief summary of their finances is required, but for the largest companies, including all plc's (public limited companies), an 'annual report' must be prepared which is sent (either physically or electronically) to all shareholders and Companies House, which is the UK government's 'storehouse' of company information. The public has a right of access to the information, for example by using the website **www.companieshouse.gov.uk**. UK companies whose shares are listed on the stock exchange will also publish an abbreviated interim statement showing their results for the first six months of the financial period. To save printing and distribution costs, companies are permitted to provide an electronic version on their website.

Many organizations regard their annual report as an opportunity to show off the best of their company, in effect treating it as a public relations exercise. The glossy photographs of the company's products and exotic locations of major contracts can give some reports the style of a travel brochure.

A key feature of UK and other EU published profit and loss accounts and balance sheets is that they have to follow specific *formats of presentation*. These formats were devised to ensure a degree of uniformity across the European Community, as they apply to all member countries. Although there is a small amount of flexibility allowed (for example a company can produce statements in either a 'vertical' or 'horizontal' format), virtually all UK companies follow the 'vertical' style format.

> Look at pp. 320–3 of the Domino's Pizza annual report. Notice how the information flows from top to bottom on each page—hence the 'vertical' format. It is sometimes also referred to as a 'columnar' format.

> Many large mainland European companies not only produce corporate reports in their 'home' language but also produce English-language versions for wider circulation. An example can be found at **www.bmw.com** (follow links to 'Investor Relations' and then click on 'Annual Report').

1.5 Diversity of international accounting practice

The method of recording day-to-day financial transactions is common throughout the world, being based on the double-entry system (see pp. 25–39). However, there are significant differences in approach when summarizing information for inclusion in published annual reports. In many countries, the accounting profession has been relatively weak, and financial reporting practices have tended to be set by formal government legislation rather than by relatively informal professional rules. A number of distinct country groupings have evolved in this respect, the principal ones being:

- United States and United Kingdom and countries historically influenced by them, e.g. Commonwealth countries such as Australia, India, and Malaysia;
- Mainland European countries, such as France and Germany—though Holland has tended towards the US/UK approach.

The reasons for the disparity of accounting procedures include:

- the relative strength of the accounting profession in the countries,
- the nature of the country's legal system,
- the main types of business organization, and
- the relationship between taxation requirements and financial reporting requirements.

The key industrialized nations have developed their own specific accounting regulations. This rarely has a major impact when applied to domestic companies within those countries, but may have dramatic implications when international investment decisions have to be made. See p. 12 for details of how accounting standards within the EU for listed companies are changing from 2005.

There are many reasons why countries developed dissimilar procedures, including:

The legal system

Some countries (e.g. France and Germany) have all-embracing sets of rules and regulations which apply to businesses, whereas countries such as the UK and the USA have more general statute laws backed up by case law, allowing more flexibility for individual companies. For example, in the USA, individual companies decide the rates at which assets depreciate, but in Germany the government decides what rates are appropriate.

Types of ownership patterns

Countries with wide share ownership (e.g. UK, USA) have developed strong independent professional accountancy associations to provide reliable financial data to shareholders. Those countries with predominantly small, family-run businesses (e.g. France) or with banks owning most shares of large companies (e.g. Germany), have had less need for providers of independent financial information.

The accounting profession

Strong independent professional associations of accountants developed in those countries (e.g. UK, USA) with the most liberal company laws and widest share ownership. Countries with restricted patterns of business ownership and rigid company legislation (e.g. France, Germany) had weak groupings of accountants, and sometimes the governments themselves controlled the profession.

Conservatism

Financial statements produced by independent accountants should ideally show a 'true and fair view'. This is open to many interpretations, not least being the problem of asset valuation. Should assets be valued at original cost, what they might be sold at today, what it would cost to replace them, or a depreciated value based on usage, wear and tear, etc.?

- US practice is conservative—don't revalue, depreciate on a reasonable basis over the asset's lifetime.
- German practice is also conservative—don't revalue, but depreciate on a basis decreed by the government.
- UK practice is liberal—allowing companies either to revalue at intervals or show assets at cost, and depreciate on a reasonable basis.

1.5.1 International accounting standards

In 1973, an International Accounting Standards Committee (IASC) was formed with the aim of harmonizing accounting practices throughout the world. Now renamed as the International Accounting Standards Committee Foundation (IASCF), its objectives are:

- to develop, in the public interest, a single set of high-quality, understandable, and enforceable global accounting standards that require high-quality, transparent, and comparable information in financial statements and other financial reporting to help participants in the world's capital markets and other users make economic decisions;
- to promote the use and rigorous application of those standards; and

- to bring about convergence of national accounting standards and International Accounting Standards[3] to high-quality solutions.

Since April 2001, the standards-setting work has been undertaken by a subsidiary of the IASCF, the International Accounting Standards Board (IASB). The IASB's responsibilities include:

- responsibility for all IASCF technical matters including the preparation and issuing of International Accounting Standards;

- publishing an 'Exposure Draft' (a preliminary version of the proposals, made available for public debate and feedback) on all projects and it normally will publish a Draft Statement of Principles or other discussion document for public comment on major projects;

- full discretion over the technical agenda of the IASCF and over project assignments on technical matters; in organizing the conduct of its work, the Board may outsource detailed research or other work to national standard setters or other organizations;

- working to identify and review all the issues related to a topic and the study of other national accounting standards and practice;

- the possible holding of public hearings to discuss proposed standards, although there is no requirement to hold public hearings for every project;

- undertaking field tests (both in developed countries and in emerging markets) to ensure that proposed standards are practical and workable in all environments, although there is no requirement to undertake field tests for every project.

The status of International Accounting Standards (IASs) was given a significant boost in 2001 when the European Commission proposed that from 2005 listed companies through-out the EU should be obliged to follow IASs rather than national standards. The other key driver in their growing acceptance may follow the accounting scandals in the USA (principally related to Enron and World Com), where the perception of weak US standards may lead to a much greater role for their international equivalent. In the UK, all new standards contain an explanation of the extent to which they are in accordance with IASs. In most respects they are closely aligned, but occasionally there are significant differences due to perceived 'national' requirements. One example is the area of *deferred taxation* (see pp. 109–10), where a UK standard issued in 2000 has key differences from the IAS, also issued in that year. As the ex-chairman of the UK Accounting Standards Board, Sir David Tweedie, was subsequently appointed chairman of the IASB, it would not be unexpected if the international standards develop in line with the UK's position rather than vice versa.

1.6 **Chapter summary**

- Accounting is defined as 'The process of identifying, measuring and communicating economic information about an organisation or other entity, in order to permit informed judgements by users of the information'.

[3] Standards 'inherited' from the old IASC. New standards will in fact be referred to as International Financial Reporting Standards (IFRSs).

- There are two main branches: financial accounting and management accounting. Financial accounting concentrates more on the recording and summarizing of financial information and compliance with GAAP and relevant legislation. Management accounting tends to concentrate on decision making, planning, and control.

- There is a 'Statement of Principles' for the preparation and presentation of financial statements.

- There are seven user groups defined in the Statement: investors; lenders; suppliers and other trade creditors; employees; customers; government and their agencies; the public.

- Qualitative characteristics of financial information are that it should be: material; relevant; reliable; comparable; understandable.

- Policies are needed which enable a true and fair view to be shown.

- Going concern and accruals concepts have a 'pervasive role' in selecting policies.

- Published accounts in the EU must follow defined formats.

- International accounting practices vary but there is great impetus towards harmonization.

- US accounting scandals have boosted the influence of international standards.

■ GLOSSARY

accounting	The process of identifying, measuring, and communicating economic information about an organization or other entity, in order to permit informed judgements by users of the information
accounting policies	Principles, bases, conventions, rules, and practices applied by an entity that specify how the effects of transactions and other events are to be reflected in its financial statements through recognizing, selecting measurement bases for, and presenting assets, l abilities, gains, losses, and changes to shareholders' funds
accounting standards	Rules to be followed by accountants when preparing financial information
Accounting Standards Board	The body which sets accounting standards within the UK
accrual concept	The non-cash effects of transactions and other events should be reflected, as far as possible, in the financial statements for the accounting period in which they occur, and not, for example, in the period in which any cash involved is received or paid
double-entry bookkeeping	A logical system which allows a record to be made of all the financial aspects of an entity
exposure draft	A preliminary version of an accounting standard, circulated for public debate and comment

financial accounting	The day-to-day recording of an organization's financial transactions and the summarizing of those transactions to satisfy the information needs of various user groups in accordance with the regulatory framework
formats	Standard layouts required by the European Union which ensure consistency of presentation of published financial information by companies in member states
going concern concept	Financial statements are drawn up on the basis that the business can continue in operational existence for the foreseeable future
International Accounting Standards	Accounting standards developed by the International Accounting Standards Board and its predecessor to harmonize and improve global financial reporting practices
management accounting	The internal accounting needs of an organization, involving planning, forecasting, and budgeting for decision-making purposes
materiality	A 'threshold quality' of financial information. To be material, its misstatement or omission might reasonably be expected to influence the economic decisions of users
published accounts	Financial information required to be disclosed by entities as a result of legislation, accounting standards, or stock exchange requirements
regulatory framework	The rules and regulations followed by financial accountants, imposed (in the UK) mainly by company legislation and the Accounting Standards Board
true and fair view	An accounting concept requiring financial summaries to reflect a reasonable and objective approach in their representation of the organization's affairs
user groups	Key groups who have a need for financial information

■ MULTIPLE CHOICE QUESTIONS

1. Financial data is recorded by means of a system known as:
    a   Management accounting
    b   Auditing
    c   Double-entry bookkeeping
    d   Generally Accepted Accounting Principles

2. Which one of the following is not specifically identified as a 'user group' by the UK's 'Statement of Principles':
    a   Management
    b   Customers
    c   Lenders
    d   Investors

3. Which of the following is a key indicator of performance for investors?

    a Number of shares issued by a company
    b Number of directors
    c Ratio of customers to suppliers
    d Earnings per share

4. According to the 'Statement of Principles', for financial information to have value it must first be:

    a Material
    b Relevant
    c Reliable
    d Comparable

5. Once an accounting policy is adopted by a company, it:

    a Must never be changed
    b Must be changed on an annual basis
    c Can be changed if another policy is more appropriate
    d Can only be changed with the government's approval

6. If a company is said to be a 'going concern', which one of the following statements is certain about that company?

    a It is about to go out of business
    b It is assumed to be able to continue in business for the foreseeable future
    c It is a company that people are concerned about
    d It is profitable and has more assets than liabilities

7. The 'accruals' concept means that, when calculating a company's profit or loss:

    a All relevant transactions, whether or not cash transfers are involved, are included
    b Any money owed by customers at the end of the period is ignored
    c Any invoices received but not paid in the period are ignored
    d Only cash paid and received in a period is included

8. The summary of company information which large UK companies have to send to Companies House is called the:

    a Profit sheet
    b Annual report
    c Cash summary
    d Tax return

9. 'Formats' are followed by EU companies when presenting published company financial information. The most common format used in the UK is the:

    a Vertical format
    b Horizontal format
    c Circular format
    d Diagonal format

10. 'Harmonization' of international accounting practice refers to:

    a International accounting standards being replaced by national standards
    b US standards being replaced by European standards

    c Non-US standards being replaced by US standards

    d National accounting standards being brought into line with international standards

(Note: answers are shown in Appendix 2.)

■ DISCUSSION QUESTIONS

To answer these, you should refer to the Domino's Pizza annual report on pp. 307–45.

1. Read the auditors' report (see p. 319) and comment on the extent to which you regard it as an objective opinion of the company's financial statements.

2. Look at the Chairman's report (see p. 307). See if you can identify any areas which give an indication as to the *future* strengths or weaknesses of the company.

3. Contrast the 'profit for the financial year' as shown in the profit and loss account (see p. 320) with the 'increase or decrease in cash' as shown in the cash flow statement (see p. 323). Are they the same? Can you think of reasons why they might be different?

(Note: Suggested answers or discussion points are available on the companion website.)

■ LONGER QUESTIONS

(Questions marked W have suggested answers on the companion website. Other questions are answered in Appendix 3.)

1. Look at the 'cash flow statement' of Manchester United plc for 2002 (with comparative figures given for 2001) shown in Fig. 1.2, then answer the questions below.

    a How did the overall cash flow differ between 2001 and 2002?

    b Which year saw more cash spent on the purchase of footballers?

    c Can you think why taxation paid in 2002 was greater than in 2001, even though the 'net cash inflow from operating activities' shown on the top line shows more in 2001 than in 2002?

2. Sandygate plc has summarized its key financial information for the past year, as follows:

	£
Total sales made in the year	560,000
Total cash received in the year from customers	490,000
Total expenses and goods bought for resale	160,000
Total cash paid in the year for expenses and goods bought for resale	170,000

    a What was the total profit which Sandygate plc made during the year?

    b How can the 'cash paid in the year for expenses and goods bought for resale' be greater than the 'total expenses and goods bought for resale'?

Consolidated cash flow statement
For the year ended 31 July 2002

		2002		2001
	£'000	£'000	£'000	£'000
Net cash inflow from operating activities		**42,807**		50,882
Returns on investments and servicing of finance				
Interest received	**521**		692	
Interest paid	**(445)**		**(146)**	
Net cash inflow from returns on investments and servicing of finance		**76**		546
Taxation paid		**(9,433)**		(7,377)
Capital expenditure and financial investment				
Proceeds from sale of players' registrations	**13,006**		4,194	
Purchase of players' registrations	**(25,089)**		(47,504)	
Proceeds from sale of tangible fixed assets	**1,165**		1,430	
Purchase of tangible fixed assets	**(15,088)**		(9,232)	
Net cash outflow from capital expenditure and financial investment		**(26,006)**		(51,112)
Acquisitions and disposals				
Investment in associated company	**–**		**(126)**	
Net cash outflow from acquisitions and disposals		**–**		(126)
Equity dividends paid		**(5,274)**		(5,013)
Cash inflow/(outflow) before management of liquid resources and financing		**2,170**		(12,200)
Management of liquid resources				
Sale of marketable securities	**–**		5,006	
Purchase of marketable securities	**–**		(5,006)	
Net cash inflow from management of liquid resources		**–**		–
Financing				
Repayment of borrowings	**–**		(1,856)	
Grants received	**–**		400	
Net cash outflow from financing		**–**		(1,456)
Increase/(decrease) in cash in the year		**2,170**		13,656

Figure 1.2 Manchester United plc

Source: Manchester United plc 2002 Annual Report.

3. Read the following extract and then answer the question that follows it.

Monotub Industries in a spin as founder gets Titan for £1

Monotub Industries, maker of the Titan washing machine, yesterday passed into corporate history with very little ceremony and only a whimper of protest from minority shareholders.

At an extraordinary meeting held in a basement room of the group's West End headquarters, shareholders voted to put the company into voluntary liquidation and sell its assets and intellectual property to founder Martin Myerscough for £1. The shares, which once reached 650p were duly suspended on Aim [*author's note: Aim is a stock market*] at 3/4p.

The only significant opposition came from Giuliano Gnagnatti, who along with other shareholders has seen his investment shrink faster than a wool twin-set on a boil wash. The not-so-proud owner of 100,000 Monotub shares, Mr Gnagnatti, the managing director of an online retailer, has referred the sale to the Department of Trade and Industry.

Yesterday he described the sale of Monotub as a 'free gift' to Mr Myerscough. This assessment was denied by Ian Green, the chairman of Monotub, who said the closest the beleaguered company had come to a sale was an offer of £60,000 that gave no guarantees against liabilities which are thought to amount to £750,000.

The quiet passing of the washing machine, eventually dubbed the Titanic, was in strong contrast to its performance in many kitchens. Originally touted as the 'great white hope' of the washing machine industry with its larger capacity and removeable drum, the Titan ran into problems when it kept stopping during the spin cycle, causing it to emit a loud bang and leap into the air.

Summing up the demise of the Titan, Mr Green said: 'Clearly, the machine had some revolutionary aspects, but you can't get away from the fact that the machine was faulty and should not have been launched with those defects'.

The usually vocal Mr Myerscough, who has promised to pump £250,000 into the company and give Monotub shareholders £4 for every machine sold, refused to comment on his plans for the Titan or reveal who his backers were. But eschewing another public listing, he did say that he intended to 'take the Titan forward'.

Lisa Urquhart, *Financial Times*, 23 Mar. 2003

For each of the seven 'user groups' identified in the Accounting Standards Board's 'Statement of Principles', suggest key areas of information which they might need concerning Monotub Industries.

4W. A company has reported record profits and increased asset values, but has also disclosed that it is unable to be considered as a 'going concern'. Suggest three reasons why a profitable company might be in imminent danger of financial collapse.

5W. 'A limited company's financial affairs should not be disclosed to anyone other than its directors and shareholders.' Criticize this statement by reference to the 'user groups' identified in the Statement of Principles.

6W. Write a brief report distinguishing between the key aspects of 'financial accounting' as contrasted with 'management accounting'.

■ **MINI CASE STUDY**

Minnie's ambitions

Minnie von Mausen is about to set up a company that deals in exotic animals, selling them to zoos throughout the world. She is ambitious and realizes that her company could one day be the global leader in its field. She wants to make sure that she understands the financial implications of her enterprise, so has consulted an accountant, and asks the following questions:

1.   How will I know if the company has made a profit?

2.   What key accounting rules and regulations have to be considered?

3. What is the main objective of providing financial statements?

What answers is the accountant likely to give to Minnie?
(Suggested solutions can be found in Appendix 4.)

■ MAXI CASE STUDY

Ahold

Read the following extract then answer the questions that follow it:

> *$500m accounts scandal engulfs Dutch retailer*
>
> Europe was last night facing one of its biggest accounting scandals when the Dutch retailer Ahold disclosed 'significant accounting irregularities' and said its chief executive and finance director would resign.
>
> The announcement, just over a year since Enron shook corporate America, fuelled speculation that the world's third-largest grocer may be broken up and fall victim to bids from rivals . . .
>
> The Dutch group, which expanded rapidly through a series of US acquisitions in the late 1990s, said income at US Foodservice, the second-largest US food distribution company, had been overstated by more than $500m (£314m). Some of its executives have been suspended and 2002 operating earnings will be reduced.
>
> Accountants are also investigating the 'accounting and legality' of transactions by Disco, an Argentine subsidiary, Ahold said.
>
> The news knocked share prices across the continent, which had hoped to avoid a US-style accounting debacle. Ahold fell nearly two-thirds to €3.59, barely a tenth of the price a year ago, leaving it with a market value of €3 bn.
>
> Analysts said Ahold might now have to sell assets even if the diminished valuation did not attract a bidder for the entire group . . .
>
> The irregularities had been discovered in the last two weeks, during the audit of the 2002 accounts. [The company chairman said] 'We believe that there are other accounting issues, but we are determined to pursue the investigation as far as possible.'
>
> Deloitte & Touche, Ahold's auditor, insisted it had done its job properly.
>
> Ahold issued two profit warnings last year, related principally to Latin American subsidiaries and slowing organic growth. It said net profit would now be 'significantly lower' and it would restate earnings for 2001 and the first nine months of 2002.
>
> Adapted from Ian Bickerton and Susannah Voyle, *Financial Times* (London), 25 Feb. 2003

Questions:

1. The company disclosed 'significant accounting irregularities', with income overstated by $500m. Do you think that there could ever be an agreed system of rules and regulations that would be able to prevent similar problems from occurring in the future?

2. Although the auditor of Ahold 'insisted it had done its job properly', the 'irregularities' still occurred. What do you consider is the auditor's role, if any, in preventing such 'accounting scandals'?

(Suggested answers and discussion areas are available on the companion website.)

■ **WEB LINKS**

American Accounting Association http://raw.rutgers.edu/raw/aaa/

Annual Report Service (to obtain copies of annual reports) http://ft.ar.wilink.com or:
www.reportgallery.com/

Chartered Institute of Management Accountants www.cimaglobal.com/

Companies House (UK government's official information registry) www.companieshouse.gov.uk/

**Company Reporting (an independent business information research company which
monitors company compliance with best financial reporting practice)**
www.companyreporting.com/home.htm

The International Accounting Standards Board www.iasb.co.uk

The UK's Accounting Standards Board www.asb.org.uk

Company websites
(Companies referred to in this chapter)

Ahold www.ahold.com

BMW www.bmw.com

Domino's Pizza www.dominos.co.uk

Enron Corporation www.enron.com

Manchester United plc www.manutd.com/corporateinformation/corporate.sps

Scoot (now part of British Telecommunications plc) www.scoot.com/

WorldCom Inc www.worldcom.com/global/about/facts/

■ **FURTHER READING**

Britton, A., and Waterston, C. (2003). *Financial Accounting*, 3rd edn. (Harlow: FT/Prentice Hall),
   chapter 1.

Dyson, J. R. (2003). *Accounting for Non-accounting Students*, 5th edn. (Harlow: FT/Prentice Hall),
   chapters 1, 2, 13.

Meek, G., and Gernon, H. (2001). *Accounting: An International Perspective*, 5th edn.
   (Maidenhead: McGraw-Hill), chapters 1–3.

Weetman, P. (2003). *Financial and Management Accounting: An Introduction*, 3rd edn.
   (Harlow: FT/Prentice Hall), chapters 1, 16.

Also:

A regularly updated website for news relating to the accounting profession:
   www.accountingeducation.com

■ **COMPANION WEBSITE MATERIALS**

 Additional materials are available for students and lecturers on the companion website, at
   www.oup.com/uk/booksites/busecon/business/

2

Recording financial transactions

OBJECTIVES

By the end of this chapter you will be able to:

- Appreciate the scope of a financial recording system.
- Understand the accounting formulae which are the basis of the system.
- Have an overview of the 'double-entry' system of recording financial information and appreciate the advantages of computerized accounting systems.

2.1 Introduction

Once a business is created, there is a need for a systematic way of recording the financial information which is generated. Even the most simple type of business—for example, a market trader buying and selling vegetables—will need to know basic financial information such as who he owes money to and who owes him money, and whether he can afford to buy stock to replace that which has been sold. At some point, he may be approached by a government agency for taxes, or he has to contact a bank for loans, in which case he may find that he has to reveal how well (or badly) his business has been trading by calculating his 'profit' (or 'loss'). If he does not have the personal skills to do this, he might approach a professional accountant who will charge him a fee. If he keeps no written records he might find that he is subject to punitive taxation charges and a large bill from his accountant, who has the task of trying to recreate a financial picture from the trader's verbal explanations, bank statements, invoices, and any other evidence available. In accountancy parlance this is referred to as 'incomplete records' and might be viewed with some suspicion by the tax authorities and the bank. Even the most unsophisticated business owner should keep basic details of what he has bought and sold, and what is owed to him and by him, as well as storing bank statements and other documents such as invoices.

When a business starts to expand, the number of financial transactions will inevitably increase as well. For example, whereas a small pizza delivery company with one shop and three employees might have sales of £200,000 a year, a major company like Domino's Pizza, with 269 stores and 800 employees, had sales of £53m in 2002.

In this chapter, we are looking at a logical system for recording financial information, which can be used by any business regardless of its size or complexity. This is known as the 'double-entry bookkeeping system' which has evolved over several hundred years. As might be expected, the key development in recent years has been the widespread introduction of computerized accounting packages, though many small businesses still prefer to keep paper-based records.

2.2 The scope of the system

To understand the scope of a financial recording system, let's consider a few transactions of a small business (we shall call it 'Moore's Stores') for a typical week in September:

1 September: starts the week with £500 in cash, £2,500 in the bank, and £3,000 unsold goods. Also owes a supplier £200 (known as a 'creditor').

2 September: buys goods for £1,100 by cheque and sells goods for £800 in cash.

3 September: pays wages £300 in cash.

4 September: buys goods for £720 on credit, receiving an invoice.

5 September: sells goods for £1,900 on credit, issuing an invoice.

6 September: buys a computer for £1,000 by cheque and stationery £80 by cash.

7 September: borrows a loan of £500 in cash from a friend. By the end of the week there is unsold stock valued at £2,900, as well as cash and bank balances.

If we look at the range of transactions during the week, we see that the business:

- bought goods, paid for stationery and a computer;
- paid wages;
- sold goods;
- borrowed money;
- has unpaid invoices received from suppliers;
- has unpaid invoices issued to customers;
- has cash and bank balances and unsold stock at the start and end of the week.

As you can see, even for a tiny business, this is a wide range of transactions, and as the business grows in size, the number of transactions might be measured in thousands, millions, or tens of millions. Our aim in maintaining a system is to ensure that *all* aspects of the business's finances are recorded so that the information needs of the various 'user groups' as referred to in Chapter 1 can be met.

The key to understanding how the system works is to look at the transactions shown above and consider how they break down into five major categories of financial information:

1. *Revenue income*: i.e. the sales of goods on 2 and 5 September. 'Revenue income' refers principally to the revenue earned from selling goods or services. Revenue income does not

include any contributions made by the owner into the business, nor the proceeds from selling fixed assets (see 'Assets' below).

2. *Revenue expenditure*: i.e. the goods bought for resale on 2 and 4 September, the wages paid on the 3rd, and the stationery paid for on the 6th. Revenue expenditure refers principally to the cost of the goods sold, and associated overheads such as wages, rent, and rates. Any value taken by the owner from the business, such as goods or personal living expenses, is excluded, as is the cost of purchasing fixed assets (see 'Assets' below).

When we compare these two categories, we can establish whether the business made a profit or a loss during the period. Businesses can make this calculation for any time period but it will be required annually for tax or other purposes. The statement showing the comparison of revenue income with revenue expenditure is referred to as a 'profit and loss account', or alternatively, 'statement of income' or 'income and expenditure account'.

Look at Domino's Pizza's profit and loss account on p. 320. Can you see if the company made a profit or a loss?

3. *Assets*: i.e. the cash and bank balances, the unsold stock of goods, the computer bought on 6 September, and the £900 owed by the customer who bought the goods on credit on 5 September. Assets are defined in the 'Statement of Principles' as 'rights or other access to future economic benefits controlled by an entity as a result of past transactions or events'. In practice they are divided between 'fixed' assets, such as machinery and land and buildings, which are 'intended for use on a continuing basis in the company's activities'[1] (often referred to as *capital expenditure*), and 'current assets' such as unsold stock, debtors, and bank balances which are not intended for continuing use.

4. *Liabilities*: i.e. the opening amount of £200 due to a creditor, the £720 owed for the goods bought on 4 September, and the loan borrowed on 7 September. Liabilities are defined in the 'Statement of Principles' as 'obligations of an entity to transfer economic benefits as a result of past transactions or events'. In practice they can be 'current liabilities' or 'long-term liabilities'. The former including amounts owed to creditors and bank overdrafts, the latter including loans due for repayment at a future date, usually at least a year away from the present time.

5. *Capital*: the value which the owner has 'tied up' in the business at any particular date. 'Capital' is referred to in the 'Statement of Principles' as 'ownership interest' and is found by deducting the liabilities (as in 4) from the assets (as in 3).

If we summarize 3, 4, and 5 we are showing the financial position of a business according to its own records at any specific moment in time. This summary is known as a 'balance sheet'.

---

[1] Companies Act 1985 s. 262 (1).

Look at Domino's Pizza's company balance sheet on p. 322. Was the 'total assets less current liabilities' figure higher or lower than the previous year?

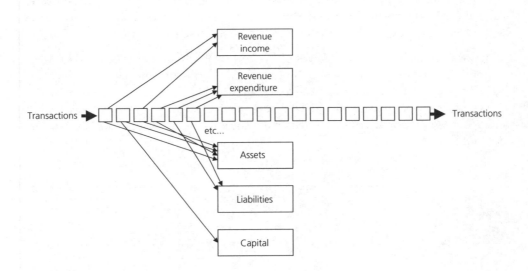

Figure 2.1 Transaction processing

Figure 2.1 shows how transactions are sorted into the key categories of financial information. When each transaction is recorded in the system, the relevant effect on income and expenditure, assets, liabilities, and capital is being shown. This is an endless process which continues for as long as the firm is in existence.

2.3 **Accounting formulae**

As we have seen in Figure 2.1, the financial transactions of a firm are being continually sorted according to the effect they have on the income, expenditure, assets, liabilities, and capital. At intervals we are able to calculate profit or loss and the financial position of the firm. In fact what we're doing is using two equations to sort the five categories:

First:

either

Revenue Income − Revenue Expenditure = Profit (or 'I − E = P'), where income is greater than expenditure

or

Revenue Expenditure − Revenue Income = Loss (or 'E − I = L'), where expenditure is greater than income.

This can be referred to as the *profit and loss equation*.

Secondly:

Assets − Liabilities = Capital (or 'A − L = C')

This can be referred to as the *balance sheet equation*.

The profit and loss equation is used to summarize transactions affecting revenue income and expenditure over a specific period of time, for example, a year, a month, six months, etc. The balance sheet equation, however, allows us to look at the firm's value of assets, liabilities and capital at a particular moment in time. For example, at the end of a year, at the end of a month, at the end of a six-month period, etc.

In practice, a firm, as a minimum, will produce a profit or loss calculation for a year, and a balance sheet at the end of that year. A 'year' does not have to be a calendar year—it can end at whatever date is convenient for the firm. This would be known as a 'financial year'.

Figure 2.2 shows how this process works.

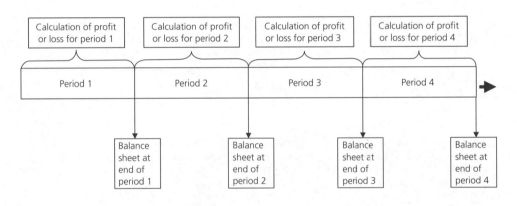

Figure 2.2 Financial summaries: time periods

> Look at Domino's Pizza's balance sheet heading on p. 321. When did their financial year end?

2.3.1 The double-entry system

As Figure 2.1 showed, the recording of transactions is a continuous process, with each transaction being sorted according to its effect on the five key categories. This 'sorting process' is known as the double-entry bookkeeping system, so called because each transaction is shown to have an effect on the business in *two* separate ways. For example, let's go back to 'Moore's Stores' shown earlier. In that business, we can analyse the effect of each day's transactions on the five categories (all amounts in £s):

September	Transaction	Revenue income	Revenue expenditure	Assets	Liabilities	Capital
1	Start of the week			Cash+500 Bank+2,500 Stock+3,000	Creditor+200	+5,800
Comment: The opening position. As A − L = C (the balance sheet equation), Capital must equal 6,000 − 200.						
2	Buys goods by cheque		+1,100	Bank−1,100		
Comment: A purchase of goods is part of revenue expenditure, but also affects the bank balance. Note that the overall value of unsold stock also changes, but we only need to consider this at the very start or very end of the period we are summarizing, not at intermediate dates.						
2	Sells goods for cash	+800		Cash+800		
Comment: A sale of goods represents revenue income, and it also affects the asset values of cash.						
3	Pays wages in cash		+300	Cash−300		
Comment: Wages are a revenue expense, but the transaction also reduces the cash balance.						
4	Buys goods on credit		+720		Creditor+720	
Comment: More goods bought increases revenue expenditure, but they haven't been paid for, hence the increase in the liability (known as a 'creditor').						
5	Sells goods on credit	+1,900		Debtor+1,900		
Comment: Selling on credit means an increase in revenue income but also, as the customer has not yet paid, an increase in what is owed to the business. Customers who owe money to a business are known as 'debtors'.						
6	Buys computer			Computer (a 'Fixed' Asset) +1,000 Bank−1,000		
	Pays for stationery		+80	Cash−80		
Comment: When a valuable item is bought which is going to be used in the firm for over a year, it is known as a 'Fixed' asset. Other types of assets are known as 'current' assets. The stationery bill is treated as a revenue expense because it is one of the 'overheads' of the firm, incurred in the day-to-day trading like wages or goods for resale.						
7	Borrows money			Cash+500	Loan+500	
Comment: A liability is created, but at the same time an asset (cash) increases.						
In addition, we are told that the closing stock was £2,900, which is £100 less than the opening stock. This must increase our overall revenue expenditure for the week, as we have 'used up' part of the stock with which we started the week.						

If we look at the transactions separately, we should realize that each transaction is neutral across the five categories: for example, an increase in income might be matched by an increase in an asset, or an increase in an expense might be matched by an increase in a liability. However, if we divide the five categories between, first, Income and Expenditure, and secondly Assets, Liabilities, and Capital, the picture starts to make sense:

Revenue Income and Expenditure
Change in income during the week: +800, +1,900 = +2,700
Change in expenditure during the week: +1,100, +300, +720, +80, +100 = +2,300
Therefore, using the profit and loss equation, I − E = P, we can see that Moore's Stores has made a profit of £400[2] in the week.

[2] For simplicity, we have ignored depreciation and a few other adjustments referred to in the next chapter.

Assets, liabilities, and capital

At the start of the week the firm had:

Assets: (Cash, Bank, Unsold goods) 500, +2,500, +3,000 = 6,000

Liabilities: (Creditors) 200

Opening Capital (A − L = C): 6,000 − 200 = 5,800

At the end of the week, assets had changed as follows:

	Computer	Stock	Debtors	Bank	Cash	Total
Opening balance	—	3,000	—	2,500	500	6,000
Effect of transactions	+1,000	−100	+1,900	−1,100	+800	
				−1,000	−300	
					−80	+1,620
					+500	
Closing balance	1,000	2,900	1,900	400	1,420	**7,620**

Liabilities changed as follows:

	Creditors	Loan	Total
Opening balance	200	—	200
Effect of transactions	+720	+500	+1,220
Closing balance	920	500	**1,420**

Therefore, using the balance sheet equation (A − L = C), the closing capital equals:

Assets 7,620 − Liabilities 1,420 = 6,200.

We can prove that this is correct by considering the effect that the week's profit has made on the owner's capital.

The business started with £5,800 on 1 September.

The firm made a profit of £400 during the week.

So his capital had increased to £6,200 (£5,800 + £400) by the end of the week.

Summary

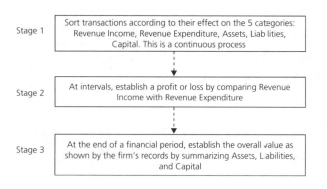

Stage 1	Sort transactions according to their effect on the 5 categories: Revenue Income, Revenue Expenditure, Assets, Liabilities, Capital. This is a continuous process
Stage 2	At intervals, establish a profit or loss by comparing Revenue Income with Revenue Expenditure
Stage 3	At the end of a financial period, establish the overall value as shown by the firm's records by summarizing Assets, Liabilities, and Capital

Figure 2.3 From transaction recording to financial summaries

2.4 Understanding the accounting process

The continuous transaction recording process known as double-entry bookkeeping is organized by creating a number of locations which receive the data generated by the system. In general terms, this is divided between *books of prime entry* which show the first stage of the process, and *the ledger* which is a collection of individual records known as 'accounts' which sort data into the key business areas.

2.4.1 Books of prime entry

In view of the mass of data generated, it is helpful for the business to keep parts of the financial data within separate areas of the bookkeeping system, in particular:

- Cash and bank transactions are shown within a 'cash book', which will record changes to the bank account and cash received and paid. The cash book will usually show an analysis of key areas of income and expenditure which are then used when completing the double-entry to the ledger. Invoice payments and receipts shown in the cash book will be 'posted' into the relevant supplier's or customer's account in the ledger.

- Sales invoices issued are shown within a 'sales journal' (also known as a 'sales day book') which acts as a continuous record of all credit sales to customers. Individual invoices are 'posted' into customers' accounts in the ledger. In addition, the sales data will be analysed into key types of sales (e.g. sales of product A separated from sales of product B) for transfer into the ledger.

- Purchase invoices received are shown within a 'purchase journal' (also known as a 'purchase day book') which acts as a continuous record of all credit purchases from suppliers. Individual invoices are 'posted' into suppliers' accounts in the ledger. In addition, the purchases data will be analysed into key types of expenditure (e.g. raw materials, goods for resale, stationery, motor fuel) for transfer into the ledger.

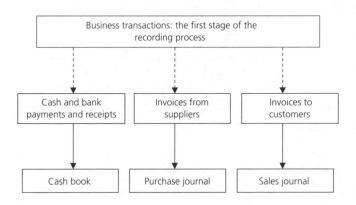

Figure 2.4 Books of prime entry

For example, consider a new business, Throttle Bikes, formed on 1 May 2004 to buy and sell motorbikes. It negotiated a £5,000 overdraft limit from its bank, and in its first few days it had the following transactions:

1 May The owner, Fred Throttle, paid a cheque of £250 to start the business's bank account. On the same day, the business paid £500 for two weeks' showroom rent by cheque and received an invoice for £5,000 relating to five motorbikes costing a total of £4,000 and also £1,000 of accessories from Wackimoto delivered today.

2 May Paid for a £600 computer by cheque and paid a cheque for stationery of £400.

3 May Sold three motorbikes to Pip Ltd. and issued an invoice to that company for £4,500.

4 May Sold accessories for £200, paid for by cheque.

5 May Paid wages to sales staff of £300.

6 May Received an invoice from Securikor Ltd. for £150 for one week's security patrols.

7 May Sold a motorbike to a customer for £1,200, receiving a cheque, and issued a sales invoice to Ranjit Chaudry for £350 worth of accessories.

The first stage in recording these transactions is to enter them in the books of prime entry, as follows (note that taxation has been ignored for simplicity).

Cash book

		Receipts						Payments					
Date	Details	Total	Capital	Motor-bikes	Accessories	SL	Date	Details	Total	Rent	Computer	Stationery	Wages	PL
1 May	Throttle	250	250				1 May	Rent	500	500				
4 May	Sales	200			200		2 May	Computer	600		600			
7 May	Sales	1,200		1,200				Stationery	400			400		
							5 May	Wages	300				300	

Explanation: Entries are made according to whether they are paid into or out of the bank account, and then analysed into the relevant column. The fact that the business negotiated an overdraft of £5,000 is not included, as this is just a facility available to the business rather than an actual transaction. Transactions on credit where invoices have been issued or received are excluded from the cash book as no payment has yet been made. The columns headed SL and PL (abbreviations for sales ledger and purchase ledger) will be used when entering cheques received from debtors or paid to creditors, as explained below.

Sales journal

Date	Details	Invoice ref.	Total	Motorbikes	Accessories
3 May	Pip Ltd	S001	4,500	4,500	
7 May	Ranjit Chaudry	S002	350		350

Explanation: Only sales on credit are entered—sales paid for by cash or cheque are entered directly into the cash book. The invoice reference is the unique identifying number for each sales invoice.

Purchase journal

Date	Details	Invoice ref.	Total	Motorbikes	Accessories	Security
1 May	Wackimoto	P001	5,000	4,000	1,000	
6 May	Securikor Ltd.	P002	150			150

Explanation: Only purchases on credit are entered—purchases paid by cash or cheque are entered directly into the cash book. The invoice reference is the unique identifying number for each purchase invoice.

2.4.2 The ledger

After the first part of the double-entry bookkeeping is entered into one of the books of prime entry above, the transaction recording is completed by a 'posting' into a *ledger account* contained within a *ledger*. In a computerized system, this is done automatically by the software, but in a non-computerized system it may be completed some time after the first entry is made.

The 'Ledger' is in fact divided into three key parts, two *personal* ledgers and the *general* ledger, as follows:

Personal ledgers

1. The sales ledger

This contains the individual personal accounts of customers ('debtors') who buy goods or services on credit terms, i.e. where there is a delay between the provision of the goods or services and payment for them. There can be as many accounts as there are customers—there is no limit to the number of accounts which can be opened. For example, if we look at the credit sales of Throttle Bikes, we see that the sales journal has recorded two invoices issued, to Pip Ltd. and Ranjit Chaudry. Throttle Bikes needs to keep a close watch on credit customers and must collect its debts within a reasonable time (say 4–6 weeks after issue of the invoice). To do this, it will open accounts within the sales ledger for each customer, as follows:

Pip Ltd.					
Date	Details	Invoice ref.	Debit	Credit	Balance
3 May	Sales: 3 motorbikes	S001	4,500		4,500 Dr

Ranjit Chaudry					
Date	Details	Invoice ref.	Debit	Credit	Balance
7 May	Sales: Accessories	S002	350		350Dr

Note that there are other formats used for ledger accounts. The one above is common for computerized systems where the 'balance' column on the right-hand side changes automatically after each entry, enabling the business to see immediately how much is owing by the customer. An alternative and simplified format often used by students is the 'T account', which shows each account in the form of a letter T, as follows:

(Name of account)

(Debit side)　　　　　　　　(Credit side)

Sometimes, the abbreviations Dr and Cr are used to denote *debit* and *credit* respectively—the debit side is always shown on the left, the credit side on the right, a tradition carried on over many centuries. In the above examples, the two ledger accounts simply show that Pip Ltd. and Ranjit Chaudry are both debtors of Throttle Bikes. Subsequently, when the debtors pay their bills, entries will be made in both the cash book and the sales ledger. For example, if Pip Ltd. pays its invoice on 10 May, the cash book will show the cheque received as follows:

Receipts							Payments							
Date	Details	Total	Capital	Motor-bikes	Accessories	SL	Date	Details	Total	Rent	Computer	Stationery	Wages	PL
1 May	F. Throttle	250	250				1 May	Rent	500	500				
4 May	Sales	200			200		2 May	Computer	600		600			
7 May	Sales	1,200		1,200				Stationery	400			400		
10 May	**Pip Ltd.**	**4,500**				**4,500**	5 May	Wages	300				300	

Notice that the cheque is entered in the 'SL' (sales ledger) column, not in the motorbikes or accessories columns—when the actual sale was made on 3 May, the details were entered in the sales journal.

The double-entry is then completed when the cheque is posted into the sales ledger, as follows:

Pip Ltd.					
Date	Details	Invoice ref.	Debit	Credit	Balance
3 May	Sales: 3 motorbikes	S001	4,500		4,500 Dr
10 May	**Cheque**			**4,500**	0

This pattern continues for all sales invoices issued to, and all cheques received, from debtors.

2. The purchase ledger

This contains the individual personal accounts of suppliers ('creditors') who sell goods or services to a business on credit terms, i.e. where there is a delay between the provision of the goods or services and payment for them. There can be as many accounts as there are suppliers—there is no limit to the number of accounts which can be opened. For example, if we look at the credit purchases of Throttle Bikes, we see that the purchase journal has recorded two invoices received, from Wackimoto and Securikor. As with its sales invoices, Throttle Bikes must keep detailed records of who it owes money to, and ensure that it pays bills within a reasonable time period. To do this, it will open accounts within the purchase ledger for each supplier, as follows:

Wackimoto					
Date	Details	Invoice ref.	Debit	Credit	Balance
1 May	Purchases: 5 motorbikes and accessories	P001		5,000	5,000 Cr

Securikor Ltd.					
Date	Details	Invoice ref.	Debit	Credit	Balance
6 May	Security patrols	P002		150	150 Cr

Explanation: In the above examples, the two ledger accounts show that Wackimoto and Securikor Ltd. are both creditors of Throttle Bikes. When Throttle Bikes eventually pays the invoices, entries will be made in both the cash book and the purchase ledger. For example, if Wackimoto's invoice is paid on 12 May, the cash book will show the cheques paid as follows:

Receipts							Payments							
Date	Details	Total	Capital	Motor-bikes	Accessories	SL	Date	Details	Total	Rent	Computer	Stationery	Wages	PL
1 May	F. Throttle	250	250				1 May	Rent	500	500				
4 May	Sales	200			200		2 May	Computer	600		600			
7 May	Sales	1,200		1,200				Stationery	400			400		
10 May	Pip Ltd.	4,500				4,500	5 May	Wages	300				300	
							12 May	Wackimoto	5,000					5,000

Notice that the cheque is entered in the 'PL' (purchase ledger) column, not in a 'motorbikes' column—when the invoice was received on 1 May, its details were entered in the purchase journal.

The double-entry is then completed when the cheque is posted into the purchase ledger, as follows:

Wackimoto					
Date	Details	Invoice ref.	Debit	Credit	Balance
1 May	Purchases: 5 motorbikes and accessories	P001		5,000	5,000 Cr
12 May	Cheque		5,000		0

This pattern continues for all purchase invoices received and all cheques paid to creditors. Figure 2.5 summarizes the information flow into the two personal ledgers.

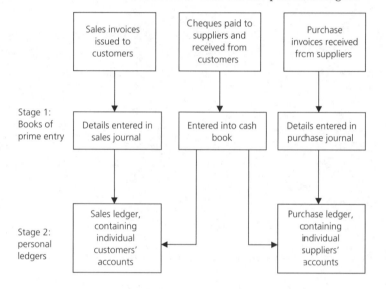

Figure 2.5 Information flow into the personal ledgers

3. The general ledger—the impersonal ledger

Also called the nominal ledger, this ledger contains accounts which reflect the major types of transactions undertaken by the business. Unlike the sales ledger and purchase ledger which show customers' accounts and suppliers' accounts respectively, the general ledger summarizes financial information into key *types* of income, expenditure, assets, and liabilities. It also shows a 'capital account' which represents the value of the owner's interest in the business. The general ledger is vital when financial summaries are needed to establish whether a profit or loss has been made or if a balance sheet has to be extracted. Typical account names include:

- Sales, which shows all sales made during the period (cash and credit);
- Purchases, which shows the cost of goods and raw materials bought during the period (whether paid for or not);

- Wages;
- Rent;
- Advertising;
- Electricity;
- Machinery;
- Computers;
- Motor cars.

The information posted into general ledger accounts comes from the books of prime entry. In the example of Throttle Bikes, the general ledger accounts will appear as follows (assuming that the business's first financial period covered its first two weeks to 14 May):

1. 'Revenue Income' accounts

Sales of motorbikes				
Date	Details	Debit	Credit	Balance
14 May	Cash Book		1,200	1,200 Cr
	Sales Journal		4,500	5,700 Cr

Sales of accessories				
Date	Details	Debit	Credit	Balance
14 May	Cash Book		200	200 Cr
	Sales Journal		350	550 Cr

2. 'Revenue Expenditure' accounts (including the cost of goods bought for sale)

Purchase of motorbikes				
Date	Details	Debit	Credit	Balance
14 May	Purchase Journal	4,000		4,000 Dr

Purchase of accessories				
Date	Details	Debit	Credit	Balance
14 May	Purchase Journal	1,000		1,000 Dr

Security				
Date	Details	Debit	Credit	Balance
14 May	Purchase Journal	150		150 Dr

Rent				
Date	Details	Debit	Credit	Balance
14 May	Cash Book	500		500 Dr

Stationery				
Date	Details	Debit	Credit	Balance
14 May	Cash Book	400		400 Dr

Wages				
Date	Details	Debit	Credit	Balance
14 May	Cash Book	300		300 Dr

3. 'Asset' accounts

Computer				
Date	Details	Debit	Credit	Balance
14 May	Cash Book	600		600 Dr

4. Liability accounts

There were no liability accounts needed in this example in the general ledger. If the business had taken out a loan, then a 'loan account' would have been created. Note that liabilities to suppliers (creditors) are shown in the purchase ledger, not the general ledger.

5. Owner's interest in the business ('Capital')

Capital				
Date	Details	Debit	Credit	Balance
14 May	Cash Book		250	250 Cr

Figure 2.6 summarizes the information flow into the General ledger.

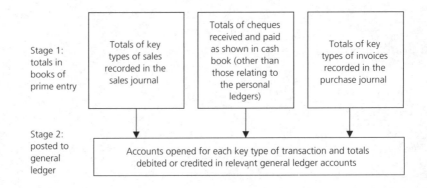

Figure 2.6 Information flow into the general ledger

2.4.3 Debits and credits

One of the puzzling things about the ledger accounts is which side—debit or credit—the information should be recorded. In the cash book we saw that receipts are shown on the left hand side—'debited'—and payments are shown on the right-hand side—'credited'. In fact this makes life even more confusing, for if we looked at a bank statement, we would expect to see money that we had paid *into* the bank on the *credit* side and money *paid out* being *debited*. The explanation for this is quite simple, as the bank statement shows the *bank's* version of our finances, so when we write our own version, this will be a mirror image of the way the bank sees it.

When we need to summarize a business's financial situation we need to look at the closing balance on each account at the end of that period. In the example of Throttle Bikes, on 14 May we could make a list of all accounts with balances, as follows:

Sales Ledger	Balance	'Type' of account
Ranjit Chaudry	350 Debit	Current asset (debtor)
Purchase Ledger		
Securikor Ltd.	150 Credit	Current liability (creditor)

General Ledger		
Sales of motorbikes	5,700 Credit	Income
Sales of accessories	550 Credit	Income
Purchase of motorbikes	4,000 Debit	Expenditure
Purchase of accessories	1,000 Debit	Expenditure
Security	150 Debit	Expenditure
Rent	500 Debit	Expenditure
Stationery	400 Debit	Expenditure
Wages	300 Debit	Expenditure
Computer	600 Debit	Fixed asset
Capital	250 Credit	Owner's interest
Cash Book		
Bank (see below)	650 Credit	Current liability (overdraft)

The bank balance is found by totalling the cash book receipts (250 + 200 + 1,200 + 4,500 = 6,150) and deducting the cash book payments (500 + 600 + 400 + 300 + 5,000 = 6,800). This leaves an excess of payments—an overdraft—of £650, which is a *credit* balance in the business's books (i.e. shown as a *debit balance* on the bank statement). Looking at the list, we see that *debit balances* comprise Asset and Expenditure accounts, whilst *credit balances* comprise, Liability, Capital, and Income accounts. In fact, the system operates by using an 'extended balance sheet equation', which combines the profit and loss equation (I − E = P) with the balance sheet equation (A − L = C) as follows:

$$\text{Assets} - \text{Liabilities} = \text{Capital} + (\text{Income} - \text{Expenses})$$

which can then be rewritten as:

$$\text{Assets} + \text{Expenses} = \text{Liabilities} + \text{Capital} + \text{Income}$$

The left-hand side of the equation (Assets and Expenses) represents accounts which will have predominantly debit entries, the right-hand side (Liabilities, Capital, and Income) represents accounts which will have predominantly credit entries. We can prove this by listing each of Throttle Bikes' accounts according to whether their closing balances were debit or credit, as follows:

Debit balances		Credit balances		
Assets	**Expenses**	**Liabilities**	**Capital**	**Income**
Bank 650	Purchase of motorbikes 4,000	Creditor (Securikor Ltd.) 150	Capital 250	Sales of motorbikes 5,700
Debtor (Chaudry) 350	Security 150			Sales of accessories 550
Computer 600	Rent 500			
	Stationery 400			
	Wages 300			

2.5 The trial balance

One of the many advantages of having a computerized accounting system is the immediate transfer of information between the books of prime entry and the ledger accounts. However, this is certainly not foolproof, as human error can creep in to misname a customer or supplier, enter the wrong amount for a cheque, treat a cheque paid as a cheque received, etc. With non-computerized systems another area of potential error is failure to complete the double-entry so that entries in a book of prime entry are not matched by their equivalent entry in the ledger. To check this aspect of the system, a *trial balance* can be extracted. This is simply a list of all balances at a particular date, shown according to whether they are debit balances or credit balances. We do not include accounts with zero balances (e.g. the sales ledger account of Pip Ltd.). If the full double-entry has been completed, then the totals of the debit balances should equal the total of the credit balances, and the trial balance is said to 'balance'. However, it still won't show if customers' names have been misspelled, invoices lost, or if wrong amounts have been both debited and credited!

The trial balance for Throttle Bikes at 14 May would be shown as follows:

Throttle Bikes Trial Balance as at 14 May 2004		
	Debit	**Credit**
Sales Ledger		
Ranjit Chaudry	350	
Purchase Ledger		
Securikor Ltd.		150
General Ledger		
Sales of motorbikes		5,700
Sales of accessories		550
Purchase of motorbikes	4,000	
Purchase of accessories	1,000	
Security	150	
Rent	500	
Stationery	400	
Wages	300	
Computer	600	
Capital		250
Cash Book		
Bank		650
Totals	**7,300**	**7,300**

If the trial balance failed to balance, we would have to check each entry until we found where the errors had occurred.

2.6 **Chapter summary**

- Businesses need to have a logical system to record financial transactions.
- The double-entry bookkeeping system is the basis of accounting information systems.
- Transactions are broken down into the effect they have on five key categories: Revenue Income, Revenue Expenditure, Assets, Liabilities, and Capital.
- Accounting formulae are used to establish overall profit or loss and the value of capital at a specific moment in time.
- Transactions are first recorded in books of prime entry.
- The double-entry is completed when information is entered in the general ledger.
- The trial balance checks whether the debit entries equal the credit entries. If they don't agree, then something must be wrong in the system.

■ GLOSSARY

accounting formulae	Income − Expenditure = Profit (where income is greater than expenditure) Expenditure − Income = Loss (where expenditure is greater than income) Assets − Liabilities = Capital
asset	Rights or other access to future economic benefits controlled by an entity as a result of past transactions or events. Usually split between *fixed and current assets*
balance sheet	A financial summary showing the assets, liabilities, and capital at a specific moment in time
book of original entry	Another name for *book of prime entry*
books of prime entry	The documents within the double-entry bookkeeping system where the first record of transactions are made. They include the *cash book* and the sales and purchase *journals*
capital	The value of the ownership interest in the business, calculated at any time by deducting the total liabilities from the total assets
capital expenditure	The purchase of fixed assets. See also *revenue expenditure*
capital income	Amounts raised from the sale of *fixed assets*. See also *revenue income*
cash book	*Book of prime entry* showing the cash and bank transactions
credit	The right-hand side of a ledger account. Accounts with, overall, more credit entries than debit entries are said to have a credit balance. Liability accounts, income accounts, and the capital account will normally have credit balances
current assets	Assets such as unsold stock, debtors, and bank balances whose values tend to change frequently, unlike *fixed* assets
current liability	Amounts owed to creditors which are repayable within a year
day books	Another name for *journals*

debit	The left-hand side of a ledger account. Accounts with, overall, more debit entries than credit entries are said to have a debit balance. Asset accounts and expenditure accounts will normally have debit balances
expenditure	See *revenue expenditure* and *capital expenditure*
financial period	The period of time covered by a financial summary
fixed assets	Assets intended for use on a continuing basis in the company's activities. They must be of a material value to be classified as a fixed asset. Examples include land, buildings, and machinery
general ledger	The ledger showing the key types of financial transactions undertaken by a business
impersonal ledger	The general ledger, where each account shows a 'type' of transaction, e.g. 'sales' or 'wages'
income	See *revenue income* and *capital income*
journals	Books of prime entry which show purchase and sales invoices
ledger	The collective name for the *sales, purchase, and general ledgers*
liability	Obligations of an entity to transfer economic benefits as a result of past transactions or events. Usually split between *current and long-term liabilities*
long-term liability	Amounts owed to creditors which are repayable after more than a year from the present date
loss	A surplus of *revenue expenditure* over *revenue income*
nominal ledger	Another name for the general ledger
personal ledger	The sales ledger and purchase ledger, containing customers' and suppliers' accounts respectively
profit	A surplus of *revenue income* over *revenue expenditure*
profit and loss account	The name given to a summary of *revenue income* and *revenue expenditure*, often abbreviated to 'P & L account'
purchase ledger	The ledger showing the accounts of the suppliers from whom the business buys goods or services on credit terms
revenue expenditure	The cost of the goods sold, and associated overheads such as wages, rent, and rates. See also *capital expenditure*
revenue income	The revenue generated by a business from selling its goods or services, plus sundry income such as bank interest receivable. See also *capital income*
sales ledger	The ledger showing the accounts of the customers who buy goods or services on credit terms
statement of income	Alternative name for the *profit and loss account*
trial balance	A check made to see if the total debits in the bookkeeping system equal the total credits

■ MULTIPLE CHOICE QUESTIONS

1. Which one of the following is not a major category of financial information?

   a Capital

   b Assets

   c Income

   d Wages

2. Which of the following formulae would be used to establish the value cf Capital at a specific moment in time?

   a Assets + Liabilities

   b Assets − Liabilities

   c Income − Expenditure

   d Assets − Expenditure

3. The first stage of the bookkeeping process is made in:

   a The balance sheet

   b The bank statement

   c A book of prime entry

   d The general ledger

4. The second stage of the bookkeeping process is made in:

   a The ledger

   b A book of prime entry

   c The profit and loss account

   d The balance sheet

5. Which one of the following is the closest definition to a 'financial year'?

   a A period of any length which ends on 31 December

   b A 12-month period ending on the last day of any month

   c A 12-month period ending on any day

   d A 12-month period ending on 31 December

6. If a business buys a machine for £10,000 with a cheque, what effect would that transaction have?

   a Only an increase in assets—nothing else.

   b An increase in an asset and a decrease in another asset

   c An increase in an asset and an increase in a liability

   d An increase in an asset and a decrease in a liability

7. A sale of goods where no invoice was issued would be first recorded in which one of the following:

   a Sales ledger

   b Sales journal

   c Purchase journal

   d Cash book

8. Accounts with more debit entries than credit entries are referred to as having 'debit balances': Which one of the following accounts is unlikely to have a 'debit balance'.
   a   Sales account in the general ledger
   b   Debtor's account in the sales ledger
   c   Machinery account in the general ledger
   d   Wages payable account in the general ledger

9. The 'personal ledgers' of a business are:
   a   General and sales ledgers
   b   Cash book and sales journal
   c   General and purchase ledgers
   d   Sales and purchase ledgers

10. Which one of the following assets would be classified as a *fixed* asset?
   a   Stock of unsold goods
   b   Motor lorry
   c   Amounts owed by debtors
   d   Bank balance

(Note: answers are shown in Appendix 2.)

■ DISCUSSION QUESTIONS

To answer these, use the Domino's Pizza annual report on pp. 307–45. Within the Directors' Report on p. 318 you will see a Statement of Directors' Responsibilities. This includes the following sentence:

> The directors are responsible for keeping proper accounting records which disclose with reasonable accuracy at any time the financial position of the group and to enable them to ensure that the accounts comply with the Companies Act 1985. They are also responsible for safeguarding the assets of the group and hence for taking reasonable steps for the prevention and detection of fraud and other irregularities.

1.   What do you think is meant by the phrase 'proper accounting records'?
2.   Why does it refer to 'reasonable accuracy' rather than 'total accuracy'?
3.   What is meant by 'safeguarding the assets of the group'?

(Note: Suggested answers or discussion points are available on the companion website.)

■ LONGER QUESTIONS

(Questions marked W have suggested answers on the companion website. Other questions are answered in Appendix 3.)

1.   On 1 November, Floella Robinson started a business buying and selling garden machinery called 'Flo-Mow'. She paid in £5,000 from her own resources to start the business bank account and

immediately took delivery of £10,000 worth of lawnmowers supplied by LawnStripe Ltd. She was also invoiced for chainsaws worth £3,000 bought from Logjam Ltd.

During the business's first week, she paid cheques for the following expenses:

2 Nov.	Rent of premises	£450
3 Nov.	Telephone rental	£200
4 Nov.	Advertising	£500
5 Nov.	Hire of office equipment	£600

She sold a lawnmower for £400 on 3 November, paid for immediately by cheque, and sales invoices were issued for the sale of three lawnmowers for a total of £1,500 on 3 November to Grimridge Council and for a £500 chainsaw to Upton Park Estate on 4 November.

On 7 November she paid Logjam's invoice and received a cheque from the Upton Park Estate in full settlement of their account.

Enter all the above transactions into the bookkeeping records of Flo-Mow and extract a trial balance at 7 November.

2. Gargoyle Ltd. sells plastic guttering systems. Its sales ledger included the following account for a major customer, Normanshaw Homes Ltd., for the month of December:

Normanshaw Homes Ltd.					
Date	Details	Invoice ref.	Debit	Credit	Balance
1 Dec.	Opening balance brought forward		1,200		1,200 Dr
2 Dec.	Sales Journal	563246	5,600		6,800 Dr
15 Dec.	Sales Journal	563315	1,923		8,723 Dr
17 Dec.	Sales Journal	563781	8,527		17,250 Dr
18 Dec.	Cash Book			1,200	16,050 Dr
30 Dec.	Sales Journal	563799	420		16,470 Dr

a Explain the terms 'Opening balance brought forward', 'Sales Journal', and 'Cash Book'.
b Why do you think Normanshaw Homes Ltd. paid £1,200 on 18 December?
c If Gargoyle Ltd. prepared a trial balance at the end of December, how would Normanshaw Homes Ltd.'s account balance be shown?
d If Gargoyle Ltd. was preparing a summary of its assets and liabilities at the end of December, under what category would the balance on Normanshaw Homes Ltd.'s sales ledger account be shown?

3. From the following list of transactions, identify their respective effect on the revenue income, revenue expenditure, assets, liabilities, and capital of the business. The first transaction has

been completed:

April	Transaction	Assets	Expenses	Liabilities	Capital	Income
1	Owner pays £500 into business bank	Bank +500			+500	
2	Goods bought on credit, £6,500					
3	Paid rent £200 by cheque					
4	Sale of goods for £2,500 by cheque					
5	Borrowed £2,000 by a loan, paid into the bank					
6	Sale of goods £1,200 on credit terms					
7	Bought a machine £2,000 on credit terms					
8	Owner drew out £100 for personal living expenses					
9	Debtor paid the sales invoice issued on 6 April					
10	Electricity bill £300 received but not yet paid					

Total the columns and then complete the following formula:

$$\text{Assets} + \text{Expenses} = \text{Liabilities} + \text{Capital} + \text{Income}$$

4W. The following is a list of all the balances (in random order) in the ledgers of Wilfred Gropius at 1 June 2004:

Name	Amount	Debit or Credit
Debtor: J. Brown	650	Debit
Rent and rates	6,400	Debit
Machinery	25,680	Debit
Capital	?	Credit
Wages	18,630	Debit
Cost of goods sold	14,560	Debit
Advertising	1,500	Debit
Creditor: P. Hunter	960	Credit
Accountancy fees	350	Debit
Sales	32,510	Credit
Bank	5,000	Debit
Creditor: L. Turner	250	Credit

a   What was the balance on Wilfred's Capital account on 1 June 2004 (show your workings)?

b Rearrange all the balances (including the capital account balance) under each of the following headings:

Assets	Expenses	Liabilities	Capital	Income

c Total the balances that appear under each of the five headings in part (b) above, and then complete and prove the following formula:

$$\text{Assets} + \text{Expenses} = \text{Liabilities} + \text{Capital} + \text{Income}$$

5W. The following are the first week's transactions of George Anderson, a trader:

1 May George started the business by paying in £4,000 into the business bank account.

1 May Bought goods for resale with a cheque for £2,000 and paid £30 by cheque for advertising.

2 May Sold goods for £2,400 cheque.

3 May Paid an £80 cheque for printing.

4 May Paid rent by cheque, £150.

5 May Sold goods for £800 cheque.

6 May Paid wages £300 cheque.

7 May Bought goods for resale costing £2,100 on credit from Jupiter p c, and sold goods worth £250 on credit to Saturn Ltd.

Enter all the above transactions into the bookkeeping records of George Anderson and extract a trial balance at 7 May.

6W. Explain the difference between 'revenue expenditure' and 'capital expenditure'. Classify each of the following as either revenue or capital expenditure:

1. The purchase of a machine.

2. Buying petrol for a van.

3. Buying stock to resell.

4. Paying an electricity bill.

5. Purchasing an office building.

6. Paying rent for an office building.

■ **MINI CASE STUDY**

Minnie plans an expedition

Minnie von Mausen (see previous mini case study) has started her business dealing in exotic animals and has named it 'MinnieBeasts'. She is planning her first expedition into the African bush to fulfil an order from the Great Rocky Zoo company for as many animals as will fit into their newly built enclosure. She knows that it will take some time to complete this order, so has bought in some elephants from Pachyderm plc which she sells on to the zoo. She is keeping records of all transactions, and in her first two weeks of business she has listed the following key financial events:

1 January She opened a bank account with a personal cheque for £20,000.

2 January She ordered eight elephants at £2,000 each from Pachyderm plc, which were delivered directly to the Great Rocky Zoo by that company. Minnie received an invoice for the order and promptly issued an invoice to the zoo, charging it £2,500 per elephant.

3 January She bought equipment from Safari Supplies Ltd. for £380, paying by cheque, and paid a £500 cheque to Aardvark Airlines as deposit for her trip to Africa.

4 January She paid office expenses of £400 by cheque and bought a computer from Micro Machines for £850 on credit terms.

5 January The zoo paid for six of the elephants by cheque and Minnie paid for half of the elephants supplied by Pachyderm plc, also by cheque.

You are required to enter this information into the cash book, journals, and ledger accounts of MinnieBeasts, and extract a trial balance at 5 January.

Note: no animals were harmed in the making of this case study.

(Suggested solutions can be found in Appendix 4.)

■ **MAXI CASE STUDY**

Jim Lawrence's Traditional Ironwork

Read the following extract then answer the questions that follow it:

> This spring, Jim Lawrence's Traditional Ironwork won the grandly titled Parcelforce Worldwide Small Business Award, at national and regional level, and banked prize money of £32,000. The eponymous founder could hardly believe it.
>
> For a decade until 1992 Mr Lawrence had struggled to make a living from beef farming outside Colchester, in Essex. But he was losing between £6,000 and £8,000 a year and getting deeper in debt.
>
> Then in 1993 he started making ironwork in one of the farm outbuildings. A friend mentioned she wanted some candlesticks and Mr Lawrence had a go. He gradually built a range of items and sold them at craft fairs held at a neighbour's house.
>
> In 1994, a fellow farmer ordered £20,000 worth of railings and tree guards, which prompted Mr Lawrence to think bigger. He decided to ditch the farming and try to make a go of the ironmongery.
>
> The first attempt at marketing was through a small advertisement in Period Living magazine, costing £90. People who responded were sent an A4 card that showed black-and-white silhouettes of the products available.
>
> Those cards cost £175 to print. Today, the 34-page colour brochure, costing £30,000, shows a wide variety of light fittings, wall brackets, curtain poles, door handles and hinges, fireside guards, grates, and tools. Turnover [sales] has risen from £4,000 in 1993 to an estimated £2.5m in the year to next March, with light fittings proving the most popular items.
>
> Mr Lawrence said: 'Although we compete with high street lighting shops, our designs are different. Our lights are not tinny, but substantial.'
>
> The company has grown without borrowing or selling equity [shares]. Capital losses from farming meant there was no tax to pay in the early years, and new machinery was funded out of cash flow.
>
> Mail-order is credit-driven with the money coming in before the goods go out, Mr Lawrence says. The farm has plenty of barns and buildings so he is not short of workshop space.
>
> He said: 'I convert the buildings myself using cash in the business. I'm fond of diggers and dumpers.' Mr Lawrence's wife, Sheena, helps with the accounts, designing and marketing new products.
>
> From Alison Eadie, 'Starting Out', *Daily Telegraph*, 10 June 2002, © Telegraph Group Limited 2002

Questions:

1. What key areas of financial information will Mr Lawrence need to cons der when setting up an accounting system for his business?

2. What is meant by 'Mail-order is credit-driven with the money coming in before the goods go out'?

(Suggested answers and discussion areas are available on the companion website.)

■ WEB LINKS

Company websites
(Companies referred to in this chapter)
Domino's Pizza www.dominos.co.uk
Jim Lawrence Traditional Ironwork www.jim-lawrence.co.uk

Websites of accounting software companies
MYOB http://www.myob.com
Pegasus http://www.pegasus.co.uk
Sage www.sage.com
Tas Books www.tassoftware.com

■ FURTHER READING

Cox, D. (1999). *Business Accounts*, 2nd edn. (Worcester: Osborne Book), chapters 2–6.

Dyson, J. R. (2003). *Accounting for Non-accounting Students*, 5th edn. (Harlow: FT/Prentice Hall), chapter 3.

Jones, M. (2002). *Accounting for Non-specialists*, 1st edn. (Chichester: Wiley), chapter 3.

Weetman, P. (2003). *Financial and Management Accounting: An Introduction*, 3rd edn. (Harlow: FT/Prentice Hall), chapter 2.

Wood, F., and Sangster, A. (2003). *Business Accounting 1*, 9th edn. (Harlow: FT/Prentice Hall), chapters 1–6.

■ COMPANION WEBSITE MATERIALS

 Additional materials are available for students and lecturers on the companion website, at **www.oup.com/uk/booksites/busecon/business/**

3

Summarizing financial information

OBJECTIVES

By the end of this chapter you will be able to:

- Appreciate the need to summarize financial information.
- Understand the accounting adjustments required to prepare a profit and loss account and balance sheet: accruals; prepayments; provisions for depreciation and doubtful debts; unsold stock.
- Compare the key features of various forms of business organizations.
- Understand the main differences between the profit and loss accounts and balance sheets prepared by different types of business organization.

3.1 Introduction

In the previous chapter we saw how nearly all businesses use a continuous accounting recording method known as double-entry bookkeeping. This ensures that the financial transactions are sorted into their effect on the five key aspects of the business: income, expenditure, assets, liabilities, and capital (ownership interest). This system will be active over the entire life of the business and is the source of such day-to-day information as who the business owes money to (creditors) and which customers owe it money (debtors). The cash book details will help to avoid unforeseen banking difficulties caused by issuing more cheques than funds available, and any queries raised by customers and suppliers on invoices can usually be resolved by looking at the information in the journals and personal ledgers.

At intervals, something else is needed. It is necessary for the managers or owners to step back from the detail and take an overview of the business performance to aid their stewardship of the organization. They can do this in a number of ways, and in this chapter we look at two of the most important financial summaries, the *profit and loss account*, which gives an overview of a business's income and expenditure and the *balance sheet*, which shows the assets, liabilities, and capital. Other important financial summaries, such as the *cash flow statement*, are considered in Chapters 9 and 11.

3.2 Financial periods

Before preparing summaries of financial information, a business must decide on the time period to be covered, known as the 'financial period'. For example, the management of a large and complex company might need to have information produced on a weekly basis, whereas a small business with an owner-manager may prepare summaries only once a year. External factors may come into play, as taxation authorities will require annual information on profits, and *limited companies* are required by legislation to publish financial summaries. Companies whose shares are listed on a stock exchange have a further duty to produce *interim* reports for the first six months of their financial year (*quarterly* reports in the USA).

The key set of financial summaries and related information is known as the 'final accounts' in a small business, or the 'annual report and accounts' in a larger one. The choice of date on which a financial year ends varies from business to business and may coincide with the calendar year (31 December), tax year (31 March), or simply a date convenient to the business (for example, a travel company might choose 30 September because it is in the 'quiet season' for holiday bookings). Many companies choose a date which is the last working day before the end of a month so that they have a complete number of weeks in each financial year.

> Look at the end date of Domino's Pizza's annual report and accounts as shown on the first line of the Directors' Report on p. 316. Why do you think they chose 29 December as the end of their financial year?[1]

3.3 The accrual basis of accounting

Company legislation, generally accepted accounting practice, and the Statement of Principles (see p. 4) state that, with the exception of cash flow information—to be considered in Chapter 9—financial statements should be prepared on the *accrual basis* of accounting. This requires the non-cash effects of transactions and other events to be reflected, as far as possible, in the financial statements for the accounting period *in which they occur*, and not, for example, in the period in which any *cash* involved is received or paid. Revenue and profits dealt with when calculating profits or losses are matched with associated costs incurred in earning them, so when calculating profit, *all* income and related expenditure, whether paid for or not, must be included. In practical terms, this means that a number of adjustments have to be made to the transaction totals disclosed in a trial balance before they can be included within the profit and loss account and balance sheet, as follows.

3.3.1 Accruals

Accruals are additional expenses incurred during the financial period which have not been paid for by the end of that period. They do not include trade creditors which have been

---

[1] To ensure an exact number of weeks in its financial year.

invoiced in the normal way. Examples would include utility charges such as electricity, gas, water, etc. which have not been fully paid for by the end of the year. If the utility companies send bills on a quarterly basis, it is likely that on the day chosen as the end of the financial period, amounts relating to those utilities will be unpaid by the business. In arriving at the amounts to be included as expenditure in the final accounts, these 'accruals' must be added to the balance in the relevant general ledger account. For example, if the financial year ends on 31 December and by that date only three quarters' electricity bills have been paid, then we have to estimate the fourth quarter's bill.

9 months paid by the year-end + 3 months' accrual = 12 months' expense

Remember '**Add an Accrual**' to get to the total expense for the year.

Figure 3.1 shows how accruals affect successive years' expense totals.

3.3.2 Prepayments

Businesses will sometimes make payments within a financial period for expenses that relate to the following financial period. These are known as *prepayments*. Typically, prepayments occur when payments are made for expenses the benefits of which accrue over a future time period. Examples include rent paid in advance, insurance premiums paid now but relating to the year ahead, and road tax which might be paid for a future period of six or twelve months. In arriving at the amounts to be included as expenditure in the final accounts, prepayments have the reverse effect to accruals, as they *reduce* the balance in the relevant general ledger account. For example, if a business has paid for eighteen months' rent by the end of its financial year, then six months' rent has been prepaid and must be deducted to arrive at the total rent for the year.

18 months paid by the year-end − 6 months prepaid = 12 months' expense

Figure 3.2 shows how prepayments affect successive years' expense totals.

3.3.3 Provisions

Another area to consider is that there may be *potential* losses or liabilities which are uncertain, in the sense that it is not clear when they may occur or what the amount might be. Despite this uncertainty, the business must accept the possibility of loss by transferring profits into specific accounts known as *provisions*. No cash transfers are involved, and provisions can decrease as well as increase. Most common examples are provisions for depreciation and provisions for doubtful debts:

1. *Provisions for depreciation*. Fixed assets such as buildings, machinery, computers, and motor vehicles will tend to lose value over time due to various factors including physical deterioration, obsolescence, or the expiry of a lease. These losses must not be ignored when preparing the profit and loss account, so a reasonable estimate must be made and included as one of the business expenses, even though there is no cash payment involved. Double-entry principles mean that the creation of a depreciation expense also results in a reduction in the value of the related fixed asset.

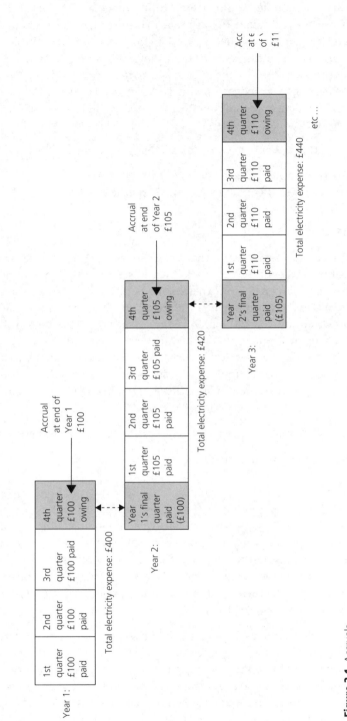

Figure 3.1 Accruals

In the example, by the end of each year, the company always has one quarter's electricity bill unpaid. Its quarterly charge has risen from £100 per quarter in Year 1, to £105 per quarter in Year 2, to £110 per quarter in Year 3. The total electricity charge to be included each year is £400, £420 and £440 respectively, as explained in the figure.

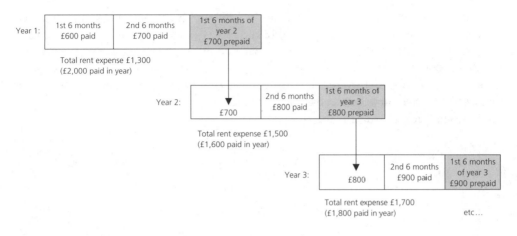

Figure 3.2 Prepayments

In the example, by the end of each year, the company has always paid six months' rent in advance. At the very start of its first year, it paid £600 for six months' rent. It then paid £1,400 for the next twelve months. The rent then increased to £1,600 p.a. half-way through Year 2, and to £1,800 half-way through Year 3. The total rent charge to be included each year is £1,300, £1,500 and £1,700 respectively, as explained in the figure.

The most common method of calculating depreciation is the *straight line method*, which is based on the following formula:

$$\frac{\text{Cost of the asset} - \text{Estimated value at end of asset's life}}{\text{Estimated life in years}}$$

This results in an even spread of the loss in value over the life of the asset. Remember that the accrual concept requires us to include all relevant transactions in the financial summaries, and the depreciation calculation is one aspect of this concept. Many businesses do not make an estimate of the value at the end of the asset's life, on the grounds of uncertainty. When estimating the potential life of the asset, the business would look at similar assets owned by the company and make an 'educated guess'. For example, a machine bought for £26,000 and estimated to have a life of five years, by which time it could be traded in for £1,000, would have a straight line annual depreciation of £5,000 p.a. for each of the five years ((£26,000 − £1,000)/5).

The next most common estimation technique is known as the *reducing balance method*, which results in higher depreciation in the early years compared to the later years of the asset's life. This method is particularly appropriate to assets such as motor cars, where most value is lost in the two years following purchase. In the first year, a depreciation percentage is applied to the cost, and in subsequent years the same percentage is applied to the 'net book value' (or 'reduced value'), which is the cost less all the previous depreciation charged on that asset.

For example, assume that the machine costing £26,000 as referred to in the above example was not to be depreciated by the straight line method, but instead by the reducing balance method using a percentage rate of 48 per cent.

The first year's depreciation would be estimated at 48% × £26,000 = £12,480. This would be shown as an expense in the profit and loss account, whilst in the balance sheet at the end of the first year, the asset's value would be shown at £26,000 − £12,480 = £13,520.

The depreciation for the second year would again use the 48 per cent, but it would be applied to the reduced value at the end of the first year, £13,520, i.e. 48% × £13,520 = £6,490. The net book value shown in the balance sheet at the end of the second year would be £26,000 − (£12,480 + £6,490) = £7,030. This pattern continues over the useful economic life of the asset, eventually writing down the asset to its estimated residual value of £1,000. It is helpful to look at bar charts for each method, based on the above example, as shown in Figures 3.3 (a) and (b):

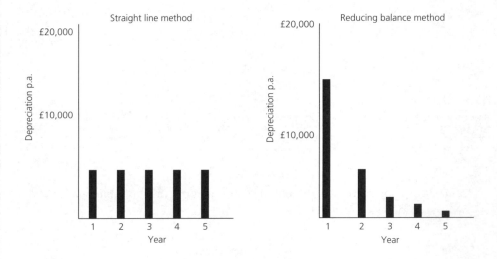

Figure 3.3 (a) Bar charts of straight line and reducing balance methods of depreciation, showing depreciation p.a. under each method

Note: Example used is of an asset costing £26,000 with a five-year life and an estimated residual value of £1,000.

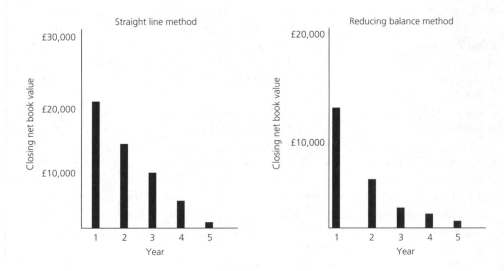

Figure 3.3 (b) Bar charts of straight line and reducing balance methods of depreciation, showing the closing net book value under each method

Note: Example used is as Figure 3.3 (a).

Note that the formula for arriving at the required percentage for the reducing balance method is as follows:

$$r = 1 - n\sqrt{\frac{s}{c}}$$

where r = percentage, n = useful life, s = residual value, and c = original cost.

In the above example, the formula was used as follows:

$$r = 1 - 5\sqrt{\frac{1,000}{26,000}}$$
$$r = 1 - 5\sqrt{0.3846}$$
$$r = 1 - (0.3846^{0.2})$$
$$r = 1 - 0.5212$$
$$r = 48\% \text{ (rounded)}$$

 Look at the note on 'depreciation' on p. 325 of Domino's Pizza's annual report and reflect on the varying time periods used to write off the tangible (i.e. 'physical') fixed assets. Which depreciation method has the company used?

2. *Provisions for doubtful debts*. When listing the assets in a balance sheet, we must ensure that we do not overstate their value. The depreciation provision allowed us to make a reasonable estimate of the fixed assets' loss in value but other assets may also be worth less than the amounts shown in the ledger. In particular, some of the amounts shown as owing by customers in the sales ledger might never be paid. For example, customers may go bankrupt or die penniless, companies go into liquidation or dispute the amounts owing. We must ensure as far as possible that the amounts shown as 'trade debtors' in the balance sheet represent only 'good' debts, i.e. those where there is a reasonable prospect of the customer actually paying.

First, the business needs to identify *bad debts*, where it is highly unlikely that the debtor will pay. Such debts must be 'written off' by deleting them from the list of the sales ledger balances, and showing the total bad debts as one of the expenses for the financial period. If there are other debts which, whilst not being 'good' debts, are not yet 'bad' debts (i.e. there is *some* possibility of getting paid), then the business will have to make a *provision for doubtful debts*, which works in a rather similar way to the provision for depreciation of fixed assets shown above. However, neither a straight line method nor a reducing balance method are applicable: instead the business calculates the total of the doubtful debts (this might be the specific 'doubtful' customer balances or an estimated percentage of the total debtors which, from past experience, the business would expect to turn bad at some time in the future), and then reduces profit to cover the total. The balance sheet will only include the 'good debts'.

For example, a business with sales ledger balances totalling £241,926 identifies that £3,026 is owed by bankrupt customers and a further £8,900 is owed by customers whose invoices have been unpaid for over six months, but are thought to be in temporary financial

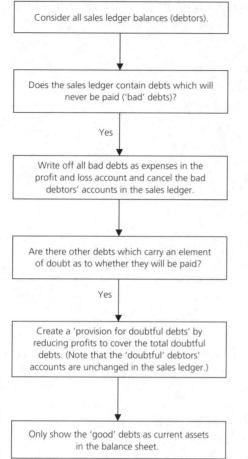

Figure 3.4 Arriving at the 'good' debts

difficulties. In the business's profit and loss account, the expenses for the year will include the bad debts of £3,026 and a provision for doubtful debts of £8,900. In the balance sheet, only the 'good' debtors must be included, i.e. £230,000 (£241,926 − (£3,026 + £8,900)).

Other types of provisions, such as for deferred taxation, are covered in Chapters 5 and 7.

3.3.4 Unsold stocks

In a trading or manufacturing company, there might be stocks of unsold goods, raw materials, and partly finished goods at the start and end of the financial period. A valuation must be made so that we can exclude unsold closing stocks from the year's profit calculation whilst including the opening stocks brought forward from the previous year in the calculation of the 'cost of the goods sold' during the year. In the balance sheet at the end of the financial period we must include the stock valuation as part of the business's current assets. The value placed on stock has a direct influence on profit levels—the higher the value of closing stock, the greater the profit. Because of this, it is vital that stock values are as accurate as possible.

In the majority of cases, stock is valued at cost price, in other words the price paid when the goods or raw materials were purchased. Sometimes it is difficult to establish the cost price, particularly in the case of raw materials or goods bought at different dates and at different prices (e.g. liquids, chemicals, ingredients). It is usual in such circumstances either to take an average cost price or to value stock on a theoretical 'First in, first out' (FIFO) basis, where it is *assumed* that the first stock into the business was the first stock to be used, thus leaving the unsold stock to be valued at the most recent prices. The use of this method is unrelated to the actual way in which physical stock moves into and out of the business.

Partly completed goods (work in progress) are valued according to the degree of completion, but again on the basis of cost price plus labour costs etc. *Stock is never normally valued at selling price*, as to do so would be to include a profit which, by definition, is unearned, as the goods in stock are unsold. Occasionally, stock has deteriorated, gone out of fashion, or otherwise been devalued so that its anticipated selling price is actually less than its cost price. Only in these circumstances can the stock be valued at what it could be sold for, less any expenses needed to be incurred to make it saleable (also known as the 'net realizable value'). The relevant accounting standard (SSAP 9 in the UK) summarizes this in the following way: 'Stock is to be stated at the total of the lower of cost and net realisable value of the separate items of stock or of groups of similar items.' For example, a lady's fashion business might have 500 orange handbags in stock which cost the company £10 each. The normal selling price was £25 each, but by the end of the financial period the company could only sell blue and yellow handbags. The only chance of selling orange handbags was to add a blue and yellow leather strap at a cost of £2 per handbag and to reduce the selling price to £8 each. The closing stocks of orange handbags would be valued at:

$$(500 \times £8) - (500 \times £2) = £3{,}000$$

Note that the original selling price is irrelevant to the calculation.

 Look at Domino's Pizza's accounting policy on stock valuation (p. 325) and relate the company's practice to the explanation given above.

3.4 The trial balance

In the previous chapter we saw how a trial balance was extracted to prove that the transaction recording process had resulted in the same value of debit entries as credit entries. In a computerized system, this would be done automatically, but in a manual system it is prepared by making a simple list of every debit balance and every credit balance. Remember that it does not prove that everything is correct, as various mistakes may still exist within the system, such as entries being made into the wrong customer's account, transactions being omitted completely, etc. However, it is still a vital stage in the preparation of the profit and loss account and balance sheet. In the previous chapter we looked at a business called Throttle Bikes, which, after fourteen days' trading, had the following trial balance:

Throttle Bikes Trial Balance as at 14 May 2003		
Sales Ledger	**Debit**	**Credit**
Ranjit Chaudry	350	
Purchase Ledger		
Securikor Ltd.		150
General Ledger		
Sales of motorbikes		5,700
Sales of accessories		550
Purchase of motorbikes	4,000	
Purchase of accessories	1,000	
Security	150	
Rent	500	
Stationery	400	
Wages	300	
Computer	600	
Capital		250
Cash Book		
Bank		650
Totals	**7,300**	**7,300**

Throttle Bikes is a 'sole trader' business, i.e. owned by one person who takes all the risks and rewards. Let's assume that Throttle Bikes has got to the end of its first year of trading, and its trial balance on 30 April 2004 (twelve months after its start date of 1 May 2003) was as follows:

Throttle Bikes Trial Balance as at 30 April 2004		
Sales Ledger	**Debit**	**Credit**
Paul Pringle	1,750	
Rita Carver	280	
Vance Sargent (owing since November)	155	
Purchase Ledger		
Securikor Ltd.		260
Wackimoto		4,860

General Ledger		
Advertising	12,000	
Bad debts written off	600	
Capital		250
Computers	1,900	
Insurance	4,000	
Motor vehicle	18,000	
Owner's drawings	22,365	
Purchase of accessories	24,560	
Purchase of motorbikes	95,200	
Rent	15,000	
Sales of accessories		42,530
Sales of motorbikes		196,700
Security	7,500	
Showroom equipment	5,600	
Stationery	2,900	
Utilities (light, heat, water)	8,420	
Wages	21,250	
Cash Book		
Bank	3,120	
Totals	**244,600**	**244,600**

As the totals of the trial balance agree, we know that, at least, the arithmetic within the double-entry bookkeeping system is correct. We shall assume that there are no mistakes which have been made whilst recording the financial transactions, and that Throttle Bikes needs to prepare its profit and loss account and balance sheet for the year ended 30 April 2004.

First, let's look at some of the entries in the trial balance:

1. The sales ledger is showing three debtors' balances, and the purchase ledger is showing two creditors' balances. Further down the trial balance we notice that during the year one or more customers didn't pay their bills, requiring their balances of £600 to be written off as bad debts.

2. The owner's capital balance has apparently not changed since 4 May 2003, when it stood at £250. However, there is a balance for 'owner's drawings', which shows that the owner, Fred Throttle, withdrew £22,365 from the business for his own purposes.

3. Several fixed assets have been purchased during the year. These are the computers, motor vehicles, and showroom equipment.

Because of the accrual concept referred to earlier, we need to make adjustments to the trial balance for the following:

- Accruals (expenses incurred but not yet paid for): assume that Throttle Bikes owed £750 for wages and £400 for electricity.

- Prepayments (expenses paid for but not yet incurred): assume that Throttle Bikes had paid £2,000 rent in advance and £500 of the insurance relates to the next financial year.

- Provisions (amounts set aside to cover potential losses): assume that the debt due from Vance Sargent is doubtful, and that depreciation is to be provided at the following rates:

    Computers: over four years, straight line basis, with no residual value. This results in an annual depreciation charge of £1,900/4 = £475 for four years.

    Motor vehicle: at 40 per cent p.a., reducing balance basis, which results in a provision being needed in the year ended 30 April 2004 of 40% × £18,000 = £7,200.

    Showroom equipment: over ten years, straight line basis, assuming a residual value of 20 per cent of initial cost. This results in an annual charge of [£5,600 − (20% × £5,600)]/10 = £448.

    Assume that in all cases, a full year's depreciation is to be charged, regardless of the date of purchase of the fixed asset within the year.

- Unsold stock (stock not sold during the current financial period, carried forward to be sold in the next financial period): As this is Throttle Bikes' first year of trading there is no opening stock brought forward from a previous financial period. At the end of the financial period, 30 April 2004, assume that there was closing stock of accessories £3,250 and closing stock of motorbikes £6,220.

3.4.1 Adjusting the trial balance

We can show the effect of these adjustments by adding a number of columns to the trial balance which show the effect of the various adjustments described above. This 'extended trial balance' also splits the ledger accounts between those affecting the profit and loss account ('income and expenditure' accounts) and those required to produce the balance sheet ('assets, liabilities, and capital' accounts):

Throttle Bikes, (Extended) Trial Balance as at 30 April 2004 (£)

	Trial balance		Adjustments		Profit and loss account		Balance sheet	
	Debit	Credit	Debit	Credit	Debit	Credit	Debit	Credit
Sales Ledger								
Paul Pringle	1,750						1,750	
Rita Carver	280						280	
Vance Sargent	155						155	
Purchase Ledger								
Securikor Ltd.		260						260
Wackimoto		4,860						4,860
General Ledger								
Advertising	12,000				12,000			
Bad debts written off	600				600			
Capital		250						250

	TB Dr	TB Cr	Adj Dr	Adj Cr	P&L Dr	P&L Cr	BS Dr	BS Cr
Computers	1,900						1,900	
Insurance	4,000			500	3,500			
Motor vehicle	18,000						18,000	
Owner's drawings	22,365						22,365	
Purchase of accessories	24,560			3,250	21,310			
Purchase of motorbikes	95,200			6,220	88,980			
Rent	15,000			2,000	13,000			
Sales of accessories		42,530				42,530		
Sales of motorbikes		196,700				196,700		
Security	7,500				7,500			
Showroom equipment	5,600						5,600	
Stationery	2,900				2,900			
Utilities (light, heat, water)	8,420		400		8,820			
Wages	21,250		750		22,000			
Increases in provisions:								
Doubtful debts				155	155			
Depreciation on computers				475	475			
Depreciation on motor vehicle				7,200	7,200			
Depreciation on showroom equipment				448	448			
Cash Book								
Bank	3,120						3,120	
Totals	244,600	244,600						
Closing stock (accessories)			3,250				3,250	
Closing stock (motor bikes)			6,220				6,220	
Accruals (400+750)				1,150				1,150
Prepayments (500+2,000)			2,500				2,500	
Provision for doubtful debts			155					155
Depreciation on computers			475					475
Depreciation on motor vehicle			7,200					7,200
Depreciation on showroom equipment			448					448
Total adjustments			21,398	21,398				
					188,888	239,230		
Net profit for the year					50,342			50,342
					239,230	239,230		
							65,140	65,140

Notice that Vance Sargent's account within the sales ledger is unaffected by it being classified as a 'doubtful debt'—the business still has hopes of recovering the amount due.

3.5 The profit and loss account of a sole trader

Once the effect of the adjustments has been considered, we can set out the profit and loss account in a way which shows both 'gross' profit (i.e. the profit made on buying and selling goods, *before* the general business expenses—also referred to as 'overhead expenses'—are deducted) and 'operating' profit (often called 'net' profit), which is the profit *after* all overhead expenses have been deducted.

Throttle Bikes' statement will appear as follows:

Throttle Bikes profit and loss account for the year ended 30 April 2004 (£)		Accessories		Motorbikes		Total
Sales (turnover)		42,530		196,700		239,230
Less cost of Sales						
Purchases	24,560		95,200		119,760	
Less closing stock	(3,250)		(6,220)		(9,470)	
		(21,310)		(88,980)		(110,290)
Gross profit		21,220		107,720		128,940
Less expenses:						
Advertising					12,000	
Bad debts written off					600	
Insurance					3,500	
Rent					13,000	
Security					7,500	
Stationery					2,900	
Utilities					8,820	
Wages					22,000	
Doubtful debts					155	
Depreciation on computers					475	
Depreciation on motor vehicle					7,200	
Depreciation on showroom equipment					448	
						(78,598)
Operating profit						50,342

The dark shaded information is optional, though many businesses will find it useful to show separate figures for the gross profit on different types of products. The figures shown in brackets are deducted from the figure immediately above in the same column—this is a convention when presenting financial summaries.

3.6 **The balance sheet of a sole trader**

Having given the overview of the year's trading performance in the profit and loss account, we can then proceed to summarize the position of the business on the last day of that period. The *balance sheet* takes the remaining balances from the adjusted trial balance and summarizes them under the key headings of Assets, Liabilities, and Capital, as follows:

Throttle Bikes balance sheet as at 30 April 2004			
Fixed assets	**Cost**	**Depreciation**	**Net book value**
Computers	1,900	475	1,425
Motor vehicle	18,000	7,200	10,800
Showroom equipment	5,600	448	5,152
	25,500	8,123	17,377
Current assets			
Stock of accessories		3,250	
Stock of motorbikes		6,220	
Trade debtors	2,185		
Less provision for doubtful debts	(155)		
		2,030	
Prepayments		2,500	
Bank balance		3,120	
		17,120	
Less current liabilities			
Trade creditors	5,120		
Accruals	1,150		
		(6,270)	
Net current assets			10,850
Total assets less current liabilities			**28,227**
Capital			
Capital introduced		250	
Add operating profit		50,342	
		50,592	
Less drawings		(22,365)	
			28,227

Again, the information in the dark shaded boxes is optional, but helps to show how we have arrived at the net book values of the fixed assets. Notice how the provisions are deducted from the relevant assets: the provision for doubtful debts is deducted from the trade debtors and the provisions for depreciation are deducted from the related fixed assets. The value of the owner's capital has changed due to the business having made an operating profit during the year, as shown in the profit and loss account. However, drawings made by the owner from the business for personal expenses serve to reduce the capital balance.

Remember the 'balance sheet equation', Assets less Liabilities = Capital, which is why the two sides of the balance sheet show the same total (£28,227).

3.7 The three main types of business organization

3.7.1 Sole traders

The profit and loss account and balance sheet of Throttle Bikes as shown above represent typical financial summaries of a small 'sole trader' business. As the owner carries all the risks and rewards of running the business, the entire operating profit (or loss) is transferred to the capital account in the balance sheet. Operating as a sole trader is the least sophisticated of all types of business organization. However, it will suit an individual who wants to run a business with a minimum of legal formalities. Sole traders, by definition, are owned by one person. Advantages of operating as a sole trader are:

- The owner has absolute control over the business.
- The business can be established without any legal formalities.
- Personal supervision by the owner may result in a better service to customers and clients.
- The owner does not have to reveal the financial results of the business to the general public.

However, there are also disadvantages, including:

- The owner has personal liability for all the debts of the business, without limit, which might lead to personal bankruptcy if the business fails and creditors claim the owner's personal assets. Contrast this with 'limited liability' companies below.
- Total control and personal supervision usually require long hours and very hard work.
- There is no co-owner with whom to share the problems and anxieties associated with running the business.
- If the owner is absent from the business due to sickness or other reasons, this may have a serious effect on the state of the business.
- Future prospects for expansion are restricted, as it is dependent on the owner's ability to raise finance.

Although many people prefer independence and quite happily continue as sole traders, it is extremely difficult to expand a business without also increasing the number of people who own it. The main types of 'multi-ownership' enterprises are partnerships and limited liability companies.

3.7.2 **Partnerships**

A partnership is defined as 'The relation which subsists between persons carrying on a business in common with a view of profit'.[2] Often partnerships are formed by professional people such as architects, accountants, and solicitors, where the rules of their profession have historically required their members to have unlimited liability for their firm's debts. This position has been softened over the years, with some limitation of liability being permitted.

Advantages of partnership include:

- Sharing of the problems and pleasures of running the business.
- Access to expertise and financial input from fellow partners.
- Sharing of losses as well as profits.
- Few legal formalities involved, though a partnership agreement should be drawn up to avoid misunderstandings.
- The financial results do not have to be made public.

Disadvantages include:

- Personality clashes may threaten the business and ultimately break up the partnership.
- In the vast majority of partnerships, there is no restriction on the personal liability of partners for the debts of the business.
- Generally there is less access to funding for expansion when compared to a limited company (see below).

Main sources of finance for a partnership are:

- Capital introduced by the partners.
- Profits ploughed back into the business.
- Loans from friends and family of partners.
- Bank borrowings, through overdrafts or loans, secured either on the partnership's assets or the personal assets of individual partners.

In most respects, including the day-to-day bookkeeping aspects, partnership accounting is identical with that of any other type of business organization. The only difference is that accounts must be opened showing the financial implications of the partnership agreement. These include details of:

- Shares of profits and losses.
- Capital introduced and withdrawn by each partner.
- Drawings made by each partner.
- Whether any partners are to receive a guaranteed salary (e.g. if only one partner works full-time for the partnership).
- Interest charged on drawings (to discourage individual partners from drawing excessive amounts).

---

[2] Partnership Act 1890.

- Interest allowed on capital balances (to reward those partners who have invested more than others).

Partnership accounting: the profit and loss account

When preparing a partnership's financial summaries, the profit and loss account will be produced in exactly the same way as that for a sole trader, such as Throttle Bikes. The only additional information, an 'appropriation account', comes in a separate section after the operating profit or loss has been determined, as the profit or loss has to be 'appropriated' (divided) between the partners according to their partnership agreement. If partners have also agreed to pay themselves salaries or charge interest on drawings or capital this is also shown in this section.

For example, if Fred Throttle, the founder of Throttle Bikes, had decided to set up the business in partnership with his sister Thora, they would have had to agree important financial arrangements such as how much capital each was to contribute, the proportions in which profits and losses were to be shared, and whether either of them was to be paid a salary. Assuming that they agreed on equal shares and no salaries, the final part (the 'appropriation account') of the profit and loss account of the partnership, 'Fred and Thora's Bikes', would have looked like this:

Operating profit		50,342
Divided as follows:		
Fred Throttle	25,171	
Thora Throttle	25,171	
		50,342

The first part of the profit and loss account would have been identical to that of the sole trader.

Partnership balance sheets

The 'top half' of a partnership's balance sheet, showing the assets and liabilities, is identical to that of a sole trader. However, the sole trader's capital account is replaced by details of the individual capital accounts of each partner. 'Fred and Thora's Bikes' would have shown the following details in the 'capital' section of their partnership's balance sheet (assuming that Fred's personal drawings were £12,365, and Thora's were £10,000):

Total assets less current liabilities			**28,227**
Capital accounts			
Fred Throttle's Capital Account			
Capital introduced		125	
Add share of operating profit		25,171	
		25,296	
Less drawings		(12,365)	
			12,931

Thora Throttle's Capital Account			
Capital introduced		125	
Add share of operating profit		25,171	
		25,296	
Less drawings		(10,000)	
			15,296
			28,227

Note that 'Capital introduced' by a partner (or sole trader) can be in the form of any asset of value, not just cash. For example, a privately owned van or computer might be given to the business as part of capital introduced, at an appropriate valuation.

3.7.3 Limited liability companies

Although there are many advantages in running a business as a sole trader or a partnership, these can be outweighed by the fact that the owner or partners have *personal* responsibility for meeting all the debts of their business. Whilst this may be of little concern to the proprietors of healthy, profitable businesses, it can have a devastating effect on the fortunes of owners of failing or loss-making enterprises, as they must meet the claims of creditors from their personal assets if the business's assets are insufficient.

Another major disadvantage for the ambitious business owner is the restricted scope sole traders and partnerships have for raising funds for expansion. To overcome these, many businesses are organized as *limited companies*. Their main features are:

1. They are separate legal entities, able to trade, own assets, and owe liabilities (including tax on their profit) in their own right independently from their owners (known as 'shareholders' or 'members').

2. Ownership is (with rare exceptions) divided into shares (the 'share capital') which can be bought and sold. The main type of shares are called *ordinary* shares (US: *common stock*), also known as the 'equity' capital of the company. Each ordinary share carries an equal right to vote in company meetings and an equal right to share in any dividends paid as a reward to the providers of the capital.

3. The owners have limited liability for the debts of the company, so even if the company fails with considerable debts, their loss is restricted to the value of their part of the share capital—their personal assets are not at risk. However, the directors of small limited companies are often required to give personal guarantees to banks or other lenders to compensate them in the event of the company failing.

4. Management is in the hands of *directors*, who are elected by the shareholders. The death or resignation of a director or shareholder does not affect the structure of the company, which may continue to trade as before.

5. Public limited companies (which have the letters *plc* after the company's name) are allowed to sell their shares to the general public, which enables them to have access to funds for expansion. *Private* limited companies (which have the letters *ltd.* after their company's name) cannot sell their shares to the public, having to raise finance by selling shares to friends, family, and business contacts. Many, but not all, plc's have their shares traded on a *stock market*, which enables shareholders and potential shareholders to buy and sell shares at a price determined by market forces. Such share sales are between one shareholder and another and no money passes to or from the company itself.

6. Limited companies can raise money by issuing *debentures*, which are fixed interest loans usually secured on the company's assets, and by issuing *convertible loan stock*, which are loans which can be converted into shares at a later date. Neither debentures nor loan stocks are part of a company's share capital.

7. Companies can keep back any part of their 'after tax' profit in the form of *reserves*— they don't have to pay it all to shareholders in the form of dividends: sole traders and partners have *all* their business profits allocated to them, which are then subject to personal income tax to be paid by the individual owners. This can result in limited companies enjoying considerable tax advantages.

Limited companies do have a number of *disadvantages* when compared to other forms of business organizations:

1. Lack of secrecy, as limited companies have to publish financial information, though large companies have to disclose more than small ones.

2. Extra costs of complying with company legislation when compared to the informality of sole trading or partnerships. For large companies this requires the appointment of an auditor, who is an independent qualified accountant responsible for reporting whether the published financial information shows a *true and fair view.*

3. Shareholders' meetings must be held and annual returns must be completed and sent to the government.

Look at Domino's Pizza's 'Notice of Meeting' on p. 341. This shows the agenda for the company's Annual General Meeting as well as details of 'special business' which requires the shareholders' approval.

4. There is a risk of 'hostile takeovers' where shares traded on a stock exchange are acquired in order to mount a takeover bid which is unwelcome to the existing owners of the company. For example, if Company A wants to take over Company B, it may buy shares in Company B over several months, gradually building up a sizeable shareholding without Company B's directors realizing. Company A will then be in a strong position to mount a bid for the rest of the company's shares.

Limited company accounting

As with partnerships, the day-to-day bookkeeping will be identical to that of sole traders. A few extra accounts will have to be opened to record payments made to directors and auditors (if any), as well as details of the share capital and reserves.

Limited company profit and loss account

The operating profit or loss needs to be allocated in a number of ways, as shown in Figure 3.5.

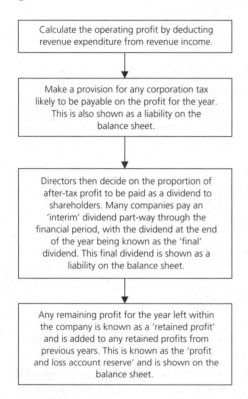

Calculate the operating profit by deducting revenue expenditure from revenue income.

Make a provision for any corporation tax likely to be payable on the profit for the year. This is also shown as a liability on the balance sheet.

Directors then decide on the proportion of after-tax profit to be paid as a dividend to shareholders. Many companies pay an 'interim' dividend part-way through the financial period, with the dividend at the end of the year being known as the 'final' dividend. This final dividend is shown as a liability on the balance sheet.

Any remaining profit for the year left within the company is known as a 'retained profit' and is added to any retained profits from previous years. This is known as the 'profit and loss account reserve' and is shown on the balance sheet.

Figure 3.5 Allocating the company's operating profit

To understand how the profit and loss account is constructed, assume that Throttle Bikes had been formed as a private limited company, with Fred and Thora Throttle as directors each owning 100 shares of £1 nominal value for which they paid £1.25 per share. Their directors' salaries were set at £12,365 for Thora and £10,000 for Fred, and taxation was estimated at £5,000. A final dividend was proposed of £20 per share. The (summarized) profit and loss account of Throttle Bikes Ltd. would appear as follows:

Throttle Bikes Ltd. profit and loss account for the year ended 30 April 2004 (£)		
Turnover		239,230
Less cost of sales		(110,290)
Gross profit		128,940

Less expenses:		
(as in Throttle Bikes)	78,598	
Directors' salaries	22,365	
		(100,963)
Operating profit before taxation		27,977
Less taxation		(5,000)
Operating profit after taxation		22,977
Less proposed dividend		(4,000)
Retained profit for the year		18,977

Look at Domino's Pizza's profit and loss account on p. 320. Find the 'Tax on profit on ordinary activities', the 'Dividends on equity shares' and the 'Profit retained for the financial year'. Refer to n. 8 on p. 329 for further details of dividends paid and proposed.

Limited company balance sheet

The top half ('total assets less current liabilities') of a limited company's balance sheet looks very similar to any other balance sheet, though often fixed assets are split between 'tangible' and 'intangible' (i.e. physical and non-physical), which is explained in Chapter 6.

Current liabilities are referred to as 'Creditors due for payment within one year', and include the taxation liability and proposed dividend.

It is the 'capital' side of a limited company's balance sheet which shows major differences compared to sole traders or partnerships. First, it is headed 'Capital and Reserves' which comprises:

1. Share capital, which is the total share capital issued to shareholders. Shares have a *nominal value* (also called a *par* value) e.g. 25p or 50p (Domino's Pizza's nominal value is 5p), which is set at the time of the company's formation (though can be subsequently changed). Sometimes dividends are expressed as a percentage of this nominal value, though they are more likely to be 'pence per share'. Each company has a maximum number of shares which it is allowed to issue (its *authorized* share capital), whilst the actual amount of share capital in the hands of shareholders is known as the *issued* or *called-up* share capital. Public limited companies must have a minimum authorized and issued share capital of £50,000. Some companies, as well as having ordinary shares, issue *preference* shares, which carry a fixed rate of dividend and have priority over the ordinary shares in respect of the payment of their dividends and the repayment of capital in the event of the company's liquidation. These shares might be *redeemable*, which means that the company can refund the preference shareholders' capital (subject to certain rules to protect the overall capital of the company) after a specified timescale. See Chapter 8 for further information on this topic.

2. Reserves, which are classified as either *capital* reserves or *revenue* reserves. The main revenue reserve is the *profit and loss account reserve*, which is the balance of all retained profits (see Figure 3.5) since the company's inception. Revenue reserves are known as

'distributable'—they can be used for paying company dividends.[3] In a lean year when the company makes losses or meagre profits, these reserves can be drawn upon to ensure that the shareholders get some reward. A key *capital reserve* is the 'share premium account', which is the amount above the nominal value paid into the company by shareholders when the company sold them the shares. For example, a company might sell its 50p nominal value shares for £3.50, in which case the 50p's go into the 'called-up share capital' section of the balance sheet whilst the remaining £3's are shown under a separate heading, 'Share premium account'. Capital reserves are referred to as being 'non-distributable', as they are not allowed to be used by a company for the payment of dividends. Some companies may have other types of capital reserves (e.g. an asset revaluation reserve), and these are considered in Chapter 8.

> Look at Domino's Pizza's capital and reserves within the group balance sheet on p. 321, and related notes on pp. 337–9. Look at the increases in share capital and the share premium account during 2002. Look at n. 20: what was Domino's *authorized* share capital at the balance sheet date?

Continuing the 'Throttle Bikes Ltd.' example, the company's (summarized) balance sheet would appear as follows:

Throttle Bikes Ltd. balance sheet as at 30 April 2004 (£)			
Fixed assets			
Tangible assets			17,377
Current assets			
Stocks		9,470	
Trade debtors		2,030	
Prepayments		2,500	
Bank balance		3,120	
		17,120	
Less creditors: amounts falling due within one year			
Trade creditors	5,120		
Accruals	1,150		
Taxation	5,000		
Dividend	4,000		
		(15,270)	
Net current assets			1,850
Total assets less current liabilities			**19,227**
Capital and reserves			
Called-up capital (200 shares at £1 each)		200	
Share premium account (200 shares at 25p premium)		50	
Profit and loss account		18,977	
			19,227

[3] Subject to detailed rules contained within companies legislation. See Companies Act 1985 ss. 263–81.

Note that, in limited company balance sheets, 'current liabilities' are usually referred to as 'Creditors: amounts falling due within one year'. Any longer-term liabilities would be referred to as 'Creditors: amounts falling due after more than one year'.

> Look again at the Domino's Pizza group profit and loss account and balance sheet on pp. 320 and 321. Familiarize yourself with the key headings (don't concern yourself with the detail at this stage).

3.8 Chapter summary

- A business's financial period can be of any length, but 'final accounts' usually cover a twelve-month period.
- The Statement of Principles requires that the accrual basis of accounting be used when producing a profit and loss account and balance sheet.
- Accruals, prepayments, provisions, and unsold stocks must be taken into account when preparing the profit and loss account and balance sheet.
- The trial balance is the starting point for preparing the profit and loss account and balance sheet.
- Partnerships and limited liability forms of business organization have various advantages and disadvantages when compared to sole traders.
- Partnerships and limited companies will require further information to be shown in the profit and loss account and balance sheet when compared to sole traders' final accounts.

■ GLOSSARY

accrual	Expenses incurred within a financial period but not paid for by the end of that financial period
accrual basis	The production of financial statements which incorporate the effects of all transactions, whether paid for or not
annual report	The collected summarized financial information for a financial year issued to shareholders
authorized share capital	The maximum share capital a limited company is allowed to issue
bad debt	A debt due to the business where there is no hope of getting paid. It is written off as a loss to profit and loss account
balance sheet	The summary of a firm's assets, liabilities, and capital at the end of a financial period
called-up share capital	The shares actually issued by a limited company. Also known as issued share capital

capital reserves	Company reserves which cannot be used for the payment of dividends
convertible loan stock	Loans raised by a limited company which may be converted into shares of that company at a future date
debentures	Loans raised by a limited company, usually secured on the company's assets
depreciation	The loss in value of a fixed asset caused by such factors as time, usage, and obsolescence caused by changing technology
directors	The individuals who act as the officers of a limited company
dividend	The reward on capital which shareholders receive from a limited company
doubtful debt	A debt due to the business where there is uncertainty as to whether the amount due will be paid, but is not yet a bad debt
equity capital	The ordinary shares of a limited company
FIFO	*First In First Out*, a method of stock valuation which assumes that the earliest stock acquired is the first to be used, resulting in closing stock being valued at the most recent prices
final accounts	Financial statements produced at the end of a financial year
financial period	The time period covered by financial summaries
financial year	A twelve-month financial reporting period
good debt	A debt due to the business which is expected to be paid
hostile takeover	A bid to take over control of a company which is unwelcome by that company's directors
interim report	Financial information published by a stock-market listed public limited company covering the first six months of a financial year
limited liability company	A type of business organization whose members' liability to meet the firm's debts is limited to the amount of capital they have invested or agreed to invest
Ltd.	Abbreviation denoting a private limited company
member	Another term for a *shareholder*
net book value	The value of a fixed asset after depreciation has been deducted
net realizable value	The selling price of stock after deducting all relevant costs to enable it to be sold
nominal value	The 'face value' of a share, e.g. £1 or 25p. Also called *par value*
ordinary shares	The most common form of shares issued by limited companies. Each share carries equal voting and dividend rights. Also known as the *equity capital*
overhead expenditure	The general expenses of a business such as those related to administration, distribution, and selling. It does not include the cost of the goods bought for resale

partnership	The relation which subsists between persons carrying on a business in common with a view of profit
partnership appropriation account	Part of the profit and loss account of a partnership, showing how profits or losses are apportioned between partners according to their partnership agreement
par value	Another term meaning nominal value
plc	Abbreviation denoting a public limited company
preference shares	A class of shares carrying a fixed rate of dividend and giving the holders preference over equity shareholders regarding payment of dividends and repayment of capital in the event of the company's liquidation
prepayment	Expenses paid for within a financial period which relate to the following financial period
private limited company	A limited company which is prohibited from selling its shares to the public, denoted by 'ltd.' after the company's name
profit and loss account	The summary of a firm's income and expenditure for a financial period
provision	A liability of uncertain timing or amount
public limited company	A company which is allowed to sell its shares to the general public, denoted by 'plc' after the company's name. It must have at least £50,000 authorized and issued share capital
published accounts	The annual report of a limited company, produced in accordance with the legislation and other relevant rules and regulations laid down by the accounting profession or the stock exchange
reduced value	The net book value of a fixed asset
reducing balance method	A method of allocating depreciation which uses the assumption that the loss in value is greater in the early years than in the later year's of the asset's life
retained profits	The profits left over after all appropriations (tax, dividends, etc.) have been made
revenue reserves	Reserves built up from retained profits via the profit and loss account of a limited company. They can be used to pay dividends
shareholder	The owner of one or more shares in a limited liability company
share premium account	The capital reserve built up from amounts paid by shareholders for their shares, in excess of the nominal value of those shares
sole trader	A business organization owned by one individual with unlimited liability
straight line method	A method of allocating depreciation which uses the assumption that the loss in value occurs evenly over the asset's life
trial balance	A list of every balance within the ledgers, divided between 'debit' and 'credit balances'. Used as a check on the arithmetical accuracy of the double-entry bookkeeping system
work in progress	Partly completed goods

■ **MULTIPLE CHOICE QUESTIONS**

1. A financial period:
    a Always ends on 31 December
    b Always ends on 31 March
    c Is always twelve months long
    d Can start or end at any time

2. A business has paid £6,000 for electricity by the end of its financial period but owes a further £1,000 for electricity used within that period. It did not owe anything for electricity at the start of the period. What relevant figures would be shown in that company's profit and loss account and balance sheet?
    a Profit and loss account expenses include £7,000 and the balance sheet shows £1,000 as a current liability
    b Profit and loss account expenses include £6,000 and the balance sheet shows £1,000 as a current liability
    c Profit and loss account expenses include £7,000 but there are no relevant entries in the balance sheet
    d Profit and loss account expenses include £6,000 but there are no relevant entries in the balance sheet

3. Straight line depreciation is calculated:
    a By using the formula:

    $$\frac{\text{Cost of the asset} + \text{Estimated value at end of asset's life}}{\text{Estimated life in years}}$$

    b By applying the same % each year to the net book value of the asset
    c By using the formula:

    $$\frac{\text{Cost of the asset} - \text{Estimated value at end of asset's life}}{\text{Estimated life in years}}$$

    d By the directors deciding each year what the asset's value is at the balance sheet date, with the year's depreciation being the estimated fall in value since the previous year's valuation

4. A theoretical stock valuation such as FIFO (First In First Out) would be used when:
    a Stock has deteriorated to a point where it is unsaleable
    b Stock is difficult or impossible to value by relating the stock to a price shown on a purchase invoice
    c Stock has been bought just after the balance sheet date
    d It is assumed that the most recent stock purchased is sold before older stock

5. In a balance sheet, stock is usually valued:
    a At average selling prices during the financial period
    b At the selling prices on the date of the balance sheet
    c At the higher of cost and net realizable value
    d At the lower of cost and net realizable value

6. The asset of 'debtors' included in the 'current assets' total in a balance sheet should contain:

   a   Good debts only
   b   All sales ledger balances
   c   All sales ledger balances less bad debts written off
   d   Bad and doubtful debts

7. Which of the following might be shown in a partnership's profit and loss account, but not a sole trader's?

   a   Wages
   b   Interest charged on drawings
   c   Provision for depreciation
   d   Bank overdraft interest

8. Which of the following might be shown in a limited company's profit and loss account, but not a partnership's?

   a   Retained profits for the period
   b   Provision for doubtful debts
   c   Bad debts written off
   d   Provision for depreciation

9. If a company issues convertible loan stock, what is it normally convertible into at a later date?

   a   Cash
   b   Debentures
   c   Shares
   d   Reserves

10. If a company issued 10,000 shares with a nominal value of 20p at a price of £2, which of the following balance sheet entries would be correct?

   a   Called-up share capital £22,000
   b   Called-up share capital £2,000, share premium account £20,000
   c   Called-up share capital £20,000, share premium account £18,000
   d   Called-up share capital £2,000, share premium account £18,000

(Note: answers are shown in Appendix 2.)

■ DISCUSSION QUESTIONS

The following is an extract from *Something Wholesale: My Life and Times in the Rag Trade* by Eric Newby:

> After the ruinous departure of Mr Lane my father had taken into partnership another man, who had been a member of Lane and Newby's since its inception. Unfortunately, although the new partner was morally blameless, he was far less competent than his predecessor and the business suffered even more. Eventually death had removed him too and my father was forced to turn the business into a Limited Company.
>
> It seems probable that no one ever succeeded in explaining to my father what the formation of a Limited Liability Company entailed. I think he believed that it was a polite fiction that divested him of the onus of liability and at the same time allowed him to be a partnership without a partner.

1. What does the first paragraph indicate about the disadvantages of partnership as a form of business organization?

2. Why do you think Eric Newby's father had been 'forced to turn the business into a Limited Company'?

3. Is the author correct in suggesting that a limited liability company is 'a polite fiction that divested him of the onus of liability and at the same time allowed him to be a partnership without a partner'?

(Note: Suggested answers or discussion points are available on the companion website.)

■ LONGER QUESTIONS

(Questions marked W have suggested answers on the companion website. Other questions are answered in Appendix 3.)

1. Avril's Artefacts is a small business buying and selling antiques. Its trial balance as at 31 October 2004 is shown below:

	Dr (£)	Cr (£)
Advertising	18,313	
Bad debts written off	250	
Bank interest	5,231	
Bank overdraft		14,852
Creditors		24,213
Debtors	27,400	
Depreciation on fixtures and fittings, at 1 November 2003		18,800
Depreciation on motor cars, at 1 November 2003		126,800
Fixtures and fittings (cost)	114,000	
Insurance	8,475	
Light and heat	6,420	
Motor cars (cost)	165,920	
Owner's drawings	52,000	
Owner's capital at 1 November 2003		328,164
Purchases	697,000	
Rent and rates	5,900	
Salaries and wages	98,500	
Sales		826,220
Stock at 1 November 2003	114,700	

Sundry expenses	13,700	
Telephone	11,240	
	1,339,049	1,339,049

Notes:

1. Closing stock at 31 October 2004 was £112,600.

2. Fixtures and fittings are to be depreciated over ten years by the straight line method (assuming a residual value of £20,000), and motor cars by 25 per cent on the reducing balance method.

3. There was an accrual for salaries and wages of £1,500, and rent and rates had been prepaid by £900.

a Prepare, on separate sheets, a profit and loss account for the year ended 31 October 2004, and a balance sheet as at that date. Show all workings.

b Avril's Artefacts is a sole trading business. Explain the advantages and disadvantages of this form of business organization.

2. The directors of Mammon plc are reviewing the final accounts of the company, which show an operating profit after tax of £600,000 and retained profits from the previous year totalling £1.4m. The balance sheet shows a bank overdraft of £100,000, and the company has maximum overdraft facilities of £500,000.

a Explain why a profitable company might show an overdraft in its balance sheet.

b The retained profit is referred to as a *revenue reserve*. What is the other type of reserve which a company might have?

c Revenue reserves can be used to pay dividends to shareholders. Why might the directors of Mammon plc be reluctant to pay the full £2m as a dividend to the shareholders?

d If the company wanted to improve its bank balance, it might consider issuing ordinary shares, preference shares, debentures, or convertible loan stock. What are the key features of each of these?

3. Ramrod plc sells computer equipment. The company accountant asks your advice about the following product lines:

(i) 20 Powerbase PCs: Original cost totalled £9,000. This stock has been unsold for three years and the company sales manager believes that the only way of selling them would be to upgrade the monitors (at a cost of £75 per machine) and sell them at £350 each.

(ii) 10 laptops: Originally bought for £400 each to meet a special order, but the customer went bankrupt before delivery. Each machine is overprinted with that customer's logo. The machines could be sold for an estimated £600 each, but only if the logo was erased at a cost of £10 per machine.

a Explain what is meant by the term 'stock should be valued at the lower of cost and net realisable value'.

b Explain, with reasons, how each of the above product lines should be accounted for in the annual accounts of the company.

c The customer who ordered the laptops went bankrupt. Explain the three terms *good debt*, *doubtful debt*, and *bad debt*, and how they affect a company's financial statements.

4W. Frodo Fashions is a small business buying and selling dresses. Its trial balance as at 31 July 2004 is shown below:

Frodo Fashions Trial balance as at 31 July 2004	Debit	Credit
Cash	531	
Shop fittings—cost	5,773	
Shop fittings—depreciation to 1 August 2003		1,959
Motor car—cost	10,997	
Motor car—depreciation to 1 August 2003		6,301
Sales		126,743
Purchases	32,183	
Opening stock at 1 August 2003	2,272	
Rent	3,828	
Electricity	2,421	
Telephone	963	
Debtors	1,411	
Creditors		795
Wages and salaries	18,299	
Owner's drawings	15,522	
Sundry expenses	445	
Capital at 1 August 2003		15,672
Bank balance	56,825	
	151,470	151,470

Notes:
1. Closing stock is £2,669.
2. Electricity charges are to be accrued at the year-end, totalling £1,398.
3. Rent has been prepaid at the year-end, amounting to £213.
4. Shop fittings are depreciated by the straight line method (no residual value) over five years.
5. Depreciation on the car is calculated using the reducing balance method at 30% p.a.

Prepare, on separate sheets, a profit and loss account for the year ended 31 July 2004, and a balance sheet as at that date. Show all workings.

5W. The sales ledger of Runaway plc included the following balances:

Total sales ledger balances	£89,600
Bad debts included within that total	£2,700
Doubtful debts identified at the end of the year	£6,200
There was also an opening provision for doubtful debts of	£4,700

Show the entries relevant to debtors that would appear in the company's profit and loss account and balance sheet.

6W. Ruby and Sapphire are partners, sharing profits and losses in the ratio 3 : 1 respectively. The partnership's operating profit for the year ended 30 September 2004 totalled £86,000, their capital balances at the start of the year were: Ruby £35,800, Sapphire £17,600, and drawings of £48,200 were made by Ruby and £16,400 by Sapphire. No salaries were payable to partners, and no interest was due on capital or charged on drawings.

The total net assets of the partnership at the end of the year amounted to £74,800.

a Prepare the section of the partnership's profit and loss showing the division of the profit between the two partners.

b Prepare the partnership balance sheet in as much detail as is possible from the above information.

c Explain the main advantages and disadvantages of operating as a partnership, as compared to sole trading and limited liability companies.

■ MINI CASE STUDY

Minnie meets Maxim

Minnie von Mausen (see previous mini case studies) has had an exciting year running 'MinnieBeasts', and not only did she succeed in catching enough animals to fill several zoos, she also captured a man—Maxim Trappenheimer. They promptly married, and Minnie and Maxim decided to relaunch 'MinnieBeasts' as a limited company, renamed 'MinnieMax Ltd.', but using 'MinnieBeasts' as a brand name. They agreed to form the company with an authorized and issued share capital of £60,000, split into shares with a nominal value of 50p each, with Minnie buying 60 per cent and Maxim 30 per cent. Minnie's sister Lottie bought the remaining 10 per cent. All the shares were issued at a premium of 10p per share and the proceeds were placed in a new bank account. £20,000 of the cash raised was then paid to Minnie, who transferred the total net assets of MinnieBeasts to the company. These comprised:

Fixed assets:
  Land Rover   £17,000
  Equipment   £3,000
  Computer   £680

Current assets:
  Stock   £2,000
  Debtors   £3,600

Current liabilities:
  Creditors   £6,280

You are required to construct the opening balance sheet of MinnieMax Ltd., after the total net assets of MinnieBeasts had been transferred.

(Suggested solutions can be found in Appendix 4.)

■ MAXI CASE STUDY

Alastair Sawday Publishing

Small publishing companies often struggle to survive among the giants, but Alastair Sawday's eponymous enterprise is flourishing. Since 1995 it has established a list of 13 guides giving highly personal and idiosyncratic descriptions of more than 3,000 special places to stay in the UK and other parts of Europe.

Mr Sawday's first book, *French Bed and Breakfast*, remains his most popular . . . [he] happily admits that eight years ago he knew nothing about publishing. Several publishers turned down the guide so Mr Sawday decided to go it alone. He borrowed £100,000 from the Midland Bank. . . . The book sold 20,000 copies in the first 18 months with minimal advertising. 'There was a magical moment when I realised that the concept worked. I was writing about places which reflected my views on travel and there were thousands of people out there who felt the same way.'

Other guides, on destinations including Ireland, Spain and Paris hotels, swiftly followed. By 2000 the business had grown to 12 employees and moved into its present base, an airy, converted barn where the younger, enthusiastic staff work at farmhouse tables of recycled pine. Three dogs are part of the team—'they're de-stressing, and stop you becoming pompous'.

Adapted from Widget Finn, *Starting Out, Daily Telegraph*, 19 May 2003, © Telegraph Group Limited 2003

You are not told in the article what form of business enterprise has been adopted by Mr Sawday's business. From your knowledge of the advantages and disadvantages of the various types of organizational structures, write a report outlining the different alternatives available.

(Suggested answers and discussion areas are available on the companion website.)

■ WEB LINKS

Company websites

Alastair Sawday Publishing www.sawdays.co.uk
Domino's Pizza www.dominos.co.uk

■ FURTHER READING

Cox, D. (1999). *Business Accounts*, 2nd edn. (Worcester: Osborne Books), chapters 12–15, 23–5.

Dyson, J. R. (2003). *Accounting for Non-accounting Students*, 5th edn. (Harlow: FT/Prentice Hall), chapters 4–6.

Jones, M. (2002). *Accounting for Non-specialists*, 1st edn. (Chichester: Wiley), chapters 4–6.

Weetman, P. (2003). *Financial and Management Accounting: An Introduction*, 3rd edn. (Harlow: FT/Prentice Hall), chapter 3.

■ COMPANION WEBSITE MATERIALS

Additional materials are available for students and lecturers on the companion website, at **www.oup.com/booksites/busecon/business**, including a 'Question Generator' file that gives unlimited practice at preparing profit and loss accounts and balance sheets from a trial balance and notes.

4

The profit and loss account: from 'turnover' to 'profit before interest and taxation'

OBJECTIVES

By the end of this chapter you will be able to:

- Understand the scope of information found within that part of a published profit and loss account relating to profit before interest and taxation.
- Assess the generally accepted accounting practices relating to key items found within a published profit and loss account relating to profit before interest and taxation.

4.1 Introduction

Companies communicate their financial performance to their shareholders by means of an annual report which is published a few months after the end of the financial period. The annual report is part general promotional material (photographs of products, company headquarters, key personnel), part financial information. For example, Domino's Pizza's annual report comprised forty-five pages, of which ten gave general information, four related to forthcoming shareholders' meetings, and the remainder dealt with the detailed financial data.

As we saw in the last chapter, the profit and loss account is one of the key statements which summarize financial performance and in this chapter we shall look in detail at its contents. Again, we shall use Domino's Pizza's published report as a starting point (see Figure 4.1, which is cross-referenced to chapter headings), though we shall refer to other companies where needed to illustrate the full range of information which might be disclosed.

4.2 — Group Profit and Loss Account

for the 52 weeks ended 29 December 2002

	Notes	2002 £000	2001 £000
TURNOVER			
Turnover: group and share of joint ventures' turnover		54,673	45,185
Less: share of joint ventures' turnover		(1,564)	(1,360)
GROUP TURNOVER	2	53,109	43,825
Cost of sales		(28,054)	(23,132)
GROSS PROFIT		25,055	20,693
Distribution costs		(8,663)	(7,150)
Administrative expenses		(11,813)	(10,230)
Other operating expenditure		(75)	(169)
GROUP OPERATING PROFIT	3	4,504	3,144
Share of operating profit in joint venture		64	75
Amortisation of goodwill on joint venture		(5)	(5)
		59	70
PROFIT ON ORDINARY ACTIVITIES BEFORE INTEREST AND TAXATION		4,563	3,214
Interest receivable		50	78
Interest payable and similar charges	6	(374)	(430)
PROFIT ON ORDINARY ACTIVITIES BEFORE TAXATION		4,239	2,862
Tax on profit on ordinary activities	7	(1,404)	(858)
PROFIT FOR THE FINANCIAL YEAR		2,835	2,004
Dividends on equity shares	8	(1,018)	(668)
PROFIT RETAINED FOR THE FINANCIAL YEAR	22	1,817	1,336
Earnings per share – basic	9	5.60p	4.00p
– diluted		5.29p	3.88p

Cross-reference boxes: 4.3, 4.4, 4.5, 4.6, 4.7, 4.8

Figure 4.1 Domino's Pizza Group: profit and loss account (cross-referenced to chapter headings). The shaded area is covered in detail in Chapter 5.

4.2 The heading

A 'group' profit and loss account is the combined summary of income and expenditure for a *group of companies*, which usually comprises, at a minimum, a *parent* company and one *subsidiary*. At its simplest, a parent company is one which holds the majority of the voting ('equity') shares in another company, which is known as its subsidiary. The word 'consolidated' is often used instead of 'group', as in 'consolidated profit and loss account'. Domino's Pizza disclosed (see n. 12 on p. 332) that it had seven subsidiaries, including two 'indirectly held' (i.e. the shares in these were themselves held by subsidiaries), which were 100 per cent owned by the parent company. More details on this topic are contained in Chapter 10, but it is important to understand at this stage that 100 per cent of a subsidiary's turnover and cost of sales (other than transactions between group companies) are included in the group profit and loss account, even if less than 100 per cent of the subsidiary's shares are owned by the parent company.

There are a number of alternatives to the term 'profit and loss account', including 'statement of income' and 'statement of operations', the latter being used in the USA. However, they have the same purpose but might be shown in slightly different formats.

The other information shown in the heading is the period of time covered by the statement, often a calendar year (e.g. for the year ending 31 December or for the year ending 31 March) but sometimes a fifty-two-week period ending on the last day of a trading week, hence Domino's Pizza's annual report ending on (Sunday) 29 December rather than (Tuesday) 31 December.

For comparison, look at a US company's statement of operations, at:
www.amrice.com/1201_Bank.pdf

4.3 Turnover

Turnover has been defined as 'the revenue resulting from exchange transactions under which a seller transfers to customers the goods or services that it is in business to provide'.[1] It might be referred to simply as 'Sales' or 'Revenue' and in most cases represents the value of goods and services sold to customers during the financial period. It does not include the sale of the company's own fixed assets, so if the company sold one of its motor vehicles, the gain or loss on the sale (sale price compared to depreciated value) would be adjusted within the 'operating expenses' rather than the gross profit calculation. Remember that turnover is not the same as 'cash received', due to the accruals concept previously explained. As turnover is a key performance indicator reflecting the success or failure of a company, there have been many instances where directors have tried to inflate sales by recognizing revenue (i.e. including it within the profit and loss account) before the company has provided the goods or services as agreed with its customers. If we look at the stages of a typical business transaction (Figure 4.2), we can see that revenue should only be recognized once the company has a *right to be paid*.

The topic of *revenue recognition* is also considered in the 'Discussion questions' on p. 98.

4.3.1 Joint ventures

Domino's Pizza's turnover refers to 'joint ventures'. A joint venture is defined as a business 'which is jointly controlled by the reporting entity and one or more other venturers under a contractual arrangement. The reporting entity's interest is on a long-term basis.'[2] In other

---

[1] Accounting Standards Board, *Amendment to FRS 5 Reporting the Substance of Transactions*, Feb. 2003.
[2] FRS 9 *Associates and Joint Ventures* (Accounting Standards Board, London, 1997); also see IAS 31, *Financial Reporting of Interests in Joint Ventures* (International Accounting Standards Board, London, 2000).

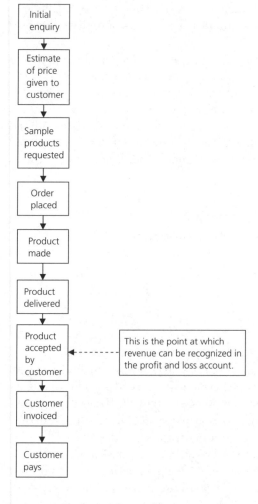

Figure 4.2 Stages of a typical business transaction

words, two or more businesses have decided to join together for a specific purpose. Under the relevant accounting standard, that part of the company's turnover which derives from the joint venture must be shown separately. Details of the joint ventures are contained within n. 12 of Domino's Pizza's annual report (see p. 332), and comprise a 41 per cent holding in a company called Full House Restaurants Ltd. and a 50 per cent holding in a company called Dominoid Ltd.

4.3.2 **Long-term contracts**

A particular problem arises with contracts for the design, manufacture, or construction of major projects (or provision of services) which extend over more than one financial period, and accounting standards have been developed to give guidance on how they should be treated. For example, a company might win a contract to build a major shopping complex, with the work expected to take several years before completion. If the revenue could only be recognized in the year of *completion* and not in the interim years, the profit and loss account would not be reflecting a true position of the company's performance, but only the impact of those contracts *completed* during the period. To get round this problem, a proportion of the contract value can be assessed at the end of each financial period, and a prudent estimate of the profit or loss achieved on that contract within that financial period will be recognized.

For example, if Bodge Builders Ltd. won a contract to build a tunnel at a cost of £40m, and the work was estimated to take two years, in each year of the contract a proportion of the contract price will be matched against the costs incurred in the same period. If, in the first year, a quarter of the contract had been completed and relevant costs were £8m, then a profit of £2m ((1/4 × £40m) − £8m) = £2m) can be recognized, by £10m being included within turnover and £8m being included within 'cost of sales'. If the tunnel is completed in the second year, and the second year's costs are £24m, the second year's profit and loss account will include turnover of £30m (3/4 × £40m) and cost of sales will include £24m, resulting in a profit in that year of £6m. Overall the profit on the contract is £8m, spread between the two years (£2m + £6m).

4.3.3 Segmental reporting

Many items of information shown in the profit and loss account are cross-referenced to notes which provide further information and detail. The entry for Group Turnover in Domino's Pizza's accounts is cross-referenced to n. 2 (see p. 326), which shows a 'segmental analysis', which is required by an accounting standard.[3] Under this standard, companies have to disclose information relating to performance in the main classes of business and geographical areas in which they trade. Domino's Pizza's segmental analysis shows the principal components of turnover as being 'royalties received, commissary and equipment sales, sale of franchises, pizza delivery sales and rental income on leasehold properties'. Further analysis is given which shows turnover by *origin* and turnover by *destination*. Turnover by origin refers to the geographical segment *from which* products or services are supplied to a third party or to another segment, whilst turnover by destination refers to the geographical segment *to which* products or services are supplied. Under international accounting standards there is no exemption from disclosures where, in the opinion of the directors, such disclosures are *seriously prejudicial* to the interests of the company. However, Domino's Pizza is a company based in the UK, where the relevant accounting standard, SSAP 25, does allow such an exemption, and that company has decided to withhold information.

For comparison, look at the segment analysis of a US corporation, Centex Construction Products Inc., at **www.centex-cxp.com/cxp-annual/cxp/1005.htm**

---

[3] SSAP 25 *Segmental Reporting* (Accounting Standards Board, London, 1990); and see IAS 14 *Segment Reporting* (International Accounting Standards Board, London, 1997).

4.4 **Cost of sales**

In a company that manufactures the goods it sells, the cost of sales will include all the costs of production such as factory wages, raw materials, and manufacturing overheads including the depreciation of machinery. Adjustments will also be made for opening and closing stocks of raw materials, work in progress, and finished stock. In a company that buys in the goods it sells (a 'trading' company) the 'cost of sales' will comprise the cost of the bought-in goods as adjusted by opening and closing stocks of those goods. Refer to Chapter 3 for details of the usual basis of stock valuation.

Look at Domino's Pizza's accounting policy relating to stock valuation shown on p. 325

4.5 **Gross profit**

Gross profit is the difference between the value of the company's sales and its cost of sales. Within the European Union, two outline formats are allowed for the profit and loss account, only one of which, Format 1, involves the calculation of gross profit. This format breaks down operating costs by *function*:

- cost of sales as previously described in section 4.4 above;
- distribution costs, see section 4.6 below;
- administrative expenses, see section 4.6 below.

The Domino's Pizza's profit and loss account follows this format. The alternative format, Format 2, breaks down operating costs by their *nature*, as follows:

- raw materials and consumables;
- staff costs (wages and salaries; social security costs; other pension costs);
- depreciation and other amounts written off fixed assets;
- other external charges;
- change in stock of finished goods and work in progress.

Note that this format does not disclose the amount of gross profit, though a reasonable estimate could be made.

An example of this type of format is given in Figure 4.3, which shows the consolidated statement of income of Hugo Boss AG.

Consolidated Statement of Income

of HUGO BOSS Aktiengesellschaft, Metzingen for the period January 1 to December 31, 2002

	Notes No.	2002 EUR thous.	2001 EUR thous.
Sales	[1]	1,093,386	1,094,716
Changes in inventories and other own costs capitalized		(36,653)	40,962
Other operating income	[2]	72,486	68,433
Cost of materials	[3]	(491,855)	(558,457)
Personnel expenses	[4]	(161,017)	(150,194)
Depreciation	[5]	(32,186)	(27,920)
Other operating expenses	[6]	(342,538)	(312,984)
Operating result		101,623	154,556

Figure 4.3 Hugo Boss AG: consolidated statement of income (format 2)

4.6 Operating costs

To arrive at the operating profit for the year, operating costs will be deducted from the gross profit. Although usually split between distribution costs and administrative expenses there is often an arbitrary allocation between the two classifications.

- Distribution costs will include wages relating to the distribution function, such as those paid to lorry drivers and packing operatives. This category will also include the cost of packaging materials as well as the overheads relating to transport such as depreciation of motor lorries, fuel, tax, and insurance.

- Administrative expenses will include all other overheads not already included within cost of sales or distribution costs. It will not include interest on bank overdrafts, as interest (paid and received) is shown separately on the profit and loss account, as it is important to see clearly what the 'cost of borrowing' has been.

There is sometimes a further category, *other operating expenditure (or income)*, which will include any further items relating to operating activities which are not included in any other category. Examples might include 'sundry income' such as rents received (where this is not a main revenue-generating activity of the company) or 'sundry expenditure' might refer to losses on the sale of fixed assets—though many companies would include this within the other cost categories.

In the UK, various items of supplementary information regarding costs must be disclosed to comply with legislation. For example, details of the amounts paid to directors must be shown (referred to as directors' *remuneration* or *emoluments*), as well as fees to auditors and depreciation of fixed assets.

 Look at n. 3 of Domino's Pizza's 'notes to the accounts' on p. 327 for this information, and also further details of directors' remuneration shown on pp. 314–5.

4.7 Operating profit

Operating profit (sometimes referred to as 'net profit') is the profit left after operating costs have been deducted from the gross profit, with any sundry income added, but before adjustments for interest and taxation. An operating loss, fairly obviously, would occur when expenditure was greater than income.

An important financial reporting standard, FRS 3 *Reporting Financial Performance*, was issued in the UK in 1992 and was designed to bring greater clarity to the profit and loss account. In particular a 'layered' format was introduced to highlight:

- results of operations *continuing* beyond the end of the financial period (including the results of businesses acquired during the financial period);
- results of operations *discontinued* by the end of the financial period;
- profits or losses on the sale or termination of a business operation, costs of a fundamental reorganization or restructuring, and profit or losses on the disposal of fixed assets.

The standard had been introduced not only to allow analysts to have greater information to inform their opinions but also to crack down on the then widespread practice of categorizing certain items as 'extraordinary', which resulted in their being omitted from the calculation of operating profit, thus boosting reported earnings. In particular, major reorganization and redundancy costs were being excluded from normal operating expenditure by that device. The accounting standard does allow companies to classify certain expenditure as *exceptional* (defined as material items which derive from events or transactions that fall within the ordinary activities of the reporting entity and which individually or, if of a similar type, in aggregate need to be disclosed by virtue of their size or incidence if the financial statements are to give a true and fair view[4]).

Look at this extract from the profit and loss account of Courts plc. Note how the 'continuing' and 'discontinuing' operations are separated, with total columns for the overall result.

	Notes	2002			2001 (as restated*)		
		Continuing operations £'000	Discontinued operations £'000	Total £'000	Continuing operations £'000	Discontinued operations £'000	Total £'000
Goods sold		545,771	46,149	591,920	572,088	50,011	622,099
Credit charges invoiced		107,134	271	107,405	116,734	304	117,038
Movement in deferred revenue		6,255	(29)	6,226	130	46	176
Credit charges earned		113,389	242	113,631	116,864	350	117,214
		659,160	46,391	705,551	688,952	50,361	739,313
Less share of joint ventures' turnover		(607)	(929)	(1,536)			
Turnover	1	658,553	45,462	704,015	688,952	50,361	739,313
Operating profit/(loss) before utilisation of provision		45,308	(9,629)	35,679	61,656	(4,572)	57,084
Less utilisation of prior year closure provision			2,626	2,626			
Group operating profit/(loss)	2	45,308	(7,003)	38,305	61,656	(4,572)	57,084

* As restated for the implementation of FRS 18 'Accounting Policies' and FRS 19 'Deferred Tax'.

Figure 4.4 Courts plc: 'layered' format of profit and loss account, to 'group operating profit/(loss)'

Domino's Pizza's profit and loss account is quite simple in comparison with Courts plc, as all its operations continued beyond the end of the financial period, it had neither acquired nor disposed of any businesses during the period, and it did not reveal any exceptional items.

[4] FRS 3 *Reporting Financial Performance* (Accounting Standards Board, London, 1992).

Look at this extract from the profit and loss account of another pizza company, PizzaExpress plc. This company showed details not only of continuing operations but acquisitions, discontinued operations, and exceptional reorganization costs.

GROUP PROFIT AND LOSS ACCOUNT

for the year ended 30 June 2002

	Notes	2002 £m	Restated 2001 £m
Turnover (including share of joint venture)	1(a)		
Continuing operations		**212.0**	185.1
Acquisitions		**1.5**	–
		213.5	185.1
Discontinued operations		**0.3**	0.8
		213.8	185.9
Less: Share of turnover of joint venture		**(0.1)**	(0.3)
Group turnover		**213.7**	185.6
Cost of sales		**(156.4)**	(129.8)
Gross profit		**57.3**	55.8
Distribution costs		**(3.9)**	(3.4)
Administrative expenses (excluding reorganisation costs)		**(14.7)**	(13.0)
Exceptional reorganization costs	1(b)	**(0.5)**	–
Administrative expenses		**(15.2)**	(13.0)
Continuing operations		38.3	39.6
Acquisitions		0.1	–
		38.4	39.6
Discontinued operations		(0.2)	(0.2)
Group operating profit	1(b)	**38.2**	39.4
Share of operating loss in joint venture		–	(0.2)
Total operating profit: group and share of joint venture		**38.2**	39.2
(Loss)/profit on disposal of fixed assets-continuing operations		**(0.2)**	0.3
Loss on termination of US operations-discontinued operations		**(0.8)**	–
Profit on ordinary activities before interest and taxation		**37.2**	39.5

Figure 4.5 PizzaExpress plc: 'layered' format of profit and loss account

4.8 Profit on ordinary activities before interest and taxation

Often referred to as 'PBIT' (profit before interest and tax), this is the profit generated from the operating activities of the group, as adjusted for items such as:

• material profits or losses on the disposal of fixed assets;

• profits or losses on the termination or sale of business segments (e.g. the sale of an overseas subsidiary);

• profits or losses from joint ventures.

Look at this further extract from the group profit and loss account of Courts plc. This shows several adjustments to the 'group operating profit/(loss)' to arrive at the 'profit/(loss) on ordinary activities before interest'. Note also the 'exceptional credit' which relates to a profit on the sale of shares in a Malaysian subsidiary company.

	Notes	2002 Continuing operations £'000	2002 Discontinued operations £'000	2002 Total £'000	2001 (as restated*) Continuing operations £'000	2001 (as restated*) Discontinued operations £'000	2001 (as restated*) Total £'000
Group operating profit/(loss)	2	45,308	(7,003)	38,305	61,656	(4,572)	57,084
Share of profit from associated undertaking		1,027		1,027	760		760
Share of losses from joint ventures		(237)	(1,453)	(1,690)			
Profit on disposal of fixed assets		93		93	122		122
Exceptional credit	4				25,705		25,705
Losses from discontinued operations			(2,405)	(2,405)			
Less utilisation of prior year closure provision			2,405	2,405			
Provision for loss on closure of discontinued operations			(6,785)	(6,785)		(6,569)	(6,569)
Profit/(loss) on ordinary activities before interest		46,191	(15,241)	30,950	88,243	(11,141)	77,102

* As restated for the implementation of FRS 18 'Accounting Policies' and FRS 19 'Deferred Tax'.

Figure 4.6 Courts plc: 'layered' format of profit and loss account, from 'group operating profit/(loss)' to 'profit/(loss) on ordinary activities before interest'

The only item in the Courts plc profit and loss account in Figure 4.6 which has not previously been referred to is the 'Share of profit from associated undertaking'. An *undertaking* is defined as a 'body corporate, a partnership or an unincorporated association carrying on a trade or business with or without a view to profit'.[5] To be classified as an *associated* undertaking, usually one company (e.g. Courts plc) has a holding of at least 20 per cent in another business, but not more than 50 per cent, as this would make it a *subsidiary* company, and other rules would apply. Courts plc would also be presumed to have a 'significant influence' over the operating and financial policies of the associate (see Chapter 10).

Within the profit and loss account, the share of the associate's operating result is included after the section showing the group's operating profit or loss. Note that the amounts of turnover, cost of sales, and operating expenses of associated companies are *excluded* from the profit and loss account—only the relevant shares of any profit or loss are included.

4.8.1 Amortization of goodwill on joint venture

In the Domino's Pizza profit and loss account, the 'share of operating profit in joint venture' has been reduced by 'amortization of goodwill'. The topic of goodwill is looked at in detail

[5] FRS 2 *Subsidiary undertakings* (Accounting Standards Board, London, 1992).

in Chapter 6, but in brief, goodwill is the difference between the cost of an investment in a business and the net assets of that business. For example, if a company had paid £15 million to buy a 10 per cent stake in a business with net assets of £120m, the 'goodwill' arising on this transaction would be £3 million (£15m − (10% × £120m)). Often goodwill represents the reputation of a business and its ability to make profits in the future. Where goodwill is regarded as having a limited useful economic life, it must be *amortized* (a word used to describe the depreciation of non-physical, intangible assets), usually on a straight line basis. Any amortization charged on goodwill other than that relating to joint ventures will be included in the operating expenses, though not always identified separately.

> Look again at n. 3 of Domino's Pizza's 'notes to the accounts' on p. 327 to see the amount charged for 'amortization of intangible fixed assets', and also n. 10 on p. 330 for the overall effect on the various types of asset.

4.9 Chapter summary

- Profit and loss account might also be called 'statement of income' or 'statement of operations'.

- Revenue should only be recognized once the company has a right to be paid.

- A *group* profit and loss account combines the results of a parent company and its subsidiaries.

- Profits or losses on long-term contracts can be recognized as the contract term progresses.

- Information relating to performance in the main classes of business and geographical areas must be disclosed in a segmental analysis.

- Gross profit is the difference between the value of the company's sales and its cost of sales.

- Operating costs are usually divided between distribution costs and administrative expenses.

- Operating profit is the profit left after operating costs have been deducted from the gross profit, plus any sundry income.

- The results of continuing, discontinued, and acquired business operations should be disclosed separately.

- Exceptional items can be disclosed separately, but are still included within the overall calculation of the operating profit or loss.

- Any profit or loss from associated undertakings or joint ventures must be disclosed separately on the face of the profit and loss account.

- Goodwill amortization is usually included as part of the operating costs, unless it relates to joint ventures, in which case it is adjusted against any profit or loss arising from that joint venture.

■ GLOSSARY

accounting standard	A component of Generally Accepted Accounting Principles (GAAP), it defines best practice for specific accounting situations
administration expenses	Other overheads not included within cost of sales or distribution costs
amortization	The depreciation of an intangible asset
annual report	The published report sent to shareholders containing financial and other company information
associated undertaking	An investment of between 20 and 50 per cent in another business
consolidated profit and loss account	An alternative term for group profit and loss account
continuing operations	Those parts of the business's operations which continue beyond the end of the financial period
cost of sales	In a manufacturing company, this comprises the costs of production such as factory wages, raw materials, and manufacturing overheads including the depreciation of machinery. In a trading company it comprises the cost of bought-in goods. In both cases, adjustments are made for opening and closing stocks of unsold goods or materials
directors' emoluments	An alternative term for directors' remuneration
directors' remuneration	The salaries, bonuses, pension contributions, fees, and other benefits paid to directors
discontinued operations	Those parts of the business's operations which do not continue beyond the end of the financial period
distribution costs	Overheads relating to the distribution function, including transport and packaging expenses
exceptional items	Transactions which, because of their size or incidence, need to be disclosed separately within the financial statements
goodwill	The difference between the cost of an investment in a business and the net assets of that business
gross profit	The difference between the value of the company's sales and its cost of sales
group	A parent company and its subsidiaries
group profit and loss account	The combined summary of income and expenditure for a group of companies
joint venture	A business operation where two or more parties jointly control the venture
long-term contracts	The contract for the design, manufacture, or construction of major projects (or provision of services) which extend over more than one financial period

operating costs	Overhead expenditure usually divided between distribution costs and administration expenses
operating profit	The profit left after operating costs have been deducted from the gross profit, plus any sundry income
parent company	The company that has invested in its subsidiaries
PBIT	Profit before interest and tax
profit on ordinary activities before interest and taxation	The operating profit for the period after adjustments for profit or losses on the disposal of fixed assets, termination or sale of business segments, or from joint ventures, but before interest and taxation
published report	The annual report sent to shareholders
segmental reporting	Analysis of performance between the main classes of business and geographical areas in which the company trades
statement of income	An alternative term (often used within the EU) for the profit and loss account
statement of operations	An alternative term (often used within the USA) for the profit and loss account
subsidiary	A company that has the majority of its shares owned by its parent company
turnover	The revenue resulting from exchange transactions under which a seller transfers to customers the goods or services that it is in business to provide
turnover by destination	The geographical segment to which products or services are supplied
turnover by origin	The geographical segment from which products or services are supplied to a third party or to another segment

■ MULTIPLE CHOICE QUESTIONS

1. Which one of the following words is often used instead of 'group', as in 'group profit and loss account'?

   a Combined
   b Consolidated
   c Connected
   d Co-ordinated

2. Which one of the following would never be seen as the heading of a profit and loss account?

   a Profit and loss account for the year ending 31 December 2003
   b Profit and loss account for the year ending 29 December 2003
   c Profit and loss account for the 52 weeks ending 29 December 2003
   d Profit and loss account as at 31 December 2003

3. Revenue should be recognized only:

    a   When the product has been manufactured
    b   When sample products have been requested by a customer
    c   When the product has been delivered to the customer
    d   When the customer has accepted liability for paying for the product

4. Level Builders have entered into a three-year contract to construct a dam, with a contract price of £210m. By the end of the first financial period within the three-year period, a third of the contract had been completed, and relevant costs incurred were £55m. What profit or loss, if any, would be recognized within the company's profit and loss account at the end of the first financial period?

    a   None, as the contract has not been completed
    b $(1/3 \times £210m) - £55m = £15m$
    c $(£210m - £55m) = £155m$
    d   A loss of £55m

5. A manufacturing company paid £8m for raw materials during its financial period. It had opening stocks of raw materials valued at £2m, and closing stocks of raw materials valued at £3m. Opening and closing creditors for raw materials were £5m and £1m respectively. What was the value of raw materials to be included in 'cost of sales' for the financial period?

    a   £3m
    b   £9m
    c   £11m
    d   £10m

6. Which of the following would *not* be classified as a '*distribution*' cost?

    a   Packaging costs
    b   Lorry drivers' wages
    c   Depreciation of factory machinery
    d   Depreciation of freight handling depot

7. Which one of the following would *not* be a term used to describe payments to directors?

    a   Remuneration
    b   Emoluments
    c   Renumeration
    d   Salaries

8. Which one of the following categories of results would *not* be disclosed in a profit and loss account which complied with the UK accounting standard *Reporting Financial Performance*?

    a   Results of operations to be acquired in the following financial period
    b   Results of operations continuing into the following financial period
    c   Results of operations discontinued during the current financial period
    d   Results of operations acquired during the current financial period

9. 'PBIT' is an acronym for:

   a Profit before interest

   b Profit before income tax

   c Profit before income and tax

   d Profit before interest and tax

10. To be classified as an 'associate undertaking', usually one company owns a specific percentage of another company's voting shares. Which of the following holdings would result in 'associate' status?

    a Between 10% and 19%

    b Between 20% and 50%

    c Between 1% and 9%

    d Between 51% and 100%

(Note: answers are shown in Appendix 2.)

■ DISCUSSION QUESTIONS

Read the following extract and then discuss the questions that follow it.

Crackdown on companies overstating turnover

Regulators have launched a belated crackdown on accounting abuses by companies that involve them exaggerating their turnover. The Accounting Standards Board, which writes UK financial reporting rules, today publishes guidance on when companies should record revenue in their accounts. Mary Keegan, ASB chairman, said some companies had 'pushed the envelope' in their recent financial reporting practices.

She did not identify particular companies, but MyTravel, Britain's biggest tour operator, last year adopted more conservative accounting practices following concern about its policy on revenue recognition. Investors have become increasingly focused on revenue growth as a yardstick of performance, and it has led to overly aggressive accounting techniques, notably in the US, and to a lesser extent in the UK . . . The UK has no comprehensive accounting standard on when companies should record revenue in their financial statements . . . The ASB has chosen to produce guidance on revenue recognition, rather than an accounting standard, partly because listed companies are due to adopt international financial reporting rules from 2005. The existing international accounting standard on revenue recognition is regarded as inadequate and out of date, and the International Accounting Standards Board is considering a new rule.

The ASB guidance focuses on how companies produce turnover figures for profit and loss statements. It sets out basic principles on revenue recognition to ensure companies record revenue at the appropriate time. MyTravel ran into difficulties over accounting practices after Deloitte & Touche replaced Andersen as the company's auditor. It had been recording income from leisure travel products when people booked their holidays. MyTravel now records the revenue when people depart for their holidays. The ASB guidance also provides detailed advice on five types of transaction which have given rise to vastly different turnover figures by companies. For example, it deals with an accounting dilemma faced by information technology companies. IT companies often sell products with long-term service contracts and, under aggressive accounting techniques, some have immediately recorded the full value of the deals instead of spreading income over a number of years.

Andrew Parker, *Financial Times*, 27 Feb. 2003

1. Why do you think 'Investors have become increasingly focused on revenue growth as a yardstick of performance, and it has led to overly aggressive accounting techniques'?

2. If shareholders want their companies to show maximum profits from maximum sales, why should a company be forced to adopt 'conservative accounting practices following concern about its policy on revenue recognition'.

3. MyTravel had 'been recording income from leisure travel products when people booked their holidays. MyTravel now records the revenue when people depart for their holidays.' Which key accounting principles are involved in the accounting policy change referred to here?

(Note: Suggested answers or discussion points are available on the companion website.)

■ **LONGER QUESTIONS**

(Questions marked W have suggested answers on the companion website. Other questions are answered in Appendix 3.)

1. Figure 4.7 is an extract from Northern Foods plc's profit and loss account for the year ended 31 March 2003.

   Briefly explain each of the items marked (i) to (viii).

2. From the following information, prepare a group profit and loss account (to 'profit on ordinary activities before interest and taxation') for the year ended 31 July 2004. Use Figure 4.1 (Domino's Pizza's profit and loss account) as a guide to presentation.

	£000
Distribution costs	5,110
Share of operating profit in joint venture	240
Total turnover	38,240
Amortization of goodwill on joint venture	10
Other operating expenditure	150
Cost of sales	15,070
Share of joint venture's turnover	1,520
Administrative expenses	6,310

3. Figure 4.8 is part of the segmental analysis of Tesco plc, an international retailer, for the years 2002 and 2003. Calculate and comment upon the key changes in the turnover (excluding VAT[6]), the operating profit, and the net operating assets of the 'Asia' segment in relation to the company as a whole.

---

[6] Value Added Tax.

	Before goodwill amortisation and exceptional items 31 March 2003 £m	Goodwill amortisation and exceptional items 31 March 2003 £m	Total 31 March 2003 £m
Group turnover			
– continuing (i)	1,421.2	—	1,421.2
– discontinued (ii)	—	—	—
Group turnover	1,421.2	—	1,421.2
Cost of sales (iii)	(1,023.3)	(31.9)	(1,055.2)
Gross profit (iv)	397.9	(31.9)	366.0
Net operating expenses (v)	(282.3)	(13.1)	(295.4)
Operating profit before goodwill amortisation			
– continuing	115.6	(42.6)	73.0
– discontinued	—	—	—
	115.6	(42.6)	73.0
Goodwill amortisation (vi)	—	(2.4)	(2.4)
Operating profit (vii)	115.6	(45.0)	70.6
Share of associated undertakings (viii)	1.4	(0.7)	0.7
Profit on disposal of businesses	—	54.0	54.0
Profit on ordinary activities before interest	**117.0**	**8.3**	**125.3**

Figure 4.7 Northern Foods plc: consolidated profit and loss account (extract)

Source: Northern Foods plc Annual report 2003.

notes to the financial statements

NOTE 1   Segmental analysis of sales, turnover, profit and net assets

The Group's operations of retailing and associated activities and property development are carried out in the UK, Republic of Ireland, France, Hungary, Poland, Czech Republic, Slovakia, Thailand, South Korea, Taiwan and Malaysia. The results for Thailand, South Korea, Taiwan, Malaysia and continental European operations are for the year ended 31 December 2002.

	Sales including VAT £m	Turnover excluding VAT £m	Operating profit £m	Net operating assets £m	Sales including VAT £m	Turnover excluding VAT £m	Operating profit £m	Net operating assets £m
				2003				2002
Continuing operations								
UK	23,407	21,615	1,297	8,445	21,685	20,052	1,213	7,131
Rest of Europe	3,032	2,689	141	1,658	2,475	2,203	90	1,079
Asia	2,174	2,033	71	1,193	1,494	1,398	29	916
	28,613	26,337	1,509	11,296	25,654	23,653	1,332	9,126

Figure 4.8 Tesco plc: segmental analysis

Source: Tesco plc Annual report 2003.

4W. Colofon plc has two divisions: Wallpaper Sales and Home Furnishing Sales. Only part of the following information relating to Colofon plc is relevant in calculating that company's 'cost of sales' to be included within the profit and loss account for its financial year. The company both buys in completed products for sale and manufactures goods for sale. You are required to calculate the cost of sales, showing your workings.

	£
Opening stock of raw materials	58,630
Closing stock of raw materials	62,152
Selling and distribution costs	65,240
Raw materials purchased in the year	358,260
Factory wages and other factory overheads	126,521
General administration overheads	205,360
Opening stock of finished goods	12,390
Closing stock of finished goods	9,520
Finished goods purchased in the year	140,750

5W. If you were informed that the Home Furnishings division of Colofon plc (see question 4W above) was permanently closed shortly before the end of its financial year, what effect if any would that closure have on the way the company's results were presented in its profit and loss account?

6W. The closure costs of the Home Furnishings division of Colofon plc (see question 4W above) were £100,000, which had been included in the total of 'general administration overheads'. The directors want to classify this as 'extraordinary expenditure' and exclude the costs when calculating the operating profit for the year. What is your view on this, and can you suggest an alternative way in which the item can be presented?

■ MINI CASE STUDY

A rare bird gets captured

MinnieMax Ltd. (see previous mini case studies) has completed its first year of trading (ended 30 September 2004), and has summarized the following information regarding its trading activities:

	£000s
Administrative expenses	62
Closing stock of animals	5
Distribution costs	46
Exceptional cost: compensation to the Wherearewe tribe of Peru for illegally capturing and selling the tribe's sacred Ibrox bird without permission	40
Expedition costs and other 'cost of sales'	130
Opening stock of animals	2
Other operating income	11
Sales of animals to zoos	486

You are required to present the information in the form of a profit and loss account (ending with 'operating profit (or loss) before interest and taxation') for the year ended 30 September 2004.

(Suggested solutions can be found in Appendix 4.)

■ MAXI CASE STUDY

Anite Group plc

Read the following extract and then answer the questions which follow.

> The shareholders in Anite Group, a small software business, should feel jolly proud of their directors; in a tough year, they managed to push up profits by more than 40 percent, so they will hardly begrudge chief executive John Hawkins the bonus that doubled his pay to £1.05m.
>
> That's the official version anyway, but it would be surprising if many shareholders agree, and Mr Hawkins deserves a rough ride at the annual meeting on September 4th. Delve further into the figures, and profits are down. After tax, there's no profit after all, merely a nasty loss, and the shares have plunged from 180p in January to 28p last night.
>
> You could almost be talking about different companies; there's the one which is justifying those fat bonuses, and the one the shareholders own. They do not seem to have much in common. The connection, up to a point, is the profit warning buried in an upbeat results statement last month.
>
> The bonuses were apparently based on declared pre-tax profits on continuing operations before goodwill amortisation (and there's a great deal of it to amortise), which only goes to show that if you link particular bonuses to targets, the executives will try and hit them, whether they are in shareholders' interests or not.

'Questor', *Daily Telegraph*, 14 Aug. 2002, © Telegraph Group Limited 2002

1. Why does the author's article state 'You could almost be talking about different companies; there's the one which is justifying those fat bonuses, and the one the shareholders own'?

2. 'The bonuses were apparently based on declared pre-tax profits on continuing operations before goodwill amortisation.' Comment on this statement and use it to explain why the shareholders may not have felt 'jolly proud' of their directors.

(Suggested answers and discussion areas are available on the companion website.)

■ WEB LINKS

Company websites

Amrice Inc www.amrice.com

Anite plc www.anite.co.uk

Centex Construction Products Inc. www.centex-cxp.com

Courts plc www.courtsretail.com

Domino's Pizza www.dominos.co.uk

My Travel Group plc www.mytravelgroup.com

Northern Foods plc www.northern-foods.co.uk

Pizza Express plc www.pizzaexpress.co.uk

Tesco plc www.tesco.com

■ **FURTHER READING**

Britton, A., and Waterston, C. (2003). *Financial Accounting*, 3rd edn. (Harlow: FT/Prentice Hall), chapter 3.

Dyson, J. R. (2003). *Accounting for Non-accounting Students*, 5th edn. (Harlow: FT/Prentice Hall), chapters 5, 6.

Elliott, B., and Elliott, J. (2003). *Financial Accounting and Reporting*, 8th edn. (Harlow: FT/Prentice Hall), chapter 8.

■ **COMPANION WEBSITE MATERIALS**

Additional materials are available for students and lecturers on the companion website, at **www.oup.com/uk/booksites/busecon/business/**

5

The profit and loss account: from PBIT to retained profit

OBJECTIVES

By the end of this chapter you will be able to:

- Understand the scope of information found within that part of a published profit and loss account which follows 'profit before interest and taxation' (PBIT).
- Assess the generally accepted accounting practices relating to key items found within a published profit and loss account that follow 'profit before interest and taxation'.
- Understand the importance of 'earnings per share' and PE ratio calculations.

5.1 Introduction

This chapter continues the analysis of the profit and loss account, the first part of which was discussed in Chapter 4. We are looking at all the items which appear below 'PBIT' (profit before interest and taxation), starting with interest receivable and payable and then the two 'appropriations' of profit, taxation, and dividends. Consideration is also given to the various profit figures identified within this section and the 'earnings per share' calculations which usually follow the profit and loss account information. One other item, minority interests, often seen in group profit and loss accounts, is also referred to.

Once again, Domino's Pizza's profit and loss account is used as our starting point (see Figure 5.1, which is cross-referenced to chapter headings), though we shall refer to other companies where needed to illustrate the full range of information which might be disclosed.

5.2 Interest receivable and payable

This part of the profit and loss account shows the costs incurred in financing the business's operations, such as bank overdraft interest and interest payable on loans, and any interest earned from such sources as investments and bank deposits. In addition, many companies,

Group Profit and Loss Account

for the 52 weeks ended 29 December 2002

	Notes	2002 £000	2001 £000
TURNOVER			
Turnover: group and share of joint ventures' turnover		54,673	45,185
Less: share of joint ventures' turnover		(1,564)	(1,360)
GROUP TURNOVER	2	53,109	43,825
Cost of sales		(28,054)	(23,132)
GROSS PROFIT		25,055	20,693
Distribution costs		(8,663)	(7,150)
Administrative expenses		(11,813)	(10,230)
Other operating expenditure		(75)	(169)
GROUP OPERATING PROFIT	3	4,504	3,144
Share of operating profit in joint venture		64	75
Amortisation of goodwill on joint venture		(5)	(5)
		59	70
PROFIT ON ORDINARY ACTIVITIES BEFORE INTEREST AND TAXATION		4,563	3,214
Interest receivable		50	78
Interest payable and similar charges	6	(374)	(430)
PROFIT ON ORDINARY ACTIVITIES BEFORE TAXATION		4,239	2,862
Tax on profit on ordinary activities	7	(1,404)	(858)
PROFIT FOR THE FINANCIAL YEAR		2,835	2,004
Dividends on equity shares	8	(1,018)	(668)
PROFIT RETAINED FOR THE FINANCIAL YEAR	22	1,817	1,336
Earnings per – basic	9	5.60p	4.00p
– diluted		5.29p	3.88p

Cross-references in left margin: 5.2 (Interest receivable / Interest payable and similar charges); 5.3 (Tax on profit on ordinary activities); 5.5, 5.6 (Profit for the financial year / Dividends on equity shares); 5.7 (Profit retained for the financial year); 5.8 (Earnings per basic/diluted).

Figure 5.1 Domino's Pizza Group: profit and loss account (cross-referenced to chapter headings). The shaded area was covered in detail in Chapter 4.

rather than buying fixed assets outright, prefer to *lease* them or buy them on *hire purchase contracts* so that valuable cash resources are not tied up in depreciating assets. The accounting treatment of leased assets on the balance sheet is dealt with in the next chapter, but within the profit and loss account, the finance charges relating to the leases are shown within the 'interest paid and received' section.

Domino's Pizza's profit and loss account shows interest receivable of £50,000 and interest payable and similar charges of £374,000. If we look at n. 6 on p. 328, we see that the latter figure comprises interest on bank loans and overdrafts £348,000, interest on joint venture (the company's share of interest charged specifically to the joint venture's operations) £17,000, and finance charges payable under finance leases and hire purchase contracts £9,000. If we look at the details contained within notes 15 to 17 on pp. 334–5, we can find out details of the loans on which interest is payable. Note 15 reveals 'short-term' bank loans of £2,400,000 and other loans of £612,000. Note 16 reveals longer-term bank loans of £5,775,000 and other loans of £1,339,000. All these loans, totalling £10,126,000, are summarized in n. 17.

By comparing the interest payable on bank loans and overdrafts (£348,000) with the average of the total loans revealed in n. 17 (the average of the closing figure of £10,126,000 and the comparable figure at the end of the previous year of £8,851,000), we can calculate the average interest rate at:

$$\frac{£348,000 \times 100}{(£10,126,000 + £8,851,000)/2}$$
$$= 3.67\%$$

(Note that we are assuming that the 'average' borrowing figures were representative of the *actual* borrowing throughout the year.)

Look at Figure 5.2 from the annual report of Tesco plc, showing that company's net interest payable. Note the many different bonds (loans) listed, their differing interest percentage rates and the final repayment dates shown as part of each bond title. For example, '6% bonds 2008' carry a 6 per cent annual interest rate and are repayable no later than a date (as specified in the bond document) in 2008. Tesco's average loans totalled £4,802.5m during the year. Can you calculate the average interest rate for the company in 2003 and how does it compare with Domino's Pizza?[1]

NOTE 7 Net interest payable

	2003		2002	
	£m	£m	£m	£m
Interest receivable and similar income on money market investments and deposits		65		66
Less interest payable on:				
Short-term bank loans and overdrafts repayable within five years	(104)		(101)	
Finance charges payable on finance leases	(5)		(4)	
4% unsecured deep discount loan stock 2006 (a)	(10)		(9)	
4% RPI bonds 2016 (b)	(12)		(15)	
3.322% LPI bonds 2025 (c)	(10)		(4)	
10¾% bonds 2002	–		(19)	
8¾% bonds 2003	(17)		(17)	
6% bonds 2006	(9)		(8)	
7½% bonds 2007	(24)		(24)	
6% bonds 2008	(15)		(9)	
5⅛% bonds 2009	(18)		(18)	
6⅜% bonds 2010	(10)		(10)	
6% bonds 2010	(12)		(12)	
0.7% Yen bonds 2006 (d)	(13)		(8)	
5¼% Euro bonds 2008	(13)		–	
4¾% Euro bonds 2010	(4)		–	
5½% bonds 2033	(2)		–	
5½% bonds 2019	(4)		–	
Other bonds (d)	(7)		(7)	
Interest capitalised	62		63	
Share of interest of joint ventures and associates	(18)		(17)	
		(245)		(219)
		(180)		(153)

(a) Interest payable on the 4% unsecured deep discount loan stock 2006 includes £5 m (2000 – £5 m) of discount amortisation.
(b) Interest payable on the RPI bonds includes £2 m (2002 – £7 m) of RPI related amortisation.
(c) Interest payable on the LPI bonds 2025 includes £1 m (2002 – £2 m) of RPI related amortisation.
(d) 2002 comparative has been separated out in line with detailed disclosure this year.

Figure 5.2 Tesco plc: interest payable and receivable

Source: Tesco plc Annual Report 2003.

---

[1] $(245 \times 100)/4,802.5 = 5.1\%$

5.3 Taxation

When, in Chapter 3, we were discussing the accounting arrangements of sole traders and partnerships, we did not refer to how such businesses were taxed. Although they would be subject to *indirect* taxation such as value added tax, any taxation on the profits of the businesses would be dealt with by the individual owners (as private liabilities) rather than by the business organization itself. Unlike limited companies, there is no legal separation between sole traders or partnerships and their owners. Consequently, any profits are transferred, without any deduction for taxation, directly to the owners' capital accounts. The individual owners would then include the businesses' profits when they declare their own annual income and will pay any taxation as a private liability. Even if the business owner uses the business's cheque book to pay the tax bill, it must be treated as *private drawings* rather than as a business expense.

The situation is different for limited companies. The company is treated as a separate legal entity from its owners, the shareholders. Because of this, it is taxed on its profits in its own right, any liability being a debt of the company, not the individual shareholders. In the UK the main rate of corporation tax is 30 per cent. However, this does not mean that you can calculate the year's taxation by simply taking 30 per cent of the profit on ordinary activities before taxation. For example, if we look at Domino's Pizza's profit before taxation and its taxation charge for the year as shown in Figure 5.1, we can calculate that its overall taxation as a percentage of profits is 33.1% ($(1,404 \times 100)/4,239$). A (very) detailed explanation is given in n. 7 on pp. 328–9. Although a full appraisal of the taxation system is outside the scope of this book, there are two key areas of which we need to be aware, *current* taxation and *deferred* taxation.

5.3.1 Current taxation

Current tax is defined as 'the amount of tax estimated to be payable or recoverable in respect of the taxable profit or loss for the period, along with adjustments to estimates in respect of previous periods'.[2] 'Taxable' profit is not usually the same as 'accounting' profit as shown in the profit loss account, for a number of reasons, known as *permanent differences*. These include:

- Income might be included in the profit and loss account which is *not taxable*, for example a government grant may have been received and added to profit, but would be excluded from the taxation calculation.

- Expenditure might be included in the profit and loss account which is *not allowed* as an expense against taxable profit. Examples include entertainment expenses and motoring fines. These 'disallowables' will be eliminated when calculating taxation.

For example, assume a company reports a pre-tax profit of £100,000 in its profit and loss account. In arriving at this figure, a non-taxable grant of £5,000 and entertainment and other disallowable expenses of £8,000 have been included. When calculating the profits which will be subject to taxation, both these items need adjustment, resulting in a net

---

[2] FRS16 *Current Tax* (Accounting Standards Board, London, 1999) and also see IAS 12 *Income Taxes* (International Accounting Standards Board, London, 2000).

£3,000 increase in the taxable profit:

$$(£100,000 + £8,000 - £5,000) = £103,000$$

Such permanent differences do not require any adjustments to be made in the profit and loss account. They merely reflect the fact that taxation law occasionally treats things in a way which is different from generally recognized accounting principles.

5.3.2 Deferred taxation

The other main component of the tax charge is *deferred taxation*. This arises because certain types of income and expenditure which are included in the measurement of *accounting* profits are not included in the measurement of *taxable* profits at the same time. These are known as *timing differences* and may have an effect stretching over several accounting periods. If no adjustment was made then the tax charge shown in the profit and loss account would be distorted and the 'true' overall liability not disclosed. A 'Provision for Deferred Taxation' literally means a recognition that at some future period a taxation liability (or asset) may need to be accounted for within the financial statements.

One of the main timing differences is that which arises due to differences between the rates of accounting depreciation on fixed assets and the government's capital allowances (i.e. 'official' percentages used to write down fixed assets for taxation purposes) on the same assets. Capital allowances tend to be more generous to companies when the assets are new, as governments usually try to encourage businesses to invest in modern plant and machinery, whereas most companies' accounting policies for depreciation will tend to spread depreciation evenly over the assets' life. This is often referred to as 'accelerated capital allowances'. This results in a generally lighter tax charge in the early years of the asset's life than in the later years, as this example shows:

Assume a company buys a £7,900 machine on the first day of year 1, and depreciates the asset on a straight-line basis over four years with a residual value of £2,500. Capital allowances are given on the asset at 25 per cent on a reducing balance basis. Assume that the taxation rate is 30 per cent. The timing differences can be calculated as follows:

Year	1	2	3	4
Accounting depreciation (as charged in profit and loss account)[3]	1,350	1,350	1,350	1,350
Capital allowance (as used in taxation computation)[4]	1,975	1,481	1,111	833
A: Originating/(reversing)[a] timing difference	625	131	(239)	(517)
B: Cumulative timing difference	**+625**	**+756**	**+517**	**0**
C: Deferred tax (30%) on annual timing difference A	**187.50**	**39.30**	**−71.70**	**−155.10**

[a] Originating difference occurs in the year in which a provision is created or increased, reversing difference occurs when the provision is reduced or eliminated.

[3] [(7,900 − 2,500)/4].
[4] Yr 1 25% × 7,900, Yr 2 25% × (7,900 − 1,975), Yr 3 25% × [7,900 − (1,975 + 1,481)], Yr 4 25% × [7,900 − (1,975 + 1,481 + 1,111)].

In Years 1, 2, and 3, a provision for deferred taxation (C) would be needed: starting at £187.50, rising by £39.30 in Year 2, falling by £71.70 in Year 3, and then it would be eliminated in Year 4. This reflects the weighting of the capital allowances towards the earlier years, when the current tax charge is lighter than in the latter years of the asset's life. The provision for deferred taxation attempts to 'equalize' the tax charge by neutralizing the timing differences.

Companies that regularly replace ageing assets have argued that generous 'early' tax allowances are continually being regenerated, thus putting off any potential tax liability. Under early accounting standards on deferred taxation, these companies did not need to provide for deferred taxation in such circumstances. However, partial provisioning, as it came to be known, was criticized as being dependent on the management's own interpretation and expectation of future events, and the International Accounting Standard (IAS 12) requires deferred tax to be provided in full, regardless of a company's policy on asset replacement.

An additional area to consider for deferred taxation is that relating to increases in value of fixed assets which have been incorporated within the balance sheet. In some countries, including the UK, companies are allowed to reassess the value of their fixed assets from time to time, to reflect a fair value which may be materially different from original cost price. As gains in value would normally be taxed when the asset is sold, the provision for deferred taxation should be adjusted for this potential liability. However, the UK accounting standard (FRS 19) does not require such a provision in cases where companies do not have any commitment to sell the asset, or if the gain on the sale of one asset is 'rolled over' as payment or part payment of a replacement asset.

 Look at Domino's Pizza's accounting policy relating to deferred taxation shown in n. 1 on p. 325. Note in particular the policy regarding tax on revaluation gains.

5.4 Minority interests

Before arriving at the profit after taxation for the financial period, we sometimes find a further heading, 'minority interests'. This will only be found in a group (consolidated) profit and loss account where fewer than 100 per cent of shares in one or more subsidiaries are owned by the parent company. For example, if company A owned 75 per cent of company B, B will be a subsidiary of A, and *all* of B's income and expenditure (other than transactions between the group companies themselves) will be consolidated with that of company A in the group profit and loss account. However, the interests of the shareholders who own the remaining 25 per cent of company B cannot be ignored, and must be recognized by calculating their proportion of company B's profit or loss and adjusting the consolidated profit figure accordingly.

Minority interests must be split between 'equity' and 'non-equity', the former referring to interests relating to minority holdings in ordinary (voting) shares, the latter referring to non-voting shares (e.g. preference shares) held by the minority.

For example, assume that company Y had issued 2m ordinary shares, 60 per cent of which were owned by its parent company X, and a further £2m 5 per cent preference shares, none of which were owned by its parent company. The after-tax profits of company Y were £300,000. The minority interests to be deducted in the group profit and loss account would be calculated as follows:

	£	Minority interests
Subsidiary's profit after tax	300,000	
Less preference dividend	(100,000)	100,000
Profit after tax and preference dividend	200,000	
Equity minority interest (40% × £200,000)		80,000
Total minority interests		180,000

£180,000 would be deducted from the after-tax profit shown in the group profit and loss account, divided between equity interest £80,000 and non-equity interest £100,000.

Look at this extract from the profit and loss account of H.P. Bulmer Holdings plc. Note the position of minority interests within the statement and the way in which equity and non-equity minority interests are disclosed in the note to the accounts.

Consolidated profit and loss account   for the year ended 26 April 2002

	Notes	After exceptional items and goodwill £000	Exceptional items and goodwill (Note 7) £000	Before exceptional items and goodwill £000
			2002	
Turnover	2	584,994	–	584,994
Operating costs	3	(572,206)	(15,308)	(556,898)
Operating profit	2	12,788	(15,308)	28,096
Share of associate's operating loss	4	(14)	–	(14)
Exceptional profit on disposal	7	–	–	–
		12,774	(15,308)	28,082
Interest	8	(8,379)	–	(8,379)
Profit on ordinary activities before taxation	5	4,395	(15,308)	19,703
Taxation on profit on ordinary activities	9	(3,878)	3,157	(7,035)
Profit on ordinary activities after taxation	10	517	(12,151)	12,668
Minority interests	31	137	–	137
Profit for the financial year		654	(12,151)	12,805
Preference dividends	11	(1,945)	–	(1,945)
Ordinary dividends	12	(3,110)	–	(3,110)
Transferred (from)/to reserves	30	(4,401)	(12,151)	7,750

Figure 5.3 (Continued overleaf)

31. Minority interests

As explained in Note 20, the Group has a controlling interest in Bulmer SA (Pty) Limited, in which Bavaria Brau has a minority interest in the profits and net assets, and a controlling interest in Qufu Bulmer Sankong Cider Company Limited, in which the Sankong Brewing Group has a minority interest on the profits and net assets.

	Bulmer SA (Pty) Limited		Qufu Bulmer Sankong Cider Company Limited	
	Equity £000	Non-equity £000	Equity £000	Total £000
At beginning of year	(125)	117	117	109
Loss on ordinary activities after taxation	(84)	–	(53)	(137)
Currency transaction adjustments	97	(20)	(2)	75
At end of year	(112)	97	62	47

Figure 5.3 H. P. Bulmer Holdings plc: minority interests

Source: H. P. Bulmer Holdings Annual Report 2003.

5.5 Profit for the financial year

Sometimes referred to by financial commentators as the 'bottom line' of the profit and loss account, this is what is left after taxation and all other costs have been deducted. It is also the basis (after deducting any preference dividends) of the 'earnings' used in the very important 'earnings per share' calculation referred to later in the chapter (see section 5.8). It is often used as the benchmark profit figure for interpreting performance between one year and the next.

 Look at Domino's Pizza's profit for each of the financial years shown in Figure 5.1. Calculate the percentage change between the two years.[5]

---

[5] Answer: $(2,835 - 2,004) \times 100/2,004 = 41.5\%$ increase.

5.6 Dividends

5.6.1 Dividends on ordinary shares

Dividends are given to the shareholders of limited companies as their reward for providing the company's share capital. Unlike the interest payable on loans, dividends do not *have* to be paid: they are at the discretion of the company's directors. In practice, the directors will endeavour to maintain good relations with the shareholders by trying to ensure regular and increasing dividends over time. Many new companies and those expanding aggressively may go years without paying a dividend. The directors of loss-making companies may not have any choice in the matter. Many factors come into play when deciding upon dividend policy, and directors must consider:

- what profits to retain within the company for future needs;
- what represents a reasonable return to shareholders;
- what comparable companies pay;
- how much cash resources the company has available to pay a dividend;
- what it is legally permissible for the company to pay.

In Chapter 7 we will be considering the question of *gearing*, which is the balance between a company's equity capital and its loan capital. One of the factors in deciding the level of gearing a company should have is the flexibility that directors of low-geared companies (those with relatively low borrowings and hence low interest commitments) enjoy regarding potential dividend payments. For example, two companies, A and B, have after-tax profits (but before interest) of £10 million. They each have £60 million invested in their companies, but company A's capital consists entirely of ordinary shares whilst company B's comprises one-quarter ordinary shares and three-quarters loan capital on which 7 per cent interest has to be paid. Potential dividends for the year are as follows:

	A	B
Profit after tax	10,000,000	10,000,000
Less interest (7% × £45m)	—	(3,150,000)
Profit available for dividend	10,000,000	6,850,000

The directors of company A can then decide what proportion if any of the £10 million available should be returned to shareholders as a dividend. Directors of the highly geared company B have less than £7 million with which to make their dividend decisions.

Note that the level of dividends has no effect on the amount of taxation charged on the company's profits: dividends come out of after-tax earnings and are therefore an *appropriation* of profits, not an expense charged against profits.

As well as considering the profit for the current year, companies which have made profits in previous years are likely to have transferred some of those profits into a reserve, referred to as the 'profit and loss account', and shown as such on the balance sheet (see Chapter 3). As this is a revenue reserve, it is fully *distributable*, meaning that it can be used for the purpose of dividend payments. This helps companies maintain dividends even in years of poor profits or loss-making periods, by paying the dividends from the accumulated reserves set aside in previous years.

5.6.2 Interim and final dividends

To ensure regular income for shareholders, many companies will pay two dividends during a financial period. The first dividend to be paid will be the final dividend of the *previous* financial period. This can only be paid after the company has received shareholders' approval for the dividend at the annual general meeting, which is held a few months after the end of the financial period to which it relates. The second dividend to be paid is the *interim* dividend for the current financial period. This does not require shareholders' approval, but the directors are likely to take a prudent approach, with the interim usually being less than half the total dividend for the period. Within the financial statements, the profit and loss account will show the interim dividend (paid during the financial period) and final dividend (proposed to be paid after the end of the financial period) as deductions from the profit for the financial period. The balance sheet will show the proposed final dividend as a 'creditor due for payment within one year'. This is shown in Figure 5.4.

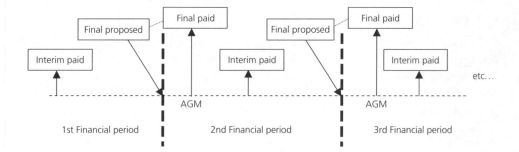

Figure 5.4 Interim and final dividends

Note: The interim dividend is paid during the year, but the final dividend is only paid *after* shareholders give their approval at the AGM following the end of the financial year.

> Look at Domino's Pizza's dividend policy as shown in n. 8 on p. 329. In the current year, what percentage of the total dividend is represented by the interim? By what percentages have the interim and final dividends increased between two years?[6]

5.6.3 Preference dividends

Some companies not only have ordinary share capital but also preference share capital (*preferred* shares in the USA), which is a class of shares carrying a fixed rate of dividend and giving the holders preference over equity shareholders regarding payment of dividends and repayment of capital in the event of the company's liquidation. In most cases these

---

[6] In the current year, the interim is 38.8% of the total. Total dividends have increased by 52.4%: the interim by 38.6%, the final by 62.7%.

shares are *cumulative*, which means that any dividends unpaid by the company in a loss-making year will be accumulated and paid if and when, eventually, the company is back in profit. Preference share dividends are always paid before those of ordinary shares. Further information is given in section 8.3.2.

5.7 Profit retained for the financial period

Sometimes referred to as the 'unappropriated' profit for the period, this represents the profit left over after all costs, taxation, and dividends have been deducted. It is added to the retained profit brought forward at the start of the period, the combined total at the end of the period being known as the 'retained profit carried forward'. This will then be shown on the balance sheet as part of the company's reserves.

5.7.1 Statement of total recognized gains and losses

Occasionally, companies may have additional gains or losses which have not resulted from *operating activities* but from occurrences such as changes in foreign currency rates and revaluations of fixed assets. In the UK they would be shown in a separate statement called the Statement of Total Recognized Gains and Losses (STRGL), which, as its name suggests, effectively serves to summarize all the gains and losses during the financial period from whatever source. In many annual reports, no STRGL is provided if the company confirms that there were no recognized gains and losses other than those disclosed within the profit and loss account.

Figure 5.5 is the Statement of Total Recognized Gains and Losses of Kingfisher PLC:

Consolidated Statement of total recognised gains and losses
For the financial year ended 1 February 2003

£ millions	2003	2002
Profit /(loss) for the financial year	**169.7**	(248.8)
Unrealised surplus on revaluation of properties (see note 14)	**39.3**	27.9
Tax on realised revaluation surplus (see note 30)	**(7.4)**	—
Minority interest movement on the issue of shares in Castorama	**(0.9)**	2.7
Net foreign exchange adjustments offset in reserves (see note 30)	**(4.1)**	(26.4)
Tax effect of exchange adjustments offset in reserves (see note 30)	**10.0**	(2.9)
Total recognised gains/(losses) relating to the financial year	**206.6**	(247.5)

Figure 5.5 Kingfisher plc: consolidated statement of total recognized gains and losses
Source: Kingfisher plc Annual Report 2003.

One of the items included in the statement is an unrealized surplus on revaluation of properties. 'Unrealized' means that the properties have not been sold, only a revised *valuation* is being incorporated within the financial statements. Note also that the related taxation which might be payable when the property is sold has been deducted, so effectively an 'unrealized gain, net of tax' is being shown.

5.7.2 **Note of historical cost profits and losses**

Another statement sometimes seen within the annual report, this is applicable for those companies which have decided to *revalue* their fixed assets to keep balance sheet values up to date. So that comparisons can be made between such companies and those companies that decide *not* to revalue their assets, the note of historical cost profits and losses shows how the reported profit or loss would have differed if no asset revaluations had been made. The starting point is the reported profit on ordinary activities before taxation, with adjustments made for relevant items such as:

- the difference between the depreciation charge based on the historical cost, and the depreciation charge as calculated on the revalued amount;
- the difference between the profit on the disposal of an asset calculated on depreciated historical cost (i.e. the original cost) and that calculated on a revalued amount.

For example, two companies, E and F, both report pre-tax profits of £20 million. Both have land and buildings which cost £40 million, but company E's land and buildings were revalued, and are shown in its balance sheet at £60 million. Both companies depreciate land and buildings over forty years by the straight line method. The note of historical cost profits and losses for company E will be shown as follows:

	£m
Reported profit on ordinary activities before taxation	20
Difference between the historical cost depreciation charge and the actual depreciation charge of the year calculated on the revalued amount $(1/40 \times £60m) - (1/40 \times £40 m)$	0.5
Historical cost profit on ordinary activities before taxation	20.5

This shows that the effect of company E's revaluation of its land and buildings on its profit and loss account was to increase costs by £0.5m.

The note of historical cost profits and losses of Somerfield plc is shown in Figure 5.6.

For the 52 weeks ended 27 April 2002

	2001/2002 £m	2000/2001 £m
Reported profit/(loss) on ordinary activities before taxation	22.2	(13.1)
Realisation of property revaluation (losses)/gains of previous years	(0.4)	1.8
Difference between a historical cost depreciation charge and the actual depreciation charge for the year calculated on the revalued amount	2.3	2.5
Historical cost profit/(loss) on ordinary activities before taxation	24.1	(8.8)
Historical cost profit/(loss) for the year retained after taxation and dividends	25.2	(2.3)

Figure 5.6 Somerfield plc: note of historical cost profits and losses

---

5.8 Earnings per share

The earnings per share (eps) calculation, shown at the foot of the profit and loss account of public companies, is widely used by investors and analysts as an indicator of a company's performance, and the *price/earnings* (PE) ratio, shown in the *Financial Times* and financial pages of certain other newspapers, is perhaps the clearest indication of the stock market's rating of any particular company. The PE ratio is simply the stock market price divided by the eps.

While market price is derived from the forces of supply and demand which exist in the stock markets, eps is, as the name implies, the proportion of a company's earnings which is attributable to each equity share, as based on the company's most recently reported profits. For the PE ratio to have meaning, the eps must be reliable, and consistently calculated both between one company and another and between one financial period and another. The basic eps calculation uses the following formula:

$$\frac{\text{Profit for the financial period (after tax, minority interests, and preference dividends)}}{\text{Weighted average number of ordinary shares outstanding during the period}}$$

Note that a company's policy regarding ordinary share dividends is irrelevant when calculating eps. This is because, as we saw in section 5.6, individual companies may have very different views on the need for, and scale of, dividend payments. By using the earnings *before* ordinary dividends, this enables comparisons to be made between companies regardless of whether or not they pay dividends.

By combining the company's own eps (which is reported twice annually—first within an interim report published to summarize the first six months' trading and secondly within the annual report) with the frequently changing stock market price, an 'instant' measure of the company's performance and risk potential as viewed by the stock market can be obtained. For example, in Figure 5.1 we see that Domino's Pizza's basic eps for the current year is 5.60p (in the UK, eps is always measured in pence). The company's stock market price at the time of writing is 110p, so the PE ratio can be easily calculated as 110p/5.60p = 19.6. The PE ratio is often referred to as a 'multiple'—it is neither a monetary amount nor a percentage. A PE ratio of 19.6 simply means that today's stock market price is 19.6 times the last reported earnings per share. To establish how this company ranks alongside other companies, we need to know average PE ratios both across the entire stock market and within the particular sector in which Domino's Pizza operates. We can find this information within the *Financial Times*: the average PE ratio across all sectors on that day was 18.11 and the average PE ratio for companies operating within the 'leisure and hotels' sector (which includes pizza companies) was 17.48. The Domino's Pizza's PE ratio of 19.6 shows that that company's stock market price is outperforming the market generally and also competing companies.

5.8.1 Diluted earnings per share

The basic eps calculation is sometimes accompanied by a second eps figure known as the *diluted* eps. Many companies offer stock options to their employees which give them the opportunity to acquire shares in the company at future dates and at prices set at the time the options are given (see p. 189). Also, some types of loan stock may carry the right of conversion into ordinary shares at future dates. So that the potential effect on eps of increasing share capital can be assessed, a diluted eps is provided, which uses the assumption that all shares subject to options, or convertible by loan stockholders, have been issued for the purpose of the calculation.

> Look at n. 9 on p. 329, which explains Domino's Pizza's eps figures, and in particular the different ordinary share totals used in the basic eps and the diluted eps calculations.

5.9 Chapter summary

- Interest payable includes the finance charges relating to leasing and hire purchase contracts.
- The taxation on the profits of sole traders and partnerships is a personal liability of the owners, but as limited liability companies have separate legal identity from its owners, the company itself is responsible for its taxation liability.
- The taxation charge shown in a company profit and loss account usually comprises two elements, the *current* tax charge and a *deferred* tax charge.
- Accounting profit is not usually the same as taxable profit.
- Any minority interests must be recognized within the profit and loss account.
- Dividend policy varies from company to company: directors in low-geared companies tend to have more flexibility in comparison with high-geared ones.
- Interim dividends are paid part way through the financial period, but final dividends can only be paid after shareholders give their approval at the annual general meeting.
- Companies may provide a statement of total recognized gains and losses and a note of historical cost profits and losses in some situations.
- Earnings per share figures are used to calculate the PE ratio, which is a widely used indicator of a company's stock market performance. If there is the possibility of the company issuing more shares at a later date due to its having issued stock options or convertible loan stock then a diluted eps figure must also be calculated.

■ GLOSSARY

accelerated capital allowances	Capital allowances which give the larger part of the allowance in the early years of the asset's life
'bottom line'	The profit for the financial year after taxation and all other costs have been deducted. Often referred to by media commentators when discussing a company's results
capital allowances	Tax allowances given by government to encourage investment in fixed assets
convertible loan stock	Loans which can be converted into equity shares at predetermined dates at the discretion of the lender
current taxation	The amount of tax estimated to be payable or recoverable in respect of the taxable profit or loss for the period, along with adjustments to estimates in respect of previous periods
deferred taxation	The estimated future tax consequences of transactions and events recognized in the financial statements of the current and previous periods
diluted earnings per share	An additional earnings per share calculation provided when there is the possibility of the company issuing more shares at a later date due to its having issued stock options or convertible loan stock
distributable reserves	Reserves that can be used for dividend payments: the same as revenue reserves
dividend	The rewards given to the shareholders of limited companies in return for their providing capital
earnings per share	The profit for the financial period after tax, minority interests, and preference dividends divided by the weighted average number of ordinary shares outstanding during the period
equity capital	The ordinary (voting) shares of a limited company
final dividend	A dividend proposed to be paid after shareholders' approval at the annual general meeting following the end of the financial period
gearing	The relative proportions of a company's equity capital and its loan capital
indirect taxation	A tax on expenditure (e.g. value added tax)
interim dividend	A dividend that relates to the first few months of a financial period
minority interests	That part of the equity share capital of a subsidiary company which is not owned by the parent company
non-equity capital	Shares in a limited company other than the ordinary (voting) shares
note of historical cost profits and losses	An additional statement provided by some UK companies showing the effect that the revaluation of fixed assets hashad on the reported profit for the period
PE ratio	The current stock market price divided by the earnings per share. It is used as a key indicator of a company's performance as shown by the stock exchange

permanent differences	Differences between a company's taxable profits and its accounting profits. They arise because certain types of income and expenditure are non-taxable or disallowable
preference shares	Non-voting shares that carry a fixed percentage dividend
statement of total recognized gains	An additional statement provided by some UK companies which summarizes *all* gains and losses for the financial period and losses
stock options	An option given to employees to purchase shares in the company at fixed prices at specified future times
timing differences	Differences between a company's taxable profits and its accounting profits which may give rise to future taxation liabilities or assets

■ **MULTIPLE CHOICE QUESTIONS**

1. If an expense has been included in the profit and loss account which is disallowable for taxation purposes, this is an example of a:
   a   Permanent difference
   b   Temporary difference
   c   Timing difference
   d   Deferred difference

2. When a government's capital allowances give greater tax benefits in the early years of the asset's life than in the later years this is known as:
   a   Reducing balance depreciation
   b   Accelerated capital allowances
   c   Deferred taxation
   d   Straight line depreciation

3. If company A owns 60% of company B, the percentage of company B's income and expenses to be included in the group profit and loss account is:
   a   100
   b   60
   c   40
   d   Nil

4. If company A owns 60% of company B, the percentage of company B's shares not owned by company A is known as:
   a   Parent's interest
   b   Majority interest
   c   Subsidiary interest
   d   Minority interest

5. If company A owns 60% of company B, how would the interests of the 40% of company B's shares not owned by company A be recognized in the group profit and loss account?
   a   40% of company B's profits must be paid to the minority shareholders
   b   40% of the group's dividends must be paid to the minority shareholders

    c 40% of company B's after-tax profits are deducted from the group's after-tax profits shown in the group profit and loss account

    d 40% of company B's pre-tax profits are deducted from the group's after-tax profits shown in the group profit and loss account

6. Which one of the following could be described as a non-equity interest in a limited company?

    a Voting shares

    b Ordinary shares

    c Preference shares

    d Equity shares

7. Which two dividends are usually paid within a financial year?

    a This year's interim dividend and this year's proposed final dividend

    b This year's interim dividend and last year's proposed final dividend

    c This year's interim dividend and next year's proposed final dividend

    d Last year's interim dividend and last year's proposed final dividend

8. If preference shares are described as cumulative, this means:

    a Dividends will definitely be paid every year

    b If dividends can't be paid in one year they will be accumulated and paid when and if the company makes sufficient profits in future years

    c Dividends will only be paid in years in which the company makes a profit

    d Dividends are not paid to shareholders, they are added to the value of the shares

9. If a company has a high PE ratio, which one of the following is certain about that company?

    a Its stock market price has been continually rising

    b Its stock market price is many times greater than its earnings per share

    c Its earnings per share for the current year is greater than that of the previous year

    d Its PE ratio is higher than competing companies

10. A *diluted* earnings per share figure is given when:

    a More company shares might be issued in future years due to the existence of stock options and/or convertible loan stock

    b Next year's forecast earnings per share is predicted to be much lower than the current year's

    c The stock market price has fallen to a level below the current earnings per share

    d A loss has been reported by the company

(*Note: answers are shown in Appendix 2.*)

■ DISCUSSION QUESTIONS

Read the following quotation and discuss the questions that follow it:

> It is time to remember that the real value of a business is simply the capital that its investors can take out of it during its lifetime. Everything else is speculation.
>
>   Anthony Nutt (director of Jupiter International Group/Jupiter Asset Management Ltd.), 'Directors must not cut their dividends carelessly', *Financial Times*, 28 Feb. 2003

1. Do you agree with Mr Nutt's definition of the 'real value of a business'?

2. Discuss the ways in which investors can 'take out [a company's capital] . . . during its lifetime'.

3. With regard to the title of the article, what factors should be considered by directors when deciding on what dividends to propose?

(Note: Suggested answers or discussion points are available on the companion website.)

■ LONGER QUESTIONS

(Questions marked W have suggested answers on the companion website. Other questions are answered in Appendix 3.)

1. Figure 5.7 is an extract from H. R. Owen plc's profit and loss account for the year ended 31 December 2002.

		2002	2001
		7000	7000
Profit on ordinary activities before interest		**4,531**	5,052
Interest receivable and similar income	(i)	**61**	1
Interest payable and similar charges		**(2,282)**	(3,042)
Profit on ordinary activities before taxation		**2,310**	2,011
Taxation on profit on ordinary activities	(ii)	**(827)**	(754)
Profit on ordinary activities after taxation		**1,483**	1,257
Dividends	(iii)	**(1,902)**	(1,878)
Retained loss for the year	(iv)	**(419)**	(621)
Basic earnings per share	(v)	**7.8p**	6.7p
Diluted earnings per share	(vi)	**7.8p**	6.7p

The Group has no recognised gains and losses other than those included in the profits above, and therefore no separate statement of total recognised gains and losses has been presented. (vii)

Figure 5.7 H. R. Owen plc: consolidated profit and loss account for the year ending 31 December 2002 (extract)

Briefly explain each of the items marked (i) to (vii).

2. You are given the following information relating to Vanquish plc for the year ended 31 October 2004:

		£000
Operating profit before taxation		456
Taxation		84
Minority interests		12
Preference dividends		6
Ordinary dividends		102
Number of ordinary shares in issue	1,770,000	
Maximum potential shares to be issued under future options	590,000	
Current stock market price	200p	

Calculate:

a basic earnings per share;

b diluted earnings per share;

c price/earnings (PE) ratio;

and

d comment on the PE ratio, assuming that the average ratio for the stock market was 17 and the average for the sector in which Vanquish plc operates is 12.

3. The accounting profit before taxation of Hoogly plc is £800,000. This includes a £50,000 grant which is not taxable and £20,000 of expenses (other than depreciation) which are disallowable for tax purposes. Depreciation charged in the profit and loss account amounted to £120,000, but this was to be replaced by capital allowances of £150,000 for the taxation computation. The tax rate for company profits is 30 per cent.

a Identify two *permanent* tax differences and one *timing* taxation difference revealed in the above information.

b Calculate the taxable profit and the amount of current taxation payable.

c Calculate the increase or decrease in the provision for deferred taxation for the year, assuming that the company had a provision brought forward at the start of the year of £5,000, and that the same assets were owned at the start and end of the year.

d What would be the overall taxation charge shown in the profit and loss account after all the adjustments had been made?

4W. Company T had issued 5m ordinary shares, 80 per cent of which were owned by its parent company U, and a further £5m 4 per cent preference shares, none of which were owned by its parent company. The after-tax profits of company T were £500,000.

Calculate the value of the minority interests to be shown in the group's profit and loss account, distinguishing between equity and non-equity interests.

5W. Yucca plc has revalued its land and buildings at £10m. They originally cost £8m, and are depreciated over a fifty-year period. In the company's latest profit and loss account, operating profit before interest and taxation was reported as £6m.

a Explain the purpose of a *note of historical cost profits and losses*.

b Prepare a note of historical cost profits and losses for Yucca plc.

6W. Two companies, Ripvan plc and Winkle plc, are comparing their financial results for the year ended 31 May 2004. They both have disclosed operating profits after taxation of £20m, but the following differences have been noticed:

1. Ripvan plc has revalued its land and buildings, and shows a revaluation reserve totalling £6m. Winkle plc shows its land and buildings at original cost. Both companies depreciate land and buildings over twenty years.

2. Ripvan plc has disclosed a separate 'diluted' earnings per share calculation whereas Winkle plc only shows its basic earnings per share.

3. Ripvan plc shows an item called 'minority interests' on its profit and loss account. Winkle plc does not make any reference to this.

4. Ripvan plc has not paid an interim dividend during the year, whereas Winkle plc has not only paid an interim dividend, but is proposing a final dividend which would make its total dividend five times greater than Ripvan plc's.

Explain the significance of each of the above differences between the two companies.

■ MINI CASE STUDY

Hard work pays dividends

MinnieMax Ltd. (see previous mini case studies) has completed its first year of trading (ended 30 September 2004), and has calculated its profit for the year before interest and taxation as £222,000. Further information has become available as follows:

	£
Final dividend (proposed)	50,000
Interest receivable	1,500
Interest payable	3,500
Interim dividend (paid)	26,000
Taxation charge (total for year)	62,500

You are required to present the information in the form of an extract from a profit and loss account (starting with 'Operating Profit before interest and taxation') for the year ended 30 September 2004.

(*Suggested solutions can be found in Appendix 4.*)

■ MAXI CASE STUDY

PE ratios

Read the following extract and then answer the questions which follow.

. . . the PE ratio of the FTSE 100 is currently about 17. This means that any share with a PE ratio lower than 17 could be regarded as offering good value. Shares can also be compared against others in the same sector and against the sector average. However, a low PE ratio is not necessarily a good guide to value. It could mean that the market expects earnings in a company with a low PE to fall this year. A high PE relative to the market could also mean that the company has had consistently higher than average profits growth, although this may not continue . . .

One of the problems with PE ratios is that they usually capture one year's earnings figures, which can be distorted by exceptional items such as one-off restructuring charges. Also, a company's earnings may be cyclical and fluctuate widely from one year to the next.

Of course, the sort of companies that cannot be valued by using a PE ratio are those with no earnings. This made it difficult to value many dotcom companies in the technology boom since none were making a profit, but had sky-high share prices. This led investors to use other sorts of valuation measures such as discounted cash flow to try and justify the rising share prices.

From Deborah Hargreaves, 'PE ratio useful, but don't rely on it too much', Financial Times, 24 May 2003

1. Explain the statement 'any share with a PE ratio lower than 17 could be regarded as offering good value'.
2. To what extent to do you agree that PE ratios are 'distorted by exceptional items such as one-off restructuring charges'?
3. If PE ratios cannot be used to measure companies without earnings, to what extent does this reduce their usefulness?

(Suggested answers and discussion areas are available on the companion website.)

■ WEB LINKS

Company websites

Companies referred to in this chapter:

Domino's Pizza www.dominos.co.uk

HP Bulmer Holdings www.bulmer.com

Kingfisher plc www.kingfisher.co.uk

H. R. Owen plc www.hrowen.com

Somerfield plc www.somerfield.co.uk

Tesco plc www.tesco.com

■ FURTHER READING

Black, G. (2003). *Students' Guide to Accounting and Financial Reporting Standards*, 9th edn. (Harlow: FT/Prentice Hall), chapters 7, 8.

Elliott, B., and Elliott, J. (2003). *Financial Accounting and Reporting*, 8th edn. (Harlow: FT/Prentice Hall), chapters 13, 23.

■ COMPANION WEBSITE MATERIALS

Additional materials are available for students and lecturers on the companion website, at **www.oup.com/uk/booksites/busecon/business/**

6

The balance sheet: assets

OBJECTIVES

By the end of this chapter you will be able to:

- Define and evaluate 'fixed assets'.
- Understand the distinction between fixed and current assets.
- Appreciate the different types of fixed assets.
- Evaluate the differing accounting treatments for the various types of fixed assets.
- Define and evaluate 'current assets'.
- Understand the way in which stock is valued within a balance sheet.
- Distinguish between the various components which might be found under the headings 'debtors' and 'cash at bank and in hand' within a balance sheet.

6.1 Introduction

Having looked in detail at the profit and loss account in Chapters 4 and 5, we now turn our attention to another major financial statement, the balance sheet. A balance sheet is a summary of every asset and liability remaining at the end of a financial period after the profit and loss account has been prepared. It has often been described as a 'snapshot' of a business at a specific moment in time, unlike the profit and loss account which summarizes information from the start to the end of the financial period. Because the balance sheet records only one moment in a business's life, we must be on our guard against 'window dressing', where a company might deliberately arrange its end of period transactions to ensure that the most favourable financial circumstances coincide with the preparation of its balance sheet.

Once again, the relevant part of Domino's Pizza's annual report is used as our starting point (see Figure 6.1, which is cross-referenced to chapter headings), though we shall refer to other companies where needed to illustrate the full range of information which might be disclosed. Note that it is usual in a group's annual report to include not only the group balance sheet but also the balance sheet of the parent company: this is explained in section 6.2 below, but remember that Figure 6.1 is the *group* balance sheet, not the parent company's balance sheet.

6.2 ⎡Group Balance Sheet
       ⎣at 29 December 2002

	Notes	2002 £000	2001 £000
6.3 — **FIXED ASSETS**			
6.4 — Intangible assets	10	2,386	2,484
6.5 — Tangible assets	11	13,685	12,181
⎡ Investments in joint venture:	12		
6.6 — Share of gross assets		717	757
⎣ Share of gross liabilities		(410)	(480)
		307	277
TOTAL FIXED ASSETS		16,378	14,942
6.7 — **CURRENT ASSETS**			
6.8 — Stocks	13	1,411	1,260
6.9 — Debtors:	14		
amounts falling due within one year		8,572	6,665
amounts falling due after more than one year		2,130	1,756
		10,702	8,421
6.10 — Cash at bank and in hand		3,885	3,231
TOTAL CURRENT ASSETS		15,998	12,912
CREDITORS: amounts falling due within one year	15	(12,919)	(10,203)
NET CURRENT ASSETS		3,079	2,709
TOTAL ASSETS LESS CURRENT LIABILITIES		19,457	17,651
CREDITORS: amounts falling due after more than one year	16	(7,152)	(7,632)
PROVISION FOR LIABILITIES AND CHARGES	7	(604)	(421)
		11,701	9,598
CAPITAL AND RESERVES			
Called up share capital	21	2,546	2,518
Share premium account	22	2,395	2,192
Profit and loss account	22	6,760	4,888
Equity shareholders' funds		11,701	9,598

Stephen Hemsley
Director

Figure 6.1 Domino's Pizza Group: balance sheet (cross-referenced to chapter headings). The shaded area is covered in detail in Chapters 7 and 8.

6.2 The heading

A 'group' balance sheet is the combined summary of assets, liabilities, capital, and reserves for a *group of companies*, which, as explained in Chapter 4, usually comprises, at a minimum, a *parent* company and one *subsidiary*. In the consolidation process, more fully explained in

Chapter 10, *all* the assets and liabilities of each group member are combined even if there are minority shareholdings in one or more subsidiaries. Any minority interest is evaluated and recognized separately on the balance sheet. Note that inter-company indebtedness is eliminated in the consolidation process—otherwise, misleadingly, loans from one group company to another would be shown as both assets and liabilities on the group balance sheet. The word 'consolidated' is often used instead of 'group', as in 'consolidated balance sheet'. The term 'balance sheet' is universal, though occasionally it may be described as a 'statement of financial position' or, more simply, 'position statement'.

The other information shown in the heading is the date of the statement, which, in the case of a published annual report, is the last day of the financial period, though, to be precise, the balance sheet is prepared at the *end of* the last day of the financial period.

The format of the balance sheet has undergone some change over the centuries. Traditionally, it was shown in an account format, but some countries (including the USA and countries of mainland Europe) showed assets on the left-hand side, with liabilities and capital on the right-hand side, whilst other countries (including the UK) reversed this. Although presentation of a balance sheet in 'account' format is still acceptable, many companies (including virtually all UK companies) have changed to a *vertical* format which allows a sub-calculation of a company's working capital (current assets less current liabilities) to be shown as part of the balance sheet information. The importance of working capital is explained in Chapter 12.

Look at the two-page 'account format' balance sheet of a US company at **www.amrice. com/1201_Bank.pdf** showing assets on one page and 'liabilities and stockholders equity' on the following page.

Balance sheet formats within the European Union have been standardized to harmonize financial reporting practice. Two formats are allowed which enable companies to choose between either vertical or account format. Domino's Pizza's group balance sheet in Figure 6.1 shows the vertical format: an example of the 'account' format used by a German company, Scholz and Friends Group, can be seen in an English-language version at **www. s-f.com/group/uk/index.html** (download the annual report and look at the consolidated balance sheet—pp. 13–14 in the 2002 report).

In addition to the *group* balance sheet, as shown in Figure 6.1, the parent company's own balance sheet will be included within the annual report. Domino's Pizza's parent company balance sheet can be seen on p. 322. It is often the case that the parent company's role is restricted to the raising of capital and the management of its investments in its subsidiaries, with the subsidiaries being responsible for the group's operating activities. However, one aspect of the parent–subsidiary relationship is that the parent company usually guarantees the debts of its subsidiaries should they get into financial difficulties. If the parent company's balance sheet shows a poor financial position, then individual creditors of subsidiary companies may be at risk of non-payment. The group balance sheet is of greater importance when analysing the company as a whole, though it may hide the fact that one or more individual subsidiaries are loss-making.

A prevalent myth is that a balance sheet shows the current value of the company—it does not. For a company whose shares are listed on a stock market, its *market value* will be the number of shares issued times the stock market price. For an unlisted company, a reasonable estimate would require an up-to-date valuation of all assets and liabilities, with possibly a premium added to allow for any extra value to reflect the company's reputation and ability to make future profits, known as *goodwill*. The balance sheet should therefore be seen as a useful accounting summary rather than as a guide to the company's market value.

> Domino's Pizza's stock market value at the time of writing was 110p. It had nearly 51m shares in issue, so its stock market value was £64.9m. Its balance sheet value (see Figure 6.1) was only £11.7m.

6.3 Fixed assets

Assets are defined in the Statement of Principles (see Chapter 1) as 'rights or other access to future economic benefits controlled by an entity as a result of past transactions or events'. In overall terms, a company's assets can be divided into two groups: those that appear on the balance sheet and those that do not. Within the former category are included the obvious 'big ticket' items such as land, buildings, machinery, and vehicles, as well as stock, debtors, and cash. It also includes less obvious assets, such as any extra amount (goodwill) paid in excess of the fair value of the net assets of a business which has been acquired. However, goodwill can only be included if a price has been paid for it—if it has been generated *internally* by the company over time, then it cannot be incorporated within the balance sheet, as there is no reliable 'cost' price which can be independently verified—any value could be manipulated to suit the purpose required. Similarly, factors such as an able and willing workforce or a motivated and successful managing director are incapable of objective valuation and cannot be shown.

Another area to be discussed is the status of *leased* assets, which are dealt with in section 6.5 below.

The whole question of what does or does not appear in a balance sheet is one of great relevance to our perception of a company's performance and viability. In the well-publicized cases of failed US companies such as Enron, 'creative' accounting techniques were said to be responsible for excluding both assets and liabilities from balance sheets, thereby making it impossible to make any reasonable and objective analysis.

Those assets that *are* included are divided between fixed assets (often referred to as *plant and equipment* in the USA), and current assets. A further distinction is between *intangible* and *tangible* fixed assets. Intangible fixed assets are those *not* having a physical substance, and include goodwill, brand names, and patents. Tangible fixed assets have physical substance and are held for use in the production or supply of goods or services on a continuing basis—usually for a period of at least one year.

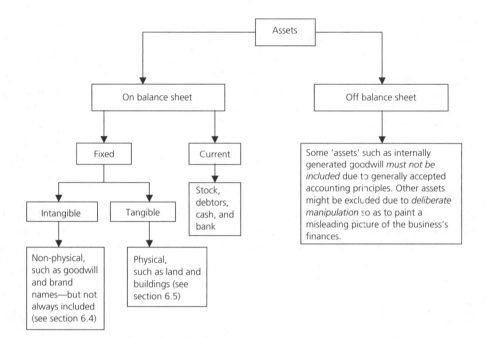

Figure 6.2 Assets: on balance sheet and off balance sheet

6.4 **Intangible fixed assets**

Note 10 of Domino's Pizza's annual report (see p. 330) gives a breakdown of the intangible fixed assets of the group at the end of its financial year, a summary of which is as follows:

£000s	Goodwill	Franchise fees	Interest in leases	Total
Cost	1,857	829	399	3,085
Amortization	206	409	84	699
Net book value	1,651	420	315	2,386

Note also that intangibles can include the cost of developing or acquiring a brand name or patent.

6.4.1 **Goodwill**

As previously stated, goodwill can only be included as an accounting value within a balance sheet when one business acquires another at a price greater than the fair values of the acquired business's assets less its liabilities. This is known as 'purchased goodwill'. Goodwill that has been *internally* generated over time, but has never been purchased, cannot be included, as its value has not been objectively valued, or tested by a market transaction.

Domino's Pizza paid £356,000 for goodwill during its financial year, as disclosed in n. 10 (see p. 330), when it acquired three stores, with stock and equipment valued at 'only' £131,000, from franchisees[1] for £487,000. Note that it is also possible for *negative* goodwill to be created when the price paid is *less than* the fair value of the net assets. For example, if Domino's Pizza had only paid £100,000 for the three stores, then *negative* goodwill of £31,000 would have been created. Negative goodwill sometimes arises when a loss-making business is being sold with few potential bidders.

The company's accounting policy regarding goodwill is set out in n. 1, the first part of which is shown below (letters in square brackets are cross-references to the explanations that follow the extract):

Goodwill

Positive goodwill arising on acquisitions of a subsidiary, associate or business is capitalized, classified as an asset on the balance sheet [A] and amortized on a straight line basis over its estimated useful economic life up to 20 years [B]. It is reviewed for impairment at the end of the first full financial year following the acquisition and in other periods if events or changes in circumstances indicate that the carrying value may not be recoverable [C].

Notes:

A. If the goodwill was *negative*, it would be disclosed on the balance sheet immediately below the value of any positive goodwill, with a sum total showing the net amount.

 Look at the extract in Figure 6.3 from the balance sheet of Courts plc, showing both positive and negative goodwill.

	Notes	Group 2002 £'000	Group 2001 as restated* £'000	Parent 2002 £'000	Parent 2001 £'000
Fixed assets					
Positive goodwill	9	1,182			
Negative goodwill	9	(7,498)			
Intangible assets		(6,316)			
Tangible assets	10	196,789	192,009	44,408	43,848
Investments	11	8,541	7,774	93,337	98,282
		198,014	199,783	137,745	142,130

Figure 6.3 Courts plc: group and parent balance sheets as at 31 March 2002 (extract)

[1] A franchisee is one who is granted a franchise (licence) to market a company's goods or services in a specific area.

B.   Intangible assets are *amortized*, not depreciated, though it has the same effect of writing down the asset over a specific time period. The international accounting standard, IAS 38 *Intangible Assets*, presumes that the useful life of goodwill does not exceed twenty years. In very rare cases goodwill may be demonstrated to have a useful life in excess of twenty years, in which case amortization is still required and the reasons for rebutting the twenty-year presumption must be disclosed. However, the UK accounting standard,[2] whilst also stating that there is a rebuttable presumption that the useful life will not exceed twenty years, permits an *indefinite* useful life, subject to extensive disclosures, and detailed impairment review requirements (see next section). Systematic amortization is not required if the goodwill is deemed to have an indefinite life.

C.   *Impairment* refers to a reduction in the value of an asset to an amount below its value as currently shown in the business's balance sheet ('the carrying amount'). A business should undertake an 'impairment review' of goodwill and other fixed assets on a regular basis to ensure that balance sheet assets are not overvalued. The policy of Domino's Pizza to review goodwill for impairment 'at the end of the first full financial year following the acquisition and in other periods if events or changes in circumstances indicate that the carrying value may not be recoverable' follows the relevant UK and international accounting standards.[3]

6.4.2 Franchise fees

These are paid by a franchisee to a franchiser. In the case of Domino's Pizza (UK & IRL) plc (the franchisee), it has had to pay a fee to Domino's Pizza Inc., the US proprietor of the brand (the franchiser), for the exclusive right to operate under the company's name in the UK and Ireland. The UK and Ireland company then, in turn, earns part of its income by selling its own franchises allowing individuals to operate a Domino's Pizza branch in a specific locality and receives a percentage of the sales made by the franchisees. These franchise fees are written off (amortized) on a straight line basis over their estimated useful lives of twenty years.

6.4.3 Interest in leases

This represents Domino's Pizza's investment in the leasehold properties of franchisees, and are written off over the life of the leases.

6.4.4 Research and development

Another area which may be included within intangible assets is *development expenditure* on new designs or products. Companies wishing to maintain or improve profitability often have to spend material amounts on research and development (R&D). Such expenditure is often highly speculative in nature, with great uncertainty being attached to the likely level, if any, of future income. For this reason, research expenditure is always written off in the profit and loss account in the year in which it is incurred. 'Development' expenditure—where products or services have progressed past the research stage and are being developed for

---

[2]   FRS 10 *Goodwill and Intangible Assets*.
[3]   FRS 11 *Impairment of Fixed Assets and Goodwill* and IAS 36 *Impairment of Assets*.

commercial use—is also usually written off but, in exceptional circumstances, may be treated as a *deferred asset*, being carried forward to future periods and ultimately amortized only when commercial production or application of the product, service, process, or system being developed has commenced. At any stage, if the project ceases to be technically feasible or is unlikely to be marketable, then the costs should be written off.

Avon Rubber plc showed development expenditure at a net book value of £2.5 million in its most recent balance sheet. Its amortization policy was to write off the development expenditure over its estimated life of five years on a straight line basis. The company's accounting policies included the following note:

Research and development

All research and development costs are written off in the year in which they are incurred, with the exception of certain major product development projects where reasonable certainty exists as regards technical and commercial viability. Such expenditure is capitalised and amortised over the expected product life, commencing in the year when sales of the product are made for the first time.

6.5 Tangible fixed assets

These are 'physical' assets such as land and buildings, motor vehicles, plant and equipment, and furniture and fittings. With a few important exceptions, they are usually depreciated by either the straight line or reducing balance methods as explained in Chapter 3. The depreciation policy of Domino's Pizza is as follows:

- freehold buildings—over fifty years;
- plant and production equipment—over ten years;
- leasehold building improvements—over the lesser of the life of the lease plus fourteen years, or thirty years;
- computers, fixtures and fittings, and other equipment—over two to ten years;
- vehicles—over three years;
- mopeds—over eighteen months.

The company's accounting policy also refers to the possibility of impairment of asset values, stating that the carrying value of tangible fixed assets is reviewed for impairment if events or changes in circumstances indicate that the carrying value may not be recoverable. For example, assume the company bought twenty vehicles for £10,000 each in February 2004 and expected them to have a useful economic life of four years, at the end of which time they would be valued at 25 per cent of cost, the depreciation to be on the straight line basis. The calculation of annual depreciation would be:

$$\frac{(20 \times £10,000) - [25\% \times (20 \times £10,000)]}{4} = \frac{150,000}{4} = £37,500 \text{ p.a.}$$

If, during the second year of ownership, it became clear that the value at the end of the four-year period (residual value) was likely to be only 15 per cent of cost, annual depreciation would have to be recalculated as follows:

Cost	200,000
Less first year's depreciation	37,500
Net book value at the end of the first year	162,500
Revised residual value (15% × £200,000)	30,000
Amount to be depreciated over remaining three years	132,500
Revised annual depreciation (£132,500/3)	44,167

The only type of tangible asset that is not normally depreciated is *freehold land*, which is land directly owned rather than leased from a landlord. All other tangible assets are usually depreciated except where the depreciation charge and accumulated depreciation are immaterial.

6.5.1 Revaluations

With many companies, the most valuable type of tangible asset is land and buildings. Often, companies decide to revalue these assets to ensure that their balance sheet reflects an up-to-date position, in which case a 'revaluation reserve' is created and shown on the company balance sheet. See section 8.5.3 for further details.

However, revaluation is not a universal practice, and even in countries where it is permitted, many companies choose not to revalue on the grounds of:

- the volatility of property prices,
- the fact that fixed assets are held for use within the business rather than for resale, and
- the costs of carrying out professional revaluations.

Also, the accounting conventions of many countries (see Chapter 1) require a very conservative valuation policy to be adopted, and so prohibit subjective revaluations being made.

In Chapter 5 we saw how UK companies which revalue their assets are expected to provide a *note of historical cost profits and losses* showing how their results would have differed if they had not revalued. One other aspect of revaluations is the effect they have on the overall balance sheet value of the company and key calculations used to analyse company results such as 'return on capital employed' (ROCE). Increasing the value of fixed assets also increases the value of the capital employed as shown in the balance sheet, so this has a depressing effect on the ROCE calculation. More details are given in Chapter 12.

Kingfisher plc showed a revaluation reserve amounting to £165.8m n its most recent balance sheet, and its note of historical cost profits and losses showed an extra £1.1m depreciation charge based on revalued amounts which were greater than the historical cost equivalent. If a revalued property is subsequently sold, that part of the revaluation reserve which relates to the sold property is taken out of the reserve, and forms part of the calculation of the gain or loss on disposal.

For example, assume a company had two plots of (undepreciated) freehold land, A and B. Each was bought for £10m. A was revalued at £12m, and B at £13m, making a balance on the revaluation reserve of £5m (£2m + £3m). If plot B was sold for £14m, the revaluation surplus on plot B of £3m would be taken out of the reserve, leaving the reserve's balance at £2m (the revaluation of plot A). The realized gain on plot B as shown in the profit and loss account would be calculated as follows:

Proceeds of sale		£14m
Less: Plot B at revalued amount	£13m	
Less transfer from revaluation reserve	(£3m)	
		£10m
Gain on sale of property B		£4m

In other words, the gain is the difference between the sales proceeds (£14m) and the original cost of the land (£10m).

6.5.2 Leased assets

Leases and hire purchase contracts are means by which companies obtain the right to use or purchase assets over a period of time. In the case of leasing, the ownership of the asset remains with the *lessor* (i.e. the original purchaser of the asset) and never passes to the *lessee* (i.e. the user of the asset). With hire purchase contracts, however, the hirer of the asset may exercise an option to purchase the asset after certain conditions contained within the agreement have been met (e.g. the payment of an agreed number of instalments).

Until the publication in the 1980s of accounting standards relating to lease accounting, companies that leased the majority of their equipment, vehicles, etc. did not show such items on their balance sheets. Only the rental payments were disclosed in the profit and loss account. This treatment was felt to be misleading to users of the financial statements and nowadays accounting standards require the company to include certain leased assets in its balance sheet despite the fact that the company does not have legal ownership of those assets. The standard accounting practice is the same for both hire purchase and leasing contracts. At the time of writing, accounting standards are being revised and are expected to require *all* leased assets (other than those on 'genuine' short-term rental arrangements) to be included as fixed assets. Currently, leases are divided into two classifications, operating leases, and finance leases.

- An operating lease involves the lessee paying the rental for the hire of an asset for a period of time which is normally substantially less than its useful economic life. The lessor retains most of the risks and rewards of ownership of the asset. Current accounting standards allow assets leased under such arrangements to be 'off-balance sheet' (i.e. the asset is not shown on the balance sheet), with the lessee needing only to show the rental as an expense in the profit and loss account.

- A finance lease usually involves payment by a lessee to a lessor of the *full cost* of the asset together with a return on the finance provided by the lessor, known as the 'finance charge'. The lessee has substantially all the risks and rewards associated with the ownership of the asset, other than its legal title. Assets leased under finance leases would be shown on the balance sheet of the lessee, in addition to the liability of the future payments to be made under the lease contract.

The treatment of leased assets recognizes that, on occasions, the *substance* of a transaction should take greater precedence than its *legal form*, to ensure that the financial statements show as fair a picture as possible for the user. In certain industries, notably airlines and shipping, the majority of planes or ships are leased, and, in some countries, these assets have not appeared on the balance sheets of the airlines or shipping companies.

British Airways is one of the world's largest airlines. The following paragraph within its annual report explains the difference in its treatment of leased aircraft with that which would have applied under US regulations:

Capitalised Leases

Under UK GAAP (Generally Accepted Accounting Principles) certain aircraft leases have been capitalised and the related liabilities included in finance lease obligations and the resulting assets are being depreciated over the remaining term of the lease. Under US GAAP, such leases would be classified as operating leases and neither the capital element nor the associated liability would be brought on to the balance sheet.

6.6 Investments in joint ventures

Joint ventures were explained in Chapter 4, where it was seen that, within a profit and loss account, the share of the profit or loss arising from joint ventures was disclosed separately. Within the balance sheet, the investment in the joint venture is shown as a fixed asset, representing the original cost of the investment, as adjusted for subsequent profits and losses. This in turn is split between the share of the joint venture's gross assets and gross liabilities respectively.

Look at n. 12 on p. 332 for further details of Domino's Pizza's joint venture.

6.7 Current assets

Unlike fixed assets which have a degree of permanence, current assets are likely to change in value within a year from the balance sheet date. In fact, the key components of stock (US: inventories), debtors (US: receivables), and cash might change thousands or tens of thousands of times within one working day. There might also be current asset investments where the investment has been made for a short-term purpose. Current assets are part of the working capital of the business, the importance of which is explained in more detail in Chapter 12. When compared with current liabilities (see Chapter 7), the important *current ratio* can be calculated which shows the relative strength or weakness of working capital within the company. If the company runs out of working capital then it will have difficulty in paying its debts and may be forced into bankruptcy.

In US balance sheets it is common for current assets to be shown before fixed assets, with cash listed first, debtors second, and inventories last. Perhaps to give truth to the cliché that the USA and UK are two nations divided by a common language, UK balance sheets show fixed assets before current assets, with the latter being shown in the order stock; debtors; cash.

6.8 Stocks and work in progress

The stocks (also known as *inventories*) and work in progress totals represent the balances remaining at the end of the financial period. As previously referred to in Chapters 3 and 4 (see p. 56 and p. 88), stocks of raw materials, partly completed production, and finished goods will be valued at the 'lower of cost and net realizable value', with separate valuations being made for each individual category of stock. When we refer to the 'cost' of stock, in the simplest case this might represent the invoiced price of easily identifiable items. However, in many cases, the price paid cannot be matched with actual goods, perhaps due to the physical nature of the stock. For example, a company might have an oil storage tank that contains 2,000 litres at the end of the financial period. The price of oil tends to fluctuate over time, so unless the price had remained constant, it would be impossible to know what was the actual cost price of the closing stock. In such circumstances, theoretical pricing models such as FIFO (First In First Out—where it is *assumed* that the first stock into the business was the first stock to be used, thus leaving the unsold stock to be valued at the most recent prices) or AVCO (Average Cost—where average cost prices are calculated) are used. 'Cost' might also comprise several other components apart from an original purchase price, particularly where the stock has been manufactured in-house. Figure 6.4 shows these.

 Hugo Boss AG is a major clothing manufacturer and retailer, trading in over 100 countries. Its most recent balance sheet showed inventories of €218m. Its relevant accounting policy was stated as follows:

Raw materials and supplies as well as merchandise are generally valued at cost as determined on the basis of average cost. Unfinished and finished goods were valued at production cost, or either the market or current price, whichever is lower. The production costs include all expenditures that are directly attributable to the production process and the share of overheads relevant to production. Financing charges were not included.

Where the inventories' cost of acquisition or production exceeds the value of the obtainable sales price minus costs incurred prior to the sale, the lower of the two values was used.

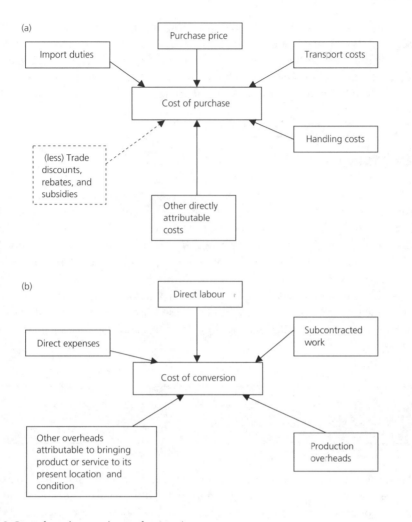

Figure 6.4 Cost of purchase and cost of conversion
(a) Cost: purchased goods
(b) Cost: where raw materials are converted into finished products

The amount of stock which a company has at its balance sheet date is often considered a measure of the efficiency of the business: too much stock is a financial drain as it has to be stored, insured, maintained in a reasonable condition (perhaps in a secure location), and finance has to be found to cover its cost. In Chapter 12, where we look at key measures of a business's performance, we shall see that one such measure is the 'stock turnover' (or 'stock turn') which shows how long it takes for the company, on average, to sell its stock. Put simply, the faster the company can sell its stock (without resorting to major price reductions) the more efficient it is.

If a company has *insufficient* stock, this can lead to other problems, such as being unable to meet production quotas or customers' orders. A suitable balance has to be struck, which is why many companies have instituted 'just in time' (JIT) stock control systems which require suppliers to deliver materials when they are actually required and not before, i.e. *just in time* to be used within the production process. This system effectively puts the onus of stock control onto the suppliers of goods and materials. The supplier has the responsibility for ensuring that it can provide what its customers need when they want it, and not before.

6.9 Debtors

The debtors figure contained within the balance sheet comprises amounts owed to the company at the end of its financial period, mainly by customers. In the USA, the term 'accounts receivable' is used. As explained in Chapter 3, trade debtors will represent the good debts of the business, after writing off any bad debts and providing for doubtful debts. Prepayments (expenses paid in the current financial period which relate to the next financial period) will also be part of the total, and any amounts that are due from joint ventures will be disclosed separately. If a company has entered into a finance lease as the lessor, then the debtors will include amounts due under those leases. Remember that, with finance leases, the value of the leased assets is included in the *lessee's* balance sheet as fixed assets, not the lessor's.

> Look at n. 14 on p. 333 of Domino's Pizza's 'notes to the accounts'. Identify each of the main components mentioned above.

Like stock, the amount of trade debtors shown within the balance sheet is used as an indicator of the company's efficiency. As a generalization, if the total debtors outstanding is an increasing proportion of the total credit sales for the period, the more inefficient the company's credit control policy is becoming. However, there may be good reason for increased debtors, including a general rise in sales before the end of the year. Normally companies will want no more than 4–6 weeks sales owing at any time and may encourage faster payment by offering cash discounts to customers. Many retail companies, such as supermarket chains, will have comparatively little that is owing by customers. This is explored in more detail in Chapter 12.

6.10 Cash at bank and in hand, and short-term investments

This heading is self-explanatory as it consists of the cash balances (notes and coins) and bank balances (current accounts and short-term deposits) at the end of the financial period. Changes in these balances during the financial period are detailed in another summary contained within the annual report, the *cash flow statement*. This is explained in

Chapter 9. As with stock and debtors, the company should not have *excessive* cash and bank balances, as this would imply that the business is failing to reinvest in fixed assets for the long-term prosperity of the company.

Note that there might be a further balance sheet category within current assets, *Investments*, which usually represents shareholdings of less than 20 per cent in one or more companies. If *greater than* 20 per cent, the other company has to be treated as either an associate (20 per cent to 50 per cent), or a subsidiary (51 per cent to 100 per cent), and different accounting rules apply as explained in Chapter 10.

6.11 Chapter summary

- For a group of companies, two balance sheets are presented within its annual report: the consolidated (group) balance sheet and the parent company's own balance sheet.

- Debts between companies of the same group are eliminated when preparing the group balance sheet.

- In some countries, balance sheets are shown in a two-sided format, with assets on one side and capital and liabilities on the other.

- The balance sheet does not show the current value of the company—it shows the value in the company's own accounting records.

- Some assets might not be included in the balance sheet as they are incapable of objective valuation. One example is goodwill generated *internally* by the company, the value of which has never been 'tested' by being sold.

- Balance sheet assets are divided between fixed (which might be either tangible or intangible) and current.

- The useful life of goodwill does not normally exceed twenty years and will be amortized. In the UK however, goodwill might have an *indefinite* useful life, in which case no amortization is needed but extensive information must be given.

- Fixed assets must be reviewed for impairment on a regular basis.

- Research and development costs are usually written off in the profit and loss account. In exceptional cases, development costs may be treated as a deferred asset on the balance sheet, with amortization starting when commercial production commences.

- Freehold land is the only type of tangible asset that is not normally depreciated.

- Some countries allow companies to revalue assets, in which case a revaluation reserve would be created, and the asset values (usually land and buildings) increased or decreased accordingly.

- Leases are divided into two classifications, operating and finance. A company leasing assets under an operating lease shows rental payments in the profit and loss account, but under a finance lease it would show the asset on the balance sheet together with the liability to the lessor. Future accounting standards are likely to require all leased assets to be included on the balance sheet.

- Current assets are likely to change in value within a year from the balance sheet date. In practice, their value might change many thousands of times during the course of the financial period.

- The amount of stocks and debtors held at the end of the financial period are key indicators of the efficiency of the company.

- 'Just in time' (JIT) stock supply systems are used increasingly by companies who want to keep their own stock to a minimum and put the responsibility for stock control onto their suppliers

■ GLOSSARY

account format	Balance sheet format which shows the assets on one side and the liabilities and capital on the other
AVCO (Average Cost)	A theoretical system of stock valuation using average prices
carrying amount	The value of an asset as currently shown in the business's balance sheet
current asset	Assets such as stock and debtors which are likely to change in value within a short period from the balance sheet date
deferred asset	In relation to development costs (q.v.), a fixed asset which is not amortized until the commercial production or application of the related product, service, process, or system has commenced
development costs	The cost of developing a product, service, process, or system. Such costs are normally written off to profit and loss account, but, exceptionally, can be included within the balance sheet as a deferred asset
FIFO (First In First Out)	A theoretical system of stock valuation which assumes that the first stock to be received is the first stock to be sold. In a period of rising prices, the unsold stock will be valued at the most recent (and highest) value
fixed asset	An asset (tangible or intangible) which is held for use on a continuing basis—usually for a period of at least one year
franchise	A licence to market a company's goods or services in a specific area
impairment	The reduction in the value of an asset to an amount below its value as currently shown in the business's balance sheet (the carrying amount)
intangible fixed asset	A fixed asset without physical substance e.g. goodwill
internal goodwill	Goodwill that has been generated internally and whose value has not been verified. It cannot be included within a balance sheet
inventory	An alternative name for unsold stock of goods and raw materials

just in time (JIT)	A stock control system which requires suppliers to deliver materials shortly before they are to be used in production
lease	A contract whereby one party (the lessor) grants the other party (the lessee) the right to use an asset that the lessor owns, in return for a rental
negative goodwill	Negative goodwill arises when the price paid for a business is less than the fair value of the net assets acquired
position statement	Alternative name for balance sheet
positive goodwill	An amount in excess of the fair value of the net assets of a business, representing the value of the reputation of the company and its ability to make future profits. It can only be included in a balance sheet if it has been paid for
revaluation	A reappraisal of the current value of a fixed asset
revaluation reserve	A reserve created if a fixed asset is revalued. It is a capital reserve and unavailable for the payment of dividends
statement of financial position	Alternative name for balance sheet
tangible fixed asset	A fixed asset with physical substance e.g. land and buildings
vertical format	Balance sheet presentation which shows the *share capital and reserves* below the *total net assets*, and allows a separate sub-calculation to be shown for net current assets
work in progress	Partly completed goods

■ MULTIPLE CHOICE QUESTIONS

1. Subsidiary X owes £2,000 to subsidiary Y. When preparing the group balance sheet, these amounts will be shown as:
   a £2,000 shown both as a current asset and a current liability
   b £2,000 shown only as a current asset
   c £2,000 shown only as a current liability
   d Neither shown as an asset nor a liability

2. Which one of the following statements is correct?
   a A balance sheet shows the current value of a company
   b A balance sheet shows the stock market value of a company
   c A balance sheet shows the value as recorded in the books of a company
   d A balance sheet shows the income and expenditure of a company

3. Goodwill can only be shown in the balance sheet of the company if:
   a It has been sold
   b It has been generated internally
   c It has been purchased
   d It has an estimated useful life of over twenty years

4. Which one of the following is a tangible fixed asset?

    a Goodwill
    b Leasehold property
    c Brand names
    d Patents

5. A business pays £750,000 to buy a rival company. The rival company's net assets had a balance sheet value of £400,000, and a fair value of £500,000. The value of goodwill purchased in this transaction was:

    a £250,000
    b £350,000
    c £150,000
    d £100,000

6. The usual accounting treatment for research and development costs is to:

    a Show the research costs as a fixed asset and the development costs as a current asset
    b Show the research costs in the balance sheet and the development costs in the profit and loss account
    c Show the total research and development costs as a fixed asset in the balance sheet
    d Write off the research and development costs entirely to profit and loss account

7. A company bought a building five years ago for £500,000 and is depreciating it over fifty years. It decides to revalue the building at the current market value of £800,000. What will the new annual depreciation charge be?

    a £6,667 [(£800,000 − £500,000)/45]
    b £17,777 (£800,000/45)
    c £16,000 (£800,000/50)
    d Nil, as it hasn't depreciated

8. If a leased asset is to be 'capitalized', this means:

    a It will be included as a fixed asset
    b It will be included under the heading 'share capital'
    c It will be part of the company's working capital
    d It will be treated as a capital reserve

9. To overcome stock control problems many companies have instituted a system known as:

    a Just in Now
    b Just in Case
    c Just in Time
    d Just in Stock

10. Which financial summary shows how the cash and bank balances have changed during the course of the financial period?

    a Note of historical cost profits and losses
    b Balance sheet
    c Profit and loss account
    d Cash flow statement

(Note: answers are shown in Appendix 2.)

■ **DISCUSSION QUESTIONS**

Lord MacNaghten, speaking in the House of Lords on 20 May 1901 stated:

> What is goodwill? It is a thing very easy to describe, very difficult to define. It is the benefit and advantage of the good name, reputation and connection of a business. It is the attractive force which brings in custom. It is the one thing which distinguishes an old-established business from a new business at its first start.
>
> *IRC v. Muller & Co Margarine Limited* (1901) AC 217

1. Explain the circumstances where you might expect to see a value for 'goodwill' in a balance sheet.

2. Why do many companies which have an excellent 'good name and reputation' have no goodwill value shown on their balance sheets?

3. What is meant by the *impairment* of goodwill, and how might this be reflected in a company's results?

(*Note: Suggested answers or discussion points are available on the companion website.*)

■ **LONGER QUESTIONS**

(Questions marked W have suggested answers on the companion website. Other questions are answered in Appendix 3.)

1. For each of the following items, explain how, if at all, they would be shown in a balance sheet:
   - **(i)** Negative goodwill.
   - **(ii)** Rentals paid under an operating lease.
   - **(iii)** A revaluation of fixed assets, adding £1m to the existing value of land and buildings.
   - **(iv)** A machine valued at £50,000 which is leased under a finance lease contract.
   - **(v)** Research costs relating to the investigation of the properties of a new scientific formula.
   - **(vi)** A short-term investment in a government bond.

2. The directors of two virtually identical companies, A and B, are discussing their respective company's results with their accountants in two separate meetings. The following is a brief summary of the advice offered by the accountants:

   Company A

   The accountant's advice was to:
   - **(i)** Amortize goodwill over twenty years. This will result in an annual amortization charge of £1m.
   - **(ii)** Capitalize development expenditure of £2m. Commercial production is expected to commence in four years' time.
   - **(iii)** Increase the value of land and buildings by £5m, to bring them in line with current market values.
   - **(iv)** Include only 60 per cent of the net assets of subsidiary X, as company A only owns 60 per cent of company X's equity share capital.
   - **(v)** Value stock at £3m, using the First In First Out (FIFO) method.

Company B

The accountant's advice was to:

(i) Write off goodwill immediately due to the uncertainty of its value.

(ii) Write off development expenditure of £2m, even though commercial production is expected to start in four years' time.

(iii) Leave the value of land and buildings at its net book value as they are considered to be permanent assets of the company and were not bought for resale.

(iv) Include 100 per cent of the net assets of subsidiary Y, even though company B only owns 60 per cent of company Y's equity share capital.

(v) Value stock at £2m, using the AVCO method.

You are required to compare and contrast the accountant's advice to the directors of the two companies.

3. Savage plc's financial year-end is 31 August 2004. When reviewing the draft balance sheet as at that date, the directors noted the following points:

1. Some stock had been omitted from the 31 August 2004 closing stock figure. The omitted stock had originally cost the company £30,000 but could be sold for only £20,000 due to changing fashions.

2. Development expenditure of £100,000, which had been capitalized in the balance sheet, related to a project which was abandoned during the year.

3. Freehold land with a net book value of £1m was to be revalued to £1.5m at 31 August 2004.

4. One of the trade debtors had become bankrupt, owing the company £100,000 which was to be regarded as non-recoverable.

5. The reputation of the company had increased considerably during the year, so the directors wanted to include a goodwill value of £2m to reflect this, and amortize it over a five-year period.

You are required to give an explanation of the appropriate treatment for each of the above items, in relation to the company's balance sheet as at 31 August 2004. For each item you should also state whether the company's operating profit for that year would be affected, and if so, by what amount.

4W. The managing directors of two companies are discussing the question of goodwill. One director, Polly, explains that her company had recently paid £500,000 for the goodwill of an existing business owned by the company's major shareholder. That shareholder had operated his business for five years prior to its sale.

The other director, Frank, relates how his company had started with virtually nothing five years ago, and had built up such a profitable business that goodwill, in his words, 'must now be in excess of £500,000'.

Comment on the permissible accounting treatments for the goodwill of the two companies, giving reasons as to why accounting practice distinguishes between 'purchased' goodwill and 'internally generated' goodwill.

5W.

a Explain the distinction between an *operating lease* and a *finance lease*.

b A company commences business on 1 June 2003. By 31 May 2004, it has the following relevant information regarding its leased assets:

Operating leases: Assets valued at £100,000, total amount paid in lease rentals to lessor: £129,900.

Finance leases: Assets valued at £300,000, total finance charges paid during the year to lessor £13,800.

The company's depreciation policy is to write off all fixed assets on the straight line basis over a five-year period, assuming no residual value.

Show how the information relating to leased assets would be shown in the company's profit and loss account for the year ended 31 May 2004, and in the 'fixed assets' section of its balance sheet as at 31 May 2004.

6W.

a Explain the circumstances where a *theoretical* stock valuation method may have to be used to value stock.

b A company in the building industry is about to value its stock of steel girders. It has 5,000 girders in stock on 30 September 2004, all of equal size and quality, which were delivered in lorry loads at 100 girders per lorry. During the financial year ended 30 September 2004, the price of girders fluctuated, as follows:

Quarter	Price per girder
October–December	£250
January–March	£280
April–June	£270
July–September	£290

Lorry loads of girders delivered during the year were as follows:

Quarter	Deliveries
October–December	60
January–March	90
April–June	170
July–September	45

Girders used on contracts were as follows:

Quarter	Girders used
October–December	3,500
January–March	8,000
April–June	9,500
July–September	10,500

There was no opening stock of girders.

The company values its stock on the 'First In First Out' basis. Calculate the value of its stock of girders at 30 September 2004.

■ MINI CASE STUDY

MinnieMax Ltd.'s assets

MinnieMax Ltd. (see previous mini case studies) is preparing its balance sheet at the end of its first year of trading, 30 September 2004. Relevant information needed to prepare the 'assets' section of the balance sheet is as follows:

	£
Brand name: cost (n. 1)	28,000
Cash and bank balances	115,120
Closing stocks	5,000
Computers: cost (n. 2)	850
Debtors and prepayments	27,200
Equipment: cost (n. 3)	16,000
Freehold land	200,000
Land Rover vehicles: cost (n. 4)	30,000
Short-term investment in government bond	50,000

Notes:

1.   This represents the legal costs of registering the brand name 'MinnieBeasts'. The estimated useful life of the brand name is twenty years.

2.   The computers are to be depreciated over five years by the straight line method, assuming no residual value.

3.   The equipment is to be depreciated at 10 per cent p.a. by the reducing balance method, assuming no residual value.

4.   The two Land Rovers are each to be depreciated over four years by the straight line method, assuming a residual value of £5,000 each. One of the vehicles is leased under a finance lease contract.

You are required to present the information in the form of an extract from the company balance sheet as at 30 September 2004, showing the assets at that date in a form suitable for inclusion within the company's annual report.

(Suggested solutions can be found in Appendix 4.)

■ MAXI CASE STUDY

Fixed assets

Read the following extract from the annual report of Carpetright plc (a carpet retailer) and then answer the questions which follow.

Outlook

Since the year end we have purchased the freehold of our new five metre width warehouse in Thurrock. The combined purchase and fit out cost was £8.6m.

The company plans to increase the store base by 32 this year. In addition, we will continue to look for opportunities for edge-of-town sites for small, sample only stores. Product development this year will continue to be focused on the ranges within our exclusive own brands, in particular new five metre width ranges which we see as key in our aim to increase the percentage of higher price carpets sold through our stores.

A nationwide television and radio advertising campaign is planned for the autumn with a Carpetright brand focus featuring television personality Ian Wright.

Carpetright plc Annual Report 2002

Explain how Carpetright plc must consider generally accepted accounting principles relating to the valuation of tangible and intangible fixed assets when deciding on balance sheet valuations. Make specific reference to the way in which freehold property, brands, and development costs might be shown.

(Suggested answers and discussion areas are available on the companion website.)

■ WEB LINKS

Company websites

(Companies referred to in this chapter)

American Rice Inc. www.amrice.com

British Airways www.british-airways.com

Carpetright plc www.carpetright.co.uk

Courts plc www.courtsretail.com

Domino's Pizza www.dominos.co.uk

Hugo Boss AG www.hugoboss.com

Kingfisher plc www.kingfisher.co.uk

Scholz and Friends Group www.s-f.com

■ FURTHER READING

Black, G. (2003). *Students' Guide to Accounting and Financial Reporting Standards*, 9th edn. (Harlow: FT/Prentice Hall), chapters 3–5.

Elliott, B., and Elliott, J. (2003). *Financial Accounting and Reporting*, 8th edn. (Harlow: FT/Prentice Hall), chapters 14–17.

■ COMPANION WEBSITE MATERIALS

 Additional materials are available for students and lecturers on the companion website, at **www.oup.com/uk/booksites/busecon/business**

7

The balance sheet: liabilities and provisions

OBJECTIVES

By the end of this chapter you will be able to:

- Define and evaluate 'liabilities'.
- Understand the way in which liabilities are recognized in a balance sheet.
- Understand the distinction between short-term and long-term liabilities.
- Explain the meaning and significance of 'provisions'.
- Analyse the typical liabilities and provisions that would be found in a balance sheet.
- Define and evaluate 'contingent liabilities', 'capital commitments', and 'post-balance sheet events'.

7.1 Introduction

We continue our exploration of the balance sheet in this chapter, by looking at the various liabilities and provisions which it is likely to contain. Remembering the basic accounting equation, Assets − Liabilities = Capital, in a 'vertical' balance sheet we find the liabilities immediately below the assets. The usual format is for short-term ('current') liabilities to be deducted from current assets to establish the net current assets (working capital) of the company. In balance sheets prepared in the USA and many mainland European countries, liabilities might be found on the opposite side to where the assets are located, without a separate working capital figure being shown. As for provisions, these have been encountered already in previous chapters within the topics of depreciation and taxation (see Chapters 3 and 5). Depreciation provisions, and provisions for doubtful debts, are deducted from the related asset values on the balance sheet (see Chapter 6), but other provisions, such as for deferred taxation or for pension liabilities, are shown as separate items within a specific balance sheet heading, 'provisions and liabilities' (see section 7.6 below).

Once again, the relevant part of Domino's Pizza's annual report is used as our starting point (see Figure 7.1, which is cross-referenced to chapter headings), though, as before, we shall refer to other companies where needed to illustrate the full range of information which might be disclosed.

Group Balance Sheet

at 29 December 2002

	Notes	2002 £000	2001 £000
FIXED ASSETS			
Intangible assets	10	2,386	2,484
Tangible assets	11	13,685	12,181
Investments in joint venture:	12		
Share of gross assets		717	757
Share of gross liabilities		(410)	(480)
		307	277
TOTAL FIXED ASSETS		16,378	14,942
CURRENT ASSETS			
Stocks	13	1,411	1,260
Debtors:	14		
amounts falling due within one year		8,572	6,665
amounts falling due after more than one year		2,130	1,756
		10,702	8,421
Cash at bank and in hand		3,885	3,231
TOTAL CURRENT ASSETS		15,998	12,912
7.2 **CREDITORS:** amounts falling due within one year	15	(12,919)	(10,203)
7.3 **NET CURRENT ASSETS**		3,079	2,709
7.4 **TOTAL ASSETS LESS CURRENT LIABILITIES**		19,457	17,651
7.5 **CREDITORS:** amounts falling due after more than one year	16	(7,152)	(7,632)
7.6 **PROVISION FOR LIABILITIES AND CHARGES**	7	(604)	(421)
7.7		11,701	9,598
CAPITAL AND RESERVES			
Called up share capital	21	2,546	2,518
Share premium account	22	2,395	2,192
Profit and loss account	22	6,760	4,888
Equity shareholders' funds		11,701	9,598

Stephen Hemsley

Director

Figure 7.1 Domino's Pizza Group: balance sheet (cross-referenced to chapter headings). The shaded areas area covered in detail in Chapters 6 and 8.

7.2 Creditors: amounts falling due within one year

Creditors are liabilities owing at the balance sheet date and are usually divided between those falling due for payment within one year of that date (referred to as *current* liabilities) and those due for payment after more than one year (referred to as *long-term* liabilities). Liabilities are defined in the Statement of Principles (see Chapter 1) as 'an entity's obligations to transfer economic benefits as a result of past transactions or events', and typical items within this category include trade creditors, accruals, taxation (other than deferred taxation), proposed final dividends, loans, obligations under finance leases, and bank overdrafts.

Look at n. 15 of Domino's Pizza's annual report (see p. 334) for that company's breakdown of the items contained within the balance sheet heading 'creditors: amounts falling due within one year'. In this group, all the liabilities, with the exception of the dividend, are owed by subsidiaries—we know this by comparing the liabilities shown in the *group* balance sheet with those shown in the *parent* company's balance sheet. This is not always the situation, and often the parent company's balance sheet shows substantial liabilities. It all depends on what proportion of the group's trading is undertaken by the parent company separately from its subsidiaries. Sometimes the parent company is the major trading vehicle of the group but in other cases, such as that of Domino's Pizza, only the subsidiaries are trading.

7.2.1 Trade creditors

Trade creditors represent the amounts owed to suppliers of goods and services. In the USA, they are known as 'accounts payable'. The balance sheet shows the total purchase ledger balances, which represent all the outstanding invoiced amounts. Creditors represent an important source of (usually) interest-free finance to a company, as there are often several weeks which elapse between the receipt of an invoice and the date of payment. The ideal business arrangement, not always achievable, is for a company to buy its goods on credit, sell them for cash as soon as possible, and then take the full interest-free credit period granted by its creditors before paying its bills.

One other aspect of the company's relationship with its creditors is revealed within the Directors' Report, where the company's policy regarding payments to trade creditors is shown.

Domino's Pizza's report states: 'It is the group's policy that payments to suppliers are made in accordance with those terms and conditions agreed between the company and its suppliers, provided that all trading terms and conditions have been complied with. As at 29 December 2002, the group had an average of 44 days (2001: 52 days) purchases outstanding in trade creditors.'

7.2.2 Accruals and deferred income

Accruals are additional expenses incurred during a financial period which have not been paid for by the end of that period (see Chapter 3). For example, a company may have received and paid an electricity bill relating to the period ending two months prior to the balance sheet date, and no further bill had been received by the year-end. The electricity costs for those remaining two months must be estimated and included as an accrual. If the next quarter's bill has been received by the time the balance sheet is being prepared, then two-thirds of it will be taken as the amount owing. For example, assume that a financial year ends on 31 December. The total electricity paid up to 31 October amounted to £4,800, with quarterly bills averaging £1,800. Assuming that the bill covering November and December has not been received by the time the balance sheet is being prepared, an estimated accrual of $2/3 \times £1,800 = £1,200$ will be shown in the balance sheet. Other typical accruals include rent, telephone charges, wages and salaries, and loan interest.

'Deferred income' represents amounts received by the company in advance of the company providing the goods or services. For example, it may represent deposits paid by customers *before* the balance sheet date which relate to goods that will be delivered *after* that date. Another possibility for inclusion within this heading would be *government grants* given towards the cost of fixed assets. Under the relevant accounting standards[1] any such grants must be written back to profit and loss account over the same time period that the related fixed asset is being depreciated. For example, a £10,000 machine being written off over five years, on which a £6,000 grant was received, would, at the end of its first year, be shown in the balance sheet as:

Fixed asset:	Machine	10,000
	Less depreciation	2,000
		8,000

Accruals and deferred income (includes):

| Government grant $[6,000 - (1/5 \times £6,000)]$ | 4,800 |

Both the machine and the related grant will be written off over the five-year period.

7.2.3 Taxation

The taxation liability at the balance sheet date might comprise several components. Within the UK, it may include:

- corporation tax;
- value added tax (VAT);
- employment taxes such as 'Pay As You Earn (PAYE)';
- social security costs.

Corporation tax is shown separately from the others, as it represents the tax on the profits of the period. VAT is normally shown as part of 'trade creditors' (if the company has collected more tax from its customers than it has paid to its suppliers, it is due to pay the balance to the tax authorities). Alternatively, it might be shown as a debtor within *current assets* if the company has paid more VAT to its suppliers than it has received from its

---

[1] IAS 20 *Accounting for Government Grants and Disclosure of Government Assistance* and (UK) SSAP 4 *Accounting for Government Grants*.

customers, in which case it will eventually get a *refund* from the tax authorities. Any liability relating to employment taxes will be shown separately. It is often quite a puzzle to reconcile the corporation tax charge as shown in the profit and loss account with the liability that appears as a creditor. First, the profit and loss account entry includes not only the current tax charge but also the provision for deferred taxation (see Chapter 5). The balance sheet liability shown within 'creditors: amounts falling due within one year', however, only represents the balance of the *current* tax charge which is unpaid by the end of the financial period. The provision for deferred taxation is shown separately under 'provisions for liabilities and charges'(see section 7.6 below). Look at the Domino's Pizza example that follows for an explanation.

Domino's Pizza's profit and loss account (see p. 320) shows an entry 'Tax on profit on ordinary activities £1,404,000' for 2002. Note 7 (see p. 328) gives the following breakdown of this amount (author's summary):

UK Corporation tax on the profit for the period	1,229,000
Adjustment in respect of the previous period	(21,000)
	1,208,000
Tax relating to joint venture	13,000
Total current tax	1,221,000
Provision for deferred tax for the period	183,000
Total tax charge	£1,404,000

However, the note to the group balance sheet (see p. 334) states that the amount owing for corporation tax at the end of 2002 was £532,000, and also shows £274,000 owing at the end of the previous year. There is also one further piece of information available—in the *cash flow statement*, which shows a summary of all the cash flowing into and out of the company during the financial period. We look at this in detail in Chapter 9, but we can see from Domino's Pizza's cash flow statement (see p. 323) that the company had a *cash outflow* relating to taxation of £950,000 during the period. UK companies with taxable profits of more than £1.5m pay their corporation tax in four quarterly instalments, with the first payment due approximately six months after the start of the financial period.

Here's how we can reconcile the figures which appear in the profit and loss account with those in the balance sheet:

Profit and loss account

	£000s
Corporation tax charge on profit for period	**1,229**
Adjustment relating to prior period	(21)
	1,208
Tax liability of joint venture	13
	1,221
Increase in provision for deferred tax	183
Total charge as shown in profit and loss account	**1,404**

Balance sheet

	£000s
Corporation tax charge on profit for period (as in profit and loss account)	**1,229**
Add: Corporation tax owing at start of the period	274
	1,503
Adjustment relating to prior period	(21)
	1,482
Corporation tax paid in the period (from cash flow statement)	(950)
Corporation tax owing at end of the period (per balance sheet)	**532**

The deferred taxation provision carried forward at the end of the period is shown under the separate balance sheet heading 'Provisions for liabilities and charges'—see section 7.6 below.

Figure 7.2 shows, in a simplified form, the way in which the information relating to taxation can be reconciled from the various financial summaries. It assumes that a company had corporation tax owing of £5,000 at the start of the period and £3,000 at the end of the period, having shown a current tax charge of £6,000 in its profit and loss account. It had paid £8,000 during the year for corporation tax. Its deferred taxation provision was £10,000 at the start of the period, and a further £1,000 was provided in the period.

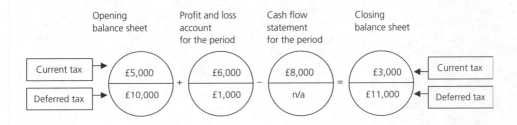

Figure 7.2 Source of taxation information in the closing balance sheet

7.2.4 **Dividends**

The dividend shown as a liability within the balance sheet is the final proposed dividend on the ordinary (equity) shares, plus dividends due on preference shares (if any). The final equity dividend, unlike the interim dividend paid part-way through the financial period, must be approved by the shareholders at the Annual General Meeting (AGM) which is held within a few months of the balance sheet date, and not more than fifteen months from the previous AGM. It is very rare for shareholders to reject or amend a proposed dividend, and in the normal course of events the dividend will be paid very shortly after it has been approved.

Like the entries for taxation, it is not always clear how the information contained within the profit and loss account relating to dividends reconciles with that shown in the balance sheet. Look at the Domino's Pizza example that follows for an explanation.

Domino's Pizza's profit and loss account (see p. 320) shows an entry 'Dividends on equity shares £1,018,000' for 2002, with a comparative figure of £668,000 for the previous year. Note 8 (see p. 000) gives the following breakdown of these amounts (author's summary):

2002:
Interim dividend paid (0.78p per share)	395,000
Proposed final dividend (1.22p per share)	623,000
	£1,018,000

2001:
Interim dividend paid (0.57p per share)	285,000
Proposed final dividend (1.22p per share)	383,000
	668,000

Note 15 to the accounts (see p. 334) shows that the balance sheet creditors included a liability for 'proposed dividend' of £624,000 at the end of 2002 (note a minor £1,000 'rounding' adjustment when compared to the profit and loss account figure), and £383,000 a year earlier. The cash flow statement (see p. 323), shows that £777,000 was paid as equity dividends during 2002, which represents the final proposed dividend of 2001 (£383,000) plus the interim dividend for 2002 paid part-way through that year (£395,000)—again with a £1,000 'rounding' adjustment.

It can be seen that the company's dividend policy has been far more generous in 2002 than the previous year. Total dividends have risen by 52 per cent, even though profit before interest and taxation rose by 'only' 42 per cent between the two years.

Figure 7.3 shows, in a simplified form, the way in which the information relating to dividends can be reconciled from the various financial summaries. It assumes that a company paid a £5,000 interim dividend and proposes a £10,000 final dividend. The previous year's proposed final dividend was £8,000, which was approved by the company shareholders at the AGM and paid shortly after.

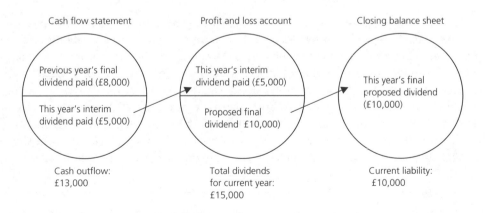

Figure 7.3 Source of dividend information in the closing balance sheet

7.2.5 Loans and overdrafts

Loans made to companies may be described in several different ways, including loan stock, loan capital, debentures, fixed term debt, and fixed interest capital. Any outstanding loans which are due for repayment within one year of the balance sheet date will be shown under the heading 'creditors: amounts falling due within one year'. More details of various types of loans are given in section 7.5. Bank overdrafts are usually repayable on demand and carry a fluctuating rate of interest. Companies are also likely to be charged an annual fee based on the maximum agreed overdraft limit, which discourages businesses from negotiating much higher limits than they need. Overdrafts have the convenience of flexibility, as companies are charged interest only on that part of the overdraft limit which is used. Those firms with a continuing and rising overdraft are likely to come under pressure from their bank to convert part of the overdraft to a fixed rate loan, repayable within a set time period. Most loans and overdrafts will be *secured*, either against specific assets, e.g. land and buildings (known as a *fixed charge*), or generally against the total assets of the business (known as a *floating charge*). This gives a safeguard to the lender, so that if the company receiving the loan defaults on interest or capital repayments, assets can be sold on the lender's behalf to recoup the amounts owing. Unsecured borrowing carries a greater risk to the lender and therefore a higher interest rate can be demanded.

7.2.6 Obligations under leases and hire purchase contracts

When, in Chapter 6, we discussed how assets held under finance leases and hire purchase contracts are shown on the balance sheet as fixed assets, we also saw how any amounts *owed* under these contracts were included within liabilities. The liability is split between that falling due within one year of the balance sheet date, and that falling due after more than one year (see section 7.5.2 below).

7.3 Net current assets (or net current liabilities)

This heading only appears in a balance sheet prepared in a 'vertical' format, as it represents the net total of the current assets less the short-term creditors (current liabilities). If the current assets exceed the current liabilities, the heading will be 'net current assets' (also known as 'working capital'). If current liabilities are greater than the current assets, it will be called 'net current liabilities' (or negative working capital). Working capital (or lack of it) is an important indicator of a company's ability to pay its debts as they fall due. This is covered in detail in Chapter 12. In an 'account' format balance sheet, although the net figure is not shown on the balance sheet, it can of course be calculated very simply by locating the short-term liabilities on one side, and deducting them from the current assets on the other side.

 Look at the balance sheet of Kimberley-Clark Corporation, a leading US paper products manufacturer, at **www.kimberly-clark.com/investorinfo/AnnualReport2002/kc02_balance.pdf.**

Calculate its net current assets for each of the two years shown, and state whether the figure has improved or declined during the period.

7.4 Total assets less current liabilities

This balance sheet heading, used in a 'vertical' style balance sheet, shows the total of fixed and current assets, less the creditors falling due within one year. It is used as an interim total before the long-term creditors and provisions are deducted, and shows the margin by which the value of a company's assets (fixed and current) exceeds its short-term liabilities.

7.5 Creditors: amounts falling due after more than one year

Also known as 'long-term creditors', this heading includes some of the items already discussed under section 7.2 above, particularly loans and obligations under finance leases. It covers any liability which is not due for repayment before one year has elapsed from the balance sheet date.

7.5.1 Loans

The loan capital of the company might comprise several different elements, including:

- Bank loans, which carry either a fixed or floating interest rate, and will usually be secured against company assets to protect the bank in the event of default. Repayments of capital and interest might be made over the entire period of the loan, or else just the interest payments might be made over the loan period with the capital amount being repaid at the end.

- Debentures, also known as *bonds*, are also likely to be secured against assets and usually carry a fixed rate of interest. Debentures can be bought and sold after issue, in the same way that shares are traded. Holders of debentures and bonds are *creditors* of the company, not *shareholders*. As with shares, the market price will depend on supply and demand, but debentures are seen as a less risky investment due to their security. However, lower risk also brings a lower reward in the form of the fixed interest rate which remains unchanged regardless of how profitable the company becomes. Another aspect of lower risk is that the interest is payable to debenture holders before any shareholders' dividends can be declared. Some loans might be convertible into ordinary shares at a date (or dates) stated in the debenture deed, which may make them more attractive to investors.

Brixton plc is a property investment and development company. In its 2002 annual report it listed the borrowings shown in Figure 7.4.

16 Borrowings

	Group 2002 £m	Group 2001 £m
Secured		
Debentures:		
10⅝% Debenture Stock 2012	**107.2**	120.0
9½% Debenture Stock 2026	**30.0**	30.0
10¾% Debenture Stock 2025	**14.8**	15.0
11¼% Debenture Stock 2023	**15.0**	15.0
11¾% Debenture Stock 2018	**15.0**	15.0
Total secured	**182.0**	195.0
Unsecured		
6% Bonds 2010 (nominal £275m)	**273.6**	273.4
Sterling bank loans and overdrafts	**243.5**	199.8
Total unsecured	**517.1**	473.2
Total borrowings	**699.1**	668.2
Falling due within one year (note 15)	**(20.0)**	(51.3)
Falling due after more than one year	**679.1**	616.9

Security for secured borrowings is provided by charges on property.

Figure 7.4 Brixton plc: borrowings

The various years which are included as part of the title of the loans in the figure indicate the year in which each loan must be repaid. In some cases, the earliest and latest redemption year is given, e.g. 2015–17, meaning that the loan cannot be repaid before 2015 nor later than 2017.

Some loans might be termed 'irredeemable', meaning that there is no set repayment date. Those loans convertible into shares will be referred to as 'convertible loan stock', with the earliest and latest years of conversion stated. Within company annual reports, the repayment dates of various loans are summarized between those falling due for repayment within one year, between one and two years, in more than two years but not more than five years, and in over five years.

Look at Domino's Pizza's breakdown of its loans shown in n. 17 of its 'Notes to the Accounts' shown on p. 335. How has the time profile of the company's loan repayments changed between the two years?

Another aspect of the disclosure requirements concerning loans is contained within accounting standards relating to 'financial instruments' and 'derivatives'. These complex standards[2] were issued to ensure transparency regarding a company's exposure to financial risk, and were specifically designed to clamp down on the practice of some companies who, by various magic accounting tricks, were able to show short-term debts as long-term, and make loan capital appear as part of share capital! The standards not only require disclosure of precisely what debts and shares have been issued (or might be issued under convertible loan stock arrangements at a future date), but also an assessment of the major financial risks that companies face and how they manage their exposure to these risks.

> Refer to Domino's Pizza's n. 19 on p. 335 for the information that it provides to comply with the accounting standards.

7.5.2 Obligations under leases and hire purchase contracts

Within long-term creditors, this heading shows that part of finance lease and hire purchase contracts which are payable after more than one year has elapsed from the balance sheet date. See section 7.2.6 above for further details. These liabilities are summarized between those falling due for payment within one year from the balance sheet date, between two years but not more than five years, and in over five years.

7.6 Provisions for liabilities and charges

A provision is either:

(a) Any amount written off by way of providing for depreciation or diminution in the value of assets; or

(b) Any amount retained to provide for any liability or loss which is either likely to be incurred, or certain to be incurred but uncertain as to the amount or as to the date on which it will arise.[3]

Provisions relating to the first part of this definition have already been included within the balance sheet, for example by the deduction of depreciation and amortization provisions from the cost of fixed assets. Any provision for doubtful debts would have been deducted in arriving at the 'trade debtors' total included within current assets.

As for the other part of the definition, this includes the closing balance on the provision for deferred taxation (see Chapter 5), and, in the case of Domino's Pizza, this is the only provision shown within the separate heading 'provision for liabilities and charges'. Some companies may create additional provisions where they use part of their profits for some specific or general purpose. For example, a company may become subject to environmental

---

[2] IAS 32 and 39 and (UK) FRSs 4 and 13.   [3] (UK) Companies Act 1985.

legislation which requires it to install costly pollution filters to its factory chimneys, with work to be completed in three years' time. To ensure that it has enough profit set aside to meet the cost when it falls due, it may create a 'Provision for Pollution Control Expenditure' and transfer profits into it over the three-year period.

7.6.1 Pension provisions

Another area where provisions may be created relates to *pension liabilities*. Many companies have pension schemes where both employers and employees make regular contributions, as a fixed annual amount or as a percentage of pay, to an independent pension company which manages the scheme on the company's behalf. This is known as a *defined contribution* scheme, and the employer has no legal obligation to pay any further contributions into the scheme if there are insufficient assets to pay all the employee pensions when they become due. The accounting treatment for such schemes is very straightforward, with pension payments being shown within the profit and loss account as part of the cost of salaries and wages. The only entries in the balance sheet would relate to any prepaid or accrued contributions, which would appear under current assets or current liabilities respectively.

The other type of pension scheme is referred to as a *defined benefit* scheme, where the benefits paid will usually depend upon either the average pay of the employees during their career (or perhaps the last few years of it) or, more usually, the employee's final pay. It is impossible to know in advance if the pension contributions plus the investment return will equal the final benefits to be paid. Any shortfall may have to be paid by the employer, either for legal reasons or else to maintain good employee relations. If a surplus arises, the employer may be entitled to either a refund of contributions or a reduction in future contributions. At the time of writing, the existing accounting standards relating to pensions disclosures[4] are under review, but the key ways in which defined benefit schemes are recognized within the balance sheet are likely to be as follows:

- A liability (the shortfall of the value of the assets in the scheme below the present value of the scheme's liabilities) should be recognized to the extent that it reflects the employer's legal or constructive obligation.

- An asset (the excess of the value of the assets in the scheme over the present value of the scheme's liabilities) should be recognized to the extent that the employer is able to recover the surplus either through reduced contributions in the future or through refunds from the scheme.

- Any unpaid contributions to the scheme should be presented in the balance sheet as a creditor due within one year.

In addition, for a defined benefit scheme, the following key disclosures should be made:

- The date of the most recent full actuarial valuation on which the amounts in the financial statements are based; and

- The contribution made in respect of the accounting period and any agreed contribution rates for future years

[4] IAS 19 and (UK) SSAP 24 and FRS 17.

In its 2002 annual report, Renishaw plc showed the accounting policy and note relating to its pension costs appearing in Figure 7.5.

Accounting policy:

Pension costs

The Group operates contributory pension schemes, of the defined benefit type, for UK and Irish based employees. The schemes are administered by trustees and are independent of the group finances. Contributions are paid to the schemes in accordance with the recommendations of independent actuaries to enable the trustees to meet from the schemes the benefits accruing in respect of current and future service.

Pension scheme assets are measured using market value. Pension scheme liabilities are measured using a projected unit method and discounted at the current rate of return on a high quality corporate bond of equivalent term and currency to the liability. The increase in the present value of the liabilities of the Group's defined benefit pension schemes expected to arise from employee service in the period is charged to operating profit. The expected return on the schemes' assets and the increase during the period in the present value of the schemes' liabilities arising from the passage of time are included in other finance income. Actuarial gains and losses are recognised in the consolidated statement of total recognised gains and losses.

The pension schemes' surpluses, to the extent that they are considered recoverable, or deficits are recognised in full and presented on the face of the balance sheet net of the related deferred tax.

Foreign based employees are covered by state, defined benefit and private pension schemes in their countries of residence. Actuarial valuations of foreign pension schemes, in accordance with FRS 17, were not obtained because of the costs involved and the smaller number of foreign employees.

19. Pension schemes

Note

The Group operates a number of pension schemes throughout the world. The major schemes, which cover over 90% of scheme members, are of the defined benefit type.

The total pension cost of the Group for the year was £4,852,000 (2001 £3,416,000), of which £254,000 (2001 £232,000) related to directors and £971,000 (2001 £930,000) related to overseas schemes. The pension cost relating to the UK scheme is assessed in accordance with the advice of a qualified actuary using the projected unit method and relates entirely to current service costs.

The latest full actuarial valuation of the scheme was carried out at July 2001 and updated to 30th June 2002 by a qualified independent actuary. The major assumptions used by the actuary were:

	30th June 2002	30th June 2001	30th June 2000
Rate of increase in pensionable salaries	3.5%	4.5%	4.5%
Rate of increase in pension payments	2.3%	2.5%	3.0%
Discount rate	5.8%	6.0%	6.5%
Inflation rate	2.5%	2.5%	3.0%
Expected return on equities	8.0%	8.0%	8.5%
Expected return on bonds	5.0%	6.2%	6.5%
Retirement age	65	65	65

The assets and liabilities in the schemes were:-

	The Group			The Company		
	30th June 2002 £'000	30th June 2001 £'000	30th June 2000 £'000	30th June 2002 £'000	30th June 2001 £'000	30th June 2000 £'000
Market value of assets:						
Equities	26,400	27,900	28,400	25,100	26,200	26,800
Bonds and cash	500	720	700	100	200	200
	26,900	28,620	29,100	25,200	26,400	27,000
Actuarial value of liability	34,200	29,170	28,600	32,400	27,300	26,800
(Deficit)/surplus in the scheme	(7,300)	(550)	500	(7,200)	(900)	200
Deferred tax thereon	2,170	230	(90)	2,160	270	(60)
Net pension (liability)/asset	(5,130)	(320)	410	(5,040)	(630)	140

Figure 7.5 (Continued overleaf)

The movements in the schemes' (deficit)/surplus were:-

	2002 £'000	2001 £'000
(Deficit)/surplus in schemes at 1st July	**(550)**	500
Current service cost (included in operating profit)	**(2,100)**	(1,800)
Contributions paid	**3,300**	1,800
Finance income	**640**	600
Actuarial loss	**(8,590)**	(1,650)
Deficit in schemes at 30th June	**(7,300)**	(550)

At the date of the latest full actuarial valuation, the market value of the assets of the UK scheme was £28,040,000 and the actuarial value of the assets was sufficient to cover 82% of the benefits that had accrued to members after allowing for expected future increases in earnings. The deficit on an ongoing basis is being reduced over members' future working lives by additional company contributions. On a minimum funding requirement basis, the scheme is 83% funded and the contributions payable are sufficient to amortise the deficit.

Figure 7.5 Renishaw plc: pensions.

Look particularly at the final paragraph which shows that the market value of the scheme's assets was only 82 per cent of likely benefits, with the company making additional contributions over the future working lives of employees.

7.7 Total net assets

This represents the grand total of all the assets less all the liabilities, as shown in a balance sheet produced in a 'vertical' format, thus representing the left-hand side of the accounting equation, Assets − Liabilities = Capital.

7.8 Contingent liabilities

Many businesses have contingent liabilities, which exist when there is uncertainty as to whether or not a future event will give rise to the company having to meet a financial obligation. For example:

- A parent company may have guaranteed the bank overdraft of a subsidiary. If at some future time the subsidiary gets into financial difficulties, the parent company must meet the debt.

- A company might be sued by customers regarding defects in products. If the legal case is still progressing through the courts at the time the balance sheet is produced, the amount of any potential loss is uncertain until the time that the judgement is made.

In such cases, in view of the uncertainty of any future loss, there is no reason why a provision should be made. However, the notes to the accounts should contain information which explains the circumstances of the contingency.

In the event of a contingent *asset* occurring, for example where the company itself is suing a supplier for compensation over defective materials, this could only be noted if there is a probability (backed up by legal opinion) that the gain will materialize.

Pace Micro Technology plc disclosed the contingent liability in its 2002 annual report shown in Figure 7.6.

32 CONTINGENT LIABILITY

The owners of patents covering technology allegedly used by the Group have indicated claims for royalties relating to the Group's use (including past usage) of that technology. Whilst negotiations over these liabilities continue, they are not concluded. The directors have made provision for the potential royalties payable based on the latest information available. Having taken legal advice, the Board considers that there are defences available that should mitigate the amounts being sought. The Group will vigorously negotiate or defend all claims but, in the absence of agreement, the amounts provided may prove to be different from the amounts at which the potential liabilities are finally settled.

Figure 7.6 Pace Micro Technology plc: contingent liability

Also, see Figure 7.7 for further examples.

7.9 Capital commitments

To give users of the annual report an indication of the company's *future* investment plans, a note is provided which discloses the amounts (or estimated amounts) of capital expenditure which, at the balance sheet date:

(a) have been contracted for, and,

(b) have been authorized by the board of directors, but no contracts have been issued.

See Figure 7.7 for an example.

7.10 Post-balance sheet events

The period between the end of the financial period and the date on which the directors meet to approve the financial statements is known as the 'post-balance sheet period'. Certain events may happen in that period—favourable and unfavourable—that might require an alteration to the amounts included in the financial statements (known as 'adjusting' events) or need to be drawn to the attention of users of the financial statements without alteration to the figures (known as 'non-adjusting' events). As always, immaterial events can be ignored. *Adjusting* post-balance sheet events provide additional evidence of conditions that existed at the balance sheet date, such as the subsequent confirmation of the purchase price of a major fixed asset bought before the end of the financial period. *Non-adjusting* events concern conditions which did *not* exist at the balance sheet date, but are important enough to affect the way in which users evaluate the company's results and future direction.

Examples of post-balance sheet adjusting events include:

- Errors discovered which show that the financial statements were incorrect.
- Debts thought to be good at the balance sheet date, but subsequently found to be bad or doubtful.
- Additional liabilities arising due to late receipt of invoices.
- Alterations to estimated values of stocks or fixed assets which show an impairment or undervaluation.

Examples of post-balance sheet non-adjusting events include:

- Takeover bids by or for the company.
- Mergers or acquisitions.
- Issues of shares and debentures.
- Calamities such as fires and floods.
- Labour disputes.
- Opening new trading activities.
- Defaulting on loans.

Adjusting post-balance sheet events will, as the name implies, change the figures in the financial statements, but do not need to be disclosed separately. Non-adjusting post-balance sheet events must be disclosed, with information being given regarding the nature of the event, and also an estimate of its financial implications, or a statement that it is not possible to make such an estimate.

 Figure 7.7 shows the capital commitments, contingent liabilities, and post-balance sheet events of Manchester United plc.

29 Commitments and contingent liabilities
a. Capital commitments
At 31 July 2002, capital commitments were:

	Group		Company	
	2002 £'000	2001 £'000	2002 £'000	2001 £'000
Contracted but not provided for	3,763	7,391	–	–

b. Transfer fees payable
Under the terms of certain contracts with other football clubs in respect of player transfers, certain additional amounts would be payable by the Group if conditions as to future team selection are met. The maximum that could be payable is £12,548,000 (2001 £5,455,000).

c. Guarantee on behalf of associate
Manchester United PLC has guaranteed a property lease of its associate, Timecreate Limited. The lease term is 35 years with annual rentals of £400,000.

Figure 7.7 (Continued overleaf)

31 Post balance sheet events

On 1 August 2002 the business and operations of MU 099 Limited (formerly Manchester United Merchandising Limited) were transferred to Nike in accordance with the terms of an agreement which grants Nike certain merchandising, promotional and sponsorship rights (including the use of the trade name Manchester United Merchandising Limited). Certain assets and liabilities of the merchandising operations were transferred at book value to Nike on that date. These assets and liabilities, which are included in the consolidated balance sheet of Manchester United PLC at 31 July 2002, are summarised below:

	£'000
Tangible fixed assets	330
Stocks	64
Debtors	286
Deferred income	(1,043)
	(363)

Figure 7.7 Manchester United plc: capital commitments, contingent liabilities, and post-balance sheet events

7.11 Chapter summary

- Liabilities are divided between those due within one year and those due after more than one year.
- The taxation charge shown in the profit and loss account is unlikely to be the same as the liability shown under current liabilities.
- The dividend owing at the balance sheet date is likely to be the final, proposed, dividend.
- Loans might be secured on a fixed or floating charge against asset values.
- 'Net current assets' is also known as 'working capital'.
- Debentures are also known as *bonds* and usually carry a fixed interest rate.
- Closing provisions relating to depreciation or doubtful debts are deducted from the related assets, but other provisions, such as for deferred taxation or pension liabilities, will be shown separately.
- Pension schemes may be either *defined contribution schemes* or *defined benefit schemes*.
- Contingent liabilities and gains must be considered, and any material capital commitments shown.

■ GLOSSARY

accruals	Additional expenses incurred during a financial period which have not been paid for by the end of that period
adjusting post-balance sheet event	A post-balance sheet event that provides additional evidence of conditions existing at the balance sheet date. It will alter the figures in the financial statements

bonds	Another term for *debentures*
capital commitments	Amounts (or estimated amounts) of capital expenditure which have, at the balance sheet date, been contracted for, and also those authorized by the board directors, but where no contracts have been issued
cash flow statement	A summary of the cash inflows and outflows during the financial period
contingent liability	An uncertain liability which may arise due to a future event giving rise to the company having to meet a financial obligation
convertible loans	Loans which may be converted into equity shares at dates stated in the loan documents
corporation tax	Taxation chargeable on company profits
current liabilities	Creditors due for payment within one year of the balance sheet date
debentures	Loans which are usually secured and carry a fixed interest rate
deferred income	Amounts received by the company in advance of the company providing the goods or services
defined benefit scheme	Pension scheme where the benefits paid will usually depend upon either the average pay of the employees during their career (or perhaps the last few years of it) or the employee's final pay
defined contribution scheme	Pension scheme where both employers and employees make regular contributions as a fixed annual amount or as a percentage of pay
discount	A deduction from an invoiced amount offered to encourage prompt payment
final dividend	A dividend proposed for approval by the shareholders at the Annual General Meeting
fixed charge	Security for a loan linked to specific assets of a company
floating charge	Security for a loan linked to general assets of a company
interim dividend	A dividend that relates to the first few months of a financial period
irredeemable loans	Loans with no set repayment date
long-term creditors	Creditors due for payment after one year from the balance sheet date
net current assets	Current assets less current liabilities
non-adjusting post-balance sheet event	A post-balance sheet event that does not require any changes to be made to the figures contained within the financial statements, but a note is provided for information only
overdraft	A borrowing facility offered by a bank which carries a fluctuating interest rate and is repayable on demand
post-balance sheet event	An event which occurs between the balance sheet date and the date on which the directors meet to approve the financial statements. It can be either *adjusting* or *non-adjusting*
provision	Any amount written off by way of providing for depreciation or diminution in the value of assets; or any amount retained to provide for any liability or

loss which is either likely to be incurred, or certain to be incurred but uncertain as to the amount or as to the date on which it will arise

redemption dates	Earliest and latest redemption or conversion dates. Shown within the description of the loan stock, e.g. 5% Convertible Loan Stock 2014–18
trade creditors	Amounts owing for goods and services
working capital	Net current assets

■ MULTIPLE CHOICE QUESTIONS

1. Which one of the following would *not* be found within the balance sheet heading 'creditors: amounts falling due within one year'?

   a   Final dividend (proposed)
   b   Interim dividend (paid)
   c   Bank overdraft
   d   Accruals

2. The closing balance on the provision for deferred taxation is usually shown within which of the following balance sheet headings?

   a   Current assets
   b   Creditors: amounts falling due within one year
   c   Provisions for liabilities and charges
   d   Creditors: amounts falling due after more than one year

3. A company had shown a current tax liability of £180,000 in its previous year's closing balance sheet. During the current financial period, the company had a cash outflow of £190,000 for corporation tax, and provided £150,000 in the profit and loss account for current taxation. Assuming that there were no other taxation adjustments, what liability would be shown in this year's closing balance sheet?

   a   £140,000
   b   £150,000
   c   £180,000
   d   £190,000

4. Companies often pay a dividend part-way through a financial period. What is it called?

   a   Preference dividend
   b   Final dividend
   c   Interim dividend
   d   Six-monthly dividend

5. In connection with a loan, what is a *floating charge*?

   a   The interest charge that the lender makes for lending the money
   b   Security given by the borrower relating to the overall net assets of the business
   c   Security given by the borrower relating to the specific assets of the business
   d   Security given by the borrower relating only to the liquid assets of the business

6. What is another term which means 'net current assets'?

   a Share capital
   b Capital expenditure
   c Negative working capital
   d Working capital

7. A debenture is also known as a:

   a Share
   b Bond
   c Lease
   d Reserve

8. If a company has a loan referred to as '5% Convertible 2018', which of the following descriptions is most accurate?

   a 5 per cent of the loan is convertible into shares every year for twenty years until 2018
   b The loan carries a 5 per cent interest rate and is convertible into shares after 2018
   c The loan carries a 5 per cent interest rate and is convertible into shares before 2018
   d The loan carries a 5 per cent interest rate and is convertible into shares in 2018

9. In a defined contribution pension scheme, the employer pays:

   a Nothing, as all the contributions are paid by the employee
   b Regular contributions which vary depending upon the predicted future pension obligations under the scheme
   c Infrequent contributions based on changing future pension obligations under the scheme
   d Regular contributions fixed as an amount or as a percentage of pay

10. A company is being sued for damages, but the case is not resolved at the balance sheet date. A material amount is involved. Which one of the following describes this situation?

    a Contingent liability
    b Adjusting post-balance sheet event
    c Capital commitment
    d Non-adjusting post-balance sheet event

(Note: answers are shown in Appendix 2.)

■ **DISCUSSION QUESTIONS**

Events within the post-balance sheet period may have an effect on the information contained within the financial statements.

1. Define 'post-balance sheet period'.

2. Explain the difference between an 'adjusting' and a 'non-adjusting' post-balance sheet event.

3. Two weeks after the balance sheet date, Peabody Products' warehouse was burned down in a suspicious fire. The stock destroyed was valued at £100,000 in the balance sheet.

On seeing the story of the blaze in a newspaper, a major creditor realized that an invoice relating to goods worth £50,000 ordered and delivered before the balance sheet date had not been sent to Peabody Products. How do the accounting standards relating to post-balance sheet events require these events to be shown in Peabody Products' financial statements?

(Note: Suggested answers or discussion points are available on the companion website.)

■ **LONGER QUESTIONS**

(Questions marked W have suggested answers on the companion website. Other questions are answered in Appendix 3.)

1. The financial director of Shrews plc recently presented the company's financial statements for approval by the shareholders at an Annual General Meeting. The shareholders voted to reject the accounting statements.

    The profit and loss account and balance sheet as presented to the meeting were as follows:

Profit and loss account for the year ended 31 December 2003	
	£
Sales	520,000
Cost of sales	(230,000)
Gross profit	290,000
Expenses	(115,000)
Operating profit before taxation	175,000
Taxation	(35,000)
Operating profit after taxation	140,000
Retained profits b/f	230,000
Retained profits c/f	370,000

Balance sheet as at 31 December 2003		
	£	£
Fixed assets (net book value):		327,000
Current assets:		
Stock	162,000	
Debtors	152,000	
Bank	24,000	
	338,000	

Less Creditors: amounts due for payment within one year:			
Trade creditors	135,000		
Taxation	35,000		
		(170,000)	
Net current assets			168,000
			495,000
Share capital			
500,000 ordinary shares of 25p each, fully paid			125,000
Reserves:			
Retained earnings (P&L a/c)			370,000
			495,000

After the meeting, the following matters relating to the accounts were discussed:

(i) A proposed dividend of 2p per share had not been included.

(ii) In the post-balance sheet period, £20,000 stock included at 31 December 2003 had proved to be worthless, but no adjustment had been made.

(iii) 'Expenses' shown in the profit and loss account excluded the directors' bonus of £18,000, which was owing at the balance sheet date.

(iv) The directors had authorized capital expenditure of £80,000 at 31 December 2003, but had not placed a contract at that date.

(v) The company's accountants informed the directors in the post-balance sheet period that they should have provided for deferred taxation amounting to £16,000.

a Redraft the profit and loss account and balance sheet, as amended by the additional information listed in (i) to (v) above, clearly showing the adjustments that you have made.

b Suggest three ways in which the directors of Shrews Limited can avoid a future situation where shareholders might reject a set of accounts.

2. Berwick plc shows the following information relating to 'creditors: amounts due after more than one year':

(i) 6% Irredeemable unsecured loan stock;

(ii) 5% Convertible debentures 2014–18, secured by a floating charge;

(iii) 4% Debentures 2008, secured by a fixed charge.

For each of these loans, explain their key features as suggested by their descriptions.

3. The finance director of Wibbley plc has recently completed the draft accounts of the company for the year ended 31 December 2003, but cannot decide on the correct treatment for the following items:

(i) On 15 January 2004, a software error was discovered in the computer program that values the company's stock. The program had undervalued stock at 31 December 2003 by £80,000.

(ii) The company had made a successful takeover bid in January 2004 for Teqno Ltd, and had issued 5 million shares for an agreed value of £10 million to buy the company.

(iii) A former employee had brought a court case against the company in November 2003. The employee claimed £55,000 compensation for wrongful dismissal. No judgement had yet been made in the case, and estimated costs to 31 December 2003 were £4,000 incurred by the company and £3,000 incurred by the ex-employee. The company's solicitors believe that it is possible that the judgement will be against the company.

(iv) The company must comply with new legislation, introduced in 2003, which requires it to spend £500,000 on improvements to a sewage treatment plant. The work must be completed by 31 December 2007 at the latest. The financial statements for the year ended 31 December 2003 had not made any reference to this.

State, with reasons, how you would account for each of items (i) to (iv) above.

4W. The following Dividends Account appeared in the ledger of Truman plc for the year ended 30 September 2004:

Dividends				
Date	Details	Debit	Credit	Balance
1 Oct. 2003	Proposed dividend brought forward		25,000	25,000 Cr
10 Jan. 2004	Bank	25,000		0
15 Mar. 2004	Bank	10,000		10,000 Dr
30 Sep. 2004	Proposed dividend carried forward	35,000		45,000 Dr
30 Sep. 2004	Profit and loss account		45,000	0

Explain each of the five entries contained within the account, and state how 'dividends' would be shown in the profit and loss account for the year ended 30 September 2004 and the balance sheet as at that date.

5W. The following Current Taxation Account appeared in the ledger of Threnody plc for the year ended 30 September 2004:

Taxation				
Date	Details	Debit	Credit	Balance
1 Oct. 2003	Current taxation liability brought forward		63,000	63,000 Cr
10 Jan. 2004	Bank: agreed liability paid	62,000		1,000 Cr
30 Sep. 2004	Estimated tax liability carried forward	105,000		104,000 Dr
30 Sep. 2004	Profit and loss account		104,000	0

Explain each of the four entries contained within the account, and state how 'current taxation' would be shown in the profit and loss account for the year ended 30 September 2004 and the balance sheet as at that date.

6W. Rooster plc, a producer of eggs and frozen poultry, has prepared draft accounts for the year ended 31 March 2004. A directors' meeting to discuss the accounts was arranged for 1 June 2004, and between the two dates the following material events occurred:

(i) A customer who owed the company £50,000 went into liquidation on 9 April. The receiver has indicated that the maximum payment to creditors would be 15 per cent of the sums owed.

(ii) A fault in the refrigeration units in April resulted in stock valued at £95,000 at 31 March being declared unfit for human consumption. It was subsequently sold as fertilizer for £4,000.

(iii) The faulty refrigeration units cost the company £80,000 to repair in May.

(iv) Animal rights protesters burned down a large chicken shed in May, causing uninsured damage of £3m.

(v) Several customers suffered food poisoning in April. They claimed that their sickness resulted from eating the company's products, and have written to the company's managing director to say that they intend to claim £2m compensation.

(vi) A legal case that the company started several years ago is nearing completion. It involved suing a competitor for infringement of copyright over an advertising slogan 'Rooster Eggs are Eggstra Special'. The company's legal advisers believe that there is a reasonable probability of winning the case, and are hopeful of being awarded £2m in compensation.

   a Comment on the extent to which any or all of the above events should be taken into account when producing the final agreed accounts for the year ended 31 March 2004.

   b Explain why accountants have to be more careful when deciding whether to anticipate gains, when compared to their attitudes regarding foreseeable losses.

■ MINI CASE STUDY

Ruffled feathers in Peru

MinnieMax Ltd. (see previous mini case studies) is preparing its balance sheet at the end of its first year of trading, 30 September 2004. Relevant information needed regarding the company's liabilities at that date is as follows:

	£
4% Debenture 2010–12	140,000
Current taxation	62,500
Finance lease obligations due after one year	12,000
Finance lease obligations due within one year	3,000
Proposed final dividend	50,000
Trade creditors due within one year	42,500
(Additional information:)	
Total fixed assets, net of depreciation	266,680
Total current assets	197,320

a You are required to present the information in the form of an extract from the company balance sheet as at 30 September 2004, showing the 'total net assets' of the company at that date. Use the 'vertical' form of balance sheet.

b The Peruvian Wherearewe tribe had received compensation from MinnieMax Ltd. for the illegal capture and sale of the tribe's sacred Ibrox bird. However, the head of the tribe, Chief Witless, decided to bring a legal action on behalf of the tribe seeking damages for mental anguish to tribe members (£500,000) and the costs of cloning a replacement bird from DNA extracted from spare tail feathers (£400,000). The directors have told you that the case was in progress at 30 September 2004 and was unlikely to be settled prior to November 2004.

How, if at all, should details of this case be shown within the annual report of MinnieMax Ltd.?

(Suggested solutions can be found in Appendix 4.)

■ MAXI CASE STUDY

Scapa Group plc

Read the following extracts from the annual report of Scapa Group plc and then answer the questions which follow.

[From the Chairman's statement]

Asbestos

There has been much written about liabilities in UK and US companies that have resulted from exposure to asbestos. As shareholders are aware, the group is involved in a number of cases in the USA arising from the alleged exposure of paper mill workers to asbestos in a product that was part of a business sold in July 1999. So far all the cases against the company have either been won, dismissed or abandoned before going to court and the directors believe, having taken advice, that it is unlikely significant liability will arise. We will continue to defend vigorously the outstanding claims and have taken an additional provision of £5 million to cover future defence costs. No Scapa group company or any of our insurance companies has admitted any liability, nor made any payment to any plaintiff. More information is given in the contingent liabilities note 27.

[From 'notes to the accounts']

27. Contingent liabilities

In the United States, various Group companies, together with numerous and diverse non-Scapa Group parties, are named as defendants in claims in which damages are being sought for personal injury arising from alleged exposure to asbestos. As at 31 March 2002: 17,933 plaintiffs (31 March 2001: 6,601 plaintiffs) have brought claims across 15 states (Georgia, Florida, Louisiana, Mississippi, North Carolina, Ohio, Alabama, California, New Jersey, Pennsylvania, Wisconsin, Oregon, Indiana, Arkansas and Texas). One lawsuit presently pending in federal court in Mississippi accounts for 7,261 of the increase in new plaintiffs, although these claims may be subject to dismissal because of the mass x-ray screening technique used by plaintiff's counsel. The claims, so far as the Scapa Group defendants are concerned, primarily relate to the Waycross business carried on by Scapa Dryer Fabrics, Inc. as part of the Paper Machine Clothing business. The Waycross business consists of the manufacture and supply of dryer fabrics to paper manufacturers. As was common with the industry between approximately 1958 and 1978, the Waycross business used yarn containing chrysotile asbestos in some of its dryer fabrics.

The plaintiffs, who are mostly former paper mill employees (or their dependants), allege that asbestos fibres were released when they cleaned the dryer fabrics by blowing compressed air across them. It is also alleged that exposure to asbestos fibres occurred during installation and removal of dryer fabrics, during the routine maintenance, and even as a result of normal wear and tear. To date there have been three sets of jury trials in the United States—in Louisiana State and Washington State (covering 5 plaintiffs each) and in Oregon State (1 plaintiff).

In Louisiana State, verdicts were returned in favour of Scapa Dryer Fabrics Inc. and another manufacturer of dryer felts, on the basis that the dryer fabrics could not have caused any of the alleged illnesses.

Subsequent to this trial in Louisiana, the plaintiffs' attorney has dismissed Scapa as a defendant in six consecutive trials (involving 58 plaintiffs), and there are currently no trials scheduled in which Scapa remains as a defendant in that state. In Washington State, Scapa Dryer Fabrics Inc. (the only remaining defendant) was exonerated by a majority verdict, which found that the relevant dryer fabrics were not 'unreasonably dangerous', and did not require any warning label for users. Subsequent Washington State cases were dismissed and none are presently pending. In Oregon State a verdict was returned in favour of Scapa Dryer Fabrics Inc. and four other defendants, including another dryer felt manufacturer. In this case, the jury found that Scapa had not been negligent with respect to its failure to put a warning concerning asbestos on its dryer felts. The jury also determined that Scapa asbestos-containing dryer felts were not unreasonably dangerous for their intended use. Finally, the jury determined that Scapa had not misrepresented anything to the Plaintiff with respect to the safety of Scapa dryer felts insofar as their asbestos content is concerned.

The only case currently scheduled for trial is in Mississippi, and involves approximately 470 plaintiffs. Trial is scheduled to begin on 6 August, 2002. Scapa Dryer Fabrics Inc. and the other Scapa Group companies named as defendants are vigorously defending the outstanding claims against them. No Scapa Group company or its insurance carrier has admitted liability to date or made any payment to any plaintiff, either as the result of any judgment or by way of settlement. The Board believes that it is unlikely that significant liabilities will arise from this litigation.

In March 2001, legal proceedings were issued in the English Courts against Scapa Group plc by J. M. Voith AG and a number of its subsidiary companies, claiming US$7.0 million plus interest. The claim has arisen under a warranty given in the sale and purchase agreement relating to the disposal in 1999 to Voith of Scapa's paper machine clothing and rolls divisions. The warranty relates to the funding of three US pension plans which were transferred in whole or in part to Voith as part of the disposal. Scapa has filed a Defence and Counterclaim seeking rectification of the sale and purchase agreement by deletion of the warranty on the grounds that it does not reflect the commercial agreement reached between Scapa and Voith. The Claim, Defence and Counterclaim, and Reply to Defence and Counterclaim have been served, and disclosure took place in December 2001. Witness statements were exchanged on 28 March 2002 and expert reports are due to be exchanged on 31 May 2002. The trial is scheduled to start on 1 October 2002. Although there can be no assurances given regarding the outcome of this dispute, after taking legal advice, the Board believes that Scapa has a good chance of success in defending the claim. Consequently, as in prior years, no provision has been made for the costs that would arise if the Group's defence was unsuccessful.

Scapa Group plc Annual Report 2002

How might the above information affect your evaluation of the company?

(Suggested answers and discussion areas are available on the companion website.)

■ **WEB LINKS**

Company websites

Companies referred to in this chapter:

Brixton plc www.brixton.plc.uk

Domino's Pizza www.dominos.co.uk

Kimberley-Clark Corporation www.kimberly-clark.com

Manchester United plc www.manutd.com

Pace Micro Technology plc www.pace.co.uk/

Renishaw www.renishaw.com

Scapa Group plc www.scapa.com

■ FURTHER READING

Black, G. (2003). *Students' Guide to Accounting and Financial Reporting Standards*, 9th edn. (Harlow: FT/Prentice Hall), chapters 7, 11.

Elliott, B., and Elliott, J. (2003). *Financial Accounting and Reporting*, 8th edn. (Harlow: FT/Prentice Hall), chapter 13.

Weetman, P. (2003). *Financial and Management Accounting: An Introduction*, 3rd edn. (Harlow: FT/Prentice Hall), chapters 10, 11.

■ COMPANION WEBSITE MATERIALS

 Additional materials are available for students and lecturers on the companion website, at **www.oup.com/uk/booksites/busecon/business/**

8

The balance sheet: capital and reserves

OBJECTIVES

By the end of this chapter you will be able to:

- Understand the meaning of 'share capital', including *authorized* and *issued* share capital, and the distinction between equity and non-equity shares.
- Explain the ways in which share capital can change: share issues; share splits; share consolidations; buy-backs.
- Appreciate the significance of shareholders' rights in their company.
- Understand the meaning of 'reserves' and the distinction between capital (non-distributable) reserves and revenue (distributable) reserves.
- Analyse the typical reserves that may appear in company balance sheets.
- Understand the ways in which reserves can be reduced or eliminated.

8.1 Introduction

Our detailed exploration of the balance sheet concludes in this chapter with the 'share capital and reserves' section. In a 'vertical' balance sheet, this will equal the 'total net assets', but in an 'account' type balance sheet, it will be added to the 'liabilities' to equal the 'total assets' on the opposite side.

Once again, the relevant part of Domino's Pizza's annual report is used as our starting point (see Figure 8.1, which is cross-referenced to chapter headings), though, as before, we shall refer to other companies where needed to illustrate the full range of information which might be disclosed.

Group Balance Sheet

at 29 December 2002

	Notes	2002 £000	2001 £000
FIXED ASSETS			
Intangible assets	10	2,386	2,484
Tangible assets	11	13,685	12,181
Investments in joint venture:	12		
Share of gross assets		717	757
Share of gross liabilities		(410)	(480)
		307	277
TOTAL FIXED ASSETS		16,378	14,942
CURRENT ASSETS			
Stocks	13	1,411	1,260
Debtors:	14		
amounts falling due within one year		8,572	6,665
amounts falling due after more than one year		2,130	1,756
		10,702	8,421
Cash at bank and in hand		3,885	3,231
TOTAL CURRENT ASSETS		15,998	12,912
CREDITORS: amounts falling due within one year	15	(12,919)	(10,203)
NET CURRENT ASSETS		3,079	2,709
TOTAL ASSETS LESS CURRENT LIABILITIES		19,457	17,651
CREDITORS: amounts falling due after more than one year	16	(7,152)	(7,632)
PROVISION FOR LIABILITIES AND CHARGES	7	(604)	(421)
		11,701	9,598
8.2 — **CAPITAL AND RESERVES**			
8.3 — Called up share capital	21	2,546	2,518
8.5.1 — Share premium account	22	2,395	2,192
8.5.4 — Profit and loss account	22	6,760	4,888
Equity shareholders' funds		11,701	9,598

Stephen Hemsley
Director

Figure 8.1 Domino's Pizza Group: balance sheet (capital and reserves) (cross-referenced to chapter headings). The shaded area was covered in detail in Chapters 6, 7, and 8.

8.2 The heading

'Capital and reserves' is the heading, in a vertical style balance sheet, which starts the second half of that statement. The total of the capital and reserves will equal, because of the accounting equation, the total of the 'assets less liabilities' (total net assets) found in the first half of the balance sheet. If the balance sheet had been drawn up in an 'account' format, the capital and reserves would be included as part of the 'equity and liabilities' side of the statement.

8.3 **Called-up share capital**

Called-up share capital, also known as *issued* share capital, is the total *nominal* (par) value of a company's shares owned by shareholders at the balance sheet date. It should be distinguished from *authorized* share capital, which is the maximum number of shares the company is allowed to issue according to its 'Memorandum of Association'. The Memorandum of Association is a book of rules which each company has, setting out basic information regarding the company's name, where the registered office of the company is situated (England, Wales, or Scotland), and what its objects are—which may simply be to carry on business as a 'general commercial company'. Note that companies also must have an 'Articles of Association' which sets out the rules for the running of the company's internal affairs. Information includes such details as company general meetings, voting rights of shareholders, and the compulsory retirement age for directors.

Private companies comprise the vast majority of limited liability enterprises, and as such are not allowed to offer their shares for sale to the general public. However, they *are* able to sell their shares, but the persons who buy are likely to be friends, relatives, or business acquaintances of existing shareholders. A public limited company (plc) wanting to raise capital by means of a share issue will usually do so by an *offer for sale*, whereby the shares are sold first by the company to a financial institution (e.g. a bank), which then offers the shares for sale to the general public by placing advertisements in national newspapers. When a company offers its shares to the public for the first time this is known as an Initial Public Offering (IPO). It is very unusual for public limited companies to sell their own shares directly to the public. Where relatively small amounts are involved, one or more financial institutions might buy all the available shares off the company and then sell the shares to their own customers. This is known as a 'placing'. Most large share sales will be *underwritten*, which means that if insufficient shares are taken up by the general public, 'underwriters' agree to buy the unsold shares at an agreed price, charging a commission to the company as their fee for taking the risks involved. The underwriters will then sell on their shares at the appropriate time through the stock market. The underwriting process guarantees that the company will sell all the shares.

Companies selling shares have to produce a *prospectus*, which contains very detailed information concerning the background of the company, its past financial performance, and profit forecasts. Those who wish to buy shares simply return an application form to the company's financial representative, together with a cheque for the appropriate amount. The price at which shares are offered will be set at the point at which, in the opinion of the company and its advisers, demand for the shares will match the supply. In practice, however, share issues tend to be either over- or undersubscribed. An oversubscription results from a high demand for shares due to such factors as a favourable price and good press comments, and leads to an increase in the share price once the shares are traded. An undersubscription results from weak demand caused by overpricing, bad press publicity, or general economic events which have worsened in the time period during which the shares have been available for purchase. Sometimes the company makes a *tender issue*, where potential shareholders are invited to decide the price at which they are prepared to buy the shares within a predetermined range, and, assuming sufficient demand, all the shares will be sold at the appropriate price within this range. The purchaser of the shares will usually be asked to pay the entire amount at the time of the offer. Occasionally, payments might be requested in instalments, with an amount due at the time of the application for the shares, another just before it allots the shares (i.e. issues them to the purchaser), and one or more further instalments (known as 'calls') at dates decided by the company. This system is useful when the company doesn't require all the capital at the time of the share issue but finds it more convenient to receive the funds over a future period.

A prospectus of a (completed) share issue can be downloaded from the following website: **http://shareoffer.willhill.com/download.asp?status=1**

It relates to a company, William Hill plc, which offered nearly 220m shares for sale in June 2003, at a price between 190p and 240p per share.

8.3.1 Equity share capital

Equity shares are the vote-carrying ordinary shares (US: common stock) which form the main type of shares issued by companies. At a company's formation, its founders will decide on various matters relating to the share capital, including:

- Whether the share capital should consist entirely of equity shares, or part equity and part non-equity shares (see below).
- The nominal value that should be given to the shares. The nominal (or par) value of a share has little significance in itself other than as a device for breaking down the totality of the share capital into individual units. For example, a company wishing to raise £100,000 could do so, in theory, by issuing one share with a nominal value of £100,000. However, if the company hopes to create a vibrant market in its shares there must be enough shares available to be bought and sold. Because of this, the £100,000 could be broken down into nominal values of whatever amount is necessary to achieve the required number of individual shares. If the company believes that 10m shares would be an appropriate number, it would make the nominal value per share 1p (£100,000 = 10 million × 1p). If it thought that one million would be sufficient then the nominal value would be 10p, and so on.

Domino's Pizza's ordinary shares have a nominal value of 5p each. The company only has equity shares. Look at Figure 8.1 above, and calculate how many individual shares (to the nearest thousand) had been issued at 29 December 2002.[1]

As each equity share carries the right to one vote, the more shares that an individual shareholder owns, the more power can be exercised within the company. Share ownership itself gives no automatic right to partake in the management of the company. Shareholders elect

---

[1] Answer: (2,546,000 × 20) = 50,920,000 shares.

directors to manage the company on their behalf, but it stands to reason that if a majority shareholder (the holder of more than 50 per cent of the voting capital) wishes to be part of the board of directors, they have the voting power to ensure this happens. The names of the owners of significant shareholdings (3 per cent and above) will be given within the Directors' Report. Details of directors' shareholdings will also be given.

 Look at p. 316 of Domino's Pizza's annual report, and note the numbers of shares that the directors own, as well as other significant shareholdings in the company.

The advantages and disadvantages of equity shares are summarized in Figure 8.2.

From the shareholders' viewpoint	
Advantages	**Disadvantages**
Carry votes, so can influence the direction of the company	No guarantee of dividend
Rising profits should result in increasing dividends	More risks than non-equity shares (in the event of company liquidation, non-equity shares have a better chance of capital repayment than equity)
Have the right to attend general meetings	Preference shareholders receive the dividend before the equity shareholders
Might gain from capital appreciation if the company does well and the stock market price increases	If the company goes into liquidation, preference shareholders stand before the equity shareholders for capital repayment purposes
Have the right to receive the annual and interim reports of the company	May have difficulty in selling shares in private companies with no stock market listing
Might get discounts on the company's products (shareholders' perks)	Might lose money if stock market share price falls due to poor results
From the company's viewpoint	
Advantages	**Disadvantages**
No obligation to pay a dividend	Pressure from shareholders to pay a dividend
Capital is not repayable at a set date	Costs of issuing new share capital may be high (legal fees, underwriters' commission, etc.)
Existing shareholders are also potential providers of future capital	Some shareholders can be 'troublemakers' at company general meetings if they disagree with the policy of the directors
Stock options can be used to incentivize staff	Existing owners of the company may lose control if other shareholders are able to get a majority shareholding
Shareholder pressure can result in better company performance	Dividends come from after-tax profit (so are not tax deductible), but interest on *loan* capital (e.g. bonds) is allowed as a taxable deduction from profit

Figure 8.2 Advantages and disadvantages of equity shares

8.3.2 Non-equity shares

The non-equity capital, usually consisting of *preference* shares (US: preferred stock), is that part of the company's capital which does not have voting rights but has greater protection in terms of dividends and repayment of capital in the event of liquidation. Although there are many varieties of preference shares, typically they will be *cumulative*, carry *fixed dividends*, and be either *redeemable* or *convertible*:

- *Cumulative* means that if the company is unable to pay a dividend in one year, the missed dividends are accumulated for payment out of any future years' profits. In such circumstances, no ordinary share dividends can be declared until the preference share dividends have been paid.

- *Fixed dividends* are calculated as percentages of the nominal value of the preference shares. The percentage is set when the shares are issued, so the total preference share dividend on £1 million 5 per cent preference share capital would be £50,000 p.a. This would remain unchanged, regardless of how high or low the company's profits were to become.

- *Redeemable* preference shares are repayable by the company either at a specific date or at some time between earliest and latest dates for redemption, set at the time of the share issue. The redemption price to be paid by the company is often the original nominal value of the preference shares, but might be set at a discount or premium to that value. For example, if a company had issued £1m 5 per cent preference share capital, redeemable at a 10 per cent premium on 10 July 2004, the amount to be returned to shareholders on that date would be £1.1m [£1m + (10% × £1m)]. If the title of the shares contains two dates, e.g. 3 per cent preference share capital, 2009–11, these are earliest and latest years in which there are dates set for redemption at the company's choosing. The actual date to be chosen by the company to redeem its preference shares will depend on how the dividend rate on the existing shares compares with the prevailing cost and availability of capital during the redemption period. In our earlier example, if a company can only replace 3 per cent preference shares with a 5 per cent loan, then it would be in the company's interest to defer the redemption for as long as possible, i.e. until 2011. If it could replace the 3 per cent shares with a new issue of 2 per cent preference shares, then it is obviously in the company's interest to replace the shares as soon as possible in 2009.

- *Convertible* preference shares can be exchanged for another category of share capital—usually equity shares—at the discretion of the preference shareholders and at a date or dates specified at the time of issue. This makes them more attractive to potential shareholders, as they can invest in relatively low-risk preference shares and eventually decide whether to convert into equity at a later time. If the convertible preference shares are traded on a stock market, the price will fluctuate in tandem with the ordinary share price, as the conversion rights become more, or less, valuable as equity prices rise or fall. As with redeemable preference shares, the title of the stock will include the earliest and latest redemption years, so the title of a typical convertible stock might be '3 per cent convertible preference shares of £1 each, 2007–10'.

The advantages and disadvantages of issuing non-equity shares are shown in Figure 8.3.

From the shareholders' viewpoint	
Advantages	**Disadvantages**
Dividend is paid before any equity share dividend	Do not carry votes, so cannot influence the direction of the company
Usually a higher rate of return than that given on loan capital (due to greater risks)	'Preference' gives no guarantee that dividends will be paid or capital returned
Fewer risks than equity shares, (in the event of company liquidation, non-equity shares have a better chance of capital repayment than equity)	Rising profits will not result in increasing dividends
If convertible, they carry the right to be exchanged for equity shares at a future date	Do not have the right to attend general meetings
Missed dividends are normally accumulated and paid out of future years' profits	Might lose value if the shares are listed on the stock market and the price decreases
Might gain from capital appreciation if the shares are listed on the stock market and the price increases	Convertible preference shares prices tend to be more volatile than non-convertibles as they reflect the price changes of the underlying equity prices

From the company's viewpoint	
Advantages	**Disadvantages**
Dividend is fixed, regardless of increasing profits	Higher cost of capital than loans
Dividends can be deferred if insufficient profits	Capital might be repayable at a set date—is cash available?
If redeemable, known date or dates for repayment	Dividends come from after-tax profit (so are not tax deductible), but interest on *loan* capital (e.g. bonds) is allowed as a taxable deduction from profit
No threat to the existing ownership of the company, unless convertible in the future into equity shares	If convertible, may affect future ownership and control

Figure 8.3 Advantages and disadvantages of non-equity shares

Aviva plc is an insurance and pensions company. Its called up share capital on 31 December 2002 was £764m, including £100m 8⅜; per cent cumulative irredeemable preference shares of £1 each.

8.4 **Changes to share capital**

When a company is first formed, it will decide upon the amount of its authorized capital, a suitable nominal value, and how many shares should be issued. It also needs to set the initial selling price, which may be the same as (but never less than) the nominal value in the first instance. As the company develops and issues more shares, the company will set the selling price at whatever it believes the market is prepared to pay. The excess of the selling price over the nominal value is known as the *share premium*, which is discussed below (see section 8.5.1). In addition to the sale of more shares, the number of shares issued might *increase* for any of the following reasons:

- rights issues;
- bonus issues;
- share splits;
- stock conversions.

Furthermore, the number of shares issued might *decrease* due to:

- the company buying back its own shares;
- the redemption of shares;
- share consolidations.

> Look at resolutions 6 and 7 in Domino's Pizza's notice of its annual general meeting shown on p. 341, and the explanatory note shown on p. 343. The directors are seeking approval to issue up to £1.5 million (nominal value) equity shares without the need to have an Extraordinary General Meeting to authorize the issue.

8.4.1 Rights issues

One of the advantages to a company of having a supportive group of equity shareholders is the potential for them to make further investments in the company by buying more shares. For a listed company, shareholders may simply decide to buy more shares from other shareholders via a stock market. In a private company, the purchase and sale of shares is more restricted and often depends on a direct approach from one shareholder to another to negotiate the deal. If the company itself wishes to raise additional capital, the cheapest and most convenient way is to make a rights issue, whereby every existing equity shareholder is given the right to buy more shares (hence *rights issue*) on a pro rata basis. If all shareholders take up the offer there would be no overall change to the company's ownership. Obviously if some shareholders were unable or unwilling to buy the additional shares, their percentage holding in the company would decrease. As an incentive to shareholders to buy the shares on offer, they are often priced at an attractive discount to the prevailing market value. Obviously, an unsuccessful, loss-making company may have difficulties in persuading the long-suffering shareholders to make further investments. Rights issues are always expressed as a ratio, i.e. x for y, where x represents the shares available for purchase, and y represents the number of shares already held. A '5 for 3' offer therefore, would mean that for every three shares held before the rights issue a *further* five shares can be bought.

For example, assume a company has made a '2 for 5' rights issue at £2 per share. A shareholder with 10,000 shares would be entitled to buy a maximum of 4,000 shares ($2/5 \times 10,000$). Assuming that they wished to buy all the shares available under the rights issue, they would send a cheque to the company for £8,000 and their total shareholding would increase to 14,000. Shareholders do not have to buy all or any of the shares they are entitled to, but can 'sell on' their rights to other existing shareholders or institutions.

Read the following news item:

Long-suffering shareholders in Laura Ashley have predictably shunned the group's £8.2m rights issue, taking up only 32% of the new shares. The fashion and household goods retailer, which yesterday parted company with chief executive KC Ng, said it had received acceptances for just 47.7m of the 149.2m shares on offer.

The ailing group will get its cash, however, as the rights issue is fully underwritten. Costs of the cash call are about £800,000 and the remaining proceeds will be used to pay for closure of the company's Continental operations . . . Laura Ashley shares were unchanged today at 6.37p. The new shares were on offer at 6p.

Adapted from the *London Evening Standard*, 9 May 2003

Note the discount to the market price and the poor shareholder take-up of the shares. Can you calculate how much cash the company would receive from the rights issue, net of costs?[2]

8.4.2 Bonus issues

A bonus issue (also known as a scrip issue, capitalization issue, or (US) stock dividend) is a *free* issue of shares to existing shareholders, pro rata to their shareholdings. Expressed in exactly the same way as rights issues (e.g. '5 for 3', '2 for 5' etc.), the major difference is that no cash changes hands. It is purely a book entry, with part of the company's reserves being transferred into share capital, hence 'capitalization'. In theory, a bonus issue should have a neutral effect on share price so that, for example, if a bonus issue was announced which doubled the share capital, this should have the effect of halving the share price. In practice this may not be the case, as the announcement of the bonus issue is often accompanied by 'good news' in the form of increased profits, new orders, etc. For example, a company announcing a '1 for 1' bonus issue when its share price is 80p would, in theory, expect the share price to reduce to 40p, as twice as many shares will be in issue after the capitalization. In practice, the markets may see the bonus issue as a positive sign and mark up the price to say 45p.

There are several reasons why a company might decide to give free shares to shareholders:

- A high stock market price may act as a deterrent to potential investors. As a bonus issue increases the number of shares traded, the price per share will decrease to a more realistic level. For example, a company with share price of £12 may decide to quadruple the number of shares issued by making a '3 for 1' scrip issue. Following the issue, the share price should come down to approximately £3.

- Bonus shares are often created by a transfer from accumulated profits. The stock market therefore tends to link bonus issues with profitable companies, thus raising the company's overall market value.

---

[2] $(149.2m \times 6p) = £8.95m$, less £0.8m costs $= £8.15m$.

- Accumulated profits in the profit and loss account (a 'revenue reserve') are *distributable*, i.e. available to pay dividends (see section 8.5.4 below). If the company wants to restrict potential dividend payouts, a bonus issue that utilises revenue reserves converts *distributable* reserves into *non-distributable* share capital. For example, a company with £100m in its profit and loss account may use £60m for a bonus issue, leaving just £40 million as distributable reserves. This reduces the pressure on directors from shareholders who otherwise might demand ever-increasing dividends.

- Over time, a company might accumulate many different reserves – distributable and non-distributable. A bonus issue serves as a convenient way of tidying up the balance sheet by transferring some or all of the reserves into share capital.

 Pendragon plc is the UK's largest motor dealership. In June 2003, it made the following announcement:

Pendragon today announces a proposed bonus issue of three new ordinary shares for every two existing ordinary shares held. The bonus issue will increase the number of ordinary shares in issue held by shareholders on a pro rata basis and will lead to an adjustment to the price at which ordinary shares are traded in the market. Pendragon believes that the increase in the number of ordinary shares in issue will enhance the liquidity and marketability of its shares. The Bonus Issue will be effected by capitalising approximately £19.7 million currently standing to the credit of Pendragon's share premium account. The Bonus Issue is subject to approval by shareholders at the extraordinary general meeting to be held on Tuesday 15 July 2003. Following such approval it is expected that dealings in the new ordinary shares will commence on Wednesday 16 July 2003. A Circular will be posted to all shareholders on Monday 16 June 2003, containing details of the Bonus Issue, shareholder's resolutions and notice of the extraordinary general meeting.

Pendragon plc website: www.pendragonplc.com

Is the company using distributable or non-distributable reserves for the bonus issue?[3]

8.4.3 Share splits

One of the reasons for making a bonus issue is the effect it has on a high stock market price. Another, simpler, way of reducing the price is to reconsider the nominal value of each share. By splitting a £1 nominal value into ten shares with a nominal value of 10p, the stock market price should reduce to one-tenth of what it was before the split. For example, a company whose £1 nominal value shares have a stock market price of £16 might decide on a reduction in the nominal value to 25p. This should cause the market price to fall to £4. There will be no adverse effect on shareholders' value as they will have four times as many shares after the split (see Figure 8.4).

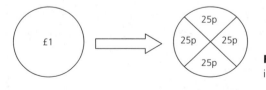

Figure 8.4 Share split (e.g. £1 nominal value split into 4 x 25p nominal value shares)

---

[3] The share premium account is non-distributable. (see Section 8.5.1.)

At the 2002 AGM of Barclays Bank plc held on 25 April 2002, a resolution was passed to divide each ordinary share of £1 each into four ordinary shares of 25p each.

8.4.4 **Stock options**

Many large corporations offer their directors and employees stock options as part of their overall remuneration package. The options give them the right to buy shares in their company at a specified price (the exercise price) within a set time period. The exercise price cannot be less than, and is likely to be considerably more than, the current share price. It will be set at a level which gives the employee an incentive to increase company profits and hence its share price. In Chapter 5 when we considered earnings per share (eps) calculations, we saw that an alternative *diluted* eps was shown to allow for the effect of options being taken up at future dates. Obviously, if the share price *falls* subsequent to the option being granted, there is no benefit to the employee and the options will lapse—they are referred to as being 'out of the money'. If share prices rise beyond the option price the option is referred to as being 'in the money' and the employee will gain from exercising the option.

Domino's Pizza granted various share options to employees, which are shown on p. 338. The exercise prices range between 42.1p and 76p, so with a current market price of over £1, all the options are 'in the money' and are likely to be exercised.

Options are especially useful in start-up companies which cannot afford large salaries but have the prospect of future growth. This was the case in the 'dotcom boom' in the late 1990s, when people were being enticed from established, secure companies to join new technology ventures at a fraction of their previous salaries. The key incentive was the granting of stock options that could be cashed in when the stock market was booming. However, when stock prices fell, many of these options proved worthless.

When options are exercised, the option holder will buy the shares from the company. The company itself will obtain the shares from one of three alternatives:

- it buys shares on the open market at the time the option is exercised,
- it has previously bought its own shares on the open market and held them in anticipation of the options being exercised (these are known as 'treasury' shares), or
- it seeks shareholder approval to make a new share issue at the option price.

In the first two cases, the company will lose money if the market price is greater than the option price. For example, if a company's current share price is £3 and a director had options over 100,000 shares at an option price of £2 each, the company would lose £100,000 if it had to buy in the shares at £3 in order to sell to the director at £2. In the third case, the existing shareholders may be uneasy at the thought of allowing employees and directors the right to buy shares at a fraction of the current market price.

At the time of writing, there is a major debate in progress as to whether the cost of granting stock options should be anticipated in the profit and loss account. Currently the only recognition of the effect of stock options is the calculation of diluted eps as referred to earlier.

8.4.5 Stock conversions

When we considered non-equity shares, we saw how some companies issue convertible stock that gives the holder the opportunity to exchange into equity shares at predetermined future dates. This gives an added attraction to the stock and makes it more marketable. Conversion rights may be attached not only to shares but also to loan stock (debentures/bonds). Whether or not the conversion rights are taken up depends upon the underlying share price. If share prices have fallen over the life of the convertible securities it may be advantageous for the holder simply to ignore the conversion rights in favour of a straight repayment of the stock.

For example, assume that a company had issued £500,000 8 per cent £1 convertible preference shares 2004. The shares have conversion rights of 50 ordinary shares for every 100 preference shares. The stock market value per ordinary share is £1.50. In such circumstances there is no incentive for preference shareholders to convert. If they wanted to invest in the ordinary shares of the company, they would ignore the conversion rights, wait for redemption of the preference shares, and then buy 67 shares per £100 (67 × £1.50 = £100) rather than receiving the 50 shares on conversion.

8.4.6 Buy-backs

If a public company with shares listed on a stock market gets permission from its shareholders, it may purchase its own shares. This might be done to meet the requirement of stock option holders (see above), hold them for future sale, or to cancel them. In the latter case, it cannot cancel all its equity capital if this would leave only *redeemable* shares in issue. When the company decides to buy back its shares, it will usually do so by buying the shares, via its broker, through the stock market. Occasionally it might make a tender offer to its shareholders, which involves the shareholders suggesting a price at which they would be prepared to sell their shares. The shares bought by the company are shown as 'treasury shares' and would be deducted from the total share capital. If cancelled, 'issued' share capital decreases, as does the total of 'treasury shares'.

 Look at how 'treasury stock' is shown on the balance sheet of Amrice, a US company, at **www.amrice.com/FinDoc_2002/ARIFin2002.pdf**

A company might decide on a buy-back if it has surplus cash which it wishes to return to shareholders. Although it could do this by increasing dividends, there might be tax advantages in buying shares in the market, thereby increasing demand, increasing the share price, and creating a capital gain for shareholders willing to sell. Once the shares are cancelled, there will be fewer shares available, which in itself might cause the price to rise. Key calculations of profitability, particularly 'earnings per share' and the PE ratio (see Chapters 5 and 12), will be improved, as the earnings for the year are divided by fewer shares.

Critics of buy-backs say that they indicate a lack of imagination on the company's part, as it should be using the surplus cash to invest in new products, take over other companies, or buy new plant and machinery.

Note that any reduction in share capital must be accompanied by an equivalent transfer into capital reserves (see below).

8.4.7 Redemption of shares

If a company has issued *redeemable* shares, the exact date of repayment is at the discretion of the company, within the earliest and latest dates stated at the time the shares were issued. The actual date will depend on the company's 'cost of capital', so that if the redeemable shares can be replaced at a lower cost to the company, the *earliest* redemption date will be chosen. If the replacement capital is more expensive, then the shares will be redeemed at the last possible date. If shares are redeemed without an equivalent amount of new shares being issued at the same time, a *capital redemption reserve* must be created to preserve the overall amount of the company's capital (see section 8.5.2).

8.4.8 Share consolidations

Poorly performing companies may have a very low share price which might act as a deterrent to potential investors, as even small price movements may lead to significant percentage changes. Also, some stock exchanges will not trade shares which fall below a specified level. To overcome this, companies can increase the nominal value per share by a process known as 'consolidation' (also known as a 'reverse split'). For example, a company with shares of 10p nominal value may have seen its share price fall to 6p. To boost the share price (though not the overall value of the company), it may change the nominal value to £1 each. Shareholders will then have only one-tenth of the number of shares following the consolidation, but each share will be valued at 60p. A share consolidation is often one part of a package of measures that struggling companies put forward to reverse their fortunes. Psychologically, a share price of 60p is a much better signal to potential investors than just 6p. See Figure 8.5.

Figure 8.5 Share consolidation (e.g. 4 x 25p shares consolidated into 1 x £1 nominal value share)

TVX Gold is a Canadian gold-mining company. It announced the following share consolidation on its website:

TVX announces that it will be seeking a special resolution from its shareholders approving a share consolidation on a one (1) new share for ten (10) old shares basis at its Annual and Special Meeting of shareholders to be held on May 16, 2002, in Toronto.

Currently, TVX has 357,223,530 common shares issued and outstanding. Upon approval of the proposed consolidation, the total number of outstanding shares will be reduced to approximately 35,722,350. The consolidation would enable TVX to maintain compliance with the NYSE's [New York Stock Exchange's] minimum trading price requirement of $1.00 per share, facilitate the Company's inclusion in the S&P/TSE [Standard & Poor's/Toronto Stock Exchange] Composite Index that is to replace the TSE 300 Index by year-end and have an indicative share price and amount of shares outstanding more in-line with its peer group. The Company's largest shareholder, which holds over 20 per cent of the outstanding common shares, has indicated its support for the proposed consolidation.

www.tvxgold.com/news

8.5 Reserves

The company's total net assets equals its share capital and reserves. Share capital, as we have seen, is the nominal value of the company's issued equity and non-equity shares. The reserves can be built up in a number of ways including:

- by the issue of shares at a price greater than their nominal value;
- by revaluing fixed assets at a value greater than that previously reported;
- by 'topping up' total capital and reserves following the redemption or buy-back of the company's own shares;
- by retaining profits within the company.

A common misconception is that reserves equal cash. In fact, the total of the share capital and reserves is represented by *all* the assets, less *all* the liabilities. Only a small part of the total net assets, if any, will be represented by cash or bank balances. A key difference between the various reserves is that usually only the closing balance on the profit and loss account is treated as *distributable*, i.e. available to be paid out as dividends. This is known as a *revenue* reserve. All the other reserves are *non-distributable*, so cannot be used to pay dividends. These are known as *capital* reserves. The combined total of share capital and capital reserves is sometimes referred to as the 'creditors' buffer' or the company's 'bedrock capital'. It is vitally important for those owed money by the company (e.g. creditors and lenders) that the capital contributed by the shareholders is not given back to them before the company's liabilities have been settled.

8.5.1 Capital reserves (1): share premium account

If a company sells its shares at a price in excess of the nominal value, it is charging a *share premium* (e.g. £2 for a share with a 25p nominal value results in a £1.75 share premium).

The share premium must be recorded separately from the nominal value, in a share premium account. As a non-distributable, capital reserve, it must not be repaid to shareholders except on the liquidation of the company or under special circumstances authorized by a court. However, it may be used for the purposes of a *bonus issue* (see above), as this would not dilute the combined total of share capital and capital reserves. For example, a company with £200,000 ordinary share capital and £600,000 in its share premium account might decide on a 3 for 1 bonus issue, with bonus shares being paid up from the share premium account. Following the bonus issue, the share premium account would no longer appear on the balance sheet, but the ordinary share capital will have increased to £800,000. The only effect is to 'tidy up' the balance sheet. The US equivalent of share premium is 'paid-in surplus'.

8.5.2 Capital reserves (2): capital redemption reserve

Due to the need to maintain a company's share capital and capital reserves, if shares have been redeemed or bought back it is necessary to 'top up' the total back to its original amount. This can be done by either issuing new replacement shares at the same time as the redemption or buy-back, or making a transfer from a distributable reserve (normally the profit and loss account) into a non-distributable reserve, called the *capital redemption reserve*. Like the share premium account, the capital redemption reserve can be used for a bonus issue.

8.5.3 Capital reserves (3): revaluation reserve

Many companies decide to revalue fixed assets at intervals to ensure that balance sheet values reflect material and permanent changes. Any increase arising on a revaluation is not available for the payment of dividends, which is a prudent policy considering that the mere fact of revaluing assets has no effect on the company's bank balances! Why then do companies revalue assets? Apart from the need to update balance sheet values, a company with significantly undervalued assets may become the target for a takeover bid, with the price offered being based on the historic values rather than current ones. Also, increased asset values may be useful when negotiating loans, as greater security values can be given to the lender. As with the other capital reserves, a revaluation reserve can be used for a bonus share issue. If the revaluation of fixed assets results in a *deficit* compared with previous values, the balance on the revaluation reserve is *negative* and must be deducted from the total of the other reserves.

Figure 8.6 shows the capital and reserves section of the balance sheet of Alvis plc, together with the relevant note to the accounts. Note how the capital redemption reserve has been created by a transfer from the profit and loss account.

(Extract from group balance sheet)		Group		Company	
Capital and reserves		**2002**	2001	**2002**	2001
Equity share capital	23	**27,265**	27,140	**27,265**	27,140
Non-equity share capital	23	**–**	31,462	**–**	31,462
Called up share capital	23	**27,265**	58,602	**27,265**	58,602
Share premium account	24	**1,164**	694	**1,164**	694
Capital redemption reserve	24	**37,014**	5,552	**37,014**	5,552
Profit and loss account	24	**(26,805)**	(1,128)	**70,163**	106,070
Shareholders' funds		**38,638**	63,720	**135,606**	170,918

23 Share capital

	31 December 2002 £000	31 December 2001 £000
Authorised:		
171,817,424 Ordinary shares of 25p each	**42,954**	42,954
Convertible Cumulative Non-Voting Redeemable Preference shares of £1 each	**–**	37,046
	42,954	80,000
Allotted, called up and fully paid:		
109,060,377 Ordinary shares of 25p each	**27,265**	27,140
Convertible Cumulative Non-Voting Redeemable Preference shares of £1 each	**–**	31,462
	27,265	58,602

The remaining Convertible Cumulative Non-Voting Redeemable Preference shares were redeemed at par on 24 April 2002 for a total cost of £31,462,000. An amount of £31,462,000 was transferred from the distributable reserves to the Capital Redemption Reserve as a result of this redemption and cancellation.

24 Reserves

	Share premium account £000	Capital redemption reserve £000	Profit and loss account £000	Total £000
Group				
At 31 December 2001	694	5,552	(1,128)	5,118
Other recognised gains and losses (exchange)	–	–	2,524	2,524
Premium on issue of new shares	470	–	–	470
Redemption and cancellation of £1 convertible preference shares	–	31,462	(31,462)	–
Profit retained in year	–	–	3,261	3,261
At 31 December 2002	1,164	37,014	(26,805)	11,373
Retained by:				
Company and subsidiaries	1,164	37,014	(26,862)	11,316
Joint ventures	–	–	57	57
	1,164	37,014	(26,805)	11,373

Figure 8.6 Alvis plc: share capital and reserves

Source: Alvis plc Annual Report 2002.

8.5.4 **Revenue reserves: profit and loss account**

This is usually the only 'distributable' reserve that a company has, and represents the maximum theoretical amount available with which a company can pay a dividend. In practice, only a small part of the accumulated profits will be declared as dividends as the directors must balance the return to shareholders with the company's need to reinvest and conserve its assets. One way in which directors can reduce the pressure from shareholders for ever-increasing dividends is to 'capitalize' part of the revenue reserves. This is achieved by making a bonus issue out of the retained profits, so that part of the distributable reserves is transformed into non-distributable share capital, and therefore taken permanently out of the reserves available for dividend payments.

Figure 8.7 shows the capital and reserves section of the balance sheet of Courts plc, together with the relevant note to the accounts. Note how the revaluation reserve changes when properties previously revalued are sold. Also, note how the value of *minority interests* (see p. 110) is shown as the final item on the balance sheet, after the subtotal of 'Shareholders' funds'.

(Extract from group balance sheet)

		Group		Parent	
	Note	2002 £000	2001 £000	2002 £000	2001 £000
Capital and reserves					
Called-up share capital		6,624	6,624	6,624	6,624
Share premium	19	149	149	149	149
Non-distributable capital reserve	19	7,734	8,379		
Capital redemption reserve	19	291	291	291	291
Revaluation reserve	19	37,075	37,843	9,022	9,194
Profit and loss account	19	139,129	153,447	45,847	54,294
		184,378	200,109	55,309	63,298
Shareholders' funds (including non-equity interests)		191,002	206,733	61,933	70,552
Equity minority interests		87,780	91,325		
Capital employed		**278,782**	**298,058**	**61,933**	**70,552**

19. RESERVES

	Share premium £'000	Non-distributable capital £'000	Capital redemption £'000	Revaluation £'000	Profit and loss £'000	Total £'000
Group						
At 1 April 2001 as previously stated	149	8,379	291	37,843	159,060	205,722
Prior year adjustment (see Accounting Policies)					(5,613)	(5,613)

Figure 8.7 (Continued overleaf)

19. RESERVES

	Share premium £'000	Non-distributable capital £'000	Capital redemption £'000	Revaluation £'000	Profit and loss £'000	Total £'000
At 1 April 2001 as restated	149	8,379	291	37,843	153,447	200,109
Retained loss for the year					(12,995)	(12,995)
Currency translation		(645)		(468)	(1,623)	(2,736)
Prior year property revaluation surplus now realised				(300)	300	
At 31 March 2002	149	7,734	291	37,075	139,129	184,378
Parent At 1 April 2001	149		291	9,194	54,294	63,928
Retained loss for the year					(8,500)	(8,500)
Currency translation					(119)	(119)
Prior year property revaluation surplus now realised				(172)	172	
At 31 March 2002	149		291	9,022	45,847	55,309

Goodwill which arose on acquisitions prior to 1990, and which was previously written off against the profit and loss reserve, has not been quantified as the information is unavailable. As permitted by s.230 Companies Act 1985 a separate profit and loss account for the Parent Company has not been included in these financial statements. The Parent Company's loss for the financial year was £5.1 million (2001: £1.1 million).

Figure 8.7 Courts plc: capital and reserves

8.6 Chapter summary

- Called-up share capital is the nominal value of all shares, equity and non-equity.
- Public companies can sell shares directly by an offer for sale, or indirectly through a placing.
- Non-equity shares might be redeemable or convertible into equity shares.
- The value of share capital might be increased by new share issues, rights issues, and stock conversions.
- The number of shares might also be increased by bonus issues and share splits.
- The value of share capital might be decreased by buy-backs or redemptions.
- The number of shares might also be decreased by share consolidations.
- Companies might give stock options as an incentive to directors and employees.
- Reserves might be non-distributable (capital reserves) or distributable (revenue reserves).
- Reserves can be reduced or eliminated by being used for bonus issues.

■ GLOSSARY

Articles of Association	Part of a company's own regulations, setting out rules for the running of the company's internal affairs. See also *Memorandum of Association*
authorized share capital	The maximum number of shares that the company is allowed to issue
bonus issue	Free shares given to existing shareholders
buy-backs	The purchase by a company of its own shares, either for cancellation or to meet the anticipated requirements of stock option schemes
called-up share capital	A company's issued share capital
calls	Instalments of a share price payable by investors following an offer for sale
capital redemption reserve	The reserve which must be created when share capital is reduced due to redemptions, or cancellations following a buy-back
capital reserves	Non-distributable reserves, e.g. share premium account, capital redemption reserve, revaluation reserve
convertible	Non-equity shares which can be converted to equity shares at future determined dates
cumulative	If dividends on non-equity shares are unpaid in one year, the missed dividends are accumulated for payment out of any future years' profits
distributable	Available for the payment of dividends
equity shares	Vote-carrying ordinary shares
exercise price	The price at which shares can be purchased under a stock option scheme
fixed dividends	Dividends of a set percentage payable to non-equity shareholders
Initial Public Offering	The first public offer of shares for sale made by a public limited company
in the money	When the exercise price of a stock option is less than the current market price
IPO	See Initial Public Offering
issued share capital	The total share capital issued to shareholders at any time, also known as 'called-up' share capital
Memorandum of Association	Part of the official rules that govern a company, including its name and objects. See also *Articles of Association*
nominal value	The face value of a share, usually set at the time of the company's formation
non-distributable	Not available for the payment of dividends
non-equity shares	Shares without voting rights

offer for sale	An offer of shares for sale made by a public limited company
out of the money	When the exercise price of a stock option is greater than the current market price
oversubscription	This occurs when potential investors have applied for more shares than are available in an offer for sale
par value	Another term for nominal value
placing	Shares sold by a company to a financial institution which then 'places' them with its own clients
preference shares	Non-equity shares carrying a preferential right to a fixed dividend and greater protection for repayment of capital in the event of liquidation
profit and loss account	Distributable revenue reserves, representing retained, realized, profits
prospectus	Detailed information given by a public company when offering shares for sale, so that potential investors have enough detail about the business to make a decision as to whether or not to buy the shares
redeemable	Shares which are repayable by the company at future determined dates
revaluation reserve	A non-distributable reserve created when fixed assets are revalued at values greater than their existing value. A *negative* revaluation reserve might arise if the assets are revalued at less than their existing value
revenue reserves	Distributable reserves, usually represented by the closing balance on the profit and loss account
reverse split	See *share consolidations*
rights issue	The right given to existing shareholders to buy more shares
share consolidations	An increase in a share's nominal value, leading to a corresponding increase in the market value
share premium	If a company sells its shares at a price greater than its nominal value, the excess is known as a share premium, and must be placed in a share premium account
share splits	The division of nominal value into smaller denominations
stock options	The right of directors and employees to buy shares in their company at a specified price within a set time period
tender issue	A company invites potential shareholders to state the price at which they are prepared to buy the shares for sale
treasury shares	A company's own shares which it has purchased in a 'buy-back' (US: Treasury stock)
undersubscription	This occurs when potential investors have applied for fewer shares than are available in an offer for sale
underwriting	An agreement by an underwriter to buy any shares left unsold following an offer for sale by a public company

■ **MULTIPLE CHOICE QUESTIONS**

1. An Initial Public Offering (IPO) is:

   a   The right given to existing shareholders to buy more shares
   b   The placing of shares by a financial institution with its own clients
   c   An offer to sell shares to the public for the first time
   d   A free issue of shares given to existing shareholders

2. If an offer for sale is undersubscribed, the likely effect following the offer will be:

   a   To increase the market price
   b   To decrease the market price
   c   To have a neutral effect on the market price
   d   The company must cancel the offer for sale

3. The nominal value of a share is the same as:

   a   Its stock market value
   b   Its book value
   c   Its asset value
   d   Its par value

4. If a company has issued £1m of 3 per cent non-cumulative preference shares 2010, which one of the following statements relating to those shares is correct?

   a   The shares will definitely be paid a 3 per cent dividend every year until 2010
   b   The shares will definitely not be paid a 3 per cent dividend every year until 2010
   c   The shares will definitely be redeemed before 2010
   d   If the company cannot afford to pay a dividend in a specific year, the shareholders will never be paid that dividend

5. If a new company has issued 200,000 ordinary shares of 20p nominal value at a price of £2, what will be the entries in the share capital and share premium accounts?

   a   Share capital £40,000, share premium £360,000
   b   Share capital £40,000, share premium £400,000
   c   Share capital £400,000, share premium £360,000
   d   Share capital £360,000, share premium £40,000

6. If a '5 for 3' rights issue is made at £1.90 per share, how much would a shareholder who owns 15,000 shares pay to the company to buy all the shares he or she is entitled to?

   a   £17,100
   b   £47,500
   c   £5,700
   d   £28,500

7. If a '2 for 3' bonus issue is made to a shareholder who originally paid £2 per share for 9,000 shares, how much would the shareholder pay for the bonus shares, if the current market value is £4 per share?

   a £72,000

   b £24,000

   c Nothing, as the shares are free

   d £12,000

8. A director has been granted stock options, giving the right to buy 50,000 shares at 80p each. The current market value is 60p per share, and the nominal value is 50p per share. If the director takes up the option to buy and then immediately resells the shares on the stock market, what profit or loss is likely to be made by the director?

   a £15,000 profit

   b £10,000 loss

   c £15,000 loss

   d £10,000 profit

9. A company's stock market price has plummeted from a high of £3 to its current value of 30p. The nominal value is 25p per share. Which one of the following techniques could be used to make an immediate boost to the company's share price?

   a A '5 for 1' share split, with the nominal value becoming 5p

   b A '10 for 1' bonus issue

   c A '1 for 4' share consolidation, with the nominal value becoming £1

   d A new share issue at a 10 per cent discount to the market price

10. A company redeems £5m preference shares, but does not make another share issue at the time of the redemption. What is the name of the reserve that must be created following the redemption?

   a Capital redemption reserve

   b Share premium account

   c Revaluation reserve

   d Profit and loss account

(*Note: answers are shown in Appendix 2.*)

■ **DISCUSSION QUESTIONS**

Over a company's life, directors have considerable flexibility over the way in which they 'engineer' the capital requirements of their companies. They might choose long-term or short-term funding, equity or non-equity shares, borrowings through debentures, or convertible securities that will eventually become part of equity.

To what extent do you agree that directors have the flexibility suggested in this comment? What constraints might exist when deciding on alternative capital-raising approaches?

(*Note: Suggested answers or discussion points are available on the companion website.*)

■ LONGER QUESTIONS

(Questions marked W have suggested answers on the companion website. Other questions are answered in Appendix 3.)

1. The share capital and reserves section of Pasteboard plc's balance sheet as at 31 December 2003 was as follows:

	£000
Called-up share capital (5p shares)	240
Share premium account	200
Profit and loss account	760
	1200

In view of the large balance in the profit and loss account, and in response to shareholder pressure, the company's chairman wants to make changes to the share capital and reserves, and has made the following *alternative* suggestions:

1. Pay a dividend of £200,000 by using the balance within the share premium account.

2. Repay all the share capital to the shareholders.

3. Use the profit and loss account balance to issue bonus shares on a 2 for 1 basis.

4. Use the profit and loss account balance to pay a dividend of £200,000.

a   Explain the extent to which each of the four alternatives is legally acceptable.

b   What are the relative advantages from the *shareholders'* viewpoint of alternatives (3) and (4)?

c   What are the relative advantages from the *company's* viewpoint of alternatives (3) and (4)?

d   Assume that the company has decided to implement alternative (3) on 5 January 2004 and then, on 12 January 2004, it implements alternative (4). Redraft the balance sheet extract as it would appear on *each* of these two dates. Assume that there were no other changes to share capital or reserves in the period.

2. After the draft trading and profit and loss accounts had been drawn up for Pitchford plc for the year ended 31 May 2004, the following balances remained in the accounts:

	Dr £000	Cr £000
Ordinary share capital (£1 shares)		40,000
3% redeemable £1 preference shares 2004–7		16,000
Bank balance	26,200	
Debtors and creditors	52,300	41,260
Tangible fixed assets	106,240	
Intangible fixed assets: goodwill	32,000	
Profit and loss account		105,300
Share premium account		35,000
Closing stock of goods	20,820	
	237,560	237,560

The directors took the following actions, in sequence, immediately after the above trial balance was extracted:

1. The existing £1 ordinary shares were split into shares with a nominal value of 25p.

2. A bonus share issue was made (based on the 'split' share capital), utilizing the £35m balance of the share premium account.

3. A rights issue was made, with shareholders able and willing to buy 100m ordinary shares of 25p each at a premium of 60p per share.

4. The 3 per cent redeemable £1 preference shares were redeemed at nominal (par) value.

5. A dividend of 5p per share was paid on all ordinary shares of 25p each, including those issued by way of bonus and by the rights issue

a Show the company's balance sheet after all the directors' decisions had been implemented.

b Explain why the directors might have decided to split the nominal value from £1 each to 25p each.

c Explain why it is so important to protect the share capital and capital reserves of a limited company

3. Parvenu plc showed the following notes to its balance sheet at 31 May 2004:

1. *Relating to share capital:*

	£m
Ordinary shares of £1 each, fully paid	520
4 per cent non-cumulative redeemable preference shares, 2005–9	50

2. *Relating to 'creditors due for payment after more than one year':*

	£m
3 per cent convertible debentures 2009–15	100

a Explain the following terms:

   (i) non-cumulative;

   (ii) redeemable;

   (iii) preference;

   (iv) convertible.

   and explain the significance of :

   (v) '2005–9' in the title of the debentures.

b Assume that Parvenu plc wanted to redeem its preference shares, but did not want to replace them with any other form of share capital. What reserve would the company have to create at the same time as the redemption, and why?

c When assessing a company's *taxable* profit, there is a major difference between the treatment of debenture interest and the treatment of dividends. What is that difference, and what is the reason for it?

4W. Many companies decide to *buy back* their own shares. Explain the advantages to a company of buying its own shares, and why such a policy might be open to criticism.

5W. The directors of Dora plc are concerned that the company's accountant may not have followed usual accounting procedures when producing the 'Reserves' figure for the company's balance sheet as at 31 October 2004.

The following is a summary of the company's reserves. The opening balance appeared in the company's audited balance sheet as at 31 October 2003, and can be assumed to be correct.

		£m
1 November 2003	Opening balance	220
1 April 2004	Bonus issue (note i)	60
1 July 2004	Rights issue (note ii)	100
1 October 2004	Dividend (note iii)	10
31 October 2004	Profit (note iv)	(240)
31 October 2004	Closing balance (note v)	150

Notes:

  (i)   The company made a bonus issue of 240m ordinary shares of 25p each, by utilizing existing reserves.

 (ii)   Shareholders had paid for a rights issue of 400 million ordinary shares, at nominal value.

(iii)   The company proposed a final dividend of £10m.

 (iv)   This represents the company's retained profit for the year.

  (v)   The closing balance is shown as a Fixed Asset on the balance sheet as at 31 October 2004.

Explain in detail the correct treatment for each of the adjustments made to the opening reserve balance shown above.

6W.

  a   Explain how a *capital reserve* differs from a *revenue reserve*.

  b   The summarized balance sheet of Clark plc as at 31 December 2003, before any provision had been made for a final dividend, was as follows:

	£000
Total net assets	670
Called-up share capital (25p nominal value)	200
Share premium account	120
Capital redemption reserve	80
Asset revaluation reserve	70
Profit and loss account	200
	670

The managing director of the company, Graham Donaldson, is under pressure from shareholders to pay large dividends each year. Graham has received a letter from a major shareholder, Sheila Tang, who says that the final dividend should be 30p per share compared with last year's final dividend of 15p per share. During 2003 an interim dividend had been paid of 5p per share (compared with 3p in 2002). The company made a bonus share issue on 1 January 2003 that doubled the share capital. No other changes to share capital occurred between 1 January 2003 and 31 December 2003.

(i) Calculate the interim dividends actually paid in 2002 and 2003, and the final dividend proposed in 2002.

(ii) Draft a reply from Graham Donaldson to Sheila Tang's suggestion that the final dividend for 2003 should be 30p per share.

(iii) Calculate the maximum possible final dividend (pence per share) for 2003 that could be paid by Clark plc, assuming that the company was to retain £50,000 in its revenue reserves.

■ MINI CASE STUDY

MinnieMax Ltd. considers a bonus issue

MinnieMax Ltd. (see previous mini case studies) was putting the finishing touches to its balance sheet at the end of its first financial year, 30 September 2004. The only part of the balance sheet to complete was the 'Share Capital and Reserves' section. When the company was formed, it had an authorized and issued share capital of £60,000, split into shares with a nominal value of 50p each. The shares were issued at a premium of 10p per share. The closing balance of retained earnings was £82,000.

a Prepare the 'Share Capital and Reserves' section of MinnieMax Ltd.'s balance sheet as at 30 September 2004.

b After a successful first year's trading, the directors of MinnieMax Ltd. feel that they should be rewarded for their efforts. Minnie suggests to Maxim that they would benefit financially if the balance remaining on the company's profit and loss account was used to issue *bonus shares*. Write a concise report to the directors explaining the nature of a bonus issue and the circumstances when it might be appropriate.

(*Suggested solutions can be found in Appendix 4.*)

■ MAXI CASE STUDY

Majestic Wine plc

Figure 8.8 is an extract from the annual report of Majestic Wine plc, and shows details of the company's share capital and share options.

a Explain each of the items (1–7) indicated.

b The company's share price at the time of writing is 690p. If the share price remains unchanged, what proportion of the share options is likely to be taken up by the holders?

(*Suggested answers and discussion areas are available on the companion website.*)

14 SHARE CAPITAL

	2003		2002	
	Number	Value £000	Number	Value £000
Authorized				
Ordinary Shares 30p each	35,000,000	10,500	35,000,000	10,500
Issued				
Ordinary Shares of 30p each	15,289,843	4,587	15,043,639	4,513

During the year, 101, 000 Ordinary Shares of 30p each were alloted for a consideration of £314,000. The Shares were allotted to satisfy the exercise of options. The Company issued 100,000 Shares to the trustees of the Company's QUEST to fulfil obligations under the Company's SAYE scheme for a consideration of £450,000 funded by the group. In addition 45,214 shares were issued to the trustees of the Company's employee share ownership trust to fulfil the requirements of the Deferred Bonus Scheme.

17 SHARE OPTIONS

The following options are outstanding for Ordinary Shares

Number of Shares	Period in which exercisable		Price per share
8,000	15 December 1997	15 December 2004	£0.75
1,000	01 November 1999	30 October 2006	£1.60
41,110	22 December 2001	21 December 2005	£3.075
17,890	22 December 2001	22 December 2008	£3.075
94,780	27 November 2003	26 November 2007	£2.425
402,220	27 November 2003	26 November 2010	£2.425
85,885	01 February 2004	31 July 2004	£1.94
1,370	01 February 2004	31 July 2004	£2.46
62,000	06 July 2004	05 July 2011	£3.05
1,020	26 November 2004	25 November 2008	£3.59
38,480	26 November 2004	26 November 2011	£3.59
12,872	01 February 2006	31 July 2006	£1.94
112,675	09 July 2005	09 July 2012	£4.58
115,325	09 July 2005	08 July 2009	£4.58
55,412	26 July 2005	26 January 2006	£3.66
7,359	26 July 2007	26 January 2008	£3.66
70,925	22 November 2005	22 November 2012	£4.80
17,575	22 November 2005	21 November 2009	£4.80

The interests of the Directors in the above options are disclosed in the Directors' Report.

Figure 8.8 Majestic Wine plc: share capital and share options

■ WEB LINKS

Company websites
(Companies referred to in this chapter)

Alvis plc www.alvis.plc.uk/

Amrice Inc www.amrice.com

Aviva plc www.aviva.com/

Barclays Bank plc www.barclays.com/

Court's plc www.courtsretail.com/

Domino's Pizza www.dominos.co.uk

Majestic Wine plc www.majestic.co.uk

Pendragon plc www.pendragonplc.com

William Hill plc www.willhill.com

A company's memorandum and articles of association can be seen at:
www.organic-countryside.co.uk/memorandum_articles.html

■ FURTHER READING

Elliott, B., and Elliott, J. (2003). *Financial Accounting and Reporting*, 8th edn. (Harlow: FT/Prentice Hall), chapter 9.

Weetman, P. (2003). *Financial and Management Accounting: An Introduction*, 3rd edn. (Harlow: FT/Prentice Hall), chapter 12.

■ COMPANION WEBSITE MATERIALS

 Additional materials are available for students and lecturers on the companion website, at **www.oup.com/uk/booksites/busecon/business/**

9

The cash flow statement

OBJECTIVES

By the end of this chapter you will be able to:

- Understand the relative importance of cash and profit.
- Evaluate the various headings typically found within a cash flow statement.
- Construct a simple cash flow statement based on past transactions.
- Appraise and assess the information contained within a cash flow statement.

9.1 Introduction

Cash is the lifeblood of a business. If it dwindles the business will die. But it is also a very difficult figure to fiddle.

This is how Professor Sir David Tweedie, then chairman of the UK's Accounting Standards Board introduced the first UK Financial Reporting Standard.[1] In our study of accounting so far, cash (by which we mean a business's cash in hand plus its bank balances, less any bank overdrafts) has perhaps taken a back seat when compared to profits. After all, accounting concepts require us to adjust 'cash' so that debtors, creditors, accruals, prepayments, unsold stock and provisions are taken into account when preparing the profit and loss account. Even within the balance sheet, cash and bank balances are just two items appearing within the list of current assets, with no special prominence.

If cash really is the 'lifeblood of the business', it is logical to give this asset a statement of its own, which is why a cash *flow statement* is prepared, giving a summary of the cash inflows and outflows over the financial period. One of the many enigmas of accounting is that it is quite possible for profitable businesses to fail through poor cash management. After all, a creditor owed £50,000 is not going to be impressed by being told that, although the business made a *profit* of £1m, the bank overdraft limit has been reached and no further cheques can be paid out! If a business has sufficient cash to draw upon to meet its liabilities as they fall due it is said to have good *liquidity*. It can also be referred to as being *solvent*. This would also apply if it could quickly change assets into cash if the need arose. Such 'liquid' assets would include investments such as shares which could be sold on a stock market, and

[1] FRS 1 *Cash Flow Statements* (Accounting Standards Board, London, 1991).

bank deposit accounts where relatively short notice could be given to gain access to the money. Surprisingly enough, it is also possible for a business to be *too liquid*: if it has excessive cash then it is not reinvesting it. Rather than hoarding cash it should be buying new fixed assets, taking over other businesses, or using the cash to fund research and development projects. In this way the business can expand and become more profitable. The ideal business is profitable and liquid, and in Chapter 12 we shall look at ways of analysing both these aspects of a company's performance.

The comment that cash is a 'very difficult figure to fiddle' relates to the widely held (though inaccurate) perception that, whilst the existence (or non-existence) of cash and bank balances can be proved with certainty, 'profit' can be adjusted up or down ('fiddled') in accordance with a business's requirements, unrelated to the underlying financial transactions. In fact, the vast majority of information contained within the financial summaries is based on objective, verifiable data. However, there is scope for subjectivity as well, for example in such areas as the amount of depreciation to be charged, how stock should be valued, and whether a provision for doubtful debts is needed. The publication of accounting standards has narrowed considerably the areas of individuality available to accountants and their scope for 'creative accounting'. Remember also that many limited companies must appoint independent auditors who report on whether or not the accounts show a 'true and fair view' of the business.

As in previous chapters, the relevant part of Domino's Pizza's annual report is used as our starting point (see Figure 9.1, which is cross-referenced to chapter headings), though, as before, we shall refer to other companies where needed to illustrate the full range of information which might be disclosed.

9.2 The format of the statement

All public limited companies have to present a cash flow statement as part of their published annual report, and it is regarded as a 'primary statement' of equal importance to the profit and loss account and balance sheet. Just as there is a set way of presenting the profit and loss account and balance sheet, there is a format to follow for the cash flow statement. Although the statement is nothing more than a summary of cash and bank transactions over the financial period, the information is made more meaningful by grouping the transactions into key headings. If we look at the headings in Figure 9.1, we can summarize Domino's Pizza's statement as follows (cash outflows are shown in brackets):

	2002	2001
	£000s	£000s
Net cash inflow from operating activities	5,128	4,475
Returns on investments and servicing of finance	(302)	(237)
Taxation	(950)	(617)
Capital expenditure and financial investment	(3,394)	(3,149)
Acquisitions and disposals	(484)	(160)
Equity dividends paid	(777)	(501)
Financing	1,433	2,422
Increase in cash	654	2,233

9.2 ──── Group Statement of Cash Flows

at 29 December 2002

	Notes	2002 £000	2001 £000
9.3 ─── **NET CASH INFLOW FROM OPERATING ACTIVITIES**	23(a)	5,128	4,475
9.4 ─── **RETURNS ON INVESTMENTS AND SERVICING OF FINANCE**			
Interest received		50	78
Interest paid		(343)	(304)
Interest element of finance lease payments		(9)	(11)
		(302)	(237)
9.5 ─── **TAXATION**			
Corporation tax paid		(950)	(617)
9.6 ─── **CAPITAL EXPENDITURE AND FINANCIAL INVESTMENT**			
Payments to acquire intangible fixed assets		(214)	(68)
Payments to acquire tangible fixed assets		(3,291)	(2,560)
Receipts from sales of tangible and intangible fixed assets		411	5
Receipts from repayment of joint venture loan		46	36
Payments to acquire finance lease assets and advance of franchisee loans		(1,247)	(1,007)
Receipts from repayment of finance leases and franchisee loans		901	445
		(3,394)	(3,149)
9.7 ─── **ACQUISITIONS AND DISPOSALS**			
Purchase of subsidiary undertaking and un-associated businesses		(484)	(160)
		(484)	(160)
9.8 ─── **EQUITY DIVIDENDS PAID**		(777)	(501)
9.9 ─── **NET CASH OUTFLOW BEFORE FINANCING**		(779)	(189)
9.10 ─── **FINANCING**			
Issue of ordinary share capital		231	164
New long-term loans		2,719	2,660
Repayments of long-term loans		(1,443)	(330)
Repayment of capital element of finance leases and hire purchase contracts		(74)	(72)
		1,433	2,422
9.11 ─── **INCREASE IN CASH**	23(c)	654	2,233

Figure 9.1 Domino's Pizza Group: cash flow statement (cross-referenced to chapter headings)

The information for 2002 can be explained, in brief, as follows:

	£000s	Explanation
Net cash inflow from operating activities	5,128	The company generated £5,128,000 from its trading operations
Returns on investments and servicing of finance	(302)	From this, net interest of £302,000 was paid on loans or charged on finance leases
Taxation	(950)	Tax was also paid during the year, amounting to £950,000
Capital expenditure and financial investment	(3,394)	Fixed assets were bought for £3,394,000 (after deducting any sale proceeds) during the year
Acquisitions and disposals	(484)	The company paid £484,000 to buy other businesses during the year
Equity dividends paid	(777)	The company paid £777,000 in dividends on its ordinary 'equity' shares during the year
Financing	1,433	The cash raised by selling shares and receiving loans exceeded the cash used to repay loans and to pay the capital element of leases by £1,433,000
Increase in cash	654	The company had an overall cash surplus of £654,000 cash in the year

The figures within the statement are arrived at by effectively stripping out all the accounting adjustments made when preparing the profit and loss account and balance sheet. By simply concentrating on cash inflows and outflows, an objective view can be taken of the overall cash surplus or deficit arising from *all* the business's transactions, regardless of whether they relate to income, expenditure, assets, liabilities, or capital. The accounting equation is irrelevant, as we are only recording one aspect of the business's transactions—cash—rather than following full double-entry principles.

Although we look in detail in Chapter 12 at the analysis of the statement, if a company has successive cash flow deficits (net outflows), this may show one of two circumstances:

- The company is expanding into new products and ventures which will (hopefully) result in increased cash inflows in future years; or

- The company is spending more than it has available and might run into financial difficulties unless cash inflows improve in the future.

In the case of Domino's Pizza, the major cash outflows in both 2002 and 2001 were connected to the purchase of fixed assets, which implies that the company is expanding, but 'within its means' as it had an overall net cash inflow in both years.

 Look at the cash flow information provided by the Colgate-Palmolive Company at **http://investor.colgatepalmolive.com/annual.cfm**
Click on 'Financial Information' then download or view the latest Annual Report—the 'dynamic' version is quicker to navigate. Look particularly at the cash outflows on 'purchase of common stock' (purchasing the company's own shares) and refer back to Chapter 8 for the reasons why companies buy back their own shares. Although the format is slightly different from the UK version shown in Domino's Pizza's statement, all the key elements are present.

9.3 Net cash inflow or outflow from operating activities

Operating activities are those that generate the net income shown within the profit and loss account and will include the trading of goods and supply of services, as well as any profits and losses arising from the sales of fixed assets. Within the profit and loss account, profits or losses arising from operating activities are shown before interest payable and receivable, and both before and after any taxation provision.

 Look at Domino's Pizza's profit and loss account on p. 320 and remind yourself of the various profit figures shown.

The starting figure on the cash flow statement (Figure 9.1) is *net cash inflow from operating activities*. This is calculated by taking the operating profit as shown in the profit and loss account and then stripping out the various adjustments which were required to comply with the accruals concept (see Chapter 3) to get back to the cash flow information. First, any depreciation and amortization charges must be added back to the operating profit figure. This is because they do not have any effect on the cash flow, they are just 'book' entries not requiring cash payments. Secondly, any other non-cash items (e.g. provisions for doubtful debts, profits or losses on the sale of fixed assets), must also be adjusted, and finally the effect of changes during the year in the levels of stocks, debtors, and creditors must also be considered.

Note 23a to Domino's Pizza's cash flow statement gives the following explanation of how the net cash inflow from operating activities for 2002 is derived:

	£000
Operating profits	4,504
Depreciation charge	1,127
Amortization charges	228
Other operating expenditure	75
(Increase) in stocks	(151)
(Increase) in debtors	(1,047)
Increase in creditors	392
Net cash inflow from operating activities	5,128

Note that the *cash inflow* from operating activities is over £500,000 more than the *profit* derived from those activities.

The adjustments to be made for stocks, debtors, and creditors depend upon whether the closing totals were greater or smaller than their opening equivalents:

- *Stock*. If a company has more unsold stock at the end of the year than the start, there is an overall *decrease* in cash flow as more cash has been tied up in unsold stock. Conversely, a higher opening stock figure results in an increase in cash flow as less cash is tied up in stock by the closing balance sheet date.

> Closing stock > Opening stock = Decrease in cash flow
> Opening stock > Closing stock = Increase in cash flow

In the case of Domino's Pizza, their closing stock was greater by £151,000 than its opening stock, so that figure was deducted from profit when calculating the cash flow equivalent.

- *Debtors*. This works in exactly the same way as stock, more debtors at the end of the year means that comparatively fewer customers have paid their bills compared with a year earlier, hence a negative effect on cash flow.

> Closing debtors > Opening debtors = Decrease in cash flow
> Opening debtors > Closing debtors = Increase in cash flow

In the case of Domino's Pizza, their closing debtors were greater by £1,047,000 than their opening debtors, so that figure was deducted from profit when calculating the cash flow equivalent.

- *Creditors*. These are adjusted in the opposite way to the debtors' figures, as more creditors at the end of the year means that the company has held on to its cash rather than paying its bills, which is of course a positive factor when considering cash flow!

> Closing creditors > Opening creditors = Increase in cash flow
> Opening creditors > Closing creditors = Decrease in cash flow

In the case of Domino's Pizza, their closing creditors were greater by £392,000 than their opening creditors, so that figure was added to profit when calculating the cash flow equivalent.

9.4 Returns on investments and servicing of finance

This heading refers to the cash inflows from interest received (the 'return' on investments) during the financial period and cash outflows relating to interest paid (the 'servicing' of borrowed money). Other items to be included are:

- The interest element of payments under finance lease contracts.
- Dividends paid on preference shares.
- Dividends paid by subsidiary companies to minority shareholders.
- Dividends received from associated companies.

Dividends paid to the holders of ordinary (equity) shares are shown in a separate heading—see section 9.8 below.

> Domino's Pizza's cash flow statement shows seven times as much interest paid as received. Notes 17 and 19 (see pp. 335 and 337) show total loan creditors outstanding of over £10 million at the balance sheet date, and cash and loan assets of £4.8m at that date. The 'returns on investments and servicing of finance' heading indicates the adverse effect that the net debt has on the company's cash flows.

9.5 Taxation

This represents the corporate taxation actually paid in the financial period, not the tax *provided* on the profits for the current year. In Chapter 7, when we were looking at the taxation liability in the balance sheet, we used the cash outflow figure as shown in the cash flow statement to reconcile the balance sheet amount with the profit and loss account provision. Look back at p. 155 to see how this reconciliation works.

9.6 Capital expenditure and financial investment

This heading shows cash flows related to acquisitions and disposals of any fixed assets (i.e. capital expenditure) other than those relating to the purchase or sale of a trade or business, which are shown separately under the heading 'Acquisitions and disposals' (see section 9.7 below). 'Financial investment' includes cash inflows arising from the repayment of loans made to other companies and cash outflows due to loans made by the company itself.

> This heading represents Domino's Pizza's largest net cash outflow, with over £3.5m being spent on acquiring both intangible and tangible fixed assets during the period. A further £1.2m cash outflow is shown, which includes loans advanced to franchisees to help finance the lump sum payments required when the franchise is granted. Cash inflows within this heading include the proceeds (£411,000) from selling fixed assets and £901,000 which includes franchisee loan repayments.

9.7 Acquisitions and disposals

If a company buys or sells another business or part of a business, related cash flows will appear under this heading. For example, if a parent company sells its shares in a subsidiary, any cash inflow arising will be shown here. Similarly, if there has been a cash outflow relating to the acquisition of investments in associated companies or joint ventures, it will appear under this heading.

9.8 Equity dividends paid

This represents the equity dividends actually *paid* in the financial period, not the dividends *provided* on the profits for the current year. In Chapter 7, when we were looking at the dividend liability in the balance sheet, we used the cash outflow figure as shown in the cash flow statement to reconcile the balance sheet amount with the profit and loss account provision. Look back at p. 157 to see how we reconciled the figures. The cash outflow for a financial period usually represents the previous year's final dividend plus the current year's interim dividend.

9.9 Net cash inflow or outflow before financing

This subtotal summarizes all the cash flows of the company before taking into account the effect of any changes to share capital, long-term loans, and other variations in the financing of the company. It is useful as it shows the overall cash flow—positive or negative—for the financial period, but without the often major effects of share sales and loans received and repaid. Companies that have continuing material cash outflows before financing over several years may be:

- In a start-up situation which requires substantial early investment.
- Expanding vigorously by investing in fixed assets or acquiring other businesses, in the hope that this investment will pay off in future years.
- Paying excessive dividends.
- Highly geared, where the cash outflows required to service borrowed finance are greater than the cash inflows generated by the extra finance.
- In a poor trading cycle which might rectify itself in future years or may lead the company into liquidation.

> Domino's Pizza's cash flow statement shows that the company had a net cash *outflow* before financing in both years, with the current year nearly four times greater than the previous year. However, the company's financing cash inflows resulted in an overall *increase* in cash for each year. Net cash outflows are not automatically a cause for alarm as they often signify an ambitious and expanding company prepared to invest heavily in new fixed assets and acquire new businesses.

9.10 Financing

Financing cash flows are receipts or repayments from or to providers of finance. The cash *inflows* under this heading include receipts from issuing:

- shares;
- debentures;
- loans;
- bonds;
- other long- and short-term borrowings (other than overdrafts).

The financing cash *outflows* include:

- repayments of amounts borrowed (other than overdrafts);
- the capital element of finance lease rental payments;
- payments to buy back or redeem the company's own shares.

Note that changes to share capital that do *not* involve cash flows, such as bonus issues or share splits (see Chapter 8) are irrelevant to the statement. Some cash flow statements show an additional heading, *Managing liquid resources*, which analyses the changes in short-term investments (such as stock market investments or bank deposits held as current assets), whereas the 'financing' heading concentrates on long-term items.

Domino's Pizza's cash flow statement shows a net financing inflow in each year, with the main funds coming from the issuing of new loans, less loan repayments. Proceeds from share issues related to share options that were exercised during the period (see Chapter 8).

9.11 Increase or decrease in cash

The final figure in the statement, it shows the overall change in the company's cash balances. Some cash flow statements may also show changes in 'cash equivalents', which are short-term, highly liquid investments that are readily convertible into known amounts of cash and which are subject to insignificant risk of changes in value. Also, the statement as a whole might be divided into the three headings 'Operating Activities', 'Investing Activities', and 'Financing Activities', but the detailed contents within these headings are identical to those explained within this chapter.

Look again at the Colgate-Palmolive cash flow statement (see p. 210) to see how this (US) company's statement is divided between 'Operating Activities', 'Investing Activities', and 'Financing Activities'. Also, note the reference to 'cash equivalents'.

A further reconciliation is often given in notes to the accounts, which analyse the movements in the 'net debt' of the company during the financial period. A second reconciliation is also provided showing how the net cash flow relates to the movement in net debt. If a group has bought or sold a subsidiary during the period, a note to the cash flow statement should show a summary of the effects of acquisitions and disposals, indicating how much of the consideration comprised cash. Where the sale or purchase of a subsidiary has a material effect on the amount reported, a note should be given showing these effects as far as practicable.

Look at nn. 23 (*b*), (*c*) and (*d*) on p. 339 to see how Domino's Pizza showed this additional information.

9.12 Preparing a cash flow statement

Now that we have looked in some detail at the contents of the cash flow statement, we can consider the practical aspects of preparing a fairly simple statement. The example that follows gives a step-by-step approach and starts with the basic information of a company's profit and loss account and balance sheet.

9.12.1 Worked example

The summarized profit and loss accounts of Mayfly plc for the two years ended 31 May 2004 are as follows:

	2004	2003
	£000	£000
Gross profit	153,340	132,200
Less operating costs	(105,640)	(94,900)
	47,700	37,300
Profit/(loss) on sale of fixed assets	(1,400)	2,800
Operating profit before interest and taxation	46,300	40,100
Less interest payable	(10,000)	(10,000)
Profit on ordinary activities before taxation	36,300	30,100
Less taxation	(14,000)	(13,000)
Profit for the financial year	22,300	17,100
Less dividends, paid and proposed	(20,000)	(11,500)
Profit retained for the financial year	2,300	5,600
Retained profit brought forward	8,500	2,900
Retained profit carried forward	10,800	8,500

Balance sheets of Mayfly plc as at 31 May 2004 and 2003 are shown below:

	2004			2003		
	£000	£000	£000	£000	£000	£000
Fixed assets (net book value)			54,000			47,000
Current assets:						
Stock		14,000			11,000	
Debtors		19,100			17,400	
		33,100			28,400	
Less **creditors: amounts**						
falling due within one year:						
Creditors	14,200			15,500		
Taxation	14,000			13,000		

Proposed dividends	16,000		8,500
Bank overdraft	3,600		2,400
		(47,800)	(39,400)
Net current liabilities		(14,700)	(11,000)
Total net assets		39,300	36,000
Capital and reserves			
Ordinary shares of 5p each		21,000	10,000
Share premium account		7,500	17,500
Profit and loss account		10,800	8,500
		39,300	36,000

Notes:

1. Ignore deferred taxation provisions.
2. A bonus issue was made during the year to 31 May 2004 by utilizing part of the balance of the share premium account.
3. A summary of the company's fixed assets account in the general ledger for the year ended 31 May 2004 is shown below (all amounts in £000s):

Fixed Assets				
Date	Details	Debit	Credit	Balance
1 June 2003	Cost brought forward	87,000		87,000 Dr
31 May 2004	Additions	14,000		101,000 Dr
31 May 2004	Disposals		12,000	89,000 Dr

The assets that were sold realized £2,400,000, which represented a loss on disposal of £1,400,000 when compared to their book value. Depreciation provided for the year was £3,200,000.

Produce a cash flow statement for the year ended 31 May 2004.

Step 1: Using Domino's Pizza's cash flow statement (see Figure 9.1) as our guide, we can start by calculating the net cash flow from operating activities. Because we show interest and taxation separately in the cash flow statement, we must start with the operating profit *before* interest and taxation.

	£000
Operating profit before interest and taxation	46,300
Depreciation	3,200
Loss on sale of fixed assets	1,400
Increase in stock (14,000−11,000)	(3,000)
Increase in debtors (19,100−17,400)	(1,700)
Decrease in creditors (15,500−14,200)	(1,300)
Net cash inflow from operating activities	**44,900**

Step 2: We can now set out the cash flow statement, starting with the net cash inflow from operating activities as calculated in Step 1:

Mayfly plc cash flow statement for the year ended 31 May 2004

	£000
Net cash inflow from operating activities	44,900
Returns on investments and servicing of finance	
Interest paid	(10,000)
Taxation	
Corporation tax paid (Note 1)	(13,000)
Capital expenditure and financial investment	
Payments to acquire tangible fixed assets	(14,000)
Receipts from sales of tangible fixed assets	2,400
	(11,600)
Equity dividends paid (Note 2)	(12,500)
Net cash outflow before financing	(2,200)
Financing	
Issue of ordinary share capital (Note 3)	1,000
Decrease in cash	(1,200)

Notes:

1. This is the amount *paid* in the year (i.e. the previous year's provision).

2. This represents the dividends actually paid in the year, being the liability in the opening balance sheet (last year's proposed final dividend £8,500) plus the part of the dividends shown in this year's profit and loss account which must have been paid during the year, found by comparing the closing liability as shown in the balance sheet with the total dividends shown in the profit and loss account.

$$(£20,000 - £16,000 = £4,000)$$

3. There was a bonus issue during the year. This is a free issue of shares so therefore does not involve a cash flow. The amount used for the bonus issue was £10,000 (the sum by which the share premium account decreased in the year), so the remaining part of the £11,000 difference between the opening and closing share capital totals must be a cash inflow resulting from a new share issue.

Step 3: We can prove the closing figure in the cash flow statement by preparing a simple reconciliation of the opening and closing cash balances:

	£000
Opening bank overdraft, 1 June 2003	2,400
Closing bank overdraft, 31 May 2004	3,600
Increase in overdraft (i.e. decrease in cash for the period)	(1,200)

9.13 Chapter summary

- A cash flow statement summarizes cash inflows and outflows over the financial period.
- Profitable businesses may fail due to poor liquidity.
- Cash flows are organized under several key headings to make the statement more meaningful.
- Operating profit is converted into a cash flow figure by adjusting for the effects of depreciation, unsold stock, debtors, and creditors.
- Analysts must monitor the net cash flows over several accounting periods, particularly if net cash *outflows* are reported on a regular basis.

■ GLOSSARY

cash	For the purposes of a cash flow statement this refers not only to cash in hand but also to bank balances, less bank overdrafts
cash equivalents	Short-term, highly liquid investments that are readily convertible into known amounts of cash and which are subject to insignificant risk of changes in value
cash flow	The cash inflows and outflows of a business over a specified period
cash flow statement	A summary of cash inflows and outflows prepared in a format set out by an accounting standard and based on historic transactions for a financial period
liquid assets	Assets that can be turned quickly into cash when needed
liquidity	The availability of cash within a business
operating activities	The income-generating activities of the business
primary financial statement	A financial summary of importance, such as the profit and loss account, balance sheet, and cash flow statement
solvency	The ability of a business to meet its debts as they fall due. The opposite is *insolvency*

■ MULTIPLE CHOICE QUESTIONS

1. The definition of cash as used in cash flow statements includes:
    a   Only cash balances
    b   Only bank balances
    c   Bank balances and bank overdrafts
    d   Cash in hand plus bank balances less bank overdrafts

2. Which one of the following is almost certainly a cause of business failure?

    a   A company cannot raise enough cash to pay its bills
    b   A company has more current liabilities than current assets
    c   A company has a bank overdraft
    d   A company has too much cash

3. The heading 'Financing' in a cash flow statement means:

    a   The cash outflow due to loan interest payments being made
    b   The cash flow from share and loan issues and repayments
    c   Cash dividends paid to shareholders
    d   The change in the level of bank balances in the period

4. If 'Taxation' is shown as a cash outflow on the cash flow statement, which one of the following will that item include?

    a   The taxation provided this year on the current year's profit
    b   The taxation payable next year on this year's profit
    c   The taxation paid this year on last year's profit
    d   The amount provided for deferred taxation as shown in the opening balance sheet

5. Depreciation is added back to profit when arriving at the cash flow from operating activities because:

    a   Depreciation is only an estimated amount
    b   Depreciation does not affect profit
    c   Depreciation does not result in a flow of cash
    d   Depreciation only affects the balance sheet, not the profit and loss account

6. If net profit before taxation and interest was £95,000, depreciation for the year was £17,000, stock has decreased during the year by £7,000, debtors have increased by £11,000, and creditors have decreased by £4,000, what is the overall cash flow from operating activities?

    a   £104,000
    b   £112,000
    c   £98,000
    d   £134,000

7. Which one of the following might be referred to as a 'cash equivalent'?

    a   Shares held in a subsidiary company
    b   A bank deposit account requiring one month's notice for withdrawals
    c   Shares held in a limited company which are not traded on a stock exchange
    d   A bank deposit account requiring one day's notice for withdrawals

8. Under which one of the following headings in a cash flow statement would 'dividends paid to preference shareholders' appear?

    a   Equity dividends paid
    b   Returns on investments and servicing of finance
    c   Financing
    d   Capital expenditure and financial investment

THE CASH FLOW STATEMENT 221

9. A company's proposed final dividends were £40,000 at the start of the year and £60,000 at the end of the year. It paid an interim dividend of £10,000 during the current year. What is the cash outflow to be recorded in the current year's cash flow statement?

   a £110,000

   b £60,000

   c £50,000

   d £40,000

10. Cash outflows relating to finance leasing contracts would be shown:

    a In total within 'Returns on investments and servicing of finance'

    b In total within 'Capital expenditure'

    c The capital element is shown within 'Capital expenditure' and the interest element is shown within 'Returns on investments and servicing of finance'

    d The capital element is shown within 'Acquisitions and disposals' and the interest element is shown within 'Returns on investments and servicing of finance'

(*Note: answers are shown in Appendix 2.*)

■ DISCUSSION QUESTIONS

1. If cash is the 'lifeblood of a business', does that make it more important than profit?

2. 'A company that shows decreases in cash in its cash flow statements will inevitably fail.' Discuss.

3. Non-accountants don't understand the double-entry system, nor the adjustments required by the accruals concept. Why not save money by just issuing a cash flow statement instead of a profit and loss account and balance sheet?

(*Note: Suggested answers or discussion points are available on the companion website.*)

■ LONGER QUESTIONS

(Questions marked W have suggested answers on the companion website. Other questions are answered in Appendix 3.)

1. From the following information for four separate companies, calculate the missing figure in each column.

(£s)	A	B	C	D
Net cash inflow from operating activities	15,800	?	19,400	50,660
Net interest paid	(5,800)	(2,900)	(6,000)	(2,950)
Tax	(7,200)	(4,500)	(7,100)	(24,880)
Capital expenditure	17,300	(2,970)	?	(6,520)
Changes in financing	800	(1,800)	14,680	(17,490)
Dividends	(9820)	(4,200)	(3,300)	?
Increase/(decrease) in cash for the period	?	7,200	11,750	(7,450)

2. Figure 9.2's cash flow statement and notes are taken from the annual report of Barnacle plc.

Write a brief report to a shareholder on the changes between the two years as disclosed by the cash flow statement. The report should include a table showing the % increases or decreases of each key heading between each year.

CONSOLIDATED CASH FLOW STATEMENT for the year ended 31 May 2004

	Notes	2004 £'000	2003 £'000
Net cash inflow from operating activities	1(a)	**7,011**	12,506
Returns on investments and servicing of finance			
Interest paid		**(53)**	(68)
Interest received		**1,035**	945
Net cash inflow from returns on investments and servicing of finance		**982**	877
Taxation			
Tax paid		**(5,083)**	(2,716)
Capital expenditure			
Purchase of tangible fixed assets		**(372)**	(320)
Sale of tangible fixed assets		**22**	16
		(350)	(304)
Acquisitions			
Purchase of subsidiary undertaking		**(2,062)**	—
Equity dividends paid		**(1,092)**	(930)
Financing			
Repayment of loans		**(1,185)**	(210)
Purchase of own shares		**(1,230)**	—
Issue of shares		**391**	97
Net cash outflow from financing		**(2,024)**	(113)
(Decrease)/Increase in cash	1(b)	**(2,618)**	9,320

Figure 9.2(a) Barnacle plc: cash flow statement

1. Cash flow statement

(a) Reconciliation of operating profit to net cash flow from operating activities

	2004 £'000	2003 £'000
Operating profit	**3,780**	7,876
Depreciation of tangible fixed assets	**316**	268
Goodwill amortisation	**1,362**	600
Profit on disposal of tangible fixed assets	**(3)**	(6)
Decrease/(increase) in stocks	**1,683**	(994)
Decrease in debtors	**5,514**	3,704
(Decrease) / increase in creditors	**(5,641)**	1,058
Net cash inflow from operating activities	**7,011**	12,506

Figure 9.2(b) (Continued overleaf)

(b) Reconciliation to net funds

	2004 £'000	2003 £'000
(Decrease)/Increase in net cash in the year	(2,618)	9,320
Decrease in debt	1,185	210
Movements in net funds in the year	(1,433)	9,530
Net funds at 1 June 2003	15,013	5,483
Net funds at 31 May 2003	13,580	15,013

Figure 9.2(b) Barnacle plc: notes to the cash flow statement

Notes to the accounts.

3. The balance sheets of Nickleby plc as at 31 October 2004 and 2003 are as follows:

	31 October 2004		31 October 2003	
	£000	£000	£000	£000
Fixed assets (net book value)		43,000		32,000
Current assets:				
Stock	19,000		18,000	
Debtors	9,000		7,500	
Bank	—		4,800	
	28,000		30,300	
Less creditors: amounts due for payment within one year:				
Creditors	6,100		9,900	
Taxation	5,000		4,000	
Proposed dividends	3,000		2,000	
Bank overdraft	2,700		—	
	(16,800)		(15,900)	
Net current assets		11,200		14,400
Total net assets		54,200		46,400
Share capital and reserves				
Ordinary shares of 25p each		24,000		33,000
Share premium account		300		200
Retained earnings		29,900		13,200
		54,200		46,400

The summarized profit and loss accounts for the two years ended 31 October 2004 are as follows:

	2004	2003
	£000	£000
Gross profit	46,100	38,900
Less expenses (including £1.2m interest)	(17,000)	(20,900)
	29,100	18,000
Less loss on sale of fixed assets	(3,200)	—
Operating profit before interest	25,900	18,000
Less interest payable	(1.200)	(1,200)
Operating profit before taxation	24,700	16,800
Less taxation	(5,000)	(4,000)
Operating profit after taxation	19,700	12,800
Less equity dividends	(3,000)	(2,000)
Retained profits	16,700	10,800
Retained profits b/f	13,200	2,400
Retained profits c/f	29,900	13,200

Notes:

A summary of the company's fixed assets account in the general ledger for the year ended 31 October 2004 is shown below:

Fixed Assets				
Date	Details	Debit	Credit	Balance
1 November 2003	Cost brought forward	76,000		76,000 Dr
31 October 2004	Additions	22,000		98,000 Dr
31 October 2004	Disposals		8,000	90,000 Dr

The assets that were sold realized £1.8m, which represented a loss on disposal of £3.2m when compared with their book value. Total depreciation charged for the year to 31 October 2004 was £6m.

Produce a cash flow statement for the year ended 31 October 2004, and reconcile the cash increase or decrease for the year as shown on the statement with the change in the bank balance shown in the balance sheets.

4W. From the following information, for four separate companies, calculate the cash flow from operating activities for each column.

(£s)	A	B	C	D
Net profit before interest	36,620	29,937	—	20,060
Net loss before interest	—	—	22,660	—
Depreciation	12,000	16,000	24,000	15,000
Increase in stock	9,650	—	—	14,850

Decrease in stock	—	5,840	5,622	—
Increase in debtors	—	—	2,240	12,795
Decrease in debtors	7,980	6,722	—	—
Increase in creditors	3,380	—	9,713	—
Decrease in creditors	—	6,840	—	11,629
Cash flow from operating activities	?	?	?	?

5W. To what extent, if at all, do the following have an effect on a company's cash flow statement?

1. Depreciation for the financial period.

2. A bonus issue.

3. A rights issue.

4. A profit made on the sale of an investment.

5. The acquisition of a business, part for shares, and part for cash.

6. A proposed final dividend for the year.

7. An interim dividend that has been paid part-way during the year.

8. Last year's tax, which is paid during the current year.

6W. The balance sheets of Kiwi plc as at 31 May 2003 and 2004 are as follows:

	31 May 2004	31 May 2003
	£000	£000
Fixed assets (net book value)	108,000	94,000
Current assets:		
Stock	28,000	22,000
Debtors	36,000	32,000
Bank	2,200	2,800
Total assets	174,200	150,800
Creditors due for payment within one year:		
Creditors	28,400	31,000
Taxation	28,000	26,000
Proposed dividends	32,000	17,000
Bank overdraft	7,200	4,800
	95,600	78,800
Total net assets	78,600	72,000
Share capital:		
Ordinary shares of 5p each	42,000	20,000
6% preference shares of £1 each	10,000	10,000
Share premium account	5,000	25,000
Retained earnings	21,600	17,000
	78,600	72,000

The summarized profit and loss accounts for the two years ended 31 May 2004 are as follows:

	2004	2003
	£000	£000
Gross profit	306,680	264,400
Less expenses	(171,280)	(149,800)
Profit/(loss) on sale of fixed assets	(2,800)	(5,600)
Profit before taxation and interest	132,600	120,200
Less interest	60,000	60,000
Profit before taxation	72,600	60,200
Less taxation	(28,000)	(26,000)
Profit after tax	44,600	34,200
Dividends, paid and proposed	(40,000)	(23,000)
Retained earnings	4,600	11,200
Retained earnings b/f	17,000	5,800
Retained earnings c/f	21,600	17,000

Notes:

1. A bonus issue was made during the year to 31 May 2004 by utilizing £20m of the share premium account. There were no other changes to share premium account in the year.

2. A summary of the company's fixed assets account in the general ledger for the year ended 31 May 2004 is shown below:

Fixed Assets (£000s)				
Date	Details	Debit	Credit	Balance
1 June 2003	Cost brought forward	174,000		174,000 Dr
31 May 2004	Additions	28,000		202,000 Dr
31 May 2004	To Disposals Account		24,000	178,000 Dr
31 May 2004	Cost carried forward		178,000	0

The assets which were sold realized £4.8m, which represented a loss on disposal of £2.8m when compared with their book value. Total depreciation for the year to 31 May 2004 was £6.4 million.

a   Produce a Cash Flow Statement for the year ended 31 May 2004. Notes should be provided, showing a reconciliation of the operating profit to the net cash flow from operating activities and an analysis of changes in cash during the year.

b   Give three reasons why companies have to publish a Cash Flow Statement in addition to other main financial statements.

■ MINI CASE STUDY

MinnieMax Ltd.'s cash flow

MinnieMax Ltd. (see previous mini case studies) is preparing its cash flow statement for its first year of trading, to 30 September 2004. Relevant information needed regarding the company's cash flows at that date is as follows:

(Summarized) balance sheet as at 30 September 2004		
	£	£
Fixed assets – cost (includes £15,000 bought via finance leases)	274,850	
Less depreciation and amortization	(8,170)	
		266,680
Current assets		
Stock	5,000	
Debtors	27,200	
Investment: government bond	50,000	
Bank balance	115,120	
	197,320	
Less: creditors due for payment within one year		
Creditors	42,500	
Leases	3,000	
Dividend	50,000	
Taxation	62,500	
	(158,000)	
Net current assets		39,320
		306,000
Less: creditors due for payment after more than one year		
Lease obligations	12,000	
Loan	140,000	
		152,000
Total net assets		154,000
Called-up share capital	60,000	
Share premium account	12,000	
Profit and loss account	82,000	
		154,000

Summarized profit and loss account for the year ended 30 September 2004				
Profit on ordinary activities before interest				222,000
Interest received			2,000	
Interest paid (including on finance leases)			(3,500)	
				(1,500)
Profit on ordinary activities before taxation				220,500
Taxation				(62,500)
Profit on ordinary activities after taxation				158,000
Dividends: interim (paid)		26,000		
final (proposed)		50,000		
				(76,000)
Retained profit for the year				82,000

You are required to prepare the cash flow statement for the year. Note that, as this was the first year of trading, the opening balances for stock, debtors, and creditors are to be taken as zero.

(Suggested solutions can be found in Appendix 4.)

■ MAXI CASE STUDY

J. Sainsbury plc

The following is an extract from the Operating and Financial Review contained within the 2003 annual report of J. Sainsbury plc, a leading UK supermarket group:

Cash flow

The Group's net debt has increased by £248 million during the year to £1,404 million. Operating cash inflow remained strong at £1,070 million. Underlying EBITDA (Earnings before Interest, Taxation, Depreciation and Amortisation), excluding exceptional items, increased by 10.3 per cent, virtually in line with earnings. Because of the timing of Easter and the introduction of new lines, working capital was broadly flat for the year, compared to an inflow of £78 million in the previous year.

The extract contains references to the company's performance relating to its debt, cash flow, earnings, and working capital. Taking each of these items in turn, explain their uses when analysing a company's results. Note that the annual report of J. Sainsbury plc can be downloaded using the web address given at the end of the chapter.

(Suggested answers and discussion areas are available on the companion website.)

■ WEB LINKS

Company websites
Companies referred to in this chapter:

Bloomsbury plc www.bloomsbury.com/
Domino's Pizza www.dominos.co.uk
J. Sainsbury plc (2003 annual report) www.j-sainsbury.co.uk/ar2003/

■ FURTHER READING

Black, G. (2003). *Students' Guide to Accounting and Financial Reporting Standards*, 9th edn. (Harlow: FT/Prentice Hall), chapter 12.

Elliott, B., and Elliott, J. (2003). *Financial Accounting and Reporting*, 8th edn. (Harlow: FT/Prentice Hall), chapter 24.

Jones, M. (2002). Accounting for non-specialists, 1st edn. (Chichester: Wiley), chapter 8.

■ COMPANION WEBSITE MATERIALS

Additional materials are available for students and lecturers on the companion website, at **www.oup.com/uk/booksites/busecon/business/**, including a 'Question Generator' file that gives unlimited practice at preparing cash flow statements.

Consolidated financial statements

OBJECTIVES

By the end of this chapter you will be able to:

- Evaluate the advantages and disadvantages of operating as a group of companies.
- Recognize the circumstances in which a parent/subsidiary relationship exists.
- Distinguish between subsidiary companies, associated companies, joint ventures, and investments, and contrast the various accounting methods required to consolidate relevant financial information.
- Explain and apply the key accounting adjustments required when consolidating financial information.
- Prepare simple consolidated accounts.
- Explain the terms *minority interests* and *related parties*.

10.1 Introduction

Most publicly traded companies operate as *groups*, which consist of a parent company and one or more subsidiary companies. These subsidiaries may have been formed for a specific purpose, such as to develop business within a specific country, or might have resulted from the parent taking over other companies. Some subsidiary companies are formed to promote a specific product or service. The shareholdings in subsidiaries owned by the parent company will usually, but not always, be over 50 per cent (see section 10.3.1 below). In addition, there may be *associated* companies with the 'investing company' owning between 20 per cent and 50 per cent of the shares, and these must also be considered when presenting the results of the group as a whole. As an example, the annual report of the Swiss-based pharmaceuticals company Roche Group listed over 200 subsidiaries and associated companies. Some of the names of these subsidiaries are self-explanatory, including:

- Roche Vitamins Europe Ltd.
- Roche (Thailand) Ltd.
- Roche Vitamins (Philippines) Inc.

- Roche Financial Market Ltd.
- Roche Laboratories Inc.
- Shanghai Roche Pharmaceuticals Ltd.

The presentation of consolidated financial statements (e.g. group balance sheet, profit and loss account, and cash flow statement) serves to effectively combine the results of all these companies. In doing so, the company's overall performance can be assessed, regardless of what the legal, political, or geographical circumstances are in the countries where the company is trading, or which products or services specific subsidiaries are providing.

In relation to the long history of accounting, the idea of consolidating the results of separate companies is a relatively new one, dating back only to the first half of the twentieth century. Individual company accounts still have to be prepared and submitted to the taxation authorities, but it is the *group* statements which are used by current and potential investors to evaluate the state of the company as a whole.

Details of Domino's Pizza's subsidiaries are shown on pp. 332–3. As well as five wholly owned subsidiaries, it lists two joint ventures (see p. 85) and two 'indirectly held' wholly owned subsidiaries (also known as sub-subsidiaries), where the shares are not owned directly by the parent company, but by one of its directly owned subsidiaries.

10.2 Advantages and disadvantages of group structures

Most companies trade in various types of products or services, often in different regions or countries. In choosing how to organize their company, there are several alternative possibilities, including:

1. Having only one company split into as many divisions as are needed, with managers responsible for each division. This has the advantage of simplicity, as there is only one company legally established and one board of directors which takes total responsibility. However, great reliance has to be placed on the skills of the divisional managers, and the centralized control may prove to be inefficient. Financial liability is not devolved to the divisions but remains with the controlling company. There may be a lack of incentive for the divisional managers if they see little chance of joining the board of directors.

2. Establishing separate companies for each key type of product or service, and for each main geographical location, with a board of directors appointed for each company. This is the most common form of business organization for large and complex companies. By establishing separate subsidiary companies, boards of directors are put in place with specific skills relevant to each company. One or more directors of the parent company will also sit on the boards of the subsidiaries. Although the parent company will often act as guarantor for the debts of the subsidiary, in extreme cases, where a subsidiary has amassed substantial debts, it might be allowed to go into liquidation thereby protecting the parent

company's business. However, this does little for the parent company's reputation and it is often the case that the parent company will pay the subsidiary's liabilities. Another advantage of the group structure is that subsidiary company directorships and (possibly) shareholdings can be offered to key employees, thereby offering them a positive incentive to remain with the company.

One other aspect to consider relates to the takeover of one company by another. For simplicity, let's say that the company making the takeover bid is Company X, and the company to be acquired is Company Y. There are three possible options in this situation:

1. Company X buys all (or most) of the shares in Company Y. A group of companies is formed as Company Y becomes a subsidiary of Company X and Company X becomes the parent company of Company Y.

2. Company X does not want to form a group of companies, but instead only purchases the assets of Company Y. Company Y then ceases to exist, its assets being added to those of Company X. If Company X pays more than the fair value for Company Y's assets, *goodwill* must be recorded and accounted for (see Chapter 6).

3. A new company, Company Z, is formed to acquire the shares of both companies, X and Y. Shareholders in X and Y then exchange their shares for shares in Company Z, with X's former shareholders having the majority of the shares. Occasionally, companies decide to *merge* their businesses on more or less equal terms, in which case they may end up with equal proportions of Company Z's equity capital. Until recently it was possible for merging companies to take advantage of a specific type of accounting arrangement, known as 'merger accounting'. This allowed two or more companies to 'combine', rather than one being treated as the parent and the others as subsidiaries. This had the effect of circumventing the normal accounting rules for consolidations (see below), usually resulting in much larger distributable reserves than would have been the case if merger accounting had not been applied. There is often not a clear-cut distinction between the terms 'merger' and 'takeover', and the same accounting procedures now apply in each case.

10.3 Group structures

Companies may decide to structure their groups in many different ways. At its simplest, a group might comprise the parent company and one or more wholly owned (100 per cent) subsidiary companies (see Figure 10.1).

Sometimes when a company takes over another, investors holding a minority of shares do not wish to sell their shares in the acquired company, preferring to remain as 'minority' shareholders in that company. As explained in Chapters 5 and 8, the group must acknowledge the financial interests of the minority shareholders within the group profit and loss account and balance sheet. Typical group structures with minority interests are shown in Figure 10.2.

Another possibility is for the subsidiaries themselves to have controlling shareholdings in other companies: from the group's viewpoint they are *sub-subsidiaries* of the parent.

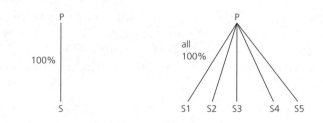

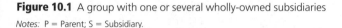

Figure 10.1 A group with one or several wholly-owned subsidiaries

Notes: P = Parent; S = Subsidiary.

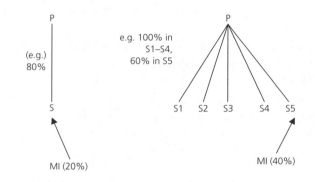

Figure 10.2 Groups with minority shareholdings in subsidiaries

Notes: P = Parent; S = Subsidiary; MI = Minority Interest.

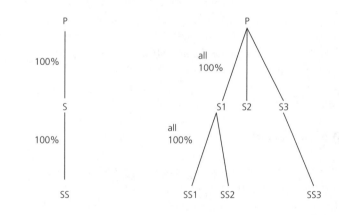

Figure 10.3 A group with one or several wholly owned subsidiaries and sub-subsidiaries

Notes: P = Parent; S = Subsidiary; SS = Sub-subsidiary.

Minority shareholdings may then exist not only in the subsidiary, but also in the sub-subsidiary. These are illustrated in Figures 10.3 and 10.4.

A further complication is that both the parent *and* the subsidiary might own shares in the sub-subsidiary: the former being referred to as a *direct* shareholding, the latter an *indirect* shareholding. This is illustrated in Figure 10.5.

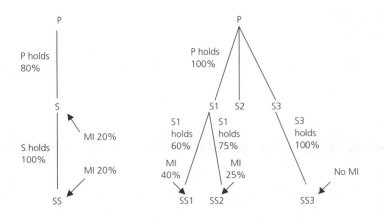

Figure 10.4 Examples of groups with minority shareholdings in one or several subsidiaries

Notes: P = Parent; S = Subsidiary; SS = Sub-subsidiary; MI = Minority Interest.

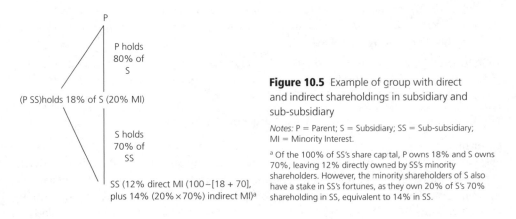

Figure 10.5 Example of group with direct and indirect shareholdings in subsidiary and sub-subsidiary

Notes: P = Parent; S = Subsidiary; SS = Sub-subsidiary; MI = Minority Interest.

[a] Of the 100% of SS's share capital, P owns 18% and S owns 70%, leaving 12% directly owned by SS's minority shareholders. However, the minority shareholders of S also have a stake in SS's fortunes, as they own 20% of S's 70% shareholding in SS, equivalent to 14% in SS.

10.3.1 Establishing the parent–subsidiary relationship

The decision as to whether companies have a parent–subsidiary relationship depends upon either the proportion of voting rights owned or the degree of influence that the would-be parent has on the other company. Once the parent–subsidiary relationship is established, it is regarded as a 'group of companies' and procedures for consolidated accounts must be followed. There are five alternative criteria to be considered when deciding if there is a parent–subsidiary relationship (assume that the potential parent is Company A, the potential subsidiary, Company B):

1. Does A hold the majority of voting rights in Company B?

2. Is A a shareholder in B with the power to appoint or remove directors holding the majority of B's voting rights?

3. Is there a clause in B's Memorandum or Articles of Association ('rule books') giving A the right to exercise dominant influence over B? (Dominant influence exists when the parent can exercise power regardless of the rights or influence of any other party.)

4. Is A a shareholder in B and actually exercises a dominant influence over B?

5. Are the operations of A and B integrated and managed as a single unit?

If the answer to any of these questions is 'yes', then the parent–subsidiary relationship is said to exist.

10.4 Accounting for consolidations: the balance sheet

Consolidated financial statements of a parent and its subsidiaries are prepared using a method known as 'acquisition accounting'. The key characteristics of this method are:

- Adjustments must be made to eliminate any inter-company indebtedness.

- *All* the net assets of the subsidiaries are included in the group's accounts, even if less than 100 per cent of the company is owned.

- If not all the shares are owned (directly or indirectly) by the parent company, the value of the *minority interest* must be calculated and disclosed on both the group profit and loss account and group balance sheet.

- Goodwill arising on consolidation (the difference between the purchase price given for the subsidiary's shares and the fair value of the net assets acquired) must be calculated and treated in accordance with accounting standards.

The following example illustrates the mechanics of a simple consolidation:

Example
Five years ago, Puddle plc bought 800 shares, representing 80 per cent of the equity share capital, in Shower Ltd. for £40,000. At the time of the purchase, Shower Ltd.'s balance sheet showed net assets (at a fair valuation) of £30,000, represented by share capital (1,000 shares) totalling £5,000 and revenue reserves £25,000. The balance sheets at the end of Year 5 of both companies are shown below:

		Puddle plc		Shower Ltd.
		£		£
Fixed assets				
Tangible fixed assets		230,000		70,000
Investment in Shower Ltd.		40,000		—
		270,000		70,000
Current assets				
Stock	40,000		22,000	
Debtors	50,000		18,000	
Due from Shower Ltd.	10,000		—	
Bank	20,000		5,000	
	120,000		45,000	

Creditors: amounts falling due within one year					
Trade creditors	40,000		15,000		
Proposed dividend	18,000		—		
Taxation	12,000		—		
Due to Puddle plc	—		10,000		
	(70,000)		(25,000)		
		50,000		20,000	
Total net assets		320,000		90,000	
Share capital and reserves					
Called-up share capital		100,000		5,000	
Profit and loss account		220,000		85,000	
		320,000		90,000	

The company's policy is to write off goodwill over a twenty-year period.

You are required to produce the consolidated balance sheet of Puddle plc.

Solution

When we look at the individual balance sheets of the two companies, we can immediately see two items relevant to the consolidation. First, in Puddle plc's balance sheet, the cost of Shower Ltd.'s shares (£40,000) is represented by the 'Investment' shown as a fixed asset. Secondly, intra-group indebtedness is reflected by the current asset appearing in Puddle plc's balance sheet and the equivalent current liability shown in Shower Ltd.'s balance sheet. Occasionally, inter-company balances do not agree and have to be reconciled by being adjusted for items such as payments made by one company but not yet received by the other, stock-in-transit, etc.

Many of the figures in the consolidated balance sheet are found by simply combining the relevant amounts in both the parent and subsidiary balance sheets, as Figure 10.6 shows.

The three key steps referred to in Figure 10.6 are:

Step 1. Calculation of goodwill

Goodwill is the difference between the price paid for the subsidiary's shares and the fair value of the subsidiary at the time the shares were bought.

In the example, at the time of acquisition, Shower Ltd.'s balance sheet showed:

Called-up share capital (1,000 shares)	£5,000
Profit and loss account	£25,000
Total (=total net assets)	£30,000

Puddle plc paid £40,000 to buy 80 per cent of Shower Ltd.'s total net assets, valued at £24,000 (80% × £30,000). The balance (£16,000) is treated as goodwill in the consolidated balance sheet, and, as it is being written off over twenty years, its net value in the Year 5 balance sheet will be shown as:

Goodwill	£16,000
Less amortization (5/20)	£4,000
	£12,000

		Puddle plc		Shower Ltd.	
		£		£	
Fixed assets					
Tangible fixed assets		230,000		70,000	Combined = 300,000
Investment in Shower Ltd.		40,000		-	Replaced by the individual assets acquired at the date the shares were bought, including any goodwil (see Step 1)
		270,000		70,000	
Current assets					
Stock	40,000		22,000		Combined = 62,000
Debtors	50,000		18,000		Combined = 68,000
Due from Shower Ltd.	10,000		-		Eliminated (see below)
Bank	20,000		5,000		Combined = 25,000
	120,000		45,000		
Creditors: amounts falling due within one year					
Trade creditors	40,000		15,000		Combined = 55,000
Proposed dividend	18,000		-		Puddle's dividend shown on group balance sheet
Taxation	12,000		-		Overall tax liability shown on group balance sheet
Due to Puddle plc	-		10,000		Eliminated (see above)
	(70,000)		(25,000)		
		50,000		20,000	
Total net assets		320,000		90,000	
Share capital and reserves					
Called-up share capital		100,000		5,000	Puddle's share capital shown on group balance sheet, not subsidiaries
Profit and loss account		220,000		85,000	Puddle's reserves shown on group balance sheet, plus subsidiaries' reserves earned since becoming a subsidiary (Step 2). Any minority interests must be calculated (Step 3)
		320,000		90,000	

Figure 10.6 Calculations for the consolidated balance sheet

Step 2. Calculation of reserves

The group's reserves at the end of Year 5 comprise the parent company's reserves and that part of the subsidiary's reserves earned since it became a member of the group. In the example, Shower Ltd.'s balance sheet five years after Puddle plc bought its shares showed that the profit and loss account had changed from £25,000 on the acquisition date to £85,000 at the latest balance sheet date, an increase of £60,000. As Puddle plc only owns 80 per cent of Shower Ltd., it can only add 80 per cent of this amount (80%×60,000=£48,000) to the combined reserves shown in the consolidated balance sheet.

The total reserves to be shown on the consolidated balance sheet will then be:

	£
Puddle plc's reserves	220,000
Less goodwill amortization	(4,000)
	216,000
Add Shower Ltd.'s reserves	48,000
Total consolidated reserves	264,000

Step 3. Minority interests

As 20 per cent of Shower Ltd. is not owned by Puddle plc but by shareholders who are 'outside' the group, the value owed to these minority shareholders must be recognized, and shown in the consolidated balance sheet. Shower Ltd.'s total net assets were valued at £90,000 at the end of Year 5, so the minority interest is valued at £18,000 (20% × £90,000).

The consolidated balance sheet of Puddle plc group can now be prepared, as follows:

Puddle plc group balance sheet as at the end of Year 5

	£	£
Fixed assets		
Intangible fixed assets (Goodwill)		12,000
Tangible fixed assets		300,000
		312,000
Current assets		
Stock	62,000	
Debtors	68,000	
Bank	25,000	
	155,000	
Creditors: amounts falling due within one year		
Trade creditors	55,000	
Proposed dividend	18,000	
Taxation	12,000	
	(85,000)	
Net current assets		70,000
Total net assets		382,000
Share capital and reserves		
Called up share capital		100,000
Profit and loss account		264,000
		364,000
Minority interests		18,000
		382,000

> Look carefully at Domino's Pizza's group balance sheet on p. 321 and the parent company's balance sheet shown on p. 322. Note how the 'investments in subsidiary undertakings' shown in the parent's balance sheet does not appear in the group balance sheet (see below for details of how the joint venture is accounted for). There are no minority interests in this company.

 Court plc's group balance sheet (see p. 195) shows minority interests of £87.8m.

10.5 Accounting for consolidations: the profit and loss account

The group profit and loss account is compiled by combining information contained within the individual profit and loss accounts of the parent company and subsidiaries. Adjustments must be made for:

- Inter-company sales and purchases (i.e. transactions made within the group), which must be eliminated on consolidation. Otherwise unrealistic totals would be shown, rather than figures just representing transactions with 'outside' customers.

- Minority interests in the profits or losses of subsidiary companies. As with the group balance sheet, *all* the relevant income and expenditure of subsidiaries will be included (after the inter-company adjustments referred to above) in the group profit and loss account, with any minority interests being shown separately.

- 'Pre-acquisition' reserves of the subsidiary must be excluded when calculating the total reserves to be carried forward and shown on the balance sheet, and any amortization of the goodwill arising on the consolidation must also be deducted.

As an example, assume that the following are the latest summarized profit and loss accounts (for Year 5) of Puddle plc and Shower Ltd.:

	Puddle plc	Shower Ltd.
	£	£
Turnover	1,100,000	569,000
Cost of sales	(725,000)	(365,000)
Gross profit	375,000	204,000
Expenses	(265,000)	(164,000)
Operating profit before taxation	110,000	40,000
Taxation	(12,000)	—

Operating profit after taxation	98,000	40,000
Proposed dividend	(18,000)	—
Retained profit for the year	80,000	40,000
Retained profit brought forward	140,000	45,000
Retained profit carried forward	220,000	85,000

Notes
1. Puddle plc sold goods worth £70,000 to Shower Ltd. during the year.
2. Puddle plc owned 80% of Shower Ltd.'s share capital.
3. Amortisation of the goodwill arising on the consolidation totalled £4,000 at the end of Year 5.
4. Shower Ltd.'s reserves were £25,000 at the time it became a subsidiary of Puddle plc, five years ago.

To prepare the consolidated profit and loss account, we must eliminate the inter-company trading, combine the remaining income and expenditure totals, and calculate the minority interest, as follows:

	Puddle plc	Shower Ltd.	Adjustments	Combined
	£	£		
Turnover	1,100,000	569,000	−70,000	1,599,000
Cost of sales	(725,000)	(365,000)	−70,000	1,020,000
Gross profit	375,000	204,000		579,000
Expenses	(265,000)	(164,000)		429,000
Amortization (current year, 1/20 × £16,000)			+800	800
				(429,800)
Operating profit before taxation	110,000	40,000		149,200
Taxation	(12,000)	—		(12,000)
Operating profit after taxation	98,000	40,000		137,200
Less Minority interests			−8000[a]	(8,000)
				129,200
Proposed dividend	(18,000)	—		(18,000)
Retained profit for the year	80,000	40,000		111,200
Retained profit brought forward (parent)	140,000			140,000
Amortization on goodwill previously written off			−3,200	(3,200)
Retained profit brought forward (subsidiary)		45,000	−20,000[b]	25,000
Less minority interests brought forward			−9,000[c]	(9,000)
Retained profit carried forward	220,000	85,000		264,000

[a] Minority interest = 20% × £40,000 = £8,000.
[b] Pre-acquisition reserves (80% × £25,000).
[c] Minority interests previously accounted for (20% × brought forward balance of £45,000).

The consolidated profit and loss account of Puddle plc group will then be shown as follows:

Puddle plc group profit and loss account for the year ending (Year 5)	
	£
Turnover	1,599,000
Cost of sales	(1,020,000)
Gross profit	579,000
Expenses	(429,800)
Operating profit before taxation	149,200
Taxation	(12,000)
Operating profit after taxation	137,200
Less minority interests	(8,000)
	129,200
Proposed dividend	(18,000)
Retained profit for the year	111,200
Retained profit brought forward	152,800
Retained profit carried forward[a]	264,000
[a] as shown on the group balance sheet	

 Look back at Figure 5.3 (p. 111) to see how H. P. Bulmer Holdings plc showed its minority interests on its profit and loss account.

10.6 Accounting for associated companies, joint ventures, and investments

In addition to subsidiary companies, consolidated financial statements must also incorporate the results of associated companies, joint ventures, and investments.

10.6.1 Associated companies

A company would be regarded as an associate when another company holds between 20 per cent and 50 per cent of its voting share capital, and it is subject to 'significant influence' by the company making the investment. For this purpose, significant influence exists when the investor is actively involved in formulating the operating and financial policies of the company in which it has invested. Such involvement may take the form of participation in such policy decisions as the expansion or contraction of the business, changes in products, and determining the balance between what proportion of the profits should be declared as dividends and what should be reinvested within the company. A typical situation for such an investment would be where one company is a major customer or supplier to the other company, and decides to take a sufficiently large shareholding to enable it to appoint a director and influence company policy.

Unlike the accounting treatment for subsidiary companies, which includes *all* income, expenditure, assets, and liabilities, only the relevant *proportion* of the associated company's operating profit or loss is disclosed in the consolidated profit and loss account. Within the consolidated balance sheet, only the investor's share of the net assets of its associates is included, classified within fixed assets as 'investments in associated companies'. This figure will be the original cost of the investment plus the appropriate proportion of the undistributed profits since the company became an associate (subject to any goodwill impairment written off). This accounting treatment is known as the 'equity method', sometimes referred to as a 'one-line' consolidation.

The Roche Group used the equity method to account for its associated companies, and Figure 10.7 shows the relevant extracts from its 2002 Annual Report:

Consolidated income statementin millions of CHF

| | Year ended 31 December | |
	2002	2001
Profit before taxes	(3,194)	4,762
Income taxes[13]	(839)	(1,038)
Profit after taxes	(4,033)	3,724
Income applicable to minority interests[28]	41	(34)
Share of result of associated companies[16]	(34)	7
Net income	(4,026)	3,597

Consolidated balance sheetin millions of CHF	2002	2001
Long-term assets		
Property, plant and equipment[14]	13,434	15,052
Intangible assets[15]	12,850	14,943
Investments in associated companies[16]	122	186
Financial long-term assets[17]	3,672	2,924
Deferred income tax assets[13]	784	1,410
Other long-term assets[18]	2,281	1,896
Total long-term assets	33,143	36,411

Note 16. Investments in associated companies and joint venturesin millions of CHF

Associated companies

The Group has investments in associated companies as listed below. These have been accounted for using the equity method.

| | Share of net income | | Balance sheet value | |
	2002	2001	2002	2001
Laboratory Corporation of America Holdings (USA)	—	44	—	—
Basilea Pharmceutica (Switzerland)	(31)	(12)	58	89
Other Investments accounted for using the equity method	(3)	(25)	64	97
Total Investments accounted for using the equity method	(34)	7	122	186

Figure 10.7 The Roche Group: associated companies

Source: The Roche Group Annual Report 2002.

10.6.2 **Joint ventures**

When two or more businesses jointly control a commercial enterprise on a long-term basis this is referred to as a 'joint venture'. Each participating company's consent would be needed for decisions on the venture's financial and operating policies—no one business alone controls the joint venture. The accounting treatment in the consolidated financial statements is similar to that of associated companies (see above), but in addition, the investor's share of the turnover of the joint venture is disclosed in the consolidated profit and loss account. In the consolidated balance sheet, the relevant share of the gross assets and liabilities is disclosed. This accounting treatment is referred to as the 'gross equity' method.

> Domino's Pizza is involved with two joint ventures, as shown in n. 12 on p. 332. In the group profit and loss account (see p. 320), note that a share of the joint ventures' turnover is shown, and also the share of the operating profit (less amortization of goodwill on the joint venture) is disclosed after the 'group operating profit'. In the group balance sheet (see p. 321), the investments in the joint ventures are shown under 'fixed assets', divided between gross assets and gross liabilities.

Type of investment	Typical shareholding	Method used	Investors' profit and loss account	Investor's balance sheet
Subsidiary	Over 50%	Acquisition accounting	All subsidiaries' income and expenditure included, with adjustments for intra-group indebtedness and any minority interests	All subsidiaries' assets and liabilities included, with adjustments for intra-group indebtedness and any minority interests
Associate	20%–50%	Equity method	Share of associates' operating result included after group operating result. Any amortization or write-down of goodwill arising on the acquisition of the associate should be disclosed separately	Investor's share of the net assets of its associates included, and separately disclosed
Joint venture	Jointly owned with other joint venturers	Gross equity method	As the equity method, but in addition, the investor's share of the turnover of the joint venture is shown	As the equity method, but the investor's share of the gross assets and liabilities of the joint venture is also shown
Investment	up to 20%	—	Dividend income shown	Investment shown at cost or valuation

Figure 10.8 Accounting for subsidiaries, associates, joint ventures, and simple investments

10.6.3 Investments

If a company owns less than 20 per cent of another company, and does not have a 'significant influence' on that company, it is treated as a simple investment. Only the dividend income from the investment is shown in the consolidated profit and loss account, and the investment's cost or valuation is included within the consolidated balance sheet.

10.6.4 Summary

Figure 10.8 shows a summary of the accounting treatment of subsidiaries, associates, joint ventures, and simple investments.

10.7 Related parties

Although consolidated statements should reflect all the relevant financial information concerning subsidiaries, associates, joint ventures, and simple investments, occasionally reported financial results may have been affected by the existence of other organizations or individuals not considered within the consolidation process. For example, the uncle of the managing director of a company might be running another company that gets the majority of its contracts from his nephew's business. This family relationship may have an influence on the decision-making policies of both businesses. Unless there is a cross-shareholding between the two companies, this influence may go unreported. However, in order to present a full picture of the financial environment within which both companies operate, the existence of the 'related parties' must be disclosed. Examples of related parties included directors and their close families, senior managers, and significant (20 per cent +) shareholders. Material transactions with related parties must be disclosed within the financial statements.

> Domino's Pizza discloses related party transactions in n. 26 on p. 340. It has disclosed transactions between the group and International Franchise Systems Inc. and Chinese Pompano Inc., as there are contractual links between two of the directors of Domino's Pizza and those companies (also, see 'Service Agreement' on p. 314).

10.8 Chapter summary

- Parent/subsidiary group structures can be advantageous for companies as they enable separate boards of directors to be established and give some financial protection if a subsidiary company fails.
- There are various ways in which groups can be structured, and sometimes companies only take over the net assets of another business, without creating a subsidiary.

- Minority shareholdings will exist if less than 100 per cent of the subsidiary's shares are owned by the parent.

- The parent–subsidiary relationship depends upon either the proportion of shares owned (over 50 per cent) or whether the parent has a 'dominant influence' on the subsidiary.

- Acquisition accounting is used to consolidate the results of a parent and its subsidiaries: all the income, expenditure, assets, and liabilities are combined, subject to adjustments for intra-group trading, minority interests, and goodwill arising on consolidation. Pre-acquisition reserves are excluded from the total of group reserves.

- Associated companies are established where an investing company owns between 20 per cent and 50 per cent of shares in another company and is subject to 'significant influence'. The equity method of consolidation is used, where only the investor's share of the associate's results are included in the group profit and loss account, and its share of the net assets plus undistributed profits is shown on the group balance sheet.

- Joint ventures exist when two or more businesses jointly control a business enterprise. Similar accounting treatment to associates, but with additional disclosures.

- Shareholdings of up to 20 per cent without 'significant influence' are treated as simple investments. Dividend income is shown in the group profit and loss account, and the cost or valuation of the shares is shown as an asset on the group balance sheet.

- Related parties are those organizations or individuals who have some influence on the operating or financial policies of the business. In most cases, the consolidated financial statements reflect the transactions with related parties, but occasionally further transactions occur which must be revealed to users of the statements.

■ GLOSSARY

acquisition accounting	The accounting method used when combining the results of the parent and its subsidiaries. All the income, expenditure, assets, and liabilities are combined, subject to adjustments for intra-group trading, minority interests, and goodwill arising on consolidation. Pre-acquisition reserves are excluded from the total of group reserves
associated company	Associated companies are established where an investing company owns between 20% and 50% of shares in another company and is subject to 'significant influence'
direct shareholding	A parent company holding shares directly in its subsidiaries
dominant influence	Dominant influence exists when the parent can exercise power regardless of the rights or influence of any other party
equity method	Accounting method used for associate companies, where the relevant proportion of the associated company's operating profit or loss is disclosed in the consolidated profit and loss account. Within the consolidated balance sheet, only the investor's share of the net assets of its associates is included
goodwill arising on consolidation	The excess of the purchase price of a subsidiary over the fair value of the net assets acquired

gross equity method	The accounting treatment of joint ventures
group	A parent and its subsidiaries
indirect shareholding	Shares in a subsidiary or sub-subsidiary owned by a group company other than the parent company
intra-group indebtedness	Debts due from one group company to another
investing company	The company which has invested in the shares of another company or venture
investment	Shareholdings of up to 20% without the 'significant influence' of one company on another
joint venture	Two or more businesses jointly controlling a business enterprise
liquidation	The sale of the net assets of a company, usually at the end of its life
merger	Two businesses combining as one, rather than one taking control of the other
minority shareholders	Shareholders owning those shares in a subsidiary (or sub-subsidiary) not owned by the parent company
parent company	The ultimate holding company of the group. It controls the shareholdings in other group companies
post-acquisition reserves	Reserves earned by a subsidiary after it became a subsidiary
pre-acquisition reserves	Reserves earned by a subsidiary before it became a subsidiary
related party	Organizations or individuals who have some influence on the operating or financial policies of the business
significant influence	Significant influence exists when the investing company is actively involved in formulating the operating and financial policies of the company in which it has invested
subsidiary	A company which is the subsidiary of its parent. The parent usually owns over 50% of the voting shares of the subsidiary or has 'dominant influence'
sub-subsidiary	A company which is the subsidiary of another subsidiary
takeover	The purchase of one company by another

■ MULTIPLE CHOICE QUESTIONS

1. A parent–subsidiary relationship will usually exist if one company holds which of the following percentages of the other company's voting rights?

   a Over 50%
   b Between 20% and 50%
   c Up to 20%
   d Up to 10%

2. Company X bought 60% of the equity share capital of Company Y for £120,000, when the fair value of Company Y was £180,000. What is the value of the goodwill arising on this acquisition?

   a £36,000

   b £60,000

   c £12,000

   d £24,000

3. Using the facts in Question 2, if Company Y's revenue reserves at the date of acquisition were £100,000 and they had increased to £200,000 at the date of the latest consolidated balance sheet, what is the value of Company Y's reserves that can be added into the total group reserves?

   a £200,000

   b £120,000

   c £100,000

   d £60,000

4. The method of accounting for associated companies within the consolidated financial statements is known as:

   a The Gross Equity Method

   b The Equity Method

   c Acquisition Accounting

   d Associated Accounting

5. Two businesses, A and B, share control of a business operation known as C Enterprises. How would C be described for the purposes of the consolidated financial statements of A?

   a Subsidiary company

   b Partnership

   c Associated company

   d Joint venture

6. A company, J, places a substantial order with another company, K, which is run by the wife of J's managing director. Which of the following will be required when preparing J's consolidated financial statements?

   a No reference need be made to the transaction

   b K's financial results must be consolidated with J's

   c Details of the related party transaction must be disclosed

   d A statement must be given stating that J will not place any further orders with K

7. If Company M owns 14% of Company N's equity capital, but does not exercise 'significant influence' on that company, M's consolidated profit and loss account will show:

   a 14% of N's operating profits before tax

   b M's dividend income from N

   c 14% of N's operating profits after tax

   d No details, as it is treated as a 'simple investment'

8. Company T has one subsidiary, Company U. During the current year, T's turnover was £400,000 and U's was £250,000. Cost of sales were: T £100,000 and U £80,000. Inter-company sales

from T to U had been made in the year amounting to £40,000. What turnover and cost of sales figures should be shown in the group profit and loss account?

a Turnover £610,000, cost of sales £140,000

b Turnover £610,000, cost of sales £180,000

c Turnover £650,000, cost of sales £140,000

d Turnover £650,000, cost of sales £180,000

9. 'Significant influence' when defining an associate company is presumed to exist if one company has at least the following percentage of another company's voting rights:

a 20

b 10

c 30

d 50

10. 'Minority interests' are:

a Shares in the parent company held other than by the company's directors

b Shares in subsidiary companies held by a fellow subsidiary company

c Shares in subsidiary companies held other than by its parent company

d Non-equity shareholders in the parent company

(*Note: answers are shown in Appendix 2.*)

■ DISCUSSION QUESTIONS

1. 'Bankers regard consolidated accounts as misleading because they disguise the individual indebtedness of particular companies.' Discuss.

2. If a parent company owns 80 per cent of a subsidiary's net assets, it is misleading to include 100 per cent of those assets in the consolidated balance sheet. Discuss.

3. Forcing companies to disclose transactions with related parties is an invasion of the privacy of those concerned and should not be required. Discuss.

(*Note: Suggested answers or discussion points are available on the companion website.*)

■ LONGER QUESTIONS

(Questions marked W have suggested answers on the companion website. Other questions are answered in Appendix 3.)

1. The annual report of a group of companies includes a consolidated prof t and loss account and a consolidated balance sheet. Explain each of the following terms which might be found within the annual report of a group of companies:

   (i)   minority interests;

   (ii) associated company;

   (iii) goodwill arising on consolidation.

2. Assume that Perkins plc bought 60 per cent of Pablo Ltd. for £100,000 on 1 January 2004, when Pablo Ltd.'s share capital and reserves stood at £80,000. During the year ended 31 December 2004 Pablo Ltd. transferred a profit of £40,000 to its reserves. There were no other changes to its share capital or reserves during 2004.

     Calculate the value of:

   (i)   The goodwill arising on consolidation.

   (ii) The minority interest in Pablo Ltd. at 31 December 2004.

   (iii) The amount of Pablo Ltd.'s reserves which can be added into the reserves of the group at 31 December 2004.

3. The summarized balance sheets of Frinton plc and its subsidiary Groudale Ltd. at 30th April 2004 were as follows:

	Frinton plc	Groudale Ltd.
	£	£
Tangible fixed assets	163,000	215,000
56,000 shares in Groudale Ltd.	80,000	
Loan to Groudale Ltd.	55,000	
Current assets	23,000	26,000
Less creditors: amounts falling due within one year	(15,300)	(46,400)
Proposed dividend	(10,000)	
Loan from Frinton plc		(55,000)
	295,700	139,600
Share capital and reserves		
Called-up share capital (£1 shares)	150,000	80,000
Revenue reserves	145,700	59,600
	295,700	139,600

When Frinton plc bought its shares in its subsidiary, Groudale Ltd.'s reserves totalled £28,000. There have been no changes to Groudale Ltd.'s share capital since it became Frinton's subsidiary. Ignore amortization of goodwill.

     You are required to prepare a consolidated balance sheet for the group as at 30 April 2004.

4W. For each of the following situations, comment on the appropriate treatment within Company A's group financial statements:

   1. Company A owns 75 per cent of Company B's voting capital and exercises a dominant influence on Company B's operating and financial policies.

   2. Company A owns 40 per cent of Company C's voting capital and exercises a significant influence on Company C's operating and financial policies.

   3. Company A owns 10 per cent of Company D's voting capital but does not exercise dominant or significant influence on Company D's operating and financial policies.

4. Company A is managing a business venture jointly with Company Z. Company A has no other connection with Company Z.

5. Company A has placed significant orders with a company owned by Peter Browne, who also owns 35 per cent of Company A's share capital.

5W. When deciding upon the structure of a company that trades in several regions or products, there are a number of alternative possibilities for the way that company is organized, including setting up divisions, or establishing subsidiaries. Explain the nature, benefits, and disadvantages of the two named types of organizational structure.

6W. The following are the summarized profit and loss accounts of Goliath Plc and its subsidiary, David Ltd., for the year ended 31 October 2004:

	Goliath plc	David Ltd.
	£	£
Turnover	2,350,000	652,000
Cost of sales	(1,230,400)	(316,000)
Gross profit	1,119,600	336,000
Expenses	(780,200)	(250,900)
Operating profit before taxation	339,400	85,100
Taxation	(95,200)	(34,100)
Operating profit after taxation	244,200	51,000
Proposed dividend	(100,000)	—
Retained profit for the year	144,200	51,000
Retained profit brought forward	356,250	122,040
Retained profit carried forward	500,450	173,040

Notes
1. David Ltd. sold goods worth £85,000 to Goliath plc during the year.
2. Goliath plc owned 75% of David Ltd.'s share capital.
3. Amortization of goodwill arising on the consolidation totalled £10,000 at 31 October 2004, including £2,000 for the current year.
4. David Ltd.'s reserves were £40,000 at the time it became a subsidiary of Goliath plc, eight years ago.

Prepare a consolidated profit and loss account for Goliath Group plc for the year ended 31 December 2004.

■ MINI CASE STUDY

Wild Life Holidays Ltd.

MinnieMax Ltd. (see previous mini case studies), after its successful first year, has entered its second year of trading with great confidence. Minnie and Maxim Trappenheimer are looking at various business opportunities. Minnie has noticed the following advertisement in the *Financial Daily Newspaper:*

Investment Opportunity

For Sale: Wild Life Holidays Ltd.

- Niche leisure travel business, specializing in safari holidays
- Turnover £2–£3m per annum, Pre-tax profits £250,000. Strong growth record
- Total net assets valued recently at £3.5m
- Established management team, who will remain with the company
- Huge potential: would suit exotic animal company wishing to expand
- Private limited company
- Sale price: in the region of £2.5m for 70% of equity, or £4m for 100% equity

Contact Box No. A 4567 for further details.

Advise MinnieMax Ltd. about the main accounting implications of:

  (i)   buying all the shares;
 (ii)   buying 70 per cent of the shares;
(iii)   buying no shares, but making an offer for the net assets of the company.

(*Suggested solutions can be found in Appendix 4.*)

■ **MAXI CASE STUDY**

History and Heraldry

Read the following article, and answer the question that follows it.

> Malcolm Ogg attributes his company's success to two things. First, rigorous targeting in the impulse-buy gift market. Second, exports. The rigorous targeting was Mr Ogg's idea. After completing a degree in design, he worked as a marketing director before founding History and Heraldry with the proceeds of the sale of his house. The biggest turning point came when Mr Ogg recruited Gerald Lakmaker in 1998 to lead the company into the export market.
>
> 'Malcolm had virtually no exports at all,' he says. At the time, the company had eight employees and a turnover of just under £2m. It was, even then, very profitable. The business, Mr Ogg says, has been self-funding from day one.
>
> But History and Heraldry needed to break into the export market to grow. It had a few overseas outlets at the time—New Zealand, Australia and Canada—but now exports to 54 countries in 24 different languages. 'We must be the only company in the world that sells acrylic products to China' says Mr Lakmaker.
>
> When Mr Lakmaker joined, he already had contacts in Austria and Denmark, so he began with those. 'You never appoint a distributor without visiting, and by the end of that year we had 14 distributors.' He has just appointed a distributor for the Baltic States and Russia—and is retiring for the third time, to cut down on the travelling. 'Last year, I travelled to 23 countries,' he says. He visited every distributor at least

twice a year. 'But it's impossible now.' On his retirement he will be replaced by five people—four to do the visiting and one to oversee them. The Lakmaker approach is tailor-made to the business and the products. He makes presentations to sales representatives, shows off the products and explains how to 'overcome sales resistance. Shops always have arguments why they shouldn't buy.'

Now the company is expanding into America, but there, unlike in other countries, History and Heraldry has decided to set up a subsidiary. So far, the company has invested some $1m in the venture and probably as much again in extended credit.

Adapted from Wendy Grossman, 'Starting Out', *Daily Telegraph* 4 Aug. 2003,
© Telegraph Group Limited 2003

Question

The company, for the first time, has decided to set up a subsidiary company. Explain why this has both advantages and disadvantages when compared with the existing ways in which the company has organized its business relationships.

(Suggested answers and discussion areas are available on the companion website.)

■ WEB LINKS

Company websites

Companies referred to in this chapter:

Courts plc www.courtsplc.com

Domino's Pizza www.dominos.co.uk

History and Heraldry www.historyheraldry.com/

Roche Group www.roche.com

■ FURTHER READING

Black, G. (2003). *Students' Guide to Accounting and Financial Reporting Standards*, 9th edn. (Harlow: FT/Prentice Hall), chapter 13.

Elliott, B., and Elliott, J. (2003). *Financial Accounting and Reporting*, 8th edn. (Harlow: FT/Prentice Hall), chapters 18–21.

■ COMPANION WEBSITE MATERIALS

Additional materials are available for students and lecturers on the companion website, at **www.oup.com/uk/booksites/busecon/business/**, including a 'Question Generator' file that gives unlimited practice at preparing simple group accounts.

The annual report

OBJECTIVES

By the end of this chapter you will be able to:

- Recognize the main components of an annual report.
- Appraise the 'public relations' aspect of annual reports.
- Understand the mixture of statutory and non-statutory information contained within the annual report.
- Appreciate the role and content of interim reports.

11.1 Introduction

The annual report is the key communication that a limited company has with its shareholders. Shareholders are entitled to receive a copy, and companies listed on stock exchanges generally issue their reports within 3–6 months of the balance sheet date. Such companies are also required to produce *interim* reports either half-yearly (e.g. in the UK) or quarterly (e.g. in the USA). There are currently proposals from the European Commission to make quarterly reports mandatory throughout the EU for publicly listed companies. Public companies' annual reports are also made freely available to potential shareholders or those generally interested in the company's performance, either as a paper copy or in an electronic format that can be downloaded from the company website. Summarized versions of the annual report can be offered as an alternative to those who do not require fully detailed information but only need the 'highlights' of what has happened during the financial year. Access to *private* limited companies' financial information is more restricted and there is usually far less 'general' information given about the company, with only the *minimum* disclosures required by law. In the UK, private companies below a certain size[1] are permitted to publish much less information than plc's, and their annual report might consist simply of a highly abbreviated profit and loss account (which might not even show the company's turnover or cost of sales), and a summarized balance sheet. However, even the shareholders in small companies are entitled to receive a more detailed version than that which is made available to the general public.

---

[1] For example, a *small* company is currently defined as having at least two of the following conditions: turnover not greater than £2.8 million, gross assets of no more than £1.4 million, and up to 50 employees (UK Companies Act 1985, s. 248).

Large listed companies often use the annual report as an opportunity for giving not only financial data but also background information about the products and services that the company provides.

For example, the annual report of the fashion company Hugo Boss AG extended to 185 pages, of which 58 pages showed photographs of fashion models, textiles, and sponsored events. Tesco plc produced a 'detailed' annual report that covered 56 pages and a separate 'annual review and summary financial statement', with many colour photos of supermarkets, products, employees, and directors, that extended to 37 pages.

Once again, the relevant parts of Domino's Pizza's annual report will be used for illustration, though, as before, we shall refer to other companies where needed to illustrate the full range of information which might be disclosed.

Figure 11.1 shows how the contents of this chapter relate to Domino's Pizza's annual report shown in Appendix 1. Note how the various parts of the report are required by different rules and regulations, or are given voluntarily by the company.

Title	Page reference	Required by:
Chairman's statement	307	(Mostly voluntary information to comply with best practice)
Chief executive's report	308–11	
Directors' and advisers' details	311–12	Stock exchange rules
Report on directors' remuneration	314–15	Stock exchange rules
Directors' report	316–18	Part stock exchange rules, part statute
Independent auditor's report	319	Statute
Group profit and loss account	320	Statute
Group statement of total recognized gains and losses	320	Accounting standards (in UK)
Group balance sheet	321	Statute
Company balance sheet	322	Statute
Group statement of cash flows	323	Accounting standards
Notes to the accounts	324–41	Statute and accounting standards
Notice of annual general meeting	341	Statute
Notes regarding resolutions at AGM	342–5	Statute
Five year record	345	Part stock exchange rules, part voluntary disclosure

Note:
1. In the UK, 'Statutory information' refers to Companies Acts.
2. The London Stock Exchange's regulations are contained in a publication known as the 'Yellow Book'.
3. 'Best practice' includes a corporate governance code issued by the 'Committee on Corporate Governance' known as 'The Combined Code'.
4. Many companies also provide additional statements including a finance director's report, an operating and financial review, and a statement of corporate governance.

Figure 11.1 The key contents of an annual report

Domino's Pizza's annual report is, in its entirety, 45 pages long, with eight of those pages (not reproduced in Appendix 1 to this book) showing colour photos of pizzas, ingredients, customers, employees, awards, and charitable and community initiatives. Access the company's website if you want to download the full report (see web link at end of chapter).

11.2 'Overview' reports, including the chairman's report and the operating and financial review

11.2.1 The chairman's report and reports of other individual directors

The chairman of a public limited company (US: company president) is the chair of the board of directors, and is usually an experienced businessman or woman who might hold similar positions with several other companies. In many companies, he or she is a member of the family that started the business, but it is equally likely that the company has appointed the chairman because he or she has had *no* previous involvement with it, and would therefore be expected to take an objective view of the role and its responsibilities. Apart from chairing directors' meetings, the company chairman will also be in charge of company general meetings, including the AGM (see section 11.6). Tact and diplomacy can be essential ingredients for a successful chairman, as well as good industry contacts. The chairman's report contained within the annual report gives the chairman an opportunity to reflect in general terms on the progress (or lack of it) in the past financial year and to comment on current and future trading prospects. Bearing in mind that the annual report is published in the financial year *following* that on which the annual report is based, users of the information look very carefully at the chairman's report to try and establish how the current trading year is progressing. As stock market prices are usually set on the basis of what the market expects the performance to be in the future rather than what it was in the past, optimistic comments in the chairman's report often lead to share price increases, whereas pessimistic or cautious remarks may push down the share price.

There is no set format to the chairman's report, and the same applies to the report of the chief executive (if a separate report is given by that director). Some companies also provide a finance director's report. In all these cases, information is voluntarily given by the company and is not subject to independent audit (see below). The directors have a responsibility, however, not to make misleading statements, and must avoid comments that are untrue or deliberately inaccurate. Do not confuse reports given by *individual* directors, such as the finance director, with the 'directors' report', which is a statutory statement containing information required by the regulatory framework that governs company reporting.

The chairman's statement of Domino's Pizza can be found on p. 307. Note that it starts with general product information (including adjectives such as 'fresh' and 'great-tasting'), gives historic market data ('10m orders . . . a quarter of all of the delivered pizza orders . . .'), and includes future predictions ('by 2010 [the home delivery pizza market] is expected to top the £800m mark'). Note the very positive tone of the entire statement.

The chief executive's report (see pp. 308–11) is a much more detailed financial analysis giving a thorough breakdown of the results for the year. Additionally, it stresses the benefit to communities in which stores operate, through employment opportunities and charitable giving. Of particular interest to users is the short paragraph headed 'Current trading and prospects', which reveals a 10.1 per cent increase in like-for-like sales in the first six weeks of the current financial year, and the optimistic conclusion to the paragraph: 'We, therefore, look forward to 2003 with confidence.'

Obviously, not all companies can be so positive. For example, look at this extract from the chairman's statement within the annual report of WILink plc:

Market conditions, which deteriorated during the second half, remained adverse and 2003 will be a challenging year and difficult to predict. We are confident about the longer term and are well positioned to benefit when the upturn comes, although the benefits of any upturn are unlikely to be before 2004.

11.2.2 The operating and financial review

Many large companies, in addition to a chairman's report, publish an 'operating and financial review' (OFR), which gives a discussion of the company's operating results, a review of the group's financial needs and resources, and a commentary on shareholder's return and share value. The overall characteristics of the OFR are that it should be fair, giving a balanced and objective statement of both good and bad news. It should focus on matters of significance, and be presented in the way most likely to help the user of the annual report in gaining an understanding of the financial circumstances of the business. The overriding purpose is to convey the 'real dynamics' of the business, including, where material, the company's relationships with stakeholders such as customers, employees, suppliers, and the community.

Tate & Lyle plc's operating and financial review for 2002 was a twelve-page summary taking an overview of the company's financial results and the related risks. The extract in Figure 11.2 explains, in non-technical language, the changes that have taken place in the company's sweeteners and starches division.

Sweeteners and Starches –
Rest of the World: continuing activities
Profits before exceptional items and interest increased from £1 million to £4 million.

Asian Sugar Businesses
Nghe An Tate & Lyle (NAT&L), the Group's cane sugar business in Vietnam, had a record season with 84,460 tonnes of sugar produced, up from 63,250 tonnes in the previous financial year. NAT&L is now the largest producer in Vietnam and the factory is working above design capacity. Sales have been expanded into the south of the country and new industrial markets penetrated. The year has been profitable and enabled early repayment of over 15% of NAT&L's project finance package. Management has been focused on improving quality by working with the 20,000 farmers who supply cane to the mill and with all factory staff. The Tate & Lyle safety awareness programme has been implemented and the operation has responded with an excellent safety record to date. The factory received the ISO 9001 accreditation in early 2002.

Well Pure Limited holds the Group's majority interest in two Chinese cane sugar factories which both experienced significant increases in cane throughput.

The United Sugar Company, in which the Group's shareholding is 10%, had a profitable year and produced 600,000 tonnes of refined sugar for the Saudi Arabian local market. The refinery capacity expansion to 760,000 tonnes will be fully operational by July 2002.

Sweeteners and Starches –
Rest of the World: discontinued activities
Profits fell from £13 million to £1 million. Zambia Sugar made £7 million in the 53 weeks to 31 March 2001 before it was sold at the beginning of April 2001. ZSR made a small loss from its sugar refining business before it was sold in February 2002, compared with a £4 million profit last year. The business suffered under adverse trading and economic conditions in Zimbabwe. Inflation exceeded 100% and price controls on sugar were reintroduced by the government.

The Group sold its 50.1% interest in ZSR to a company led by ZSR's senior management, and the business is now effectively owned by indigenous interests. In the circumstances of the economic and political environment in Zimbabwe, combined with Group strategy to focus on core businesses, this outcome was considered the most advantageous for all parties. The Group's 20% shareholding in United Farmer & Industrial Company in Thailand and 15% shareholding in East Asia Properties, the holding company of five other sugar factories in southern China, were sold in the final quarter of the year.

Adverse exchange rate movements, primarily in Zimbabwe, reduced profit by £3 million.

Figure 11.2 Tate & Lyle plc: operating and financial review

11.3 **The directors' report**

In the UK, most of the information contained within the directors' report is required by statute—particularly the Companies Act 1985. Much of the information, for example the group profit for the year and the total dividend, can be found in other parts of the annual report. However, details such as the directors' shareholdings, significant shareholdings above 3 per cent of the issued capital, the company's policy regarding payment to suppliers, and payments to political parties and charities are usually only found within this part of the annual report.

For public limited companies listed on a stock market, a further section on 'corporate governance' is required, which explains the way in which the board of directors operates, what its responsibilities are, and how the board maintains internal control to safeguard the company's assets. Most large companies have an audit committee, whose primary responsibilities include monitoring the system of internal control, approving the company's accounting policies, and reviewing the interim and annual financial statements before their submission to the main board of directors. The whole area of corporate governance has been strengthened in recent years in the wake of financial scandals. In the USA, the Sarbanes-Oxley Act 2002 has brought in several measures to strengthen the role of audit committees in that country to improve investor protection. In particular, it requires audit committees:

1. to have independence, so that no member of the committee accepts any advisory, consulting, or other fee from the company, other than as a member of the audit committee;

2. to have at least one 'financial expert' as a member of the committee—or give a reason why not;

3. to have adopted a code of ethics for their principal financial officers—or give a reason why not;

4. to have adopted GAAP (Generally Accepted Accounting Principles)—or explain the ramifications of not using GAAP, and also to reveal the accounting treatment preferred by the outside auditors, if not followed by the company's own procedures;

5. not to appoint a chief executive officer or chief financial officer who had been employed by the company's outside auditors, if they had participated in the company's audit in the prior year;

6. to have pre-approved all auditing services and non-audit services to be provided by their outside auditors;

7. to have procedures in place for the receipt and treatment of complaints and concerns regarding questionable accounting or auditing matters, including confidential and anonymous submissions by employees.

Similar proposals within the UK (the 'Smith Report') have been put forward and are currently being debated. Note that public limited companies listed on a stock exchange are expected to have several *non-executive* directors who are appointed for their wide experience of business, and objectivity in considering the company's affairs. A report published in the UK in January 2003 (The 'Higgs Report') recommended that at least half of a company's board members should be independent, that the roles of the chairman and chief executive should be separate, and that directors should not act as chairman of more than one company.

Look at Domino's Pizza's Directors' Report shown on pp. 316–18. In particular, read the sections headed 'Corporate Governance' and 'Statement of Directors' Responsibilities'. Note the functions of the audit and remuneration committees, and the statement referring to 'going concern'. Look also at p. 311, which lists the six directors, including three non-executive directors.

11.4 **The auditor's report**

The auditor's report is that of an *external* auditor:[2] an independent qualified accountant or (more usually) a firm of accountants, who reports to the shareholders as to whether or not the financial statements and related notes show a true and fair view of the company's state of affairs. The auditor also states whether the statements comply with relevant legislation and accounting standards. Until relatively recently, *every* limited company in the UK had to appoint an independent auditor, but this requirement no longer applies to small unlisted companies. Sole traders and partnerships have never been subject to a statutory audit, and the removal of the requirement for small companies was seen to be a logical step in reducing 'red tape'. Any company, however small, can, however, choose to appoint an auditor, and shareholders may insist on such an appointment if they believe that it would safeguard their interests.

Auditors do not check *every* financial transaction, though an auditor has 'a right of access at all times to the books, accounts and vouchers, and is entitled to require from the company's officers such information and explanations as he thinks necessary for the performance of the auditor's duties'.[3] In practice, sampling and statistical techniques are used to test the reliability and accuracy of the company's systems, and physical inspections will be made to verify the existence of material assets such as stock and tangible fixed assets.

The key elements of the auditor's report are outlined in a 'Statement of Auditing Standards' which was first published in May 1993. The report should contain:

- a title identifying the person or persons to whom the report is addressed;
- an introductory paragraph identifying the financial statements audited;
- separate sections, appropriately headed, dealing with:

  (i) the respective responsibilities of directors and auditors;

  (ii) the basis of the auditor's opinion;

  (iii) the auditor's opinion on the financial statements (see below);

- the signature of the auditors;
- the date of the report.

Once the auditors have completed their audit, they must decide upon the wording of their opinion, which can be either unqualified or qualified. An unqualified opinion is given when the financial statements give a 'true and fair view' and comply with legislation and accounting standards. The vast majority of auditors' reports on public listed companies contain unqualified opinions. Occasionally, a qualified opinion must be given where there has been a 'limitation of scope' or a 'disagreement'.

- A *limitation of scope* exists when the auditors have been unable to carry out all their intended procedures because information is not made available to them, or because

---

[2] Not to be confused with *internal* auditors, who are employed by the company to check the efficiency of financial reporting procedures and internal financial control.   [3] Companies Act 1985, s. 237.

the directors or others impose limitations upon their work. Examples are:

- loss or corruption of records due to poor control;
- lack of access to the records of overseas branches;
- refusal to allow the auditors to attend a stocktake.

- A *disagreement* exists when the auditors have a difference of opinion with the directors over the way in which items have been treated within the financial statements. For example, the auditors' valuation of a company's intangible fixed assets may be significantly higher or lower than the directors' valuation.

> Domino's Pizza's auditors' report is shown on p. 319. Note the three separate sections: respective responsibilities of directors and auditors, basis of audit opinion, and opinion. The latter is unqualified, as it states that the financial statements 'give a true and fair view and have been properly prepared in accordance with the relevant legislation'.

As stated previously, qualified opinions are unusual for public listed companies, and could be damaging to a company's reputation, particularly where it has not complied with accounting standards or legislation. The wording of qualified opinions depends upon the severity of the situation, and ranges from a relatively mild caveat where the auditor states that the financial statements show a true and fair view 'except that (e.g.) inventory records of the Bolivian subsidiary were unavailable for the purposes of our audit, and there were no other satisfactory audit procedures that we could adopt to confirm the stock valuation', to an *adverse* opinion which states (with reasons) that the financial statements do *not* show a true and fair view.

The auditing firm Deloitte & Touche issued a qualified audit opinion in respect of the financial statements of the Constellation Corporation plc for the year ending 31 December 2000. The following is an extract from the auditor's report:

Basis of opinion

. . . We planned and performed our audit so as to obtain all the information and explanations which we considered necessary in order to provide us with sufficient evidence to give reasonable assurance that the financial statements are free from material misstatement, whether caused by fraud or other irregularity or error. However, the evidence available was limited in respect of the results of a number of subsidiary companies which were sold on 6 November 2000. As stated in note 1 the results of these subsidiaries for the period from 1 August 1999 to 29 July 2000 and subsequently up to their sale in November 2000 are based on unaudited management accounts drawn up to 30 October, being the latest financial information available before the sale. Upon sale the subsidiaries were excluded from the Group. Because of the sale and the related difficulties of obtaining information, it was not practicable for the Directors or ourselves to obtain adequate assurance regarding the results of these subsidiaries included with the profit and loss account or the proper allocation of these results being operating results (and the relevant statutory headings) and the exceptional loss on disposal required by FRS 2. This limitation also applies to the appropriate parts of the cash flow statement and in particular to the net cash inflow from operating activities and the disposal of subsidiary undertakings. The overall loss for the financial period itself for these subsidiaries is not affected by this limitation in scope. There were no other satisfactory audit procedures that we could adopt to verify this allocation of results . . .

Qualified opinion arising from limitation in scope

Except for any adjustments required to the disclosure of the profit and loss account in the accounts that might have been found to be necessary had we obtained sufficient information and explanations concerning the results of the subsidiary companies before sale, in our opinion the accounts give a true and fair view of the state of the Company and the Group's affairs as at 31 December 2000 and of the loss of the Group for the period then ended and have been properly prepared in accordance with the Companies Act 1985.

Constellation Corporation plc 2000 Annual Report

11.5 Financial statements

The financial statements within the annual report comprise, for a group, the group profit and loss account, the group balance sheet, the parent company's balance sheet, the group statement of cash flows, the group statement of total recognized gains and losses, and the related notes to the accounts. These have been covered in Chapters 4–10.

11.6 General meetings

11.6.1 Annual general meetings

As its name implies, the annual general meeting (AGM) is held once per year. Its purpose is to put resolutions to a shareholders' vote, relating to such matters as:

- approval of the financial statements and directors' and auditors' reports;
- approval of the final dividend;
- election or re-election of directors;
- appointment or reappointment of auditors.

In the UK, prior to the Companies Act 1989, all companies were required to hold an annual general meeting, but since then, private limited companies may decide not to hold one. For all other companies, an AGM should be held in each calendar year, not later than fifteen months after the preceding AGM. A new company need not hold an AGM in the year of its incorporation, or in the following year, provided that the first AGM is held within eighteen months of the date of incorporation. The AGM may be held at the company's offices, a hotel or other suitable venue.

Shareholders have the opportunity to question the directors on any aspect of company policy, but in practice only a small percentage usually attend. However, voting rights can be exercised by proxy, so that a shareholder's attendance is not necessary to vote on resolutions. The shareholder is sent a reply-paid card (see Figure 11.3(a)) with the resolutions listed, and simply ticks a 'for' or 'against' box, and returns the card to the company. Occasionally the AGM might be a bad-tempered occasion, particularly if the company is engaged in ethically dubious practices when the chairman and fellow directors may be subject to robust questioning from protesting shareholders. In recent years, the level of financial rewards paid to some directors has been criticized, resulting in heated debate—particularly where a company's financial results are in decline yet directors' remuneration has increased.

Severn Valley Railway (Holdings) plc issued a proxy form (to be returned to the company), as well as a poll card and attendance card (for those actually attending the AGM) prior to its annual general meeting. These are shown in Figures 11.3(a) and (b).

Severn Valley Railway (Holdings) PLC
A.G.M. 12TH JULY 2003 – POLL CARD

In connection with the **ORDINARY RESOLUTIONS**, please indicate below your vote

		For	Against
1.	Approval of the minutes of the previous AGM		
2.	Vote for a maximum of **THREE** from the following:		
	EXISTING DIRECTORS		
	2.1 Re-election of Alvin Barker		
	2.2 Election of Nicholas Campbell Paul (confirmation of appointment)		
	OTHER CANDIDATES		
	2.3 Election of Ian Baxter		
	2.4 Election of Richard Kitley Power		
3.	To approve the Report and Accounts		
4.	Re-appointment and remuneration of the Auditors		

Please complete the following section. (If attending as a Proxyholder, please give the name and address of the person(s) you represent)

Name: _____

Address: _____

_____Postcode_____

FOR SCRUTINEERING OFFICIALS ONLY

Share Certificate No. _____   No. of Shares _____
_____   _____
_____   _____

Severn Valley Railway (Holdings) PLC

ATTENDANCE CARD

Annual General Meeting
on
12th July 2003
at
The Castle Hall, Bridgnorth
at 8.00 pm.

If you wish to attend, please sign this card, bring it with you and hand it in on arrival. This will facilitate entry to the Meeting.

Signature _____

Print name: _____

Shareholder Number: _____
(if known)

Figure 11.3(a) Severn Valley Railway (Holdings) plc: poll card and attendance card

Severn Valley Railway (Holdings) PLC
Proxy Form 2003

I/We hereby appoint the Chairman of the Meeting

or _____

as my/our proxy to attend and, on a poll, vote on my/our behalf at the Annual General Meeting to be held on 12th July 2003 and at any adjournment thereof.

Ordinary Resolutions:		For	Against
1.	Approval of the minutes of the previous AGM		
2.	Vote for a maximum of **THREE** from the following:		
	EXISTING DIRECTORS		
2.1	Re-election of Alvin Barker		
2.2	Election of Nicholas Campbell Paul (confirmation of appointment)		
	OTHER CANDIDATES		
2.3	Election of Ian Baxter		
2.4	Election of Richard Kitley Power		
2.	To approve the Report and Accounts		
3.	Re-appointment and remuneration of the Auditors		

Please sign here _____ Date: _____

Please state your Name _____

Address _____

If the proxy form is signed by someone else on your behalf, their authority to sign must be returned with the form. In the case of joint holdings, any one holder may sign the form. If the member is a corporation the proxy should be executed under its common seal or under the hand of an officer or attorney duly authorised in writing.

If you complete and return the proxy form, you may still attend the Meeting and vote in person should you later decide to do so.

Please detach and post this form once you have completed it. To be valid, the proxy form must be received no later than 4.30 pm on 10th July 2003.

NOTES:

1. If you cannot attend the Annual General Meeting but wish to vote on the resolutions, you can appoint another person (a proxy, who need not be a member of the Company) who will, on a poll, vote according to your instructions. A proxy cannot vote on a show of hands. If you wish to appoint someone other than the Chairman of the Meeting please write their name and address in the space provided. You may appoint more than one proxy. In the absence of instructions, the proxy may vote or abstain as he/she thinks fit on the resolutions or on any other business (including amendments to resolutions) which comes before the Meeting.

2. Please indicate by a tick (✔) in the space provided how you wish your votes to be cast. If you do not do so the proxy may vote or abstain as he thinks fit.

Figure 11.3(b) Proxy form

Domino's Pizza's AGM notice (see pp. 341) shows that the meeting was held at the company's head office. The first five resolutions cover the standard matters of re-electing directors, receiving the financial reports, and re-electing or reappointing directors and auditors. It also lists a further four resolutions, two of which relate to share issues, another requiring authority to purchase the company's own shares, and a further resolution giving the company permission to distribute annual reports to shareholders by electronic means.

11.6.2 **Extraordinary general meetings**

An extraordinary general meeting (EGM) is any meeting of shareholders other than the AGM. A company's articles of association usually provide for the calling of EGMs at the discretion of the directors, or at the request of the members. If the directors refuse to hold an EGM, there is a statutory right for members to call for such a meeting, whereby holders of 10 per cent of the paid-up share capital of the company deposit a requisition at the company's registered office stating the objects of the meeting. The company's directors must proceed to convene the general meeting within twenty-one days from the deposit of the requisition. If they fail to do so, those making the requisition can themselves convene the meeting. Typical reasons for holding an EGM are when approval is needed from shareholders:

- to pursue a takeover bid for another company;
- to accept a takeover approach from another company;
- to make major changes to share capital.

 Read this news bulletin from the website of Heart of Midlothian plc, a football club based in Scotland:

This morning's EGM, lasting all of eleven minutes, passed without any incident of note. Approximately 100 shareholders sat passively in the Gorgie Suite whilst Club Chairman, Douglas Smith, outlined the reasons for the meeting. Shareholders were advised that the Board had decided to transfer the operating activities of the Company from 'Heart of Midlothian plc' to a wholly owned subsidiary, Heart of Midlothian Commercial Limited. In turn this non-trading subsidiary was to be renamed 'Heart of Midlothian Football Club Limited'. All day to day trading activities of the football club will in future operate under/within the subsidiary company.

The Chairman stated that the Board believed that it is more appropriate that all football activities are handled by a subsidiary company. There is no change of ownership, and accounts of the subsidiary will be consolidated at the year-end and presented to shareholders.

Shareholders were also advised that a technical issue has arisen in relation to the Company's erosion of capital where net assets had fallen below 50% of called up share capital. The erosion had occurred as a result of a number of reasons but mainly due to player's wages and/or early settlement of contracts. The Directors were satisfied that steps taken in recent months are addressing the trading position of the Company, and that the Club can look forward to improved trading conditions as a result.

Questions from those shareholders present were few but perhaps the most interesting was from ex-chairman, Wallace Mercer, who made it known that he fully supported the Club's recent proposals to move the stadium to an out of town site.

www.heartsfc.co.uk, 6 Aug. 2001

11.7 Financial summary and other information

Although not a statutory requirement, many companies provide a summary of what they regard as the financial highlights of previous years. Information may be given in graphical form, numerical tables, or a mixture of the two. In some cases, data for as many as twenty years is given. Some caution should be exercised though, as the summary is not covered by the auditor's report, and less than flattering information might be omitted. However, it can be useful as a quick guide to the company's progress over the period.

> Domino's Pizza's financial summary covers five years and is shown on p. 345. Key figures of turnover, profit, earnings per share, and dividends are given, as well as balance sheet totals, net debt, gearing as a percentage, and the number of stores. The final line shows the annual percentage increase in sales, year on year.

11.8 Interim reports

Public limited companies listed on the stock exchange within the UK are required not only to publish an annual report, but also an interim report covering the first half year's trading. Equivalent companies in the USA publish quarterly reports. These reports are not audited, but will contain an 'independent review' from the company's auditors stating whether or not the report contains any apparent misstatements or material inconsistencies. A typical interim report contains:

- financial highlights for the period (similar to the financial summary in the annual report);
- operating review and/or chief executive's statement giving an overview of the first six months' trading and the outlook for the rest of the financial period;
- profit and loss account covering the first six months;
- balance sheet as at the end of the six-month period;
- cash flow statement covering the first six months.

Interim reports are extremely important in providing investors with credible (though unaudited) financial information part way through the financial period. The earnings per share figure disclosed in the interim report will be used to recalculate the PE ratio (see p. 117), and this may lead to significant share price changes. The market will look particularly at the trading pattern of the first six months in comparison with that of the similar period in the previous year. The operating review is also considered very carefully and any hint of above or below average sales or profits will lead to share price changes.

Domino's Pizza's interim results for the half-year to 30 June 2003 were contained in a twelve-page booklet published in July of the year. It can be viewed at **www.dominos.co.uk** (click on 'Investor Relations' and follow the links to 'financial reports').

11.9 Chapter summary

- The annual report is the key communication that a limited company has with its shareholders. Interim reports are published either half-yearly or quarterly.

- Some parts of the annual report are required by statute, others by accounting or stock exchange regulations, and there may also be voluntary disclosure of information.

- Many companies publish an 'operating and financial review' which gives an objective commentary on the company's performance.

- Most large companies have an audit committee, whose primary responsibilities include monitoring the system of internal control, approving the company's accounting policies, and reviewing the interim and annual financial statements before their submission to the main board of directors.

- Independent, qualified accountants act as external auditors, reporting to the shareholders as to whether or not the financial statements show a true and fair view. The auditors' report might be either unqualified or qualified.

- Annual and extraordinary general meetings are held so that shareholders can vote on company resolutions. Examples of such resolutions include the approval of a dividend and the election or re-election of directors.

- Financial summaries showing the financial highlights of several years are often provided within the annual report, but they are unaudited and the company itself selects the information to be included.

■ **GLOSSARY**

annual general meeting (AGM)	Formal company meetings held once per year, at which resolutions are put forward for shareholders' approval
annual report	Summarized financial and other information issued to shareholders in accordance with statute, accounting, or stock exchange regulations
audit committee	An internal company committee which monitors the system of internal control, approves the company's accounting policies and reviews the interim and annual financial statements prior to their submission to the main board of directors
auditor	See *external auditor* and *internal auditor*

auditor's report	The external auditor's report to shareholders contained within the annual report, stating whether or not the financial statements and related notes show a true and fair view of the company's state of affairs. The report may be either unqualified or qualified
chairman	A person who chairs the board of directors
chairman's report	A general report of the company's performance given by the company's chairman
chief executive	A company's senior managing director
company president	US equivalent of 'company chairman'
directors' report	Statement included within the annual report containing information required by statute or the regulatory framework which is not contained elsewhere within the financial statements
external auditor	An independent qualified accountant or firm of accountants who reports to the shareholders as to whether or not the financial statements and related notes show a true and fair view of the company's state of affairs
extraordinary general meeting (EGM)	Any meeting of shareholders other than the annual general meeting
financial summary	Highlights of the company's performance included within an annual report. The summary is unaudited and the company itself selects the information
interim report	Unaudited summaries of quarterly or half-yearly financial information issued to shareholders in accordance with stock exchange regulations
internal auditor	Individuals employed by the company to check the efficiency of financial reporting procedures and internal financial control
non-executive director	A member of the board of directors who does not take an active role in managing the company but is appointed for his or her objectivity in considering the company's affairs, and wide experience of business
operating and financial review	An objective commentary on the company's performance contained within the annual report
qualified auditor's report	An external auditor's report to shareholders that contains a qualified opinion. Qualifications range from a disagreement on specific matters, to a full-scale adverse opinion stating that the accounts do not show a true and fair view
Sarbanes-Oxley Act 2002	US legislation designed to strengthen investor protection
unqualified auditor's report	An external auditor's report to shareholders, stating that the financial statements show a true and fair view and comply with the relevant regulatory framework

■ MULTIPLE CHOICE QUESTIONS

1. Which one of the following most closely defines an external auditor:

   a An independent qualified accountant who reports to the shareholders

   b An accountant employed by the company who reports to the directors

   c A non-executive director who takes an independent and objective view of the company's affairs

   d An independent qualified accountant who prepares the financial statements

2. Which one of the following is *not* a key element of an external auditor's report:

   a The signature of the auditors

   b The date of the report

   c The address of the company's head office

   d A title identifying the person or persons to whom the report is addressed

3. Which one of the following gives an objective overview to help the user of an annual report to gain an understanding of the financial circumstances of the business:

   a Directors' report

   b Auditors' report

   c Operating and financial review

   d Financial summary

4. A non-executive director is someone who:

   a Audits the company's financial statements

   b Checks the internal financial controls of the company

   c Chairs the annual general meeting

   d Is appointed to the board of directors to give unbiased advice and expertise

5. Annual reports are usually published:

   a 3–6 months before the end of the financial year

   b Within 3–6 months after the end of the financial year

   c On the same day that the financial year ends

   d On the day of the annual general meeting

6. Interim reports are usually published:

   a To comply with accounting rules

   b To comply with stock exchange regulations

   c To comply with company legislation

   d As voluntary information provided by companies

7. If the external auditors give an unqualified audit opinion, they are reporting that:

   a The financial statements give a true and fair view and comply with legislation and accounting standards

   b The financial statements do not give a true and fair view and do not comply with legislation and accounting standards

c The financial statements give a true and fair view but do not comply with legislation and accounting standards

d The financial statements do not give a true and fair view but do comply with legislation and accounting standards

8. When a public limited company is first incorporated, its first annual general meeting must be held within which of the following time periods from the date of incorporation:

   a 24 months
   b 6 months
   c 12 months
   d 18 months

9. What name is given to the voting method that is available to shareholders who cannot attend a general meeting?

   a Proxy voting
   b Postal voting
   c Prior voting
   d Preferential voting

10. Which one of the following statements is *not* contained within a published interim report?

    a Cash flow statement
    b Profit and loss account
    c Auditor's report
    d Balance sheet

(*Note: answers are shown in Appendix 2.*)

■ DISCUSSION QUESTIONS

1. As such a large proportion of the annual reports of leading companies consists of glossy colour photos of directors, products, stores, factories, and offices, the financial information seems to be of secondary importance. Discuss.

2. The annual general meeting is a genuinely democratic event that gives shareholders the opportunity to question the way in which their company is managed. Discuss.

3. Company financial information is of little use to potential investors because it is out of date by the time it is published. For example, an annual report for 2004 will probably not be published until late 2005, by which time the directors will be planning for the year 2006. Discuss.

(*Note: Suggested answers or discussion points are available on the companion website.*)

■ LONGER QUESTIONS

(Questions marked W have suggested answers on the companion website. Other questions are answered in Appendix 3.)

1. A shareholder with no accounting knowledge has received a very detailed annual report, and is unsure about the following parts of the document:

   a the chairman's report;

   b the directors' report;

   c the auditor's report;

   d the operating and financial review.

   Explain the significance of each of the above sections of the annual report.

2. The 2002 auditor's report to the shareholders of Marconi plc contained the following paragraph:

   Going Concern—fundamental uncertainty

   In forming our opinion, we have considered the adequacy of the disclosures made in note 1 of the accounts concerning the Group's current borrowing facilities and ongoing negotiations with its bankers and bond-holders. As indicated in note 1, the going concern assumption is dependent on the Directors reaching a satisfactory resolution of the re-financing negotiations with the Group's bankers and bondholders. Should the Group's bankers and bondholders not continue to provide support until a re-financing of the Group is achieved, the going concern basis of preparation would no longer be applicable and adjustments to the Group profit and loss account and Group balance sheet would be required to record additional liabilities and write down assets to their recoverable amount. Furthermore, the contingent liabilities relating to the indebtedness and obligations guaranteed by Marconi plc described in note 28 (a) to the accounts would crystallise, resulting in additional liabilities in the Company balance sheet. It is not practicable to quantify these potential adjustments. In view of the significance of this fundamental uncertainty, we consider that it should be drawn to your attention. Our opinion is not qualified in this respect.

   Marconi Corporation plc website

   The above auditor's report is unqualified even though there is a 'fundamental uncertainty' regarding the applicability of the going concern concept. To what extent would this uncertainty affect your view of the company's financial results?

3. Sir Richard Sykes, the former chairman of GlaxoSmithKline yesterday said small shareholders should be excluded from annual general meetings (AGMs) as he lambasted large shareholders for being inactive.

   Institutional investors have been 'pathetic and it is a sin' according to Sir Richard, the rector of Imperial College of Science and newly appointed head of an independent inquiry into the relationship between investment and wealth creation.

   However, he said those investors who hold large blocks of shares should take better advantage of AGMs to grill management. 'Why should one person with one share be able to have a cup of coffee and a sandwich and disrupt the company when the investors with control are not bringing it to task?' he asked.

   Small shareholders should have their own platform to air views, he added. Sir Richard's inquiry is sponsored by Tomorrow's Company, an independent think tank. However, his criticisms may embarrass the government, which has appointed him as an adviser to the Department of Trade and Industry (DTI). The DTI said Sir Richard is 'not speaking for the DTI in any shape or form on this particular issue'.

   Lina Saigol 'Large investors pathetic, says Sykes', *Financial Times*, 4 Feb. 2003

   Critically comment upon Sir Richard Sykes's comments. Do you agree with the suggestion that small shareholders should be excluded from AGMs?

4W. Publicly listed companies must not only produce an annual report, but also an unaudited interim report. Explain the purpose of interim reports, their typical contents, and their use in stock market evaluation of a company's performance.

5W. Explain the function of an 'audit committee', particularly in relation to the aim for improved corporate governance.

6W. To what extent, if at all, do the information needs of a shareholder with 80 per cent of a company's equity shares differ from a shareholder with only 5 per cent?

■ MINI CASE STUDY

Foskitt or Quavers?

Lottie von Mausen is the owner of 10 per cent of the equity share capital of MinnieMax Ltd. (see previous case studies). She has received notice of the first annual general meeting of the company, which includes the following resolution: 'To replace Foskitt, Tryste & Co., who were appointed as the company's auditors on its formation, with Quaver, Lipperman & Co. to act as the company's auditors until the next annual general meeting.'

Lottie had read the audit report of Foskitt, Tryste & Co., which contained the following paragraphs:

Basis of opinion

We conducted our audit in accordance with United Kingdom Auditing Standards issued by the Auditing Practices Board. An audit includes examination, on a test basis, of evidence relevant to the amounts and disclosures in the financial statements. It also includes an assessment of the significant estimates and judgements made by the directors in the preparation of the financial statements, and of whether the accounting policies are appropriate to the company's circumstances, consistently applied and adequately disclosed.

We planned and performed our audit so as to obtain all the information and explanations which we considered necessary in order to provide us with sufficient evidence to give reasonable assurance as to whether the financial statements are free from material misstatement. In forming our opinion we also evaluated the overall adequacy of the presentation of information in the financial statements. We believe that our audit provides a reasonable basis for our opinion.

Qualified opinion: adverse opinion

A legal case brought against the company by the Peruvian Wherearewe tribe was settled out of court on 30 September 2004 for the sum of £250,000, payable in ten equal annual instalments commencing on 1 January 2005. This has been excluded from the financial statements as the directors take the view that the payments are not relevant to the financial statements for the financial year ended 30 September 2004. We disagree with the directors' position.

In view of the effect of the failure to provide for the matters referred to above, in our opinion the financial statements do not give a true and fair view of the state of the company's affairs as at 30 September 2004 and of its profit for the year then ended. In our opinion the financial statements give a true and fair view of the company's cash flows for the year ended 30 September 2004. In all other respects, in our opinion the financial statements have been properly prepared in accordance with the Companies Act 1985.

Foskitt, Tryste & Co

Registered auditor

London

12 December 2004

You are required to advise Lottie how she should respond to the proposed resolution.

(*Suggested solutions can be found in Appendix 4.*)

■ MAXI CASE STUDY

Annual report review

To complete this case study, you need to obtain a recent annual report of a public limited company. In the UK, you can obtain free annual reports by accessing the website of the *Financial Times* annual report service at **www.wilink.com**, you can contact a company directly, or find its website (usually there is a link to 'investor information'). Avoid companies in the banking, insurance, or financial services sector, as their annual reports tend to be highly specialized. A manufacturing or retailing company is preferable.

Read carefully through the following statements and reports of your chosen company, and then answer the questions that follow:

1. Chairman's statement
   Question: What is the overall tone of the report? Identify those parts that are optimistic, pessimistic, and neutral. What, if any, praise does the chairman give to employees, fellow directors, shareholders, or others?

2. Operating and financial review (this might be called simply 'review of operations')
   Question: The OFR should be fair, giving a balanced and objective statement of both good and bad news. To what extent does your company's OFR reflect good practice?

3. Auditor's report
   Question: Is the auditor's opinion qualified in any way? Do the financial statements show a true and fair view? What are the respective responsibilities of the directors and auditors?

4. Notice of annual general meeting
   Question: What is the date of the AGM? How long after the end of the financial year is it being held? Where is it being held? What is the ordinary business at the AGM? Is there any special business being considered? What are the voting arrangements?

(*Suggested answers and discussion areas are available on the companion website.*)

■ WEB LINKS

Company websites
(Companies referred to in this chapter)

Constellation Corporation plc www.constellationcorporation.com

Domino's Pizza www.dominos.co.uk

Heart of Midlothian Football Club www.heartsfc.co.uk

Hugo Boss AG www.hugoboss.com

Marconi Corporation plc www.marconi.com

Severn Valley Railways (Holdings) plc www.svr.co.uk

Tate and Lyle plc www.tateandlyle.co.uk

WILink plc www.wilink.com

Other links:

An interesting website showing how a major pension fund decides upon its vot ng strategy at company general meetings: **www.westmids-pensions.org.uk/pdfs/corpgovernancepolicyapril2003.pdf**

■ FURTHER READING

Dyson, J. R. (2003). *Accounting for Non-accounting Students*, 5th edn. (Harlow: FT/Prentice Hall), chapter 11.

Jones, M. (2002). *Accounting for Non-specialists*, 1st edn. (Chichester: Wiley), chapter 12.

McKenzie, W. (2003). *FT Guide to Using and Interpreting Company Accounts* (Harlow: FT/Prentice Hall), chapters 6, 7.

■ COMPANION WEBSITE MATERIALS

 Additional materials are available for students and lecturers on the companion website, at **www.oup.com/uk/booksites/busecon/business/**

12

Understanding and analysing the annual report

OBJECTIVES

By the end of this chapter you will be able to:

- Undertake preliminary research prior to analysing company accounts.
- Distinguish between, and compute, a vertical and horizontal analysis of financial information and interpret the data revealed by the analysis.
- Prepare ratios within five main groupings and analyse the data revealed.
- Summarize and draw up a conclusion on a company's performance.
- Understand concerns regarding the validity of accounting information.

12.1 Introduction

The purpose of this chapter is to help you make sense of the information contained in the financial summaries—to analyse them, interpret them, and come to a conclusion about how well or badly the company has performed. It is easy to be overwhelmed by the mass of information that companies include within their annual and interim reports. We have already seen within this book that, in addition to the financial summaries, there are several reports of a general nature (such as the chairman's review, and chief executive's report) that may be useful in giving a non-technical overview of the company's progress in the past period, and its potential for the future. The independent auditor's report is also vital to give assurance that the statements show a true and fair view, and if they don't, the reasons why the auditors came to that conclusion. For public limited companies listed on stock exchanges, there is likely to be much information and comment available in the financial pages of daily newspapers, and from internet-based sources. For example, the following is a typical newspaper article following the announcement of a plc's annual results.

Holmes Place staggers in with dividend decline and banking covenant problems

Holmes Place yesterday piled additional woe on its weary shareholders with a 76 per cent fall in full-year profits, a dividend cut and news it still had not renegotiated its banking covenants.

The health club operator, which faced having its shares suspended if it had not released its last year's results yesterday, indicated there would be little recovery beyond the current year.

Graham Reddish, chairman, said: 'the previously hoped-for marked improvement in overall group profitability and cash generation beyond 2003 has declined.'

But the group continued to dangle the carrot of a possible management buy-out and said takeover talks were at an 'advanced stage'. It thought that venture capital groups Bridgepoint and Permira would make an offer in the next ten days.

Pre-tax profit in the year to December 31 fell from £18.9m to £4.6m, on turnover up 17 per cent to £144.1 million. Net debt stood at £116 million at the end of the year. However, the group's breaching of its banking covenants meant the accounts were qualified.[1]

Allan Fisher, chief executive, said that the company was still in discussions with its banks but declined to give further details. Nick Batram, at Robert W. Baird,[2] called the results a 'catalogue of ugliness' . . .

There was no final dividend, giving a total of 1.9p (5.1p). Losses per share were 0.81p (9.21p).

FT Comment

Holmes Place increasingly looks like a dog that needs to be put out of its misery. Unfortunately for shareholders, the comprehensive catalogue of woes means Bridgepoint and Permira will do that cheaply if they do it at all. The dire trading and forecasts of no recovery for the next two years mean that any take-out price would be near the current price of 37½p, down 5p. At six times enterprise value to ebitda,[3] this looks expensive compared with a similar ratio for the much healthier Fitness First,[4] but the lower share price should take some of the sting out of it for the VCs.[5] Given the poor chance of returns, investors should take what they can get.

Lisa Urquhart, *Financial Times,* 1 May 2003

Looking at the information contained within the newspaper article, we can identify the following as key areas for comment (in the order they appear in the article):

- profit level;
- dividend level;
- company borrowings;
- future prospects;
- chairman's remarks, including comments on cash flow;
- takeover possibilities;
- amounts of profit, turnover, and net debt for current and previous years;
- the auditor's report;
- dividend per share and losses per share.

[1] i.e. the auditor's opinion was qualified.   [2] A US-based financial adviser.
[3] Earnings before interest, tax, depreciation, and amortization.   [4] A rival health club operator.
[5] Venture capitalists.

Although the company that is the subject of the article was having difficulties, the key areas identified are typical for virtually all companies. In this chapter, we shall be looking at a systematic analysis of a company's results, based first on preliminary research, secondly by horizontal, vertical, and 'trend' analysis, and finally by a detailed ratio analysis.

As in previous chapters, the relevant parts of Domino's Pizza's annual report are used, though, as before, we shall refer to other companies where needed to illustrate the full range of information which might be used for analysis.

12.2 The first stage: preliminary research

There are many reasons for analysing financial statements, including:

- Investment—you may be an existing shareholder or potential shareholder.

- Commercial relationship—you may have an existing trading link, or are considering a future relationship with the business.

- Lending decisions—banks and other financial institutions need to know if a business is capable of repaying loans.

- Self-interest—you might work (or consider working) for the company, and you want to find out more about the company that pays your salary.

- Business rivalry—how well or badly is a competitor doing compared with your company?

- Curiosity—you may have used a business's products or services and want to find out more about what it does.

- Taxation—the taxation authorities may need to be satisfied that the accounts appear complete and trustworthy.

- Environmental factors—local communities and pressure groups may wish to find out more about local companies, including their employment and ecological attitudes.

- Economic analysis—business trends can be ascertained by analysing company results.

Those wishing to make the analysis may already know a great deal about the company, as shareholders, employees, or by virtue of publicly available information such as newspaper comment. The key background information that is needed prior to starting a detailed numerical analysis of the financial statements includes:

- Type of trade—what does the company do?

- Competitors—who are the company's main competitors? What share of the market do they have?

- Geographical spread—in which areas are the company's goods and services bought and sold?

- Management—how experienced and well qualified are they?
- Quality of products—how reliable and innovative are the company's products and services?

Much of this information can be gleaned from the 'non-financial' parts of the annual report, by accessing data via the internet or in libraries, or even by visual inspection of products, stores, advertisements, etc. All this preliminary research is useful in placing the business in an appropriate context prior to making any detailed financial calculations, and the 'general' statements of the chairman and other key directors can be very helpful in giving a non-technical overview.

Having obtained a good general impression of the scope and nature of the business, the analyst should then read through the latest annual report, making a note of any unusual or interesting items such as changes in accounting policies, businesses acquired in the year, etc. By looking at the 'bottom lines' of the three main financial summaries, an immediate impression can be gained of the business's progress in the year:

- The increase or decrease in operating profit before taxation and interest as shown in the profit and loss account.
- The change in the total net assets shown in the balance sheet.
- The overall net cash inflow or outflow as shown in the cash flow statement.

> Domino's Pizza's chairman's statement (see p. 307) is very upbeat, without any negative comments to worry an analyst. Similarly, the chief executive's report (see pp. 308–11) is uniformly positive, with a helpful summary of trading results showing substantial increases in turnover, operating profit, earnings per share, and dividends. Total net borrowings increased due to 'the expanding activities of our leasing company', but actually declined when compared with total shareholders' funds (see 'Gearing' below). The section on 'current trading and prospects' is also extremely positive, and it is not surprising that the company's share price showed a steady increase during the period following the announcement of the results.

12.3 The second stage: horizontal, vertical, and trend analysis

Having gathered the background information, the next stage is to start the detailed numerical analysis of the financial statements. Horizontal, vertical, and trend analysis is a relatively simple means of comparing the relative size of individual components within each of the main summaries. Horizontal analysis achieves this by calculating the percentage change from the preceding year to the current year, whilst vertical analysis expresses each profit and loss account item as a percentage of the sales total, each balance sheet item as a percentage of the total net assets, and cash flow statement items as a percentage of the net cash flow from operating activities. Trend analysis is similar to horizontal analysis, but instead of percentage increases year on year, a base year is set at 100 (usually the earliest year being analysed) and subsequent years are related to this base year. Figure 12.1 shows an example, using a simplified profit and loss account extract.

	(A)	(B)	'Horizontal' analysis % change between the 2 years [(A–B) as a % of B]	'Vertical' analysis (Each item as a % of turnover)		'Trend' analysis (Using 2003 as Base 100)	
	2004 £000s	2003 £000s		2004	2003	2004	2003
Turnover	2,000	1,750	+14	100.00	100.00	114	100
Less cost of sales	(1,600)	(1,450)	+10	(80.00)	(82.86)	110	100
Gross profit	400	300	+33	20.00	17.14	133	100
Administrative expenses	(80)	(80)	0	(4.00)	(4.57)	100	100
Distribution costs	(20)	(22)	–9	(1.00)	(1.26)	91	100
Operating profit on ordinary activities before interest etc...	300	198	+52	15.00	11.31	152	100

Figure 12.1 Horizontal, vertical, and trend analysis

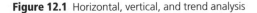

Using slightly simplified versions of Domino's Pizza's three key financial statements, Figures 12.2 (a), (b), and (c) show respectively a horizontal, vertical, and trend analysis of the group profit and loss account, balance sheet, and cash flow statement.

Domino's Pizza (UK & IRL) plc (summarized) Group profit and loss account for the 52 weeks ended 29 December 2002			Horizontal analysis	Vertical analysis		Trend analysis	
	2002	**2001**		**2002**	**2001**	**2002**	**2001**
	£000s	£000s	%	%	%		
Turnover	53,109	43,825	+21.18	100	100	121	100
Less cost of sales (see note 1)	−28,054	−23,132	+21.28	−52.82	−52.78	121	100
Gross profit	25,055	20,693	+21.08	47.18	47.22	121	100
Distribution costs	−8,663	−7,150	+21.16	−16.31	−16.31	121	100
Administrative expenses	−11,813	−10,230	+15.47	−22.24	−23.34	115	100
Other operating income and expenditure	−16	−99	−83.84	−0.03	−0.23	16	100
Profit on ordinary activities before interest and taxation	4,563	3,214	+41.97	8.59	7.33	142	100
Interest receivable	50	78	−35.90	0.09	0.18	64	100
Interest payable and similar charges	−374	−430	−13.02	−0.70	−0.98	87	100
Profit on ordinary activities before taxation	4,239	2,862	+48.11	7.98	6.53	148	100
Taxation	−1,404	−858	+63.64	−2.64	−1.96	164	100
Profit for the financial year	2,835	2,004	+41.47	5.34	4.57	141	100
Dividends (note 2)	−1,018	−668	+52.40	−1.92	−1.52	152	100
Profit retained for the financial year	1,817	1,336	+36.00	3.42	3.05	136	100

Notes:
1: Taken as 'credit purchases' for 'creditor payment period' calculation.
2: Dividends per share 2002: 2p, 2001: 1.33p.

Figure 12.2(a) Horizontal, vertical, and trend analysis of group profit and loss account

Comment

(a) Group profit and loss account

Taking each analysis in turn, it is clear that 2002 was a very successful year for the company. The horizontal analysis shows gross profit increasing by 21.08 per cent, with turnover and cost of sales broadly keeping pace. Although distribution and administrative costs increased by 21.16 per cent and 15.47 per cent respectively, the vertical analysis shows that these costs were almost exactly the same proportion of the turnover in each of the two years. There were large percentage changes in 'other operating income and expenditure' and the 'interest' figures, but the amounts involved are relatively immaterial in the context of the company as a whole. Profit on ordinary activities before and after taxation showed healthy increases, and shareholders were rewarded by a 52 per cent hike in their dividends. The 'final line' showed a creditable 36 per cent increase in the profit retained for the financial year. As for the vertical analysis, another way of interpreting these figures is to regard the 'turnover' percentage as equivalent to £100. The other figures listed then represent the costs and profits associated with each £100 of turnover. For example, in 2002, for every £100 of turnover, there was £22.24 expended on administrative costs, compared with £23.34 in the previous year. On this measure, gross profit was slightly down as a percentage of turnover (due to the slightly greater increase in cost of sales than the increase in turnover, as shown by the horizontal analysis) from £47.22 per £100 sales in 2001 to £47.18 per £100 sales in 2002. The good news for the company, again, is the 'final line', which shows that, despite increasing dividends by over 50 per cent, the company was able to retain £3.42 profit per £100 of sales in 2002, compared with 'only' £3.05 in 2001.

The trend analysis gives a quick and simple indicator of the progress during 2002 compared to the index year, 2001.

Domino's Pizza (UK & IRL) plc Group balance sheet as at 29 December 2002			Horizon-tal analysis	Vertica analysis		Trend analysis	
	2002	**2001**		2002	2001	2002	2001
	£000s	£000s	%	%	%		
Fixed assets							
Intangible assets	2,386	2,484	−3.95	20.39	25.88	96	100
Tangible assets	13,685	12,181	12.35	116.96	126.91	112	100
Investments in joint venture (net)	307	277	10.83	2.62	2.89	111	100
	16,378	14,942	9.61	139.97	155.68	110	100
Current assets							
Stocks	1,411	1,260	11.98	12.06	13.13	112	100
Debtors due within one year (see note 1)	8,572	6,665	28.61	73.26	69.44	129	100
Debtors due after more than one year	2,130	1,756	21.30	18.20	18.30	121	100
Cash at bank and in hand	3,885	3,231	20.24	33.20	33.66	120	100
	15,998	12,912	23.90	136.72	134.53	124	100
Creditors due within one year (see note 2)	12,919	10,203	26.62	110.41	106.30	127	100
Net current assets	3,079	2,709	13.66	26.31	28.22	114	100
Total assets less current liabilities	19,457	17,651	10.23	166.28	183.90	110	100
Creditors due after more than one year	−7,152	−7,632	−6.29	−61.12	−79.51	94	100
Provision for liabilities and charges	−604	−421	43.47	−5.16	−4.39	143	100
Total net assets	11,701	9,598	21.91	100.00	100.00	122	100
Capital and reserves							
Called-up share capital	2,546	2,518	1.11	21.76	26.23	101	100
Share premium account	2,395	2,192	9.26	20.47	22.84	109	100
Profit and loss account	6,760	4,888	38.30	57.77	50.93	138	100
Equity shareholders' funds	11,701	9,598	21.91	100.00	100.00	122	100

Notes:
1. Of which trade debtors: 2,533 2,621
2. Of which trade creditors: 3,956 4,006
3. No. of equity shares issued at year-end (m) 50,920 50,360
4. Assume stock market price (p) 110 75

Figure 12.2(b) Horizontal, vertical, and trend analysis of group balance sheet

(b) Group balance sheet

Again, the 'bottom line' gives us a quick impression of healthy progress in 2002. The equity share-holders' funds increased by nearly 22 per cent, with the total retained profits within the profit and loss account increasing by over 38 per cent. Total fixed assets show a relatively modest 9.61 per cent increase, but individual current assets, notably debtors and cash, show major increases. To balance this, short-term creditors have increased by nearly 27 per cent, though net current assets have increased by a respectable 13.66 per cent. The vertical analysis uses the 'total net assets' as the benchmark figure. Tangible fixed assets, although increasing by 12.35 per cent as shown in the horizontal analysis, represent a lower proportion of the value of the company in 2002 compared with 2001 (116.96 per cent against 126.91 per cent). Another significant change is the reduction in long-term creditors from just under 80 per cent in 2001 to just over 60 per cent a year later.

Domino's Pizza (UK & IRL) plc Group cash flow statement for the 52 weeks to 29 December 2002			Horizontal analysis	Vertical analysis		Trend analysis	
	2002	**2001**		2002	2001	2002	2001
	£000s	£000s	%	%	%		
Net cash inflow from operating activities	**5,128**	**4,475**	+14.59	100	100	115	100
Returns on investments and servicing of finance							
Interest received	50	78	−35.90	0.98	1.74	64	100
Interest paid	−343	−304	+12.83	−6.69	−6.79	113	100
Interest element of finance lease payments	−9	−11	−18.18	−0.17	−0.25	82	100
	−302	**−237**	+27.43	−5.88	−5.30	127	100
Taxation	**−950**	**−617**	+53.97	−18.53	−13.79	154	100
Capital expenditure and financial investment							
Payments to acquire intangible fixed assets	−214	−68	+214.71	−4.17	−1.52	315	100
Payments to acquire tangible fixed assets	−3,291	−2,560	+28.55	−64.18	−57.20	129	100
Receipts from sales of fixed assets	411	5	+8,120.00	8.01	0.11	8,220	100
Receipts from repayment of joint venture loan	46	36	+27.78	0.90	0.80	128	100
Payments to acquire finance lease assets and advance of franchisee loans	−1,247	−1,007	+23.83	−24.32	−22.50	124	100
Receipts from repayment of finance leases and franchisee loans	901	445	+102.47	17.57	9.94	202	100
	−3,394	**−3,149**	+7.78	−66.19	−70.37	108	100
Acquisitions and disposals							
Purchase of subsidiary undertaking and unassociated businesses	**−484**	**−160**	+202.50	−9.44	−3.57	303	100
Equity dividends paid	**−777**	**−501**	+55.09	−15.15	−11.19	155	100
Net cash outflow before financing	**−779**	**−189**	+312.17	−15.19	−4.22	412	100
Financing							
Issue of ordinary share capital	231	164	+40.85	4.50	3.66	141	100
New long-term loans	2,719	2,660	+2.22	53.02	59.44	102	100
Repayments of long-term loans	−1,443	−330	+337.27	−28.14	−7.37	437	100
Repayments of capital element of finance leases and hire purchase contracts	−74	−72	+2.78	−1.44	−1.61	103	100
	1,433	**2,422**	−40.83	27.94	54.12	59	100
Increase in cash	**654**	**2,233**	−70.71	12.75	49.90	29	100

Figure 12.2(c) Horizontal, vertical, and trend analysis of group cash flow statement

(c) Group cash flow statement

Within the statement, the 'bottom line' shows that the year's increase in cash is 70 per cent lower than the equivalent figure for 2001. However, the horizontal analysis shows significant cash outflows relating to the purchase of a subsidiary (up 202.5 per cent) and long-term loan repayments (up 337.27 per cent). Other cash flows relating to interest, taxation, and dividends had a negative effect, though offset by the large inflows from the sale of fixed assets, and receipts from leases and loans. The vertical analysis shows a broadly similar pattern between the two years, using the net cash flow from operating activities as the benchmark.

12.4 The third stage: ratio analysis

Having established the percentage movements between the two years, and assessed the relative strengths of the component parts of the three key financial statements, the next step is to calculate specific percentages and ratios to reveal further aspects of the business's performance. With such a mass of financial information available, the data is usually made manageable by being segregated into five main groupings:

- profitability;
- efficiency;
- long-term solvency and liquidity;[6]
- short-term solvency and liquidity;
- investment ratios.

These are shown in the Table 12.1.

12.4.1 Profitability group of ratios

The four ratios within the profitability group can be calculated for Domino's Pizza, as follows (using the data as shown in Figures 12.2 (a) and (b) above):

		2002		2001	
		£000s	**%**	**£000s**	**%**
ROCE (return on capital employed)	$\dfrac{\text{Operating profit before interest and tax}}{\text{Share capital} + \text{Reserves} + \text{Long-term loans}^a}$	$\dfrac{4,563}{18,853}$	24.2	$\dfrac{3,214}{17,230}$	18.65
Gross margin (or gross profit margin)	$\dfrac{\text{Gross profit}}{\text{Turnover}}$	$\dfrac{25,055}{53,109}$	47.18	$\dfrac{20,693}{43,825}$	47.22
Mark-up	$\dfrac{\text{Gross profit}}{\text{Cost of goods sold}}$	$\dfrac{25,055}{28,054}$	89.31	$\dfrac{20,693}{23,132}$	89.46
Net margin (or net profit margin)	$\dfrac{\text{Operating profit before interest and tax}}{\text{Turnover}}$	$\dfrac{4,563}{53,109}$	8.59	$\dfrac{3,214}{43,825}$	7.33

[a] Equity shareholders' funds plus 'creditors due after more than one year'.

[6] 'Solvency' refers to a company's capacity to meets its financial obligations; 'Liquidity' to its ability to raise enough cash when needed.

Table 12.1 Key groups of data

Group	Name of ratio	Formula[a]	Expressed as
Profitability	ROCE (return on capital employed)[a]	$\dfrac{\text{Operating profit before interest and tax}}{\text{share capital} + \text{reserves} + \text{Long-term loans}}$	%
	Gross margin (or gross profit margin)	$\dfrac{\text{Gross profit}}{\text{Turnover}}$	%
	Mark-up	$\dfrac{\text{Gross profit}}{\text{Cost of goods sold}}$	%
	Net margin (or net profit margin)	$\dfrac{\text{Operating profit before interest and tax}}{\text{Turnover}}$	%
Efficiency	Fixed assets turnover	$\dfrac{\text{Turnover}}{\text{Fixed assets at net book value}}$	multiple
	Stock turn	$\dfrac{\text{Stock (average or closing)}}{\text{Cost of goods sold}} \times 365$	days
	Trade debtors collection period	$\dfrac{\text{Trade debtors (average or closing)}}{\text{Credit sales}} \times 365$	days
	Trade creditors payment period	$\dfrac{\text{Trade creditors (average or closing)}}{\text{Credit purchases}} \times 365$	days
Short-term solvency and liquidity	Current ratio (aka 'working capital' ratio)	Current assets : Current liabilities	ratio
	Acid test (aka 'quick assets' ratio)	(Current assets − Stock) : Current liabilities	ratio
Long-term solvency and liquidity	Gearing[a]	$\dfrac{\text{Long-term loans} - \text{Cash and bank balances}}{\text{Share capital} + \text{reserves} + (\text{long-term loans} - \text{cash and bank balances})}$	%
	Interest cover	$\dfrac{\text{Profit before interest}}{\text{Interest payable}}$	multiple
Investment ratios	Eps (earnings per share)[a]	$\dfrac{\text{Profit available for ordinary dividend}}{\text{No. of equity shares issued}}$	pence per share
	PE (price/earnings)	$\dfrac{\text{Stock market price}}{\text{Earnings per share}}$	multiple
	Dividend cover	$\dfrac{\text{Profit available to pay dividend}}{\text{Dividends paid and proposed}}$	multiple
	Dividend yield	$\dfrac{\text{Dividend per share}}{\text{Market price per share}}$	%

[a] There are alternative formulae which might be used in these cases, explained when discussing each ratio below.

Comments:

1. *Return on capital employed* (ROCE) is a fundamental measure of business performance as it compares the profit before interest and tax with the overall capital used to generate that profit. Notice that we have used year-end figures for capital employed rather than average figures for the year, though it is permissible to use the average. A viable business should generate a considerably higher return than the interest charges they would have to pay on borrowed money. In the case of Domino's Pizza, the return has increased significantly during the year, and is significantly higher than, for example, bank overdraft rates. However, for a full assessment to be made (and this applies to all the ratios which we calculate), we would also need to know comparative figures for other businesses operating in the same business sector. For example, if other pizza businesses were generating only 15 per cent ROCE, we could assume that Domino's Pizza was doing relatively better than its competitors.

If competitors were reporting ROCE of 30 per cent, we might consider Domino's Pizza as underperforming. What is certain is that we cannot make any meaningful statement about any ratio without having some comparable figure (previous year, competitors' results, etc.) to use as a yardstick. There are several variations of the ROCE formula, but the one given is that which best reflects the overall return that the business has achieved. If the return was to be calculated purely from the viewpoint of the ordinary shareholders, we might define the numerator as 'operating profit after interest, taxation, and preference dividends (if any)', and the denominator as 'equity share capital plus reserves'. We would then be comparing the amount earned during the period that was available for the ordinary shareholders' dividend with the total value of equity capital within the company.

One important point to bear in mind is the potential effect of revaluations of fixed assets on the ROCE figure. If assets have been revalued upwards (see Chapter 6 p. 135), the overall amount of capital employed will increase, as it will include a revaluation reserve. However, the profit is likely to be reduced due to the increased depreciation on the revalued amounts. This effect on ROCE should be considered carefully when comparing two companies, only one of which has revalued its fixed assets.

2. *Gross margin* shows the proportion of turnover that resulted in a gross profit to the company. It is affected by various factors including changing price levels and different products being sold (the 'sales mix'). The margin might be reduced by aggressive companies wanting to expand their share of the market, or increased if there is reduced competition. Inaccurate stock valuations or the theft of goods may also affect the ratio. In the case of Domino's Pizza, the margin has remained virtually unchanged in the two years, resulting in £47 of gross profit out of every £100 sales.

3. *Mark-up* indicates the pricing policy of the business, as it shows the percentage addition to cost price in order to arrive at the selling price. For Domino's Pizza, the mark-up remained constant at 89 per cent, so that every £100 represented within 'cost of sales' was converted into goods with a saleable value of £189. Mark-up and gross margin move in tandem, so that a change in one is automatically reflected in the other.

4. *Net margin* shows the proportion of sales that resulted in a profit after all overheads (other than interest) have been deducted. In 2001, £8.59 out of every £100 sales resulted in net (operating) profit, an increase on the previous year's £7.33. Net profit can be improved by reducing overheads, but a balance has to be achieved between cutting expenses and maintaining business efficiency.

12.4.2 Efficiency group of ratios

							2002						2001
Fixed assets turnover	$\dfrac{\text{Turnover}}{\text{Fixed assets at net book value}}$	$\dfrac{53,109}{16,378}$	=	3.24	times	$\dfrac{43,825}{14,942}$	=	2.93	times
Stock turn	$\dfrac{\text{Closing stock} \times 365}{\text{Cost of goods sold}}$	$\dfrac{1,411 \times 365}{28,054}$	=	18.36	days	$\dfrac{1,260 \times 365}{23,132}$	=	19.88	days
Trade debtors collection period	$\dfrac{\text{Trade debtors} \times 365}{\text{Credit sales}}$	$\dfrac{2,533 \times 365}{53,109}$	=	17.41	days	$\dfrac{2,621 \times 365}{43,825}$	=	21.83	days
Trade creditors payment period	$\dfrac{\text{Trade creditors} \times 365}{\text{Credit purchases}}$	$\dfrac{3,956 \times 365}{28,054}$	=	51.47	days	$\dfrac{4,006 \times 365}{23,132}$	=	63.21	days

Comments:

1. *Fixed assets turnover* indicates that the company's fixed assets are generating more sales in 2002 than 2001, as every £1 of fixed assets generated £3.24 of sales in 2002, but only £2.93 in the previous year. This is quite a crude measure of efficiency as it is affected by the company's revaluation, depreciation, and amortization policies. However, it is reasonable to assume that an investment in fixed assets should be matched by increasing turnover.

2. *Stock turn* shows the effect of changing stock levels and indicates the efficiency of the company's stockholding policies. A pizza company will, by its nature, need to keep food stocks for the minimum possible period, and Domino's Pizza's average of just over two weeks is compatible with this. By comparison, engineering or other industrial companies may have to keep several months' worth of stock. In our calculations, we have used the closing stock figure as the numerator, but often an average figure is taken, achieved by simply adding the opening and closing stock figures together and then dividing by two. In many companies, the balance sheet figures for stock, debtors, and creditors might be lower than the average during the year, as the date chosen as the end of the financial period often coincides with a relatively quiet trading period.

3. *Trade debtors collection period* shows an improved time period for collecting outstanding debtors, down from nearly twenty-two days to just over seventeen days. This could be because more resources have been applied to credit control, or prompt-payment discounts have been offered. Efficient businesses collect their debts as quickly as possible, but care should be taken in comparing the results of businesses with high volumes of cash sales (e.g. supermarkets) and those whose sales are on credit terms and issue invoices for every transaction. In 1998, a survey showed that the average figure of 'debtor days' for all the UK's privately owned companies with turnover between £2m and £60m was 69 days. The same survey put the average number across all companies as 42 days.[7]

4. *Trade creditors payment period* shows that the company paid its creditors faster in 2002 than in 2001. This may have resulted from being offered discounts for prompt payment. It is good practice not to pay creditors too quickly, as it is a form of interest-free credit to the business. However, great care must be taken not to alienate suppliers by delaying payment beyond a reasonable time. The figure may be misleading, however, as although 'trade creditors' will be shown in the notes to the accounts, the figure for 'credit purchases' is not disclosed separately. In our example, we have assumed that the credit purchases total is equivalent to the cost of sales figure, though in practice this will not be the case. In fact, Domino's Pizza's directors' report (see p. 317) shows different figures for its creditors payment period from those calculated above: 44 days in 2002 and 52 days in 2001, though the trend is identical.

12.4.3 Short-term solvency and liquidity group of ratios

		2002	2001
Current ratio	Current assets: Current liabilities	15,998 : 12,919 = 1.24 : 1	12,912 : 10,203 = 1.27 : 1
Acid test	Current assets (−Stock): Current liabilities	14,587 : 12,919 = 1.13 : 1	11,652 : 10,203 = 1.14 : 1

[7] *UK Ltd—Financial and Business Performance—KPMG, July 1998.*

Comments:

1. The ideal *current ratio* (also known as the working capital ratio) is often quoted as somewhere between 1.5 : 1 and 2 : 1 (i.e. between one and a half and twice as many current assets as current liabilities), but it depends upon the type of business, and many successful companies (notably those with a high proportion of cash sales) operate on current ratios of 1 : 1 or less. The ratio gives a measure of the ability of a company to meet its current liabilities as they fall due, so in theory at least, having more current assets than short-term creditors makes sense. In practice, efficient control of working capital will mean that:

- Stock is kept to a minimum, otherwise too much stock may be held, resulting in high costs for storage and security, plus interest on overdrafts and loans used to pay for the stock.
- Debtors are encouraged to pay as soon as possible, otherwise inadequate control of debtors may result in uncollected debts.
- 'Surplus' cash or bank balances should be reinvested or returned to investors in the form of increased dividends.
- Trade creditors' payment periods might be lengthened to take advantage of interest free credit periods.

If a company (particularly a young business) expands aggressively to gain market share, it might have to invest in fixed assets such as machinery and buildings, build up stock levels, and sell on extended credit terms, without having first built up sufficient working capital to enable it to service the finance charges on the amounts borrowed. For example, a business may get a lot of new orders beyond its existing capacity. After investing in new plant it may have no working capital left, and have to resort to heavy borrowing and reliance on extended credit terms from suppliers. If the creditors and lenders demand payment, the company may be forced to sell its fixed assets and go out of business. This is known as 'over-trading'.

In most cases, the new orders bring in enough additional profit, cash flow, and working capital to weather the storm.

Note that current ratios can be too high as well as too low. A company with a 6 : 1 ratio might have too much stock, poor credit control of debtors, or uninvested cash surpluses. For Domino's Pizza, the ratios for both years show roughly a quarter more current assets than current liabilities, which is acceptable.

Leading UK supermarkets group Tesco plc showed a current ratio of only 0.45 : 1 in its most recent balance sheet.

---

2. The *acid test* (also known as the 'quick assets ratio') is the crucial measure of whether a business seems able to meet its debts as they fall due for payment. 'Quick' assets are those which can be converted quickly into cash as the need arises, and it is normal to define these as current assets other than stock and work in progress. This is on the basis that stock and work in progress may be difficult to convert into cash in a short period. The 'ideal' ratio is

sometimes quoted as 1 : 1 (£1 of 'quick' assets to every £1 of current liabilities), but look at the supermarket's calculations below to see how viable businesses can survive on much lower ratios. In the case of Domino's Pizza, the exclusion of the stock does not result in a great variation from the current ratio, and having 13 per cent (2001: 14 per cent) more quick assets than current liabilities is a strong position. Remember that one of the current liabilities is the proposed dividend, so a company showing a weak acid test ratio may have to rethink the level of its rewards to shareholders.

 Tesco plc's acid test was only 0.24 : 1 in its 2003 balance sheet. Put in simple terms, in that year Tesco had only 24p of quickly cash-convertible assets to meet each £1 of current liabilities! The strong cash inflows of the company should ensure enough day-to-day liquidity to meet creditors as they fall due. However, there may come a point when any company is threatened with liquidation if it cannot ensure that suppliers are paid on time.

In contrast, Cobham plc is an engineering company in the aerospace industry. Its working capital ratio was 1.5 : 1, and its acid test ratio was 0.98 : 1.

12.4.4 Long-term solvency and liquidity group of ratios

	2002		2001	
Gearing				
$\dfrac{\text{Long-term loans} - \text{Cash and bank balances}}{\text{Share capital} + \text{reserves} + (\text{long-term loans} - \text{cash and bank balances})}$	$\dfrac{(7,152 - 3,885)}{11,701 + (7,152 - 3,885)}$	21.83%	$\dfrac{(7,632 - 3,231)}{9,598 + (7,632 - 3,231)}$	31.44%
(or)				
$\dfrac{\text{Long-term loans} - \text{Cash and bank balances}}{\text{Share capital} + \text{reserves}}$	$\dfrac{(7,152 - 3,885)}{11,701}$	27.92%	$\dfrac{(7,632 - 3,231)}{9,598}$	45.85%
(or)				
$\dfrac{\text{All loans} - \text{Cash and bank balances}}{\text{Share capital} + \text{reserves}}$	$\dfrac{6,308}{11,701}$	53.91%	$\dfrac{5,760}{9,598}$	60.01%
Interest cover				
$\dfrac{\text{Profit before interest}}{\text{Interest payable}}$	$\dfrac{4,563}{374}$	12.2 times	$\dfrac{3,214}{430}$	7.47 times

Comments:

1. *Gearing* (US: *leverage*) reflects the relationship between a company's equity capital (ordinary shares and reserves) and its other forms of long-term funding (including preference shares, debentures, etc.). A company may exist solely on its equity shareholders' funds (i.e. have no gearing), but to expand it may have to issue preference shares or take out long-term loans on which interest must be paid. A company with relatively high borrowings in relation to its equity shareholders' capital is called a 'high-geared' company. Those with a relatively small proportion of borrowings are 'low-geared' companies. Management

strategy may be to run a high-geared company, making use of a high proportion of borrowed funds to expand. This has its risks, as many companies have gone into liquidation due to borrowing money and then finding that insufficient profits are generated to repay the interest, and ultimately the loan capital itself. However, the rewards for ordinary shareholders can often be much greater in a successful high-geared company than its low-geared equivalent, as the increased profits, less the interest due on the borrowing, should result in higher dividend payments. As a general rule, in terms of potential for company failure, high gearing equals higher risk, lower gearing equals lower risk.

Table 12.2 explains the advantages and disadvantages of different gearing levels.

Table 12.2 Advantages and disadvantages of gearing

	Advantages		Disadvantages	
	To the company	To equity shareholders	To the company	To equity shareholders
High gearing	Prospect of higher profit using borrowed money to expand, e.g. by taking over other businesses or investing in new machinery. Interest is 'tax deductible' whereas dividends are not.	Potential of high dividends if the return on the capital employed exceeds the cost of servicing the debt.	High interest burden, which must be paid in priority to equity dividends; Loan capital will have to be repaid eventually; Security is usually required—often relating to tangible fixed assets.	Risk of dividends not being paid due to high interest burden; possible company failure if profits can't cover high interest and repayments.
Low gearing (or no gearing)	Lower interest payments than a high-geared company; lower risk of defaulting on loans.	Less risk of the company not paying dividends due to heavy interest commitments.	Company reliant on internal funding and profit retention; less scope to expand.	Less potential for growth than a higher-geared company.

There are a number of different ways to calculate gearing levels, and three of them are shown in the table. Other textbooks may show further variations, but the principle underlying each one will be consistent. The ratio is establishing the relationship between the company's borrowed capital and its equity shareholders' capital, and each variation of the formula is investigating this, albeit from a slightly different angle. To take each of the three formulae shown above in turn:

$$(1) \quad \frac{\text{Long-term loans} - \text{Cash and bank balances}}{\text{Share capital} + \text{reserves} + (\text{long-term loans} - \text{cash and bank balances})}$$

This shows the *net* value of the long-term indebtedness of the company (i.e. after deducting the cash and bank balances found within current assets) and compares it with the grand total of the equity shareholders' funds and the net long-term indebtedness. In the case of Domino's Pizza, this gearing measure has dropped from 31.44 per cent in 2001 to 21.83 per cent a year later. This means that in the current year, net long-term loans are less than a quarter of the total capital (equity and borrowed) net of cash and bank balances.

$$(2) \qquad \frac{\text{Long-term loans} - \text{Cash and bank balances}}{\text{Share capital} + \text{reserves}}$$

The second formula compares the net long-term indebtedness (again after deducting cash and bank balances) with the value of the equity shareholders funds. This is sometimes referred to as the 'debt/equity' ratio. This will inevitably return a higher percentage than the first formula and could even be greater than 100 per cent if the equity capital was less than the net indebtedness.

$$(3) \qquad \frac{\text{All loans} - \text{Cash and bank balances}}{\text{Share capital} + \text{reserves}}$$

The third formula is the one that Domino's Pizza itself uses to calculate the 'capital gearing' percentage shown in its five-year record at the end of its annual report (see p. 345). This looks at all loans (short and long term), again deducts cash and bank balances, and compares the total with the equity shareholders' funds. As with the second formula, this could return a percentage greater than 100 per cent if the total of the net loans exceeded the equity shareholders' value.

It is not possible to say that there is one 'correct' formula to use: the key is to be consistent, when comparing one year's gearing with the next, and also when contrasting the gearing of one company with that of another. Note that if a company has preference shares, these are treated as 'loan capital' for the purposes of the gearing calculations. A final point to note is that other textbooks might not show 'cash and bank balances' deducted from the total loans, but it is now conventional practice within companies to show a 'net loans' figure when calculating gearing.

2. *Interest cover* indicates the relative safety of the interest payments by comparing the interest payable with the profit available to make the interest payments. Domino's Pizza's available profit is over 12 times the interest payments payable, which appears very safe (particularly in view of its increase from 7 times in the previous year) and will give assurance to lenders that there would have to be a very dramatic decline in profit before their interest payments were threatened.

12.4.5 Investment group of ratios

	2002		2001	
Earnings per share (basic)				
$\dfrac{\text{Profit available for ordinary dividend}}{\text{No. of equity shares issued}}$	$\dfrac{2,835}{50,920}$	5.6p	$\dfrac{2,004}{50,360}$	4.0p
PE (price/earnings) ratio				
$\dfrac{\text{Stock market price}}{\text{Earnings per share}}$	$\dfrac{110}{5.6}$	19.6 times	$\dfrac{75}{4.0}$	18.8 times

Dividend cover				
Profit available to pay dividend / Dividends paid and proposed	$\dfrac{2,835}{1,018}$	2.8 times	$\dfrac{2,004}{668}$	3.0 times
Dividend yield				
Dividend per share / Market price per share	$\dfrac{2}{110}$	1.82%	$\dfrac{1.33}{75}$	1.77%

1. *The earnings per share (eps) and the price/earnings (PE) ratios* have already been considered in section 5.8 (see p. 117). Refer to that section for details of a further *diluted* eps calculation, required when a company's capital might increase at some future time due to the existence of stock options or convertible loans. Many analysts use another earnings per share calculation, *ebitda*—which stands for 'earnings before interest, taxation, depreciation, and amortization'. This eliminates any inconsistencies relating to depreciation and accounting policies when comparing different companies. Although it has no 'official' recognition within accounting standards, it is used widely as an alternative measure of a company's performance.

Both eps and the PE ratio are important indicators of a company's performance. The PE ratio, where the market price per share is expressed as a multiple of the eps, is the clearest indication of how the stock market rates a particular company: the higher the multiple, the greater the expectation of future profits, with investors having pushed up the market price in anticipation. A low PE ratio results from losses or poor profits, with a depressed share price. The average PE ratio across all sectors at the time of these calculations was 18.11 and the average PE ratio for companies operating within the 'leisure and hotels' sector (which includes pizza companies) was 17.48. The Domino's Pizza's PE ratio of 19.6 shows that the company's stock market price was outperforming the market generally, and also competing companies.

2. *Dividend cover* is similar to interest cover, in that it indicates the relative safety of the dividends for the year by comparing them with the profit available to make the payments. Domino's Pizza's available profit increased by 41 per cent in the year, but the 52 per cent rise in dividends resulted in the cover decreasing slightly from 3 to 2.8 times.

3. *Dividend yield* measures the actual rate of return obtained by investing in an ordinary share at the current market price. Someone buying a Domino's Pizza share at 110p would obtain a yield of 1.82 per cent, which is a slight increase on that of the previous year.

12.5 Summarizing the information

After completing the detailed analysis, it is helpful to summarize the information and then draw a conclusion. The numerical analysis is shown in Table 12.3. As can be seen, all the ratios, with the sole exception of the dividend cover, show a very positive trend, and this ties in with the summary of the horizontal and vertical analyses above.

(Note: the companion website includes an Excel spreadsheet showing the basis of the calculations.)

Table 12.3 Summary of ratios

	2002	2001	Trend (immaterial changes ignored)
Profitability group			
ROCE (return on capital employed)	24.20%	18.65%	⇑
Gross margin (or gross profit margin)	47.18%	47.22%	—
Mark-up	89.31%	89.46%	—
Net margin (or net profit margin)	8.59%	7.33%	⇑
Efficiency group			
Fixed assets turnover	3.24 times	2.93 times	⇑
Stock turn	18.36 days	19.88 days	⇑
Trade debtors collection period	17.41 days	21.83 days	⇑
Trade creditors payment period	51.47 days	63.21 days	See comment[a]
Short-term solvency and liquidity			
Current ratio (aka 'working capital' ratio)	1.24 :1	1.27 :1	—
Acid test (aka 'quick assets' test)	1.13 :1	1.14 :1	—
Long-term solvency and liquidity			
Gearing	21.83%	31.44%	⇑
Debt/equity	27.92%	45.85%	⇑
Capital gearing (company's formula)	53.91%	60.01%	⇑
Interest cover	12.20 times	7.47 times	⇑
Investment ratios			
Eps (earnings per share)[a]	5.6 p	4.0 p	⇑
PE (price/earnings)	19.6 times	18.8 times	⇑
Dividend cover	2.8 times	3.0 times	⇓
Dividend yield	1.82%	1.77%	⇑

[a] A decrease in the trade creditors' payment period could be interpreted in two ways. It could be seen in a positive light if excessive credit periods have been taken in the past, as faster payment would benefit customer–supplier relations. However, it is normal business practice to take as long a time period as the supplier is prepared to give: paying too quickly is detrimental to cash flow.
Key:
⇑ Trend considered positive for company.
⇓ Trend considered negative for company.

 When the results of Domino's Pizza were announced in February 2003, the *Financial Times* made the following comment:

Dough rises as Domino's turns up the heat

Hard-up yuppies helped Domino's Pizza boost pre-tax profits by almost 50 per cent last year.

Stephen Hemsley, chief executive of the franchised home delivery chain, said the economic downturn and the shift away from fine dining over the past year had helped the company maintain double-digit growth.

'When times are tough our socio-economic customer base changes. Some of the D's and E's are lost and the A's and B's become our core market. They are no longer eating in restaurants, but have a disinclination to cook for themselves.'

That may explain the company's latest departure—it has added a Thai green curry pizza to its classic repertoire, even though it is sticking to its target audience and continuing its television advertising policy of sponsoring *The Simpsons*.

Pre-tax profits rose from £2.9m to £4.2m in the year to December 29, as (diluted) earnings per share increased 36 per cent to 5.29p (3.88p).

Mr Hemsley said that as the continued roll-out of stores involved minimal capital expenditure—because of the franchise structure—the company had become sufficiently cash generative to recommend a final dividend of 1.22p (0.76p), giving a total up 50 per cent at 2p (1.33p).

The group has also raised the prospect of using surplus cash to buy back shares later in the year. However, there was some disappointment that Domino's showed no inclination to increase liquidity in the stock. Colin Halpern, the chairman, retains a stake of just under 30 per cent.

Domino's has also had to increase the royalty payments to its U.S. parent from 1.94 per cent of sales to 2.5 per cent, and that has added impetus to the drive to open more outlets. It opened 34 branches last year and aims to add another 50 to its current total of 272 this year. The first UK store was opened in 1985. Like-for-like sales in the first six weeks were up by just over 10 per cent

The shares rose 3½p to close at 98½.

Peter John, *Financial Times*, 26 Feb. 2003

12.6 The validity of the financial statements

In the analysis of company reports, it has been assumed that the information is accurate and reliable and provides a suitable basis for study. Whilst it is true that the published financial statements of a plc will be audited and thus, with very rare exceptions, show a 'true and fair view' according to an independent firm of qualified accountants, many objective observers have questioned the validity of financial statements for various reasons, including:

1. Financial summaries are usually drawn up under the *historic cost convention*, whereby items are included at their purchase price at the time of acquisition, and no account is taken of inflation on the replacement price of assets such as stock or machinery. This problem is more acute when inflation rates are high, and attempts at introducing alternative inflation-adjusted accounting methods were tried in the 1970s and 1980s when inflation in the UK peaked at over 25 per cent p.a. No method was felt reliable enough to replace the traditional historic cost convention, though it was felt acceptable to allow revaluations of certain assets (notably land and buildings) where market values had changed significantly when compared to book values. The use of asset revaluation reserves to record such changes was explained in Chapter 8.

2. The rules and regulations of accounting allow a certain measure of flexibility, so that companies faced with the same accounting problem may come to differing solutions. This flexibility is seen by some as a strength of accounting procedures, where the requirements of specific companies allow individual accounting treatments to be adopted where appropriate. An example is depreciation, where the judgement of the length of a time period over which assets should be depreciated is left to the discretion of the directors. In some countries, governments decree the time period for depreciating different types of asset.

The issuing of national and international accounting and financial reporting standards has greatly reduced the scope for 'creative accounting', but unscrupulous directors will always try and find a loophole.

3. Information is based on past events, but it is argued that meaningful decisions can be taken only on the basis of forecasts of future performance. Unfortunately, the future is rather harder to verify than the past, so historic documents tend to be seen as a more reliable guide to future prospects than future predictions, however well researched. The ideal is perhaps a balance between the two, with a company's forecasts being published alongside the conventional historic information. However, companies are naturally reluctant to divulge information that may be of use to competitors, so the forecast information may be so vague and generalized as to be of little use to anybody. The possible move to quarterly reporting of results will help to overcome this, but will add considerably to the amount of data to be digested by analysts and the workload of the accountants who have to produce it.

12.7 Chapter summary

- There are three stages to the analysis of a company's results: preliminary research, horizontal, vertical, and trend analysis, and ratio analysis.

- Preliminary research investigates the company's background, including what it does, who manages it, and where it sells its products or services.

- Horizontal analysis is a percentage analysis showing the change between the current and previous year's figures.

- Vertical analysis is an analysis showing the percentage that each item comprises in each year, related to a key component of that statement.

- Trend analysis uses one year as the base year, and shows subsequent years in relation to that base year.

- Ratio analysis looks at five key areas for analysis: profitability, efficiency, long- and short-term liquidity and solvency, and investors' ratios.

- Information must be summarized, and a suitable overall conclusion drawn.

- Consideration must be given to concerns about the basic validity of the information contained within annual reports.

■ GLOSSARY

acid test	The comparison between the 'quick' assets and the current liabilities (creditors due for payment within one year)
current ratio	The comparison between current assets and current liabilities (creditors due for payment within one year)
dividend cover	The ability of a company to pay its dividends, measured by expressing the profit available for dividends as a multiple of the dividends paid and proposed

earnings	The profit for the financial period that is available to meet equity dividends
earnings per share (eps)	Earnings divided by the number of ordinary shares issued. Eps is always measured in pence and forms part of the PE ratio
ebitda	Earnings before interest, taxation, depreciation, and amortization. An alternative, 'unofficial' method of calculating eps
fixed assets turnover	The relationship between a company's sales and its fixed assets
gearing	The relationship between a company's equity shareholders' funds and its other forms of long-term funding (preference shares, debentures, etc.)
historic cost convention	The traditional accounting convention which values assets at their purchase price at the time of acquisition with no allowance made for subsequent inflation
horizontal analysis	Comparison of values within financial statements by calculation of percentage changes between one year and the next
interest cover	The ability of a company to meet its interest commitments, measured by expressing the profit before interest as a multiple of the interest paid and payable
margin	Profit as a percentage of sales
mark-up	The percentage added to the cost price of goods or services to arrive at the selling price
PE ratio	See *price/earnings ratio*
preliminary research	Investigating the company's background prior to a detailed numerical analysis
price/earnings ratio	Market price as a multiple of the latest earnings per share. Used as a relative measure of stock market performance
quick assets	Assets that can be turned quickly into cash. Usually the current assets, other than stock and work in progress
ratio analysis	Detailed numerical analysis of a company's financial statements
ROCE	Return on capital employed
stock turn	The speed at which stock is sold by a company
trade creditors' payment period	How quickly the company pays its trade creditors
trade debtors' collection period	How quickly trade debtors pay their bills to the company
trend analysis	A numerical analysis of a company's results, using one year as the base year, and showing subsequent years in relation to that base year
vertical analysis	Analysis of the relative weighting of components within financial statements by expressing them as a percentage of a key component in that statement
yield	The percentage return obtained from an investment

■ MULTIPLE CHOICE QUESTIONS

1. Vertical analysis is:

   a The calculation of the relative weighting of components within a particular financial period

   b The comparison of the current year's figures with the previous year's figures

   c The comparison of one company's results with another company

   d The comparison of the profit and loss account with the balance sheet

2. An analyst is preparing a trend analysis of a company, whose turnover for three successive years is: 2002: £25 million, 2003: £38 million, 2004: £22 million. Which of the following shows the correct trend analysis for that company's turnover?

   a 2002: 100   2003: 152   2004: 58

   b 2002: 100   2003: 152   2004: 88

   c 2002: 88   2003: 173   2004: 100

   d 2002: 66   2003: 100   2004: 58

3. Which one of the following would cause a company's gross margin to be overstated?

   a The profit on the sale of a fixed asset has been omitted

   b Interest on loans has been wrongly calculated

   c Closing stock has been overvalued

   d Taxation on profit has been understated

4. A company's interest cover has decreased from 6 times to 3 times. Which one of the following is certain about that company?

   a Interest has increased

   b Interest has decreased

   c Profit before interest has decreased

   d The relative safety of the interest payments has halved when compared to last year

5. Which one of the following refers to the ability of a company to raise enough cash to meet its needs?

   a Solvency

   b Gearing

   c Liquidity

   d Cover

6. If a company calculates its gearing level by using the formula:

$$\frac{\text{Long-term loans} - \text{Cash and bank balances}}{\text{Share capital} + \text{reserves} + (\text{long-term loans} - \text{cash and bank balances})}$$

   Which one of the following could *not* be the company's gearing percentage?

   a 75%

   b 110%

   c 25%

   d 40%

7. Two companies, A and B, have PE ratios of 16 and 19 respectively. Which one of the following is certain about the companies?

   a B's profit was greater than A's
   b B's share price was greater than A's
   c B's earnings per share was greater than A's
   d B's share price was a greater multiple of its earnings per share than A's

8. Ebitda is an alternative eps calculation used by some analysts. Ebitda is an acronym for:

   a Earnings before interest and depreciation
   b Earnings before interest, taxation, and debtors
   c Earnings before interest, taxation, and depreciation on assets
   d Earnings before interest, taxation, depreciation, and amortization

9. A company has total net assets of £420,000. It has no long-term liabilities or provisions, current liabilities of £125,000, stock of £15,000, and fixed assets (net book value) of £340,000. What is the acid test ratio?

   a 1.52 : 1
   b 1.64 : 1
   c 1.56 : 1
   d 0.8 : 1

10. One of the criticisms of accounting information has been:

   a The information is always incorrect
   b Accountants' rules and regulations are too complex
   c Inflation is not normally reflected within the financial statements
   d Directors will always try and find loopholes to show the best profit

(*Note: answers are shown in Appendix 2.*)

■ DISCUSSION QUESTIONS

1. 'The chairman's report gives an excellent overview of the company's results in non-technical language, often in less than one page. Preparing a detailed numerical analysis is an unnecessary luxury.' Discuss.

2. 'Aggressive, successful, companies will always have high gearing levels.' Discuss.

3. 'It is impossible to summarize a complex commercial organization's performance by only referring to its PE ratio, yet many analysts attempt to do just that.' Discuss.

(*Note: Suggested answers or discussion points are available on the companion website.*)

■ LONGER QUESTIONS

(Questions marked W have suggested answers on the companion website. Other questions are answered in Appendix 3.)

1. The management of Aldridge plc has calculated the following statistics from its results for the year ended 31 October 2004. Equivalent average figures from a survey of other similar companies are also given.

		Aldridge plc	Trade average
(i)	Gross profit margin	50%	40%
(ii)	Net profit margin	10%	8%
(iii)	Return on capital employed	16%	12%
(iv)	Acid test	1 : 1	1.5 : 1
(v)	Gearing percentage	80%	30%

  a Explain the significance of, and the basis of calculation for, each of the five statistics listed above.

  b Explain why, if you were informed that Aldridge plc's current ratio was 5 : 1, compared with a trade average of 2 : 1, this would not necessarily indicate a satisfactory situation.

2. An individual is deciding whether to make a substantial investment in Jancis plc, a company founded many years ago and which, until relatively recently, has had an unbroken record of growth and profitability. Some relevant ratios are given below:

	2004	2003	2002
Dividend cover (times)	0	2.3	3.4
PE ratio (times)	0	18	19
Basic eps (p)	(2.4) loss	3.5	4.2
Diluted eps (p)	(1.2) loss	2.7	3.1
Dividend yield (%)	6	4.1	1.4
Stock market price at end of year (p)	110	160	180

  a Prepare a trend analysis table for the above statistics, using 2002 as the base year.

  b Comment on the possible reasons for the trends shown in your answer to (a) above.

3. The sales director of Caribou plc is an expert at selling the company's products, but at directors' meetings, he is often confused by many of the terms that the financial director uses. In brief, at a recent board meeting, he heard comments about three customers, that 'company A (a relatively new business) is over-trading, company B has a high gearing ratio, and company C has a high PE ratio despite a low return on capital employed'.

    The sales director is concerned that future sales to these companies might be risky, and has asked for your advice.

    Explain to the sales director the significance of the comments made by the finance director.

4W–6W. Use the data contained within the financial statements shown in Figure 12.3 to answer questions 4W–6W below.

Farsight plc (summarized) Group profit and loss account for the year ended 30 September 2004	2004 £000s	2003 £000s
Turnover	620	540
Less cost of sales (see note 1)	–240	–280
Gross profit	380	260
Distribution costs	–40	–35
Administrative expenses	–60	–50
Other operating income and expenditure	+20	+10
Profit on ordinary activities before interest and taxation	300	185
Interest receivable	+15	+40
Interest payable and similar charges	–35	–10
Profit on ordinary activities before taxation	280	215
Taxation	–80	–50
Profit for the financial year	200	165
Dividends (see note 2)	–50	–35
Profit retained for the financial year	150	130

Notes:

1: Taken as 'credit purchases' for 'trade creditor payment period' calculation.
2: Dividends per share 2004: 7.14p, 2003: 5.83p.

Farsight plc Group balance sheet as at 30 September 2004	2004 £000s	2003 £000s
Fixed assets		
Intangible assets	120	125
Tangible assets	1,620	1,285
	1,740	1,410
Current assets		
Stocks	80	70
Debtors due within one year (see note 1)	165	89
Cash at bank and in hand	30	1
	275	160
Creditors due within one year (see note 2)	–190	–210
Net current assets (2003: liabilities)	85	–50
Total assets less current liabilities	1,825	1,360
Creditors due after more than one year	–420	–200
Provision for liabilities and charges	–25	–20
Total net assets	1,380	1,140
Capital and reserves		
Called-up share capital (50p nominal value)	350	300
Share premium account	190	150
Profit and loss account	840	690
Equity shareholders' funds	1,380	1,140
1. Of which trade debtors:	135	85
2. Of which trade creditors:	60	90
3. 'Net indebtedness' (for gearing calculation)	580	409
4. No. of equity shares issued at year-end (000)	700	600
5. Assume stock market price (p)	135	100

Figure 12.3 (Continued overleaf)

Farsight plc Group cash flow statement for the year to 30 September 2004		
	2004	**2003**
	£000s	**£000s**
Net cash inflow from operating activities	**174**	**118**
Returns on investments and servicing of finance		
Interest received	13	35
Interest paid	−32	−12
	−19	**+23**
Taxation	**−50**	**−35**
Capital expenditure and financial investment		
Payments to acquire tangible fixed assets	−368	−200
Receipts from sales of fixed assets	+24	+80
	−344	**−120**
Equity dividends paid	**−42**	**−30**
Net cash outflow before financing	**−281**	**−44**
Financing		
Issue of ordinary share capital	90	20
New long-term loans	300	50
Repayments of long-term loans	−80	−20
	+310	**50**
Increase in cash	**29**	**6**

Figure 12.3 Farsight plc financial summaries for analysis

4W. Prepare a horizontal, vertical, and trend analysis of Farsight plc.

5W. Calculate the relevant ratios within the five groupings of: profitability, efficiency, long- and short-term liquidity and solvency, and investors' ratios.

6W. Summarize your analysis of the company's results in the form of a report to a potential investor. The report should be no more than 1,500 words in length.

■ **MINI CASE STUDY**

Analysing Wildlife Holidays Ltd.

MinnieMax Ltd. (see previous case studies) is still considering whether or not to purchase shares in Wild Life Holidays Ltd. (see p. 252). To help their decision, that company has provided financial statements for its last two years of trading, as shown in Figure 12.4.

The directors of MinnieMax Ltd. have asked you to analyse the accounts of Wild Life Holidays Ltd. and report to them on the progress shown during the two years that have been made available. Your report should give your overall impression of the company's performance, as well as a fully detailed numerical analysis.

(Suggested solutions can be found in Appendix 4.)

Wild Life Holidays Ltd. Profit and loss account for the year to 31 August	2004	2003
	£000s	£000s
Turnover	2,600	2,800
Less cost of sales (see note 1)	(2,200)	(2,250)
Gross profit	400	550
Distribution costs	(10)	(10)
Administrative expenses	(95)	(85)
Other operating income and expenditure	(5)	(15)
Profit on ordinary activities before interest and taxation	290	440
Interest receivable	10	25
Interest payable and similar charges	(50)	(30)
Profit on ordinary activities before taxation	250	435
Taxation	(70)	(120)
Profit for the financial year	130	315
Dividends (see note 2)	(120)	(120)
Profit retained for the financial year	50	195

Notes:

1: Taken as 'credit purchases' for 'creditor payment period' calculation.

2: Dividends per share 2004: 6p, 2003: 7.5p.

Figure 12.4(a) Profit and loss account of Wild Life Holidays Ltd.

Wild Life Holidays Ltd. Balance sheet as at 31 August	2004	2003
	£000s	£000s
Fixed assets		
Tangible assets	4 500	3,300
Current assets		
Stocks	4	4
Debtors due within one year (see note 1)	105	120
Cash at bank and in hand	5	20
	114	144
Creditors due within one year (see note 2)	(414)	(104)
Net current liabilities (2003: assets)	(300)	40
Total assets less current liabilities	4,200	3,340
Creditors due after more than one year (loans)	(700)	(500)
Total net assets	3,500	2,840
Capital and reserves		
Called-up share capital	2,000	1,600
Share premium account	1,000	800
Profit and loss account	500	440
Equity shareholders' funds	3,500	2,840
Notes:		
1. Of which trade debtors:	85	100
2. Of which trade creditors:	20	80
3. No. of equity shares issued at year-end (m)	2	1.6
4. Assume 'notional' stock market price (p)	90	250

Figure 12.4(b) Balance sheet of Wild Life Holidays Ltd.

Wild Life Holidays Ltd. Cash flow statement for the year ended 31 August	2004	2003
	£000s	£000s
Net cash inflow from operating activities	403	72
Returns on investments and servicing of finance		
Interest received	12	18
Interest paid	(40)	(25)
	(28)	(7)
Taxation	(120)	(80)
Capital expenditure and financial investment		
Payments to acquire tangible fixed assets	(1,100)	(140)
Receipts from sales of fixed assets	150	20
	(950)	(120)
Equity dividends paid	(120)	(100)
Net cash outflow before financing	(815)	(235)
Financing		
Issue of ordinary share capital	600	100
New long-term loans	200	50
	800	150
Decrease in cash	(15)	(85)

Figure 12.4(c) Cash flow statement of Wild Life Holidays Ltd.

■ **MAXI CASE STUDY**

Renishaw plc

You have been asked by a colleague for your opinion on the performance of Renishaw plc, an engineering company. You have been given only thirty minutes to spend on this task, and accordingly have decided to ask for a copy of the '10 year financial record' contained within that company's annual report. This is reproduced in Figure 12.5.

Within your time allocation of thirty minutes, make a list of five key trends disclosed by the report (stating whether they are favourable or adverse). List a further five items of information contained within a full annual report that you would request if you had sufficient time to make a full analysis.

(Suggested answers and discussion areas are available on the companion website.)

	2003	2002	2001	2000**	1999	1998	1997	1996	1995	1994
Results	£'000	£'000	£'000	£'000	£'000	£'000	£'000	£'000	£'000	£'000
Overseas sales	100,969	94,769	113,133	94,106	85,958	82,684	72,063	69,633	57,267	46,130
UK sales	9,671	9,721	12,215	11,488	10,361	9,665	9,338	7,444	5,395	4,744
Total sales	110,640	104,490	125,348	105,594	96,319	92,349	81,401	77,077	62,662	50,874
Operating profit	15,644	13,448	27,943	25,677	23,339	20,859	14,247	17,636	11,865	7,173
Profit on ordinary activities before tax	17,799	16,062	30,795	28,261	25,829	22,380	18,034	20,115	13,535	8,222
Taxation	3,454	880	6,082	7,065	6,716	6,280	4,653	4,207	3,831	2,379
Profit for the financial year	14,345	15,182	24,713	21,196	19,113	16,100	13,381	15,908	9,704	5,843
Dividends	12,156	11,573	11,020	9,572	8,184	7,242	6,292	5,242	3,880	3,372
Retained profit for the year	2,189	3,609	13,693	11,624	10,929	8,858	7,089	10,666	5,824	2,471
Capital employed										
Share capital	14,558	14,558	14,558	14,558	14,558	14,557	14,548	12,123	10,765	9,776
Share premium	42	42	42	42	42	40	4	66	145	1,041
Revenue reserves	93,085	93,085	94,722	82,498	70,443	59,712	52,797	52,044	40,273	35,763
Shareholders' funds	107,685	107,685	109,322	97,098	85,043	74,309	67,349	64,233	51,183	46,580
Deferred taxation	2,548	2,548	2,380	4,175	3,775	3,110	3,003	2,209	4,672	4,815
Capital employed	110,233	110,233	111,702	101,273	88,818	77,419	70,352	66,442	55,855	51,395
Statistics										
Overseas sales as a percentage of total sales	91.3	90.7	90.3	89.1	89.2	89.5	88.5	90.3	91.4	90.7
Basic earnings per share *	19.7p	20.9p	34.0p	29.1p	26.3p	22.1p	18.4p	21.9p	13.4p	8.1p
Dividend per share *	16.7p	15.9p	15.14p	13.16p	11.44p	9.95p	8.65p	7.21p	5.34p	4.65p

* Figures for 1996 and prior years have been amended for the one for five capitalisation issue in November 1996 and previous capitalisation issues.

** The 2000 figures have been restated to reflect the impact of the adoption of FRS 17–Retirement benefits. Figures for 1994 to 1999 have not been restated.

Figure 12.5 Renishaw plc: 10 year financial record

Source: Renishaw plc 2003 Annual Report.

■ **WEB LINKS**

Company websites

(Companies referred to in this chapter)

Cobham plc www.cobham.com/

Domino's Pizza www.dominos.co.uk

Holmes Place plc www.holmesplace.co.uk/

Renishaw plc www.renishaw.com

Tesco plc www.tesco.com/

■ **FURTHER READING**

Britton, A., and Waterston, C. (2003). *Financial Accounting*, 3rd edn. (Harlow: FT/Prentice Hall), chapter 11.

Elliott, B., and Elliott, J. (2003). *Financial Accounting and Reporting*, 7th edn. (Harlow: FT/Prentice Hall), chapter 25.

Jones, M. (2002). *Accounting for Non-specialists*, 1st edn. (Chichester: Wiley), chapter 9.

Weetman, P. (2003). *Financial and Management Accounting: An Introduction*, 3rd edn. (Harlow: FT/Prentice Hall), chapters 13–14.

■ COMPANION WEBSITE MATERIALS

 Additional materials are available for students and lecturers on the companion website, at **www.oup.com/uk/booksites/busecon/business/**, including a 'Question Generator' file that gives unlimited practice at preparing horizontal and vertical analyses, and accounting ratios.

APPENDIX 1

 Domino's Pizza UK & IRL plc
Annual Report 2002

Chairman's statement:

Delivering more quality growth . . .

Even as you read this report, people all over the country are picking up their telephones, logging onto the internet and using their digital remote controls to order a delivery from Domino's Pizza. Their made-to-order pizzas will usually arrive in less than 30 minutes, fresh-baked and straight out of the oven.

When one thinks for a moment, it's amazing how new technology, quality ingredients, skilled professionals and a focus on service can work together to make an experience that's so special yet so perfectly straightforward for the customer.

At Domino's, we are becoming quite accomplished at making something complex look seemingly effortless. After all, delivering fresh, great-tasting pizza on time would appear to be such a simple transaction when it is, in actual fact, a very intricate one that is only made possible by ongoing innovation, invention and product development.

In 2002 alone, we responded to almost ten million orders from customers—that's around a quarter of all of the delivered pizza orders placed in the UK and Republic of Ireland in the last year. As our share of the pizza delivery market continues to grow, so does the market itself. Today, the home delivery pizza market is estimated to be around £400 million per annum. By 2010, it is expected to top the £800 million mark. And Domino's is the leader in this market thanks to our vigorous commitment to using the freshest, finest ingredients and our total dedication to impeccable service with every order. (Source: Future Foundation).

Thanks to our commitment to quality in all areas of the business, our like-for-like sales have continued to grow significantly over the last three years. In the past year, our system sales have increased more than 20%, from £98 million at the end of 2001 to nearly £119 million in 2002. We have also continued to add stores at an aggressive clip, 34 stores opened in 2002 compared to 24 in 2001.

Furthermore, our pool of franchise applicants is growing as word of our success spreads. In 2002, we had over 2,300 franchise applicants and we accepted 14. With a selection that large, we are able to select only the most competent and experienced franchisees to add to our family tree.

It is our commitment to quality that has made Domino's what it is today, but it is national TV that has made Domino's Pizza such a familiar name. In 2003, our national advertising fund will spend in excess of £5.5 million and our stores will deliver to approximately 35–40% of all households within our potential reach. As we open more stores, each of our new and existing ones will benefit from coming under the umbrella of our existing nationwide TV campaigns.

Opening more stores, driving up like-for-like sales, increasing e-commerce revenues and growing market share—all of these things have been accomplished in 2002 without our raising any new capital. This means our shareholders will see the benefits of our labour even faster. This year our dividend will increase by 50% on last year to two pence per share. That's more than our entire earnings per share in 1999. Our cashflow will continue to grow as we continue to drive our business and profitability. We believe we can sustain our growth without any increase in our current share capital in the years ahead.

We are proud to share the details of our success with you, our valued shareholders. As always, we look forward to years of continued growth and success. We thank you for your commitment to Domino's and we pledge our continued devotion to you.

Colin Halpern
Chairman

"Domino's is the leader in this market thanks to our vigorous commitment to using the freshest, finest ingredients and our total dedication to impeccable service with every order."

Chief executive's report:

Record success . . .

Introduction

2002 was the most successful year on record for your company. It was also a year during which we passed several significant milestones which helped to ensure that Domino's Pizza remained the leading pizza delivery company in the UK and Republic of Ireland. How did we achieve this? Simply, by *delivering more*.

At its heart, Domino's is a partnership between our franchisees, their teams and our corporate team members. Working together we have delivered more to our customers by further increasing our focus on fresh food and high in-store standards. Together we have delivered record store sales and a record number of store openings. Our corporate team members have delivered more by exceeding the majority of our internal targets for the year and we will be sharing the resulting rewards with them. And, of course, we delivered more to shareholders, with a 40% increase in earnings per share and a 50% increase in dividend this year.

One milestone of which I am particularly proud is the opening of our third commissary in Penrith, the final addition to the infrastructure required to sustain our ever-growing community of stores in the North of England and Scotland. It is in these local markets that we see one of our greatest opportunities for expansion and such growth would not be possible without the Northern commissary to produce and deliver fresh dough and ingredients to the stores.

I have highlighted in previous statements the benefits that should arise from the continued roll-out of stores and sales increases in a fixed cost business such as ours. With the majority of our higher royalty payments and infrastructure costs absorbed, it is very encouraging to see that a 20.8% increase in system sales has delivered a 43.2% increase in operating profit.

Sales

Continued positive sales performance in 2002 means that Domino's Pizza has retained its position as the UK's leading pizza delivery company in terms of both total sales and number of stores.

System sales, which are the sales of all stores in the Domino's system in the UK and Republic of Ireland, rose by 20.8% to £118.9m (2001: £98.4m) in the 52 weeks ended 29 December 2002. Average weekly unit sales grew 8.1% (2001: 19.0%). Like-for-like sales in the 215 stores open for twelve months or more in both periods grew by 11.2% (2001: 21.4%).

System expansion & re-imaging

2002 saw a significant acceleration in the rate of new openings with 34 delivery stores opened (2001: 24 stores). Two delivery stores were closed (2001: two). This took the year-end store count to 269.

We opened more stores in 2002 than in any other year, of which 11 were in the South of England, five in the Midlands, six in the North of England, six in the Republic of Ireland, one in Northern Ireland and five in Scotland.

In addition to opening new delivery stores, we continued to focus on re-imaging existing stores. At the year-end a further 42 stores had been re-imaged, bringing the total stores with the latest image standards to 85% of the system. Such improvements have helped to convey to customers our contemporary and exciting brand values and have also underlined our commitment to high standards in all areas of our operation.

Trading results

Group turnover, which includes the sales generated by the group from royalties, fees on new store openings, food sales and rental income, as well as the turnover of corporately owned and operated stores, grew by 21.2% to £53.1m from £43.8m.

Group operating profit was up 43.2% to £4.50m from £3.14m. 2002 saw the second of three phased increases in the rate of royalty paid to Domino's Pizza International Inc. in the USA under the Master Franchise agreement. The rate increased from an average rate of 1.94% in 2001 to 2.5% in the year. The final increase to 2.7% occurred on 1 January 2003.

The net interest charge fell slightly in the year to £0.32m (2001: £0.35m). The total net interest charge was covered a comfortable 14.1 times by operating profit (2001: 9.1 times).

Profit before tax was up 48.1% to £4.24m from £2.86m. The tax charge increased from 30% to 33% principally as a result of the full provision for deferred taxation and the reduction in tax losses available from an acquired subsidiary.

> "At its heart, Domino's is a partnership between our franchisees, their teams and our corporate team members."

Earnings per share and dividend

Basic earnings per share were up 40.0% to 5.60 pence from 4.00 pence. Diluted earnings per share increased by 36.3% to 5.29 pence from 3.88 pence.

With the completion of the infrastructure, the company has moved into a period in which it should generate strong positive cashflows. As a result, the Board is pleased to recommend to shareholders a 50.4% increase in the dividend per share for the year. If approved, this will give a final dividend of 1.22p per share (2001: 0.76p per share) and result in a total dividend for the year to 2.00 pence per share (2001: 1.33 pence per share). The proposed dividend is 2.8 times covered by profits after tax (2001: 3.0 times).

Subject to shareholders' approval the final dividend will be payable on 29 April 2003 to shareholders on the register on 11 April 2003.

Cash flow & balance sheet

Operating activities generated net cash of £5.1m (2001: £4.5m). Capital expenditure (including intangibles) totalled almost £4.0m during the year. Of this, £1.3m was expended on the completion of the freehold commissary facility in Penrith which, together with the commissaries in Milton Keynes and Naas in Ireland, gives the group the infrastructure necessary to service in excess of 500 stores. Investment in corporate stores of £1.6m was broadly matched with proceeds from disposals, although most of these funds were received after the year end or were reinvested in a further joint venture.

The group further extended the leasing finance provided to franchisees, to fit-out new stores and refit existing stores. In the year further advances of £0.9m were made which, after repayments, resulted in a balance outstanding at the year-end of £2.0m (2001: £1.6m). These facilities are financed by a limited recourse facility which at the year-end stood at £2.0m (2001: £1.4m).

At the year-end, the group had total net borrowings of £6.3m (2001: £5.8m) of which borrowings used to finance group operating assets, including freehold properties, declined slightly to £4.3m from £4.4m in the previous year. The increase in overall borrowing resulted from the expanding activities of our leasing company as noted above. Total borrowings represented 53.9% (2001: 60.0%) of shareholder funds of £11.7m (2001: £9.6m).

Corporate stores

The initial purpose of expanding the portfolio of corporate stores was to generate additional income to meet the increased royalty payment to the US. The portfolio of stores successfully delivered this with a contribution to group profits of £633,000 (2001: £787,000) in the year. However, now that the infrastructure has been completed and the economies of scale available from the expanding store base are apparent, we wish to concentrate our efforts on the roll-out of stores which we feel is best achieved in partnership with our franchisees.

We therefore expect to reduce the number of corporate stores from the year-end total of 35. As part of this process, we have established a joint venture with an existing franchisee in Scotland to whom we sold our two corporate stores in Edinburgh. Subsequently, other transactions have been agreed, in principle, which we will complete in the current year, and the cash flow generated will be re-invested in the franchise business, used to repay bank borrowings or returned to shareholders.

The market

The total home-delivered food market is estimated to have been worth £1.1 billion in 2002, a 56% increase in value since 1997. Pizza is the single largest category in the home delivered food market, presently accounting for 36% of the total, or £400m. (Source: Future Foundation).

In December 2002, we commissioned the Future Foundation, an independent think-tank, to track the factors that will impact on the food delivery industry during the rest of this decade. The key findings indicate that more people will be seeking to order delivered food to save time and, in other instances, to accompany an increasing portfolio of at-home entertainment choices.

I am delighted to report that the key 'new' opportunities identified in the report are already incorporated into our own strategy. For example, the Future Foundation indicates that, over the next five years, 90% of the population will have access to interactive technologies. These people will become more experienced and confident about e-commerce and online home food deliverers such as Domino's are likely to benefit.

Building the brand

During the third quarter of 2002, we undertook a far-reaching strategic review of our marketing communications activity. This process reinforced our understanding of the maturing and developing audiences who are in the market for delivered pizza today and in the future.

The review also involved a thorough appraisal of the Domino's Pizza brand, product and service attributes that appeal strongly to these audiences. We will continue to translate these unique attributes into new creative themes for future marketing communications activity and, in doing so, will continue to set Domino's apart from the competition.

In 2002 there was further evidence of the 'virtuous circle' effect created by our national advertising fund. In brief, this means that every time store sales increase, the national advertising fund increases too. This provides us with more money to invest in high impact marketing such as national terrestrial TV, which further increases sales.

Whilst it is both exciting and effective, national advertising is only made so powerful when it works alongside equally successful local marketing campaigns. The 120 million menus we distribute every year and in particular, the strategically focused local store marketing activities we execute, help to reinforce brand values at store level.

The community

At the heart of our business is a commitment to the communities we serve and a belief that our presence should benefit local people in many more ways than just via the provision of a pizza delivery service.

On average, every store opening creates between 25 and 30 new jobs and every store team is trained to think about its positive impact on the local area. Our franchisees and stores aim to deliver greater value to their communities by showing support for local charities and organisations, enabling local schools and groups to visit stores and conducting business in a responsible, friendly manner.

Current trading and prospects

Trading at the start of 2003 is off to a very good start with like-for-like sales up 10.1% in the first six weeks of the year. The rollout of new stores remains a key part of our strategy in delivering improving shareholder returns. We plan to further accelerate the rate of openings in the current year and have a strong pipeline of both new properties and franchisees to help us achieve this. We, therefore, look forward to 2003 with confidence.

Conclusion and thanks

The results we have achieved in 2002 would not have been possible without a team of exceptional people working in partnership. Any business that develops using a franchising model has to be keenly aware that the success of the business depends on the strength of that partnership. It is testament to the strength of the underlying business, and the spirit of co-operation that exists between our franchisees and us, that we continue to successfully build this business together. I thank all our franchisees and their staff for their support and hard work during the year.

Such growth would also not be possible without the talented and dedicated people in the corporate team. This team's constant commitment to the targets we set for ourselves has been one of the most positive aspects of the last year. To recognise this commitment we have put in place revised bonus arrangements and will shortly be bringing forward for shareholder approval a revised share option arrangement and long-term incentive plan for key team members. I should like to thank each and every team member for their continuing dedication.

To close where we opened, it is our continuing objective to *deliver more* for all the stakeholders in this great business we are creating, in particular for our franchisees, our team members, our shareholders and, most importantly of all, our customers.

Stephen Hemsley
Chief Executive

"The results we have achieved in 2002 would not have been possible without a team of exceptional people working in partnership."

Directors and Advisors

Directors

Colin Halpern	*Executive Chairman*
Stephen Hemsley	*Chief Executive*
Christopher H R Moore	*Sales and Marketing Director*
Nigel Wray	*Non-Executive*
Yoav Gottesman	*Non-Executive*
Gerald Halpern	*Non-Executive*

Secretary

Andrew Mallows

Nominated advisor and nominated broker

Numis Securities Limited, Cheapside House
138 Cheapside, London, EC2V 6LH

Auditors

Ernst & Young LLP, 400 Capability Green
Luton, LU1 3LU

Bankers

National Westminster Bank PLC
Exchange House, 478 Midsummer Boulevard
Milton Keynes, MK9 2EA

Solicitors

McDermott, Will & Emery
7 Bishopsgate, London, EC2N 3AR

Registrars

Capita Registrars, Bourne House
34 Beckenham Road, Beckenham
Kent, BR3 4TU

Registered office

Domino's House, Lasborough Road
Kingston, Milton Keynes, MK10 0AB

Registered number

3853545

Report and Accounts

Report on directors' remuneration

The remuneration committee consists of Yoav Gottesman, Nigel Wray and Colin Halpern. It has the primary responsibility to review the performance of executive directors and similar employees and set the scale and structure of their remuneration.

Service agreement

Stephen Hemsley and Christopher Moore have entered into service agreements with the company, which are subject to a twelve month notice period by both parties. The remuneration packages consist of basic salary, bonus, pension contributions, health and life insurance benefits and the use of a company car or cash equivalent allowance.

Colin Halpern is seconded to the company from International Franchise System Inc. ("IFS") as executive chairman under the terms of a management agreement. The agreement is reviewed annually and the level of compensation paid to IFS agreed.

The non-executive directors are appointed on three-year agreements with the company terminable at one week's notice. Fees for non-executive directors are set by the board.

Directors' remuneration

	Salary or fees 2002 £000	Bonus 2002 £000	Benefits 2002 £000	Pension contributions 2002 £000	Total 2002 £000	Total 2001 £000
EXECUTIVE DIRECTORS:						
Colin Halpern	165	—	36	—	201	165
Stephen Hemsley	182	43	11	17	253	194
Christopher Moore	151	25	13	12	201	150
NON-EXECUTIVE DIRECTORS:						
Gerald Halpern	65	—	6	—	71	65
Nigel Wray	15	—	—	—	15	15
Yoav Gottesman	24	—	—	—	24	26
	602	68	66	29	765	615

The value of benefits relates primarily to the provision of company car or equivalent allowance. Colin Halpern is not remunerated by the company. A management fee of £165,000 (2001: £165,000) was paid to IFS in respect of his services. Gerald Halpern is not remunerated by the company. A management fee of £65,000 (2001: £65,000) was paid to Chinese Pompano Inc in respect of his services. The company makes contributions of up to 10% of annual basic salary to personal pension plans of Stephen Hemsley and Christopher Moore.

Remuneration in 2001 included £15,000 for Stephen Hemsley and £4,000 for Christopher Moore in respect of pension contributions.

Interest in options

The interests of the directors under the company's share option schemes are as follows.

DIRECTORS	No. of ordinary shares under option	Date of grant	Expiry date of option	Exercise price per ordinary share
Stephen Hemsley	415,654	31/03/1999	30/03/2009	42.10p
	432,973	24/11/1999	23/11/2009	50.00p
	105,000	04/08/2000	03/08/2010	53.00p
	336,934	01/01/2001	31/12/2010	33.50p
	1,290,561			
Christopher Moore	415,654	31/03/1999	30/03/2009	42.10p
	207,827	24/11/1999	23/11/2009	50.00p
	90,000	04/08/2000	03/08/2010	53.00p
	278,794	01/01/2001	31/12/2010	33.50p
	992,275			
Gerald Halpern	519,568	31/03/1999	30/03/2009	42.10p
	103,914	24/11/1999	23/11/2009	50.00p
	130,000	04/08/2000	03/08/2010	53.00p
	753,482			
Yoav Gottesman	237,269	31/03/1999	30/03/2009	42.10p
	109,110	24/11/1999	23/11/2009	50.00p
	346,379			

No options have been exercised or lapsed during the year.

The remuneration committee has resolved that the exercise of these options which have been granted under the Share Option Schemes will be subject to the condition that the growth in normalised earnings per share in any financial year between grant and vesting exceeds the growth in the Retail Price Index in the previous financial year by at least 5%.

The market price of the Companys shares on 29 December 2002 was 90.5p per share and the high and low share prices during the year were 102.5p and 59.5p respectively.

Director's Report

The directors present their report and the group accounts for the 52 weeks ended 29 December 2002.

Results and dividends

The group profit for the year, after taxation, amounted to £2,835,000 (2001: £2,004,000).

The directors recommend a final ordinary dividend amounting to £623,000 making a total dividend for the year of £1,018,000 (2001 : £668,000).

The final ordinary dividend, if approved, will be paid on 29 April 2003 to ordinary shareholders whose names appear on the register on 11 April 2003.

Principal activity and review of the business

The principal activity of the group is the development of the Domino's franchise system in the UK and Republic of Ireland.

The review of the business is contained in the Chief Executive's Report on pages 308 to 311.

Branches

The group operates a branch in the Republic of Ireland in order to service that market.

Directors and their interests

The directors during the year under review and their interest in the share capital of the company, other than with respect to options to acquire ordinary shares (which are detailed in the analysis of options included in the Report on Directors' Remuneration) were as follows:

	At 29 December 2002 Ordinary shares	At 30 December 2001 Ordinary shares
Colin Halpern (i)	14,974,006	19,274,006
Stephen Hemsley (ii)	2,060,109	1,472,109
Christopher Moore	103,235	15,000
Nigel Wray (iii)	14,029,725	13,741,411
Gerry Halpern	50,000	50,000
Yoav Gottesman	300,000	—

(i) shares are held 14,041,515 by International Franchise Systems Inc., beneficially for HS Real Company LLC and 932,491 by HS Real Company LLC (HS Real Company LLC is owned by a discretionary trust, the beneficiaries of which are the adult children of Colin and Gail Halpern).

(ii) 1,472,109 shares are held by CTG Investment Limited, which is beneficially owned by a discretionary trust of which Stephen Hemsley and his family are potential beneficiaries.

(iii) 7,614,000 shares are held by Abacus (CI) Ltd, which is beneficially owned by the family trusts of Nigel Wray, principal beneficiaries of which are Nigel Wray's children.

During the period from the end of the financial year to 25 February 2003, there have been no changes in directors' shareholdings.

Other significant shareholders

Directors' interests in the shares of the company have been disclosed above. The other significant shareholder holding more than 3% of the shares in the company, which has been disclosed to the company is RBS Mezzanine Limited which holds a 5.2% interest and Moonpal Grewal a franchisee who is the beneficial holder of a 3.9% interest.

Share option schemes

In order to provide employee share incentives in the future the group has adopted two share option schemes, one of which, the Domino's Pizza Group Limited (Unapproved) Share Option Scheme, has been in place since 30 March 1999. The Domino's Pizza Share Option (Unapproved) Scheme was introduced on 24 November 1999 (the Share Option Schemes).

All participants in the Domino's Pizza Group Limited (Unapproved) Share Option Scheme were, on Admission of the company to the Alternative Investment Market, offered the chance to release their options over shares in Domino's Pizza Group Limited in return for equivalent options over ordinary shares in the company under the Domino's Pizza Share Option (Unapproved) Scheme. Further details of options outstanding at the year end are contained in note 20.

The remuneration committee has resolved that the exercise of these options which have been granted under the Share Option Schemes will be subject to the condition that the growth in normalised earnings per share in any financial year between grant and vesting exceeds the growth in the Retail Price Index in the previous financial year by at least 5%.

Creditor payment policy

It is the group's policy that payments to suppliers are made in accordance with those terms and conditions agreed between the company and its suppliers, provided that all trading terms and conditions have been complied with. At 29 December 2002, the group had an average of 44 days (2001: 52 days) purchases outstanding in trade creditors.

Corporate Governance

The directors acknowledge the principles set out in the Combined Code issued by the committee on Corporate Governance and intend to comply over time with the main provisions in-so-far as they are appropriate for smaller quoted companies. At present the main facets are:

• The Board—during the year the company had three executive and three non-executive directors. The directors hold regular board meetings at which operating and financial reports are considered. The board is responsible for formulating, reviewing and approving the group's strategy, budgets, major items of capital expenditure and senior personnel appointments.

• Audit Committee—which consists of Nigel Wray, Yoav Gottesman and Colin Halpern. It meets at least twice each year and is responsible for ensuring that the financial performance of the group is properly reported on and monitored, for meeting the auditors and reviewing the reports from the auditors relating to accounts and internal control systems.

• Remuneration Committee—which consists of Nigel Wray, Yoav Gottesman and Colin Halpern. It meets at least twice each year and has a primary responsibility to review the performance of executive directors and senior employees and set the scale and structure of their remuneration having due regard to the interests of shareholders. It also has responsibility for administering the share option schemes.

• Going Concern—the directors are satisfied that the group has adequate resources to continue in existence for the foreseeable future and for this reason, they continue to adopt the going concern basis of preparing the accounts.

• Internal Control—the directors have overall responsibility for ensuring that the group maintains internal controls to provide reasonable assurance on the reliability of the financial information used within the business and for safeguarding the assets. There are limitations in any system of internal controls and accordingly, even the most effective system can only provide reasonable and not absolute assurance with respect to preparation of the financial information and the safeguarding of the assets.

The key elements of financial control are as follows:

- Control Environment—the presence of a clear organisational structure and well-defined lines of responsibility and delegation of appropriate levels of authority.
- Risk Management—business strategy and plans are reviewed by the board.
- Financial Reporting—a comprehensive system of budgets and forecasts with monthly reporting of actual results against targets.
- Control Procedures and Monitoring Procedures—ensuring authorisation levels and procedures and other systems of internal financial controls are documented, applied and regularly reviewed.

Statement of directors' responsibilities

Company law requires the directors to prepare accounts for each financial year which give a true and fair view of the state of affairs of the company and of the group and of the profit or loss of the group for that period. In preparing those accounts, the directors are required to:

- select suitable accounting policies and then apply them consistently;
- make judgements and estimates that are reasonable and prudent;
- state whether applicable accounting standards have been followed, subject to any material departures disclosed and explained in the accounts; and prepare the accounts on the going concern basis unless it is inappropriate to presume that the group will continue in business.

The directors are responsible for keeping proper accounting records which disclose with reasonable accuracy at any time the financial position of the group and to enable them to ensure that the accounts comply with the Companies Act 1985. They are also responsible for safeguarding the assets of the group and hence for taking reasonable steps for the prevention and detection of fraud and other irregularities.

Employees

Employees of group companies are encouraged to participate in the success of the business through incentive and share option schemes. Progress is regularly communicated to the management of subsidiary companies and all management and staff are expected to communicate fully within their own area of responsibility.

Disabled employees

The group gives full consideration to applications for employment from disabled persons where the requirements of the job can be adequately fulfilled by a handicapped or disabled person.

Where existing employees become disabled, it is the group's policy wherever practicable, to provide continuing employment under normal terms and conditions and to provide training, career development and promotion to disabled employees wherever appropriate.

Auditors

A resolution to re-appoint Ernst & Young LLP as the company's auditor will be put to the forthcoming Annual General Meeting.

By order of the board

Andrew Mallows
Secretary

Independent auditors' report

We have audited the group's financial statements for the 52 weeks ended 29 December 2002 which comprise the Group Profit and Loss Account, Group Balance Sheet, Company Balance Sheet, Group Statement of Cash Flows, Group Statement of Total Recognised Gains and Losses, and the related notes 1 to 26. These financial statements have been prepared on the basis of the accounting policies set out therein.

This report is made solely to the company's members, as a body, in accordance with Section 235 of the Companies Act 1985. Our audit work has been undertaken so that we might state to the company's members those matters we are required to state to them in an auditors' report and for no other purpose. To the fullest extent permitted by law, we do not accept or assume responsibility to anyone other than the company and the company's members as a body, for our audit work, for this report, or for the opinions we have formed.

Respective responsibilities of directors and auditors

The directors' responsibilities for preparing the Annual Report and the financial statements in accordance with applicable United Kingdom law and accounting standards are set out in the Statement of Directors' Responsibilities.

Our responsibility is to audit the financial statements in accordance with relevant legal and regulatory requirements and United Kingdom Auditing Standards.

We report to you our opinion as to whether the financial statements give a true and fair view and are properly prepared in accordance with the Companies Act 1985. We also report to you if, in our opinion, the Directors' Report is not consistent with the financial statements, if the company has not kept proper accounting records, if we have not received all the information and explanations we require for our audit, or if information specified by law regarding directors' remuneration and transactions with the group is not disclosed.

We read other information contained in the Annual Report and consider whether it is consistent with the audited financial statements. This other information comprises the Directors' Report, Chairman's Statement and Chief Executive's Report. We consider the implications for our report if we become aware of any apparent misstatements or material inconsistencies with the financial statements. Our responsibilities do not extend to any other information.

Basis of audit opinion

We conducted our audit in accordance with United Kingdom Auditing Standards issued by the Auditing Practices Board. An audit includes examination, on a test basis, of evidence relevant to the amounts and disclosures in the financial statements. It also includes an assessment of the significant estimates and judgements made by the directors in the preparation of the financial statements, and of whether the accounting policies are appropriate to the group's circumstances, consistently applied and adequately disclosed.

We planned and performed our audit so as to obtain all the information and explanations which we considered necessary in order to provide us with sufficient evidence to give reasonable assurance that the financial statements are free from material misstatement, whether caused by fraud or other irregularity or error. In forming our opinion we also evaluated the overall adequacy of the presentation of information in the financial statements.

Opinion

In our opinion the financial statements give a true and fair view of the state of affairs of the company and of the group as at 29 December 2002 and of the profit of the group for the 52 weeks then ended and have been properly prepared in accordance with the Companies Act 1985.

Ernst & Young LLP
Registered Auditor
Luton
25 February 2003

Group profit and loss account

	Notes	2002 £000	2001 £000
TURNOVER			
Turnover: group and share of joint ventures' turnover		54,673	45,185
Less: share of joint ventures' turnover		(1,564)	(1,360)
GROUP TURNOVER	2	53,109	43,825
Cost of sales		(28,054)	(23,132)
GROSS PROFIT		25,055	20,693
Distribution costs		(8,663)	(7,150)
Administrative expenses		(11,813)	(10,230)
Other operating expenditure		(75)	(169)
GROUP OPERATING PROFIT	3	4,504	3,144
Share of operating profit in joint venture		64	75
Amortisation of goodwill on joint venture		(5)	(5)
		59	70
PROFIT ON ORDINARY ACTIVITIES BEFORE INTEREST AND TAXATION		4,563	3,214
Interest receivable		50	78
Interest payable and similar charges	6	(374)	(430)
PROFIT ON ORDINARY ACTIVITIES BEFORE TAXATION		4,239	2,862
Tax on profit on ordinary activities	7	(1,404)	(858)
PROFIT FOR THE FINANCIAL YEAR		2,835	2,004
Dividends on equity shares	8	(1,018)	(668)
PROFIT RETAINED FOR THE FINANCIAL YEAR	22	1,817	1,336
Earnings per share – basic	9	5.60p	4.00p
– diluted		5.29p	3.88p

Group statement of total recognised gains and losses

	2002 £000	2001 £000
Profit attributable to the financial period	1,817	1,336
Unrealised gain on exchange of properties for interest in joint venture	55	—
Total gains and losses recognised since the last annual report	1,872	1,336

Group balance sheet

	Notes	2002 £000	2001 £000
FIXED ASSETS			
Intangible assets	10	2,386	2,484
Tangible assets	11	13,685	12,181
Investments in joint venture:	12		
Share of gross assets		717	757
Share of gross liabilities		(410)	(480)
		307	277
TOTAL FIXED ASSETS		16,378	14,942
CURRENT ASSETS			
Stocks	13	1,411	1,260
Debtors:	14		
amounts falling due within one year		8,572	6,665
amounts falling due after more than one year		2,130	1,756
		10,702	8,421
Cash at bank and in hand		3,885	3,231
TOTAL CURRENT ASSETS		15,998	12,912
CREDITORS: amounts falling due within one year	15	(12,919)	(10,203)
NET CURRENT ASSETS		3,079	2,709
TOTAL ASSETS LESS CURRENT LIABILITIES		19,457	17,651
CREDITORS: amounts falling due after more than one year	16	(7,152)	(7,632)
PROVISION FOR LIABILITIES AND CHARGES	7	(604)	(421)
		11,701	9,598
CAPITAL AND RESERVES			
Called up share capital	21	2,546	2,518
Share premium account	22	2,395	2,192
Profit and loss account	22	6,760	4,888
Equity shareholders' funds		11,701	9,598

Stephen Hemsley
Director

Company balance sheet

	Notes	2002 £000	2001 £000
FIXED ASSETS			
Investments in subsidiary undertakings	12	2,475	2,475
Investments in joint venture	12	205	205
		2,680	2,680
CURRENT ASSETS			
Debtors	14	2,885	2,412
Cash at bank and in hand		—	1
		2,885	2,413
CREDITORS: amounts falling due within one year	15	(624)	(383)
NET CURRENT ASSETS		2,261	2,030
TOTAL ASSETS LESS CURRENT LIABILITIES		4,941	4,710
CAPITAL AND RESERVES			
Called up share capital	21	2,546	2,518
Share premium account	22	2,395	2,192
Profit and loss account	22	—	—
Equity shareholders' funds		4,941	4,710

Stephen Hemsley
Director

Group statement of cash flows

	Notes	2002 £000	2001 £000
NET CASH INFLOW FROM OPERATING ACTIVITIES	23 (a)	5,128	4,475
RETURNS ON INVESTMENTS AND SERVICING OF FINANCE			
Interest received		50	78
Interest paid		(343)	(304)
Interest element of finance lease payments		(9)	(11)
		(302)	(237)
TAXATION			
Corporation tax paid		(950)	(617)
CAPITAL EXPENDITURE AND FINANCIAL INVESTMENT			
Payments to acquire intangible fixed assets		(214)	(68)
Payments to acquire tangible fixed assets		(3,291)	(2,560)
Receipts from sales of tangible and intangible fixed assets		411	5
Receipts from repayment of joint venture loan		46	36
Payments to acquire finance lease assets and advance of franchisee loans		(1,247)	(1,007)
Receipts from repayment of finance leases and franchisee loans		901	445
		(3,394)	(3,149)
ACQUISITIONS AND DISPOSALS			
Purchase of subsidiary undertaking and un-associated businesses		(484)	(160)
		(484)	(160)
EQUITY DIVIDENDS PAID		(777)	(501)
NET CASH OUTFLOW BEFORE FINANCING		(779)	(189)
FINANCING			
Issue of ordinary share capital		231	164
New long-term loans		2,719	2,660
Repayments of long-term loans		(1443)	(330)
Repayment of capital element of finance leases and hire purchase contracts		(74)	(72)
		1,433	2,422
INCREASE IN CASH	23(c)	654	2,233

Notes to the Accounts

1. Accounting Policies

Basis of preparation

The accounts are prepared under the historical cost convention and in accordance with applicable accounting standards.

Basis of consolidation

The group accounts consolidate the accounts of Domino's Pizza UK & IRL plc and all its subsidiary undertakings drawn up to the nearest Sunday to 31 December each year. No profit and loss account is presented for Domino's Pizza UK & IRL plc as permitted by Section 230 of the Companies Act 1985.

Entities in which the group holds an interest on a long-term basis and are jointly controlled by one or more ventures under a contractual agreement are treated as joint ventures in the group accounts. Joint ventures are accounted for using the gross equity method. The group accounts include the appropriate share of assets and liabilities and earnings, based on management accounts for the period to 29 December 2002.

Goodwill

Positive goodwill arising on acquisitions of a subsidiary, associate or business is capitalised, classified as an asset on the balance sheet and amortised on a straight-line basis over its estimated useful economic life up to 20 years. It is reviewed for impairment at the end of the first full financial year following the acquisition and in other periods if events or changes in circumstances indicate that the carrying value may not be recoverable.

If a subsidiary, associate or business is subsequently sold or closed, any goodwill arising on acquisition that has not been amortised through the profit and loss account is taken into account in determining the profit or loss on sale or closure.

Intangible assets

Intangible assets acquired separately from a business are capitalised at cost. Intangible assets acquired as part of an acquisition of a business are capitalised separately from goodwill if the fair value can be measured reliably on initial recognition, subject to the constraint that, unless the asset has a readily ascertainable market value, the fair value is limited to an amount that does not create or increase any negative goodwill arising on the acquisition. Intangible assets, excluding development costs, created within the business are not capitalised and expenditure is charged against profits in the year in which it is incurred.

Intangible assets are amortised on a straight-line basis over their estimated useful lives as follows:

Franchise fees   –   over 20 years

Interest in leases   –   over the life of the lease

The carrying value of intangible assets is reviewed for impairment at the end of the first full year following acquisition and in other periods if events or changes in circumstances indicate the carrying value may not be recoverable.

Significant property developments

Interest incurred on finance provided for significant property development is capitalised up to the date of completion of the project. Where employees participate in the development, the incremental staff costs directly attributable with the time spent on those projects are capitalised. These costs are then depreciated in accordance with the group's policy for the relevant class of tangible fixed assets.

Depreciation

Depreciation is provided on all tangible fixed assets, at rates calculated to write off the cost less residual value of each asset evenly over its expected useful life as follows:

Freehold buildings	–	over 50 years
Plant and production equipment	–	over 10 years
Leasehold building improvements	–	over the lesser of the life of the lease plus 14 years, or 30 years
Computers, fixtures and fittings and other equipment	–	over 2 to 10 years
Motor vehicles	–	over 3 years
Mopeds	–	over 18 months

The carrying values of tangible fixed assets are reviewed for impairment in periods if events or changes in circumstances indicate that the carrying value may not be recoverable.

Stocks

Stocks comprise raw materials, consumables and goods for resale (being equipment for resale to franchises) and are stated at the lower of cost and net realisable value. Cost of stock is determined on the average cost basis or, for computer and food stock, the first-in, first-out basis.

Deferred taxation

Deferred tax is recognised in respect of all timing differences that have originated but not reversed at the balance sheet date where transactions or events have occurred at that date that will result in an obligation to pay more, or right to pay less or to receive more, tax, with the following exceptions:

- Provision is made for tax on gains from the revaluation (and similar fair value adjustments) of fixed assets, or gains on disposal of fixed assets that have been rolled over into replacement assets, only to the extent that, at the balance sheet date, there is a binding agreement to dispose of the assets concerned. However, no provision is made where, on the basis of all available evidence at the balance sheet date, it is more likely than not that the taxable gain will be rolled over into replacement assets and charged to tax only where the replacement assets are sold.

- Deferred tax assets are recognised only to the extent that the directors consider that it is more likely than not that there will be suitable taxable profits from which the underlying timing differences can be deducted.

Deferred tax is measured on an undiscounted basis at the tax rates that are expected to apply in the periods in which timing differences reverse, based on tax rates and laws enacted or substantively enacted at the balance sheet date.

Foreign currencies

Transactions in foreign currencies are recorded at the rate ruling at the date of the transaction or at the contracted rate if the transaction is covered by a forward foreign currency contract. Monetary assets and liabilities denominated in foreign currencies are retranslated at the rate of exchange ruling at the balance sheet date or if appropriate at the forward contract rate. All differences are taken to the profit and loss account.

Leasing and hire purchase commitments

As lessee

Assets held under finance leases, which are leases where substantially all the risks and rewards of ownership of the asset have passed to the group, and hire purchase contracts, are capitalised in the balance sheet and depreciated over their useful lives. The capital elements of future obligations under leases and hire purchase contracts are included as liabilities in the balance sheet. The interest elements of the rental obligations are charged in the profit and loss account over the periods of the leases and hire purchase contracts and represent a constant proportion of the balance of capital repayments outstanding.

Rentals payable under operating leases are charged in the profit and loss account on a straight-line basis over the lease term.

As lessor

Amounts receivable under finance leases are included under debtors and represent the total amount outstanding under lease agreements less unearned income. Finance lease income, having been allocated to accounting periods to give a constant periodic rate of return on the net cash investment is included in turnover.

Rental

Income and expenditure from the rental of leasehold properties and equipment have been included in the gross income in turnover and the related expenditure within cost of sales.

Other operating income and expenditure

Certain stores are acquired from poor performing franchises. Where the store is not intended to form part of the long-term portfolio of corporate stores, it is included as a current asset, as it is held with a view to subsequent resale. Profits or losses on the disposal of these stores are treated as other operating income or expense.

Exchange of non-monetary assets

Exchange of non-monetary assets for an interest in joint venture, associate or subsidiary are accounted for in accordance with UITF 31. Gains are recognised to the extent that the fair value of consideration received exceeds that part of the non-monetary assets no longer owned, including related goodwill. If the gain is unrealised, this is reported in the Statement of Total Recognised Gains and Losses.

Pensions

The company makes contributions to certain individuals' personal pension plans. Contributions are charged in the profit and loss account as they become payable.

2. Turnover and segmental analysis

The principal components of turnover are royalties received, commissary and equipment sales, sale of franchises, pizza delivery sales and rental income on leasehold properties stated net of value added tax after eliminating inter-company transactions. All of the turnover is in one continuing business segment and originates in the United Kingdom and the Republic of Ireland. The directors believe that full compliance with the requirements of SSAP 25 'Segmental Reporting' would be seriously prejudicial to the interests of the group as it would require disclosure of commercially sensitive information.

Geographical analysis	Turnover by origin		Turnover by destination	
	2002 £000	2001 £000	2002 £000	2001 £000
Group Turnover				
United Kingdom	50,679	42,156	50,141	41,894
Republic of Ireland	2,430	1,669	2,968	1,931
	53,109	43,825	53,109	43,825

3. Operating profit

This is stated after charging:		2002 £000	2001 £000
Auditors' remuneration	– audit services	75	70
	– non-audit services	273	116
Depreciation of owned assets		1,066	972
Depreciation of assets held under finance leases and hire purchase contracts		61	72
Amortisation of intangible fixed assets		228	146
Operating lease rentals	– land and buildings	3,372	2,949
	– plant, machinery and vehicles	1,153	832
Other operating expenses		75	169
Foreign exchange loss/(profit)		(38)	10

4. Directors' emoluments

	2002 £000	2001 £000
Emoluments	736	596
Pension contributions	29	19
	765	615

Further information concerning directors' emoluments are disclosed on page 314.

5. Staff costs

	2002 £000	2001 £000
Wages and salaries	10,171	8,083
Social security costs	766	590
Other pension costs	102	87
	11,039	8,760

The average monthly number of employees (including directors) during the year was made up as follows:

	2002 No.	2001 No.
Administration	109	98
Production and distribution	100	88
Corporate stores	684	569
	893	755

6. Interest payable and similar charges

	2002 £000	2001 £000
Bank loans and overdrafts	348	394
Interest on joint venture	17	25
Finance charges payable under finance leases and hire purchase contracts	9	11
	374	430

7. Tax on profit on ordinary activities

a) Analysis of tax charge in the year.

The charge based on the profit for the year comprises:	2002 £000	2001 £000
UK Corporation tax:		
Profit for the period	1,229	788
Adjustment in respect of the previous period	(21)	(185)
Joint venture tax	13	16
Total current tax	1,221	619
UK deferred tax:		
Origination and reversal of timing differences in respect of:		
Profit in the period	183	239
Total deferred tax	183	239
Tax on profit on ordinary activities	1,404	858

b) Factors affecting tax charge for the period.

	2002 %	2001 %
Corporation tax at the statutory rate	30.0	30.0
Effects of:		
Expenses not deductible for tax purposes	1.1	1.4
Rolled over gains	(3.3)	—
Accounting depreciation not eligible for tax purposes	3.3	4.1
Goodwill amortised	3.5	1.0
Utilisation of tax losses	(2.3)	(5.3)
Tax depreciation in excess of accounting depreciation	(5.2)	(5.5)
Adjustments relating to prior years corporation tax	(0.5)	(6.5)
Originating timing differences	2.2	2.4
Total current tax rate	28.8	21.6

c) Deferred taxation – group

Deferred tax provided in the accounts is as follows:

	2002 £000	2001 £000
Accelerated capital allowances	855	623
Other timing differences	(251)	(154)
Losses	—	(48)
	604	421
Deferred tax provided at 30 December 2001		421
Charges to profit and loss account		183
Deferred tax provided at 29 December 2002		604

d) Factors that may affect future tax charges

No provision has been made for deferred tax where potentially taxable gains have been rolled over into replacement assets. Such gains would become taxable only if the assets were sold without it being possible to claim rollover relief. The amount not provided is £156,000 (2001: £18,000) in respect of this. At present, it is not envisaged that any tax will become payable in the foreseeable future.

8. Dividends

	2002 £000	2001 £000
Equity dividends on ordinary shares:		
Interim paid 0.78p (2001: 0.57p)	395	285
Final proposed 1.22p (2001: 0.76p)	623	383
	1,018	668

9. Earnings per ordinary share

The calculation of basic earnings per ordinary share is based on earnings of £2,835,000 (2001: £2,004,000) and on 50,620,687 (2001: 50,043,018) ordinary shares.

The diluted earnings per share is based on earnings of £2,835,000 (2001: £2,004,000) and on 53,577,582 (2001: 51,561,552) ordinary shares. All of the difference relates to share options which takes into account theoretical ordinary shares that would have been issued, based on average market value if all outstanding options were exercised.

10. Intangible fixed assets

Group	Goodwill £000	Franchise fees £000	Interest in leases £000	Total £000
Cost:				
At 31 December 2001	2,011	813	209	3,033
Additions	356	24	190	570
Disposals	(510)	(8)	—	(518)
At 29 December 2002	1,857	829	399	3,085
Amortisation:				
At 31 December 2001	127	366	56	549
Provided during the year	156	44	28	228
Disposals	(77)	(1)	—	(78)
At 29 December 2002	206	409	84	699
Net book value:				
At 29 December 2002	1,651	420	315	2,386
At 30 December 2001	1,884	447	153	2,484

During 2002, three stores were purchased from franchisees. The provisional fair value of assets acquired with this business is as follows:

	Provisional fair value £000
Equipment	128
Stock	3
Net assets	131
Goodwill	356
	487
Discharged by	
Cash	487

11. Tangible fixed assets

Group	Freehold land and buildings £000	Leasehold improvements £000	Motor vehicles £000	Equipment £000	Total £000
Cost:					
At 31 December 2001	5,633	2,678	276	6,493	15,080
Additions	1,130	200	29	2,060	3,419
Disposals	—	(535)	(157)	(577)	(1,269)
At 29 December 2002	6,763	2,343	148	7,976	17,230
Depreciation:					
At 31 December 2001	204	333	229	2,133	2,899
Provided during the year	89	84	42	912	1,127
Disposals	—	(113)	(151)	(217)	(481)
At 29 December 2002	293	304	120	2,828	3,545
Net book value:					
At 29 December 2002	6,470	2,039	28	5,148	13,685
At 30 December 2001	5,429	2,345	47	4,360	12,181

The net book value of tangible fixed assets includes an amount of £261,000 (2001: £325,000) in respect of assets held under finance leases and hire purchase contracts, the depreciation charge on which was £61,000 (2001: £72,000).

Included within freehold land and buildings is an amount of £1,684,000 (2001: £1,552,000) in respect of land which is not depreciated. Also included is an amount of £154,000 (2001: £154,000) of capitalised interest.

12. Investments

Group	2002 £000	2001 £000
Investments:		
Joint venture	307	277
At 30 December 2001		277
Share of profit retained by joint venture		30
At 29 December 2002		307

Included within the investment in joint venture is an amount of £237,000 (2001: £91,000) of goodwill arising on acquisition.

Company	Subsidiary undertaking £000	Joint venture £000	Total £000
Fixed asset investment			
Cost:			
At 29 December 2002 and 30 December 2001	2,475	205	2,680

At 29 December 2002 the company held directly more than 20% of the nominal value of the share capital of the following:

Name of company Subsidiary undertakings	Country of incorporation	Proportion held	Nature of business
Domino's Pizza Group Limited	England	100% ordinary	Operation and management of franchise business
DPGS Limited	England	100% ordinary	Management of pizza delivery stores
DP Realty Limited	England	100% ordinary	Property management
DP Group Developments Limited	England	100% ordinary	Property development
DP Capital Limited	England	100% ordinary	Leasing of equipment
Joint ventures			
Full House Restaurants Limited	England	41% ordinary	Management of pizza delivery stores
Dominoid Limited	Scotland	50% ordinary	Management of pizza delivery stores
Indirectly held subsidiaries			
Livebait Limited	England	100% ordinary	Property management
American Pizza Company Limited	England	100% ordinary	Management of pizza delivery stores

On 24 October 1998, a 41% interest in Full House Restaurants Limited was acquired for £205,000. Additionally, a loan of £345,000 was advanced to Full House Restaurants Limited, which is repayable by equal quarterly instalments of £12,000, which commenced on 30 June 2001. The loan bears interest at a rate of 2% above National Westminster base rate. At 29 December 2002 the balance outstanding on the loan was £263,000 (2001: £309,000).

Sales of £1,323,000 (2001: £1,062,000) were made to Full House Restaurants Limited during the year. The company received interest of £17,000 (2001: £23,000) in respect of the loan.

At 29 December 2002, there was a receivable of £50,000 (2001: £54,000) from Full House Restaurants Limited, which has arisen through normal trading activities.

On 11 November 2002, a 50% interest in Dominoid Limited was acquired. Two stores were sold to Dominoid Limited and the group recognised an unrealised gain of £55,000. The consideration for the sale was satisfied by the issue of a Loan Note by Dominoid Limited of £442,000 which is repayable on demand at least one year after the date of the agreement. The loan bears interest at a rate of 2.5% above Royal Bank of Scotland base rate. At 29 December 2002 the balance outstanding on the loan was £442,000.

Sales of £135,000 were made to Dominoid Limited during the year.

At 29 December 2002, there was a receivable of £12,000 from Dominoid Limited, which has arisen through normal trading activities.

13. Stocks

		Group
	2002 £000	2001 £000
Raw materials and goods for resale	1,411	1,260

14. Debtors

	Group		Company	
	2002 £000	2001 £000	2002 £000	2001 £000
Trade debtors	2,394	2,392	—	—
Amounts owed by group undertakings	—	—	2,885	2,412
Amounts owed by joint venture	699	309	—	—
Other debtors	3,661	2,608	—	—
Prepayments and accrued income	2,035	1,511	—	—
Net investment in finance leases	1,913	1,601	—	—
	10,702	8,421	2,885	2,412

Amounts falling due after more than one year included above are:

	Group		Company	
	2002 £000	2001 £000	2002 £000	2001 £000
Trade debtors	139	229	—	—
Amounts owed by joint venture	632	261	—	—
Other debtors	43	65	—	—
Net investment in finance leases	1,316	1,201	—	—
	2,130	1,756	—	—

The aggregate rentals receivable in respect of finance leases was £725,000 (2001: £352,000).

The cost of assets acquired for the purpose of letting under for finance leases was £2.781,000 (2001: £1,844,000).

15. Creditors: amounts falling due within one year

	Group 2002 £000	Group 2001 £000	Company 2002 £000	Company 2001 £000
Bank loans (note 17)	2,400	900	—	—
Other loans (note 17)	612	379	—	—
Finance lease creditors (note 18)	29	81	—	—
Trade creditors	3,956	4,006	—	—
Corporation tax	532	274	—	—
Other taxes and social security costs	719	906	—	—
Other creditors	931	512	—	—
Accruals and deferred income	3,116	2,762	—	—
Proposed dividend	624	383	624	383
	12,919	10,203	624	383

16. Creditors: amounts falling due after more than one year

Group	2002 £000	2001 £000
Bank loans (note 17)	5,775	6,525
Finance lease creditors (note 18)	38	60
Other loans (note 17)	1,339	1,047
	7,152	7,632

Bank loans

The group has entered into an agreement to obtain bank loans and mortgage facilities. These are secured by a fixed and floating charge over the group's assets. At 29 December 2002 the balance due under these facilities was £8,175,000 (2001: £7,425,000). The loans will bear interest at 1.1% over base.

Other loans

The other loans are repayable in equal instalments over a period of up to five years. These are unsecured.

17. Loans

Group	2002 £000	2001 £000
Amounts falling due:		
In one year or less or on demand	3,012	1,279
Due between one and two years	511	1,306
In more than two years but not more than five years	6,603	6,266
	10,126	8,851

18. Obligations under leases and hire purchase contracts

Amounts due under finance leases and hire purchase contracts:

Group	2002 £000	2001 £000s
Amount payable:		
Within one year	35	90
In two to five years	38	66
	73	156
Less: finance charges allocated to future periods	(6)	(15)
	67	141

Annual commitments under non-cancellable operating leases are as follows:

	Land and buildings		Other	
	2002 £000	2001 £000	2002 £000	2001 £000
Operating leases that expire:				
Within one year	23	—	100	42
In two to five years	330	293	782	351
In over five years	3,390	3,038	—	—
	3,743	3,331	882	393

19. Derivatives and other financial instruments

The group's principal financial instruments are bank loans, other loans, finance leases and cash.

The financial instruments are principally in place to finance the head office facility and associated equipment and provide finance to franchisees. The group has other financial instruments such as trade debtors and trade creditors that arise directly from its operations. As permitted by FRS 13 short-term debtors and creditors have been excluded from the disclosure of financial liabilities and financial assets.

The group has not entered into any derivative transactions such as interest rate swaps or financial foreign currency contracts. In view of the low level of foreign currency transactions, the board does not consider that there are significant risks in respect of this. All financial assets and liabilities are denominated in £ sterling. The main risk area is in respect of any change in interest rates on the floating rate loans, which the board will continue to monitor.

Interest rate risk profile of financial assets
The interest rate profile of the financial assets of the group as at 29 December was as follows:

2002	Total £000	Fixed rate financial asset £000	Floating rate financial asset £000	Financial asset on which no interest is paid £000	Average period to maturity
Trade debtors	139	—	139	—	
Other debtors	43	—	—	43	80 months
Joint venture loan	699	—	699	—	
Finance lease receivable	1,913	1,913	—	—	42 months
Cash	3,885	—	3,885	—	
	6,679	1,913	4,723	43	

The floating rate financial assets are based on the group's bank base rate plus a fixed percentage.

The average interest on the fixed rate financial asset is 12%.

2001	Total	Fixed rate financial asset £000	Floating rate financial asset £000	Financial asset on which no interest is paid £000	Average period to maturity
Trade debtors	229	—	229	—	
Other debtors	65	—	—	65	71 months
Joint venture loan	309	—	309	—	
Finance lease receivable	1,601	1,601	—	—	51 months
Cash	3,232	—	3,232	—	
	5,436	1,601	3,770	65	

The fair value of the financial assets is not considered materially different from book value.

Interest rate risk profile of financial liabilities

The interest rate profile of the financial liabilities of the group as at 29 December was as follows:

2002	Total £000	Fixed rate financial liability £000	Floating rate financial liability £000
Bank loan	8,175	—	8,175
Other loan	1,951	1,951	—
Finance leases	67	67	—
	10,193	2,018	8,175

2001	Total £000	Fixed rate financial liability £000	Floating rate financial liability £000
Bank loan	7,425	—	7,425
Other loan	1,426	1,426	—
Finance leases	141	141	—
	8,992	1,567	7,425

The average interest on the fixed rate financial liability is 7.1% (2001: 8.4%). The bank loan attracts interest at a rate of 1.1% over base rate.

The maturity profile of the group's financial liabilities is set out in notes 17 and 18.

The fair value of the financial liabilities is not considered materially different from book value.

Un-drawn committed facilities at 29 December 2002 amounted to £219,000 (2001: £1,319,000)

20. Share capital

	Number	Issued allotted and fully paid £	Number	Authorised £
At 30 December 2001	50,359,063	2,517,953	80,000,000	4,000,000
Additions in the year	563,234	28,162	—	—
At 29 December 2002	50,922,297	2,546,115	80,000,000	4,000,000

During the year 563,234 shares with a nominal value of £28,162 were issued at between 33.5p and 55.0p for total cash consideration received of £231,000 to satisfy options that were exercised.

As at 29 December 2002, the following share options were outstanding:

Date of grant	Option price £	Outstanding at 30 December 2001	Granted during the year	Exercised or lapsed during the year	Outstanding
24 November 1999	42.1p	3,245,566	–	395,675	2,849,891
24 November 1999	50.0p	1,570,363	–	78,811	1,491,552
4 August 2000	53.0p	713,000	–	48,533	664,467
1 January 2001	33.5p	1,065,728	–	450,000	615,728
25 October 2001	55.0p	524,750	–	80,000	444,750
11 March 2002	74.5p	—	100,000	–	100,000
2 April 2002	760.p	—	75,000	–	75,000
		7,119,407	175,000	1,053,019	6,241,388

On 24 November 1999 participants in the Domino's Pizza Group Limited (Unapproved) Share Option Scheme (which had been in place since 31 March 1999) had the option of exchanging options over shares in Domino's Pizza Group Limited in return for equivalent options over ordinary shares in the company under Domino's Pizza Share Option (Unapproved) Scheme.

All of the share options outstanding are in the Domino's Pizza Share Option (Unapproved) Scheme.

Options under this scheme may be exercised as follows:
One year after date of grant—maximum 1/3 of options held
Two years after date of grant—maximum 2/3 of options held
Three years after date of grant—in full
The options expire 10 years after the date granted.

21. Reconciliation of shareholders' funds and movement on reserves

Group	Share capital £000	Share premium account £000	Profit and loss account £000	Total shareholders' funds £000
At 31 December 2000	2,500	2,046	3,552	8,098
Proceeds from share issue	18	146	—	164
Profit for the year	—	—	2,004	2,004
Dividends	—	—	(668)	(668)
At 30 December 2001	2,518	2,192	4,888	9,598
Proceeds from share issue	28	203	—	231
Unrealised gain on exchange of properties for interest in joint venture			55	55
Profit for the year	—	—	2,835	2,835
Dividends	—	—	(1,018)	(1,018)
At 29 December 2002	2,546	2,395	6,760	11,701

Company	Share capital £000	Share premium account £000	Profit and loss account £000	Total shareholders' funds £000
At 31 December 2000	2,500	2,046	—	4,546
Proceeds from share issue	18	146	—	164
Profit for the year	—	—	668	668
Dividends	—	—	(668)	(668)
At 30 December 2001	2,518	2,192	—	4,710
Proceeds from share issue	28	203	—	231
Profit for the year	—	—	1,018	1,018
Dividends	—	—	(1,018)	(1,018)
At 29 December 2002	2,546	2,395	—	4,941

22. Profit and loss account

Profit after taxation amounting to £1,018,000 (2001: £668,000) has been dealt with in the accounts of the company.

23. Notes to the statement of cash flows

(a) Reconciliation of operating profit to net cash inflow from operating activities

	2002 £000	2001 £000
Operating profit	4,504	3,144
Depreciation charge	1,127	1,044
Amortisation charge	228	146
Other operating expenditure	75	168
(Increase) in stocks	(151)	(66)
(Increase) in debtors	(1,047)	(690)
Increase in creditors	392	729
	5,128	4,475

(b) Analysis of net debt

	At 31 December 2001 £000	Cash flow £000	Other non-cash movements £000	At 30 December 2002 £000
Cash at bank and in hand	3,231	654	—	3,885
Bank loans (within one year)	(900)	(1,500)	—	(2,400)
Bank loans (due after one year)	(6,525)	750	—	(5,775)
Other loans (within one year)	(379)	566	(799)	(612)
Other loans (due after one year)	(1,046)	(1,092)	799	(1,339)
Finance leases	(141)	74	—	(67)
Net debt	(5,760)	(548)	—	(6,308)

(c) Reconciliation of net cash flow to movement in net debt

	2002 £000	2001 £000
Increase in cash	654	2,233
Cash inflow from increase in loans	(2,719)	(2,660)
Repayment of long-term loans	1,443	330
Repayments of capital element of finance leases and hire purchase contracts	74	72
Inception of finance leases	—	(72)
Movement in net debt	(548)	(97)
Net debt at 31 December 2001	(5,760)	(5,663)
Net debt at 29 December 2002	(6,308)	(5,760)

(d) Major non-cash transactions

During the year, the company transferred two stores to Dominoid Limited in exchange for a 50% interest in this new joint venture. Further details of the transaction are contained in note 12.

24. Capital commitments

Amounts contracted for but not provided in the accounts amounted to £nil for the group and £nil for the company (2001: £943,000 and £nil respectively)

25. Contingent liabilities

Additional consideration up to a maximum of £500,000 in cash, may become payable for the acquisition of American Pizza Company Limited, dependent upon certain conditions being met. Due to the remote probability of these conditions being met, the directors consider a provision of these amounts to be inappropriate.

26. Related Parties

Transactions between the group and International Franchise Systems Inc, are set out below:

	2002 £000	2001 £000
Current account:		
Costs incurred by Domino's Pizza Group Limited on behalf of International Franchise Systems Inc.	126	178
Costs incurred by International Franchise Systems Inc., on behalf of Domino's Pizza Group Limited	91	(43)
Transfer of funds to/from International Franchise Systems Inc.	(16)	30
Management charges from International Franchise Systems Inc.	(201)	(165)
Closing debt due to International Franchise Systems Inc.	—	—

During the period, the group purchased services to the value of £71,000 (2001: £65,000) in the normal course of business and at normal market prices from Chinese Pompano Inc., a company in which Gerald Halpern is a director. At the balance sheet date the amount due to Chinese Pompano Inc., was £nil (2001: £nil).

Transactions between the group and its joint ventures are set out in note 12.

Notice of meeting

Notice of annual general meeting

Notice is hereby given that the fourth Annual General Meeting of the Company will be held at Domino's House, Lasborough Road, Kingston, Milton Keynes, MK10 0AB on 24th April 2003 at 12pm for the following purposes:

As ordinary business

1. To receive the reports of the directors and the auditors and the audited accounts of the Company for the 52 weeks ended 29 December 2002;

2. To approve a final dividend of 1.22 pence per ordinary share in the capital of the Company ("Ordinary share");

3. To re-elect as a director of the Company Mr Gerald Halpern;

4. To re-elect as a director of the Company Mr Stephen Hemsley;

5. To re-appoint Ernst & Young as auditors to hold office from the conclusion of this meeting until the conclusion of the next general meeting at which accounts are laid before the Company and to authorise the directors to fix the remuneration of the auditors.

As special business

6. To consider and if thought fit to pass the following resolution which will be proposed as an ordinary resolution:

   THAT, for the purpose of section 80 of the Companies Act 1985, the directors of the Company be and they are hereby generally and unconditionally authorised to exercise all powers of the Company to allot, grant options over, offer or otherwise deal with or dispose of relevant securities (as defined in the said section) up to an aggregate nominal amount of £1,500,000 provided that this authority shall expire at the close of the next Annual General Meeting of the Company after the passing of this resolution (or, if sooner, at the expiration of 15 months after the passing of this resolution), save that the Company may before such expiry make an offer or agreement which would or might require relevant securities to be allotted after such expiry and the directors of the Company may allot relevant securities in pursuance of such an offer or agreement as if the authority conferred hereby had not expired;

7. To consider and if thought fit to pass the following resolution which will be proposed as a special resolution:

   THAT subject to the passing of the previous resolution the directors of the Company be and they are hereby empowered pursuant to section 95 of the Companies Act 1985 (the "Act") to allot equity securities (within the meaning of section 94 of the Act) for cash pursuant to the authority conferred by the previous resolution as if sub-section (1) of section 89 of the Act did not apply to any such allotment, provided that this power shall be limited to

   (a) the allotment of equity securities in connection with a rights issue in favour of Ordinary shareholders where the equity securities respectively attributable to the interests of all

Ordinary shareholders are proportionate (as nearly as may be) to the respective numbers of Ordinary shares held by them; or

(b) the allotment (otherwise than pursuant to sub-paragraph (a) above) of equity securities up to an aggregate nominal value of not more than 10% of the issued Ordinary share capital, and shall expire at the close of the next Annual General Meeting of the Company after the passing of this resolution (or, if sooner, at the expiration of 15 months after the passing of this resolution), save that the Company may before such expiry make an offer or agreement which would or might require equity securities to be allotted after such expiry and the board may allot securities in pursuance of such an offer or agreement as if the power conferred hereby had not expired; and

8. To consider and if thought fit to pass the following resolution which will be proposed as a special resolution:

THAT the regulations, in the form produced to the Meeting and signed for the purposes of identification by the Chairman of the Meeting, be adopted as the new Articles of Association of the Company to replace in their entirety the existing Articles of Association of the Company, with effect from the conclusion of the Meeting.

9. To consider and if thought fit to pass the following resolution which will be proposed as a special resolution:

THAT The Company be generally and unconditionally authorised to make one or more market purchases (within the meaning of section 163(3) of the Companies Act 1985) of Ordinary shares of five pence each in the capital of the Company ("Ordinary Shares") provided that;

(a) the maximum aggregate number of Ordinary Shares authorised to be purchased is 5,000,000 (representing 10% of the issued Ordinary share capital);

(b) the minimum price which may be paid for an Ordinary Share is five pence;

(c) the maximum price which may be paid for an Ordinary Share is an amount equal to 105% of the average of the middle market quotations for an Ordinary Share as derived from The London Stock Exchange Daily Official List for the five business days immediately preceding the day on which that Ordinary share is purchased; and

(d) this authority expires at the close of the next Annual General Meeting of the Company after the passing of this resolution (or, if sooner, at the expiration of 15 months after the passing of this resolution), save that the Company may before such expiry make an offer or agreement to purchase Ordinary Shares under this authority which would or might require to be executed wholly or partly after such expiry, and the Company may make a purchase of Ordinary Shares in pursuance of such an offer or agreement as if the power conferred hereby had not expired.

By order of the Board
Andrew Mallows
Secretary
26 March 2003

Notes

Resolution 1—Report and Accounts
The Directors are required to present the Accounts for the 52 weeks ended 29 December 2002 to the Meeting.

Resolution 2—Declaration of a Dividend
A Dividend can only be paid if it is recommended by the Directors and approved by the shareholders at a General Meeting. The Directors propose that a final dividend of 1.22 pence per Ordinary share be paid on 29 April 2003 to Ordinary shareholders who are on the register at the close of

business on 11 April 2003. An interim dividend of 0.78 pence per Ordinary share was paid on 4 September 2002.

Resolutions 3 and 4—Re-appointment of Directors

The Articles of Association of the Company requires one-third of the Directors to retire at each Annual General Meeting (generally those who have been longest in office since their last appointment). At this Meeting, Gerald Halpern and Stephen Hemsley will retire by rotation and seek re-election.

Resolution 5—Re-appointment of Auditors

The Company is required to appoint auditors at each Annual General Meeting to hold office until the next such meeting at which accounts are presented. This Resolution proposes the re-appointment of the Company's existing Auditors, Ernst & Young, and authorises the Directors to agree their remuneration.

Resolutions 6 and 7—Authority to Allot and Disapplication of Section 89(1) of the Companies Act 1985

The Directors only have general authority to allot relevant securities as permitted by the Company. This Resolution seeks to grant (until the next Annual General Meeting or the expiration of 15 months if sooner) the Directors authority to allot equity securities up to an aggregate nominal amount of £ 1,500,000 otherwise than in accordance with certain statutory pre-emption provisions, provided the authority is limited to an allotment of equity securities either in connection with an issue or offering by way of rights issue to existing Ordinary shareholders, pro-rata, or to the issue of securities up to an aggregate nominal value of not more than 10% of the issued Ordinary share capital of the Company. In proposing this resolution, the Directors consider that it is in the best interests of the Company and its shareholders that Directors should retain the ability to take advantage of business opportunities as they arise without the cost and delay of an Extraordinary General Meeting to seek specific authority for an allotment.

Resolution 8—New Articles of Association

The existing Articles of Association were adopted on 15 November 1999. Following various amendments to company law as a result of The Companies Act 1985 (Electronic Communications) Order 2000, formal electronic communication with shareholders became legally possible. The Order provides that, where a company and a shareholder agree, the Annual Report and Accounts, Summary Financial Statements and Notices of Meetings may be sent to the shareholder electronically. Alternatively, where the company and the shareholder agree, the company can publish the relevant documents on a website and send a notice by e-mail informing shareholders that these documents are available electronically from a website. The Order also allows, where a company and a shareholder agree, the shareholder to appoint a proxy by electronic means. It is therefore proposed that new Articles of Association be adopted to reflect the changes in company law to allow the Company to communicate with its shareholders through electronic media and to allow electronic proxy appointment.

The principle underlying the new legislation is permissive: electronic communications will only be used if both the Company and its shareholders agree. In the absence of agreement, the Company will continue to use printed documents to send Annual Accounts and Notices of Meetings to shareholders and shareholders will send printed proxy cards to the Company.

Details of the more important differences between the proposed new Articles of Association and the existing Articles of Association are set out in the Explanatory Notes below.

A copy of the new Articles of Association incorporating all the amendments will be available for inspection at the registered office of the Company during normal business hours from the date of the Notice of Annual General Meeting until [25 April 2003] and at the place of the Meeting from fifteen minutes prior to, and until the conclusion of, the Meeting.

New Articles of Association

These notes explain the more important differences between the proposed new Articles and the existing Articles. The changes are aimed at bringing the Articles into line with recent legislation permitting electronic communications between the Company and its shareholders, with the corresponding amendments to the United Kingdom Listing Authority listing rules and with best practice guidance issued by the Institute of Chartered Secretaries and Administrators.

The number identifying each Article, unless otherwise indicated, corresponds to the numbering used in the existing Articles. References to the 'Act' are to the Electronic Communications Act 2000, and references to the 'Order' are to the Companies Act 1985 (Electronic Communications) Order 2000.

Article 2 (Interpretation): There is a new definition of 'address' which now includes electronic addresses and a new definition of 'electronic signature' which reflects the meaning given to that term in the Act. Further interpretation clauses have been inserted in order to deal with references to 'document', 'electronic communication' and to a document being 'executed'.

Article 29 (Amendments to Resolutions): Article 29 will provide for notice of amendments proposed by shareholders to the terms of resolutions to be received in an electronic communication where the Company has given an address for this purpose.

Article 31 (Proxies): Article 31 will permit the appointment of proxies to be contained in an electronic communication, executed in such manner as the board may approve, and will permit the directors to send forms of proxy and invitations to appoint a proxy in electric format. For the purposes of these Articles, electronic communications appointing proxies need not contain writing if the directors so determine.

Article 31 will provide for appointments of proxy contained in an electronic communication, where the Company has specified an address for receipt of the electronic communication in the notice convening the meeting, in the form of proxy or in any invitation contained in an electronic communication. The appointment of proxy should be received at that address not less than 48 hours before the meeting. Where a poll is taken more than 48 hours after it is demanded, a proxy form contained in an electronic communication must be delivered or received after the poll has been demanded and not less than 24 hours before the time for the taking of the poll. A proxy appointment which is not delivered or received in accordance with these provisions is invalid.

Article 31 will also permit a notice of revocation of a proxy appointment to be sent either by instrument or by means of an electronic communication (which need not be written if the board so approves) regardless of how the original appointment was effected.

Article 44.2 (Notice of board meetings): Article 44 will permit notices of board meetings to be sent to directors by means of electronic communication where the director has notified an address for that purpose. For the purposes of this Article, electronic communications need not comprise writing if the board so determines.

Article 44.11 (Resolution in writing): Article 44 will permit written resolutions of the directors to be made by means of an instrument or contained in an electronic communication, and the resolution may consist of several such instruments or electronic communications, or a combination of both.

Article 54 (Service of notices and other documents): Article 54 will provide that any notices required to be given by the Articles may be sent using electronic communications where an address for this purpose has been notified to the person giving the notice by the person entitled to receive it. Article 54 provides that the Company may also send notices or other documents to shareholders by electronic communications and by publishing them on a website where the Company and the shareholder have agreed that the shareholder will have access to the website and the shareholder is notified of the publication of the notice or document on the website and the website address. The notice or document must be available on the website for (in the case of a notice adjourned meeting) not less than seven clear days before the date of the adjourned meeting beginning on the day following that on which the notification is sent or (in any other case) not less than 21 days from that time. Failure to display the notice or document on the website throughout this period is excused if it is wholly attributable to circumstances which it would not have been reasonable to have expected the Company to prevent or avoid. Shareholders whose registered address is outside the United Kingdom but who agree an address for electronic communications within the United Kingdom are entitled to receive notices and other documents at that address provided the Company so agrees. Otherwise, overseas shareholders shall not be entitled to receive such notice or documents, and any notices of general meetings sent to overseas shareholders will be ignored in determining the validity of proceedings at the general meeting.

Article 54 will also provide that compliance with the current guidance issued by the Institute of Chartered Secretaries and Administrators (or, if the directors so resolve, any subsequent guidance) constitutes conclusive proof that notices or other documents dispatched by means of an electronic communication were sent. Notices or documents sent by the Company to shareholders contained in electronic communications are deemed to be sent to the member on the day following that on which the electronic communication was sent.

Article 55 (Terms and conditions for electronic communications): New Article 55 allows the board to issue or adopt terms and conditions relating to the use of the electronic communications for the sending of notices, documents and proxy appointments by the Company to members and by members to the Company.

Resolution 9—Authority to Purchase Company's own shares
The Articles of Association of the Company provide that the Company may from time to time purchase its own shares subject to other consents required by law. Such purchases must be authorised by the shareholders at a General Meeting. This Resolution seeks to grant (until the next Annual General Meeting or the expiration of 15 months if sooner) the Directors authority to purchase the Company's own shares up to a maximum of 10% of the issued Ordinary share capital of the Company. In proposing this Resolution, the Directors consider that it is in the best interests of the Company and its shareholders that Directors should retain the ability to make market purchases of the Company's own shares without the cost and delay of an Extraordinary General Meeting to seek specific authority for a share purchase.

Five year record

	2002	2001	2000	1999	1998
Trading Weeks	52	52	53	52	52
System sales (£m)	118.9	98.4	76.1	63.5	54.9
Group sales (£m)	53.1	43.8	32.5	25.6	20.7
Operating profit (£000)*	4,563	3,214	2,457	2,058	1,576
Profit before tax (£000)*	4,239	2,862	2,189	1,848	1,548
Basic earnings per share (pence)	5.60	4.00	2.61	1.91	2.54
Dividends per share (pence)	2.00	1.33	0.80	0.71	0.60
Shareholders funds (£000)	11,701	9,598	8,098	7,412	3,689
Net (indebtedness) (£000)	(6,308)	(5,760)	(5,663)	(156)	(2,623)
Capital gearing	53.9%	60.0%	69.9%	2.1%	71.1%
Stores at start of year	237	215	201	175	153
Stores opened	34	24	22	29	27
Stores closed	(2)	(2)	(8)	(3)	(5)
Stores at year end	269	237	215	201	175
Corporate stores at year end	35	34	31	14	6
Like-for-like sales growth (%)	11.2%	21.4%	4.8%	5.6%	6.3%

*Including joint venture but excluding discontinued operations and exceptional items.

■ APPENDIX 2

Answers to multiple choice questions

Chapter	1	2	3	4	5	6	7	8	9	10	11	12
Question												
1	C	D	D	B	A	D	B	C	D	A	A	A
2	A	B	A	D	B	C	C	B	A	C	C	B
3	D	C	C	D	A	C	A	D	B	D	C	C
4	A	A	B	B	D	B	C	D	C	B	D	D
5	C	C	D	A	C	A	B	A	C	D	B	C
6	B	B	A	C	C	D	D	B	A	C	B	B
7	A	D	B	C	B	B	B	C	D	B	A	D
8	B	A	A	A	B	A	D	B	B	A	D	D
9	A	D	C	D	B	C	D	C	C	A	A	A
10	D	B	D	B	A	D	A	A	C	C	C	C

Answers to longer questions

Chapter 1

Question 1

(a) The bottom lines of the cash flow statement indicate that in 2001, Manchester United plc had an overall decrease in cash for the year of £13,656,000. In 2002, the company achieved an increase in cash of £2,170,000. Remember that 'cash flow' is not the same as 'profit'.

(b) Strictly speaking, football clubs do not buy footballers, they are purchasing the right to register them as players for the team. The cash flow statement indicates that Manchester United paid out just over £47.5 million in 2001 and just over £25 million a year later. Note that these sums were offset by the proceeds from selling players' registrations: just over £4 million in 2001 and £13 million in 2002.

(c) Company taxation is based on the *profit* that the organization makes, not its cash flow. The cash flow statement shows the actual taxation payments during the year, but these will be based largely on the profit made in the previous financial period. There is no direct linkage between a year's cash flow and the taxation payments made during the same year.

Question 2

(a) The total profit is calculated by comparing the total sales with the total of the expenses and the cost of goods bought for resale. All relevant transactions are included in this calculation, regardless of whether the related cash has been paid or received. Sandygate plc's profit was therefore £560,000 − £160,000 = £400,000.

(b) 'Total expenses and goods bought for resale' as used in the profit calculation includes all relevant transactions, whether or not cash has been paid or received. At the start and end of the year, there will be amounts owing to suppliers (creditors), non-cash expenses such as the depreciation on the company's assets, and also expenses incurred where bills have not yet been received (e.g. electricity or telephone) or paid in advance for future periods. All these have to be taken into consideration when calculating the total expenses and the cost of the goods bought for resale.

To take a simple example, if a company started the year owing suppliers £5,000, bought £75,000 worth of goods from them during the year, paid cheques to suppliers totalling £70,000 in the year, and owed them £10,000 at the year-end, the amount to be included in the profit calculation will be the £75,000 of goods actually bought during the year, even though the cash paid is only £70,000.

Question 3

The user groups may require the following areas of information concerning Monotub Industries:

Investors. Investors will want assurances regarding the company's sale for just £1. What attempts were made to sell the company for a higher amount? What guarantees are there regarding Mr Meyerscough's offer to pay shareholders £4 for every machine sold in future?

Lenders. The company was thought to have liabilities amounting to £750,000, but the product appeared to be defective with little prospect of immediate profit with which to repay them. The promise of £250,000 being paid into the company by Mr Meyerscough would appear to be quite attractive in the circumstances.

Suppliers and other trade creditors. The same considerations apply here as to lenders.

Employees. There is no mention made of employees in the article, and when a company fails it is often the workers who have little protection. At least the company will continue under the proposed arrangements, which should preserve some if not all of the jobs.

Customers. There have been obvious problems with the washing machine and customers will no doubt have complained to the company. They will need to know if guarantees given when they bought the machine will be honoured under the new arrangements.

Government and other agencies. With the liquidation of the company, there may be unpaid tax bills outstanding. However, if the company has been loss-making, there might be no tax liability. The article states that one of the shareholders has referred the sale to the Department of Trade and Industry, possibly on the grounds that the sale is prejudicial to the interests of the minority shareholders, and this may lead to a government inquiry into the circumstances of the sale.

The public. If the closure leads to job losses and factory closures in a particular community, this may cause severe problems, and local representatives (such as elected councillors) may wish to discuss with company representatives ways in which the effects can be mitigated.

Chapter 2

Cash book

	Receipts						Payments						
Date	Details	**Total**	Capital	Mowers	SL	Date	Details	**Total**	Rent	Phone	Adverts	Hire	PL
1 Nov.	Capital	**5,000**	5,000			2 Nov.	Rent	**450**	450				
3 Nov.	Sales	**400**		400		3 Nov.	Phone	**200**		200			
7 Nov.	Upton Park Estate	**500**			500	4 Nov.	Advertising	**500**			500		
						5 Nov.	Equipment hire	**600**				600	
						7 Nov.	Logjam Ltd.	**3,000**					3000
		5,900						**4,750**					

Sales journal

Date	Details	Invoice ref.	Total	Mowers	Chainsaws
3 Nov.	Grimridge Council	S001	1,500	1,500	
4 Nov.	Upton Park Estate	S002	500		500
			2,000	1,500	500

Purchase journal

Date	Details	Invoice ref.	Total	Mowers	Chainsaws
1 Nov.	Lawnstripe Ltd.	P001	10,000	10,000	
1 Nov.	Logjam Ltd.	P002	3,000		3,000
			13,000	10,000	3,000

Sales ledger

Grimridge Council					
Date	Details	Invoice ref.	Debit	Credit	Balance
3 Nov.	Sales: 3 lawnmowers	S001	1,500		1,500 Dr

Upton Park Estate					
Date	Details	Invoice ref.	Debit	Credit	Balance
4 Nov.	Sales: chainsaw	S001	500		500 Dr

Purchase ledger

Logjam Ltd.					
Date	Details	Invoice ref.	Debit	Credit	Balance
1 Nov.	Purchase Journal	P001		3,000	3,000 Cr
7 Nov.	Bank		3,000		0

Lawnstripe Ltd.					
Date	Details	Invoice ref.	Debit	Credit	Balance
1 Nov.	Purchase journal	P002		10,000	10,000 Cr

General ledger

Capital				
Date	Details	Debit	Credit	Balance
1 Nov.	Cash book		5,000	5,000 Cr

Sales of lawnmowers				
Date	Details	Debit	Credit	Balance
3 Nov.	Cash book		400	400 Cr
7 Nov.	Sales journal		1,500	1,900 Cr

Sales of chainsaws				
Date	Details	Debit	Credit	Balance
7 Nov.	Sales journal		500	500 Cr

Purchase of mowers				
Date	Details	Debit	Credit	Balance
7 Nov.	Purchase journal	10,000		10,000 Dr

Purchase of chainsaws				
Date	Details	Debit	Credit	Balance
7 Nov.	Purchase journal	3,000		3,000 Dr

Rent				
Date	Details	Debit	Credit	Balance
2 Nov.	Bank	450		450 Dr

Phone				
Date	Details	Debit	Credit	Balance
3 Nov.	Bank	200		200 Dr

Advertising				
Date	Details	Debit	Credit	Balance
4 Nov.	Bank	500		500 Dr

Office equipment hire				
Date	Details	Debit	Credit	Balance
5 Nov.	Bank	600		600 Dr

Flow-Mow trial balance as at 7 November

	Debit	Credit
Sales ledger		
Grimridge Council	1,500	
Purchase ledger		
Lawnstripe Ltd.		10,000
General ledger		
Sales of lawnmowers		˙,900
Sales of chainsaws		500
Purchase of lawnmowers	10,000	
Purchase of chainsaws	3,000	

Rent	450	
Phone	200	
Advertising	500	
Office equipment hire	600	
Capital		5,000
Cash book		
Bank	1,150	
Totals	**17,400**	**17,400**

Question 2

(a) **'Opening balance brought forward'** shows that on 1 December, Gargoyle Ltd. was owed £1,200 by Normanshaw Homes Ltd.

The **'sales journal'** is the book of prime entry that summarizes all the sales invoices issued by Gargoyle Ltd. The entries in Normanshaw Homes Ltd.'s account which have been transferred from the sales journal are the sales invoices issued to that company by Gargoyle Ltd.

The **'cash book'** is the book of prime entry that records all bank (and cash) transactions prior to posting to a ledger account.

(b) It appears that Normanshaw Homes Ltd. paid the amount to clear the opening balance. Often companies receive a summary of their account (a 'statement') at the end of one month, and this is expected to be paid some time within the following month.

(c) Normanshaw Homes Ltd.'s account balance would appear in Gargoyle Ltd.'s trial balance in the debit column, as:
'Debtor: Normanshaw Homes Ltd. £16,470'

(d) Debtors are treated as part of current assets.

Question 3

April	Transaction	Assets	Expenditure	Liabilities	Capital	Income
1	Owner pays £500 into business bank	Bank + 500			+500	
2	Goods bought on credit, £6,500		Goods +6,500	Creditors +6,500		
3	Paid rent £200 by cheque	Bank −200	Expenses +200			
4	Sale of goods for £2,500 by cheque	Bank +2,500				+2,500
5	Borrowed £2,000 by a loan, paid into the bank	Bank +2,000		Loan +2,000		
6	Sale of goods £1,200 on credit terms	Debtors +1,200				+1,200
7	Bought a machine £2,000 on credit terms	Machine (fixed asset) +2,000		Creditor +2,000		
8	Owner drew out £100 for personal living expenses	Bank −100			−100	
9	Debtor paid the sales invoice issued on 6 April	Bank +1,200 Debtors −1,200				
10	Electricity bill £300 received but not yet paid		Expenses +300	Creditor +300		
		+7,900	+7,000	+10,800	+400	+3,700

$$\text{Assets} + \text{Expenses} = \text{Liabilities} + \text{Capital} + \text{Income}$$
$$(7900 + 7000) = (10800 + 400 + 3700)$$
$$14900 = 14900$$

Chapter 3

Question 1

Avril's Artefacts Trading and profit and loss account for the year ended 31 October 2004		
Sales		826,220
Less cost of goods sold		
Opening stock	114,700	
Add purchases	697,000	
	811,700	
Less closing stock	(112,600)	
		(699,100)
Gross profit		127,120
Less expenses		
Advertising	18,313	
Bad debts written off	250	
Bank interest	5,231	
Insurance	8,475	
Light and heat	6,420	
Rent and rates (5,900 − 900)	5,000	
Salaries and wages (98,500 + 1,500)	100,000	
Sundry expenses	13,700	
Telephone	11,240	
Depreciation: fixtures and fittings (10% × 94,000)	9,400	
Depreciation: motorcars (25% × 165,920 − 126,800)	9,780	
		(187,809)
Net loss		(60,689)

Avril's Artefacts Balance sheet as at 31 October 2004			
	Cost	Accumulated depreciation	Net book value
Fixed assets			
Fixtures and fittings	114,000	28,200	85,800
Motor cars	165,920	136,580	29,340
	279,920	164,780	115,140

Current assets			
Stock		112,600	
Debtors		27,400	
Prepayments		900	
		140,900	
Less current liabilities			
Creditors	24,213		
Accruals	1,500		
Bank overdraft	14,852		
		(40,565)	
Net current assets			100,335
Total net assets			215,475
Capital			
Opening balance		328,164	
Less net loss		(60,689)	
		267,475	
Less drawings		(52,000)	
			215,475

Question 2

(a) The accruals concept is of paramount importance when calculating the figure of profit. According to this concept, all relevant income and expenditure transactions are included, regardless of when the related cash inflows or outflows take place. Consequently, factors such as unpaid purchase invoices or sales invoices, unsold stock, depreciation on fixed assets, and accruals and prepayments all have to be taken into the profit calculation. Items excluded from the calculation include the actual cost of purchasing fixed assets, dividend payments made to shareholders, and loans received and repaid. Inevitably, the difference between the income and expenditure used in the profit calculation will result in a different figure when contrasted with the net cash flowing into or out of the business.

A bank overdraft of £100,000 shown in the balance sheet simply means that at that particular moment in time the business owed that amount to the bank. Bank balances are not permanent, and increase, decrease, or are eliminated in the normal course of the business's life. A well-managed profitable business will be expected to keep its bank borrowings to the minimum necessary which is consistent with the efficient management of the organization.

(b) In addition to revenue reserves, a company may have capital reserves. The main capital reserve is the share premium account, which represents amounts paid in by shareholders over and above the nominal value of shares. Capital reserves are not normally allowed to be used by a company for the payment of dividends. (Note that the topic is covered in more detail in Chapter 8.)

(c) As stated in part (a) above, profit is not the same as cash, and although a company might have a seemingly healthy balance of retained profits, it is represented by *all* assets (fixed and current), less liabilities, not just a cash balance. In the example given, the company had a bank *overdraft* at the balance sheet date, so the company must consider very carefully what it can afford to pay to shareholders as dividend, bearing in mind what its overdraft limit is, what previous dividends have been paid, and what other factors might affect the bank balance before the date that any dividend is due for payment.

(d)

● Ordinary shares represent the most common type of shares in a company. They are also known as the 'equity' capital of the company. Each ordinary share carries an equal right to vote in company meetings and an equal right to share in any dividends paid as a reward to the providers of the capital.

- Preference shares carry a fixed rate of dividend and have priority over the ordinary shares in respect of the payment of their dividends and the repayment of capital in the event of the company's liquidation. These shares might be *redeemable*, which means that the company can refund the preference shareholders' capital (subject to certain rules to protect the overall capital of the company) after a specified timescale.

- Debentures are fixed interest loans usually secured on the company's assets. In most cases, they are repayable by a specific date. They are not part of the company's share capital, and the interest payments must be paid before any dividends can be considered.

- Convertible loan stock is a loan that gives the lender the possibility of converting the loan into shares at a later date. This is often an attractive option for the lender. Like debentures, convertible loan stock is not part of a company's share capital.

Question 3

(a) Unsold stock is never normally valued at selling price, as this anticipates that it will be sold at a profit. The normal valuation will be based on cost price (even though this may have to be calculated on a theoretical basis such as *FIFO—First In First Out*). Occasionally, stock has deteriorated, gone out of fashion, or otherwise been devalued so that its anticipated selling price is actually less than its cost price. Only in these circumstances can the stock be valued at what it could be sold for, less any expenses needed to be incurred to make it saleable (also known as the 'net realizable value').

(b) The usual method of stock valuation is 'at the lower of cost and net realizable value'. In the case of the Powerbase PCs, the selling price is lower than cost, and additional costs will need to be incurred to sell them. Their valuation will therefore be:

Anticipated selling price	20 × £350	£7,000
Less upgrade costs	20 × £75	(£1,500)
		£5,500

With regard to the laptops, as the cost is less than the 'net realizable value', they must be valued at cost price: 10 × £400 = £4,000.

(c)

- *Good debts* are those customer balances in the sales ledger where it is expected that they will be paid in the normal course of business. The current assets total within the balance sheet must only include good debts.

- *Bad debts* are those amounts due from customers who are highly unlikely to pay their debts. Such debts must be 'written off' by deleting them from the list of the sales ledger balances, and the total bad debts for the period will be shown as one of the expenses for the financial period. They must not be included within the balance sheet debtors' total.

- *Doubtful debts* usually occur where there has been some concern over payment, but they have not yet got to the point where they are considered as 'bad' debts. The business will have to make a *provision for doubtful debts* to cover the potential loss to the business if they do turn bad in the future. The business calculates the total of the doubtful debts and then reduces profit to cover the total. The provision is adjusted up or down each year depending upon how the total at the end of the year compares with that at the beginning.

Chapter 4

Question 1

(i) Continuing group turnover is that part of the total turnover that relates to business activities that were in existence during *and beyond* the financial year.

(ii) The part of group turnover identified as 'discontinued' relates to business activities that will not form part of the following financial period's business activities, as they have been sold or terminated. They were, however, in existence for all or part of the current financial year.

(iii) 'Cost of sales' represents the cost of purchasing or manufacturing the goods that have been sold during the financial period. It might include the cost of raw materials, manufacturing overheads such as production workers' wages, and the general costs of running a factory. For a trading business, it might consist of the opening unsold stock of goods, plus the purchases of goods during the year, less the value of any unsold stock at the end of the year.

(iv) Gross profit is the difference between the income generated from sales and the cost of those sales. It is the profit that the business makes before the 'general' overheads (such as administration expenses) are deducted, or any 'sundry' income is added.

(v) Net operating expenses are the general overheads of the business and normally consist of administration expenses and selling and distribution costs.

(vi) Goodwill amortization represents the estimated reduction in value of goodwill (an intangible fixed asset) during the financial period. It is the equivalent of depreciation charged on a tangible fixed asset.

(vii) Operating profit is also known as 'net profit', and is the profit left after the net operating expenses have been deducted from the gross profit. It represents the profit on operating activities after all relevant expenditure has been deducted from turnover.

(viii) 'Share of associated undertakings' relates to the proportion of an associated company's profit attributable to the shareholding of the investing company, i.e. Northern Foods plc. An associated company is one where the investing company owns between 20 per cent and 50 per cent of the share capital. The accounting treatment is different from that of a subsidiary company, whose results would be fully consolidated with its parent company, rather than the 'one-line' consolidation used for an associate.

Question 2

Group profit and loss account for the year ended 31 July 2004	
	£000
Turnover	
Turnover: group and share of joint venture's turnover	38,240
Less: share of joint venture's turnover	(1,520)
Group turnover	36,720
Cost of sales	(15,070)
Gross profit	21,650
Distribution costs	(5,110)
Administrative expenses	(6,310)
Other operating expenditure	(150)
Group operating profit	10,080
Share of operating profit in joint venture	240
Amortization of goodwill on joint venture	(10)
	230
Profit on ordinary activities before interest and taxation	10,310

Question 3

The relative amounts and percentages relating to turnover for the two years are as follows:

	2003		2002		Change in monetary amount in the two years(%)
Turnover excluding VAT	£m	%	£m	%	
UK	21,615	82.1	20,052	84.8	+7.7
Rest of Europe	2,689	10.2	2,203	9.3	+22.1
Asia	2,033	7.7	1,398	5.9	+45.4
	26,337	100	23,653	100	

This shows that the turnover of the Asian segment of operations has increased from 5.9 per cent of the total to 7.7 per cent of the total between the two years. The actual monetary total of the turnover in this segment has increased by 45.4 per cent, a much greater increase than either of the other two segments.

The relative amounts and percentages relating to operating profit for the two years are as follows:

	2003		2002		Change in monetary amount in the two years(%)
Operating profit	£m	%	£m	%	
UK	1,297	85.9	1,213	91.1	+6.9
Rest of Europe	141	9.4	90	6.8	+56.7
Asia	71	4.7	29	2.1	+144.8
	1,509	100	1,332	100	

This shows that the operating profit of the Asian segment of operations has increased from 2.1 per cent of the total to 4.7 per cent of the total between the two years. The actual monetary total of the turnover in this segment has increased by 144.8 per cent, again a much greater increase than either of the other two segments.

The relative amounts and percentages relating to net operating assets for the two years are as follows:

	2003		2002		Change in monetary amount in the two years(%)
Net operating assets	£m	%	£m	%	
UK	8,445	74.7	7,131	78.2	+18.4
Rest of Europe	1,658	14.7	1,079	11.8	+53.7
Asia	1,193	10.6	916	10.0	+30.2
	11,296	100	9,126	100	

Although the Asian segments have increased only slightly in comparison to the group as a whole, there has been a 30 per cent increase in the actual amount invested. However, considering that the Asian turnover increased by 45.4 per cent, and the operating profit was up by nearly 145 per cent, this is a very impressive set of results from that segment.

Chapter 5

Question 1

(i) Interest receivable and payable shown within the profit and loss account shows the costs incurred in financing the business's operations, such as bank overdraft interest and interest payable on loans, and any interest earned from such sources as investments and bank deposits. Also, any finance charges relating to leasing contracts are shown within this section.

(ii) The taxation charge shown in the profit and loss account comprises a current tax charge and any deferred taxation. Current tax is defined as 'the amount of tax estimated to be payable or recoverable in respect of the taxable profit or loss for the period, along with adjustments to estimates in respect of previous periods'. Limited companies are liable to pay corporation tax on their *taxable profits*, and adjustments must be made to the *accounting profit* to convert it into a taxable profit, as taxation laws treat certain types of income and expenditure in ways which are different from normal accounting conventions. The other main component of the tax charge is *deferred taxation*. Deferred tax arises because certain types of income and expenditure which are included in the measurement of accounting profits are not included in the measurement of taxable profits at the same time. These are known as *timing differences* and may have an effect stretching over several accounting periods. If no adjustment was made, then the tax charge shown in the profit and loss account would be distorted and the 'true' overall liability not disclosed. A deferred tax provision is created, which is adjusted (up or down) via the profit and loss account each year, depending on whether the potential deferred tax liability has increased or decreased.

(iii) A company pays dividends as a reward to its shareholders for their contribution to its success. Ordinary shareholders might receive two dividends in a financial year, an interim and a final dividend. The final dividend can only be paid after the shareholders have given their approval at an annual general meeting, but the interim dividend does not need such approval. The interim dividend is usually less than the final, as it is based on an estimate of profits, whereas the final dividend relates to actual profits. Preference shareholders receive a fixed percentage dividend, which does not fluctuate with the company's profit levels. However, in the case of both ordinary and preference shares, the company is not bound to pay dividends if the directors believe that it is against the company's best interests. In the case of H. R. Owen plc, their dividends total more than the profit on ordinary activities after taxation for the year. This is possible because they have drawn upon the accumulated profits of previous periods to maintain dividend levels.

(iv) The retained loss for the year shows that the total dividends (paid and proposed) were greater than the profit on ordinary activities after taxation for the year. This has caused a reduction in the company's reserves of £149,000—obviously a company cannot continue indefinitely to subsidize dividends out of previous years' accumulated profits. Either profits must increase in the future, or dividends must be reduced or abandoned.

(v) The basic earnings per share figure represents the profit on ordinary activities after taxation divided by the average number of ordinary shares that the company had in issue during the year. The figure has increased from 6.7p to 7.8p during the year, a 16.4 per cent increase. This seems a good performance, and might explain the company's optimism in increasing the year's dividends.

(vi) The diluted earnings per share figure is a recalculation of the basic earnings per share, as adjusted for the potential effects of stock options and convertible loan stocks which will cause an increase in the total share capital at some future date. As the company's basic and diluted eps figures are identical, we can assume that there is no material change to the basic calculation of eps.

(vii) In the UK, companies have to prepare a statement of total recognized gains and losses if there are any additional gains and losses other than those disclosed within the profit and loss account. Examples include any gains or losses on foreign currency transactions or from the revaluation of fixed assets. In the case of H. R. Owen plc, the footnote is merely confirming that all gains and losses have been disclosed within the profit loss account itself.

Question 2

(a) Basic eps $\dfrac{£354,000}{1,770,000} = 20p$

(b) Diluted eps $\dfrac{£354,000}{2,360,000} = 15p$

(c) PE ratio 200p/20p = 10 times

(d) In comparison with both the stock exchange as a whole, and the sector in which Vanquish plc operates, Vanquish is underperforming. A PE ratio of 10 for Vanquish signifies that its current share price is 10 times the last reported basic earnings per share figure. Share prices increase due to greater demand than supply, so if other companies have PE ratios of 12 or 17, this means that more investors are demanding those shares when compared to market demand for shares in Vanquish plc.

Question 3

(a) Examples of permanent taxation differences are the grant which is not taxable, and the expenses which are not allowable. The timing difference is the 'reversible' difference between the company's depreciation, and the capital allowance which is determined by government.

(b)		£
Accounting profit before taxation		800,000
Less non-taxable grant		(50,000)
		750,000
Add non-allowable expenses		20,000
		770,000
Add depreciation	120,000	
Less capital allowances	(150,000)	
		(30,000)
Taxable profit		740,000
Current tax @ 30%		**222,000**
(c) Deferred taxation		
30% × (150,000 − 120,000)	9,000	
Provision brought forward	(5,000)	
Provision for the year		**4,000**
(d) Total charge		**226,000**

Chapter 6

Question 1

 (i) Negative goodwill, which arises when a business pays *less than* the fair value of the net assets of a business being acquired, is shown as a deduction from any positive goodwill total included on the balance sheet.

 (ii) Rentals paid under an operating lease are shown as an overhead expense in the profit and loss account. They are not shown on the balance sheet, unless some of the rentals were unpaid, in which case they would be shown as part of trade creditors.

 (iii) A revaluation surplus of £1m would be shown by adding that amount to the value of land and buildings under the heading 'tangible fixed assets', and by the creation of an Asset Revaluation Reserve of £1m, which would be shown as part of the 'called-up capital and reserves' section of the balance sheet.

 (iv) Assets leased under finance lease contracts are included as fixed assets in the normal way, and are depreciated. Any outstanding amounts due under the contracts will be shown as part of 'liabilities' on the balance sheet, split between short-term and long-term creditors.

 (v) All research costs are written off to the profit and loss account and are never included on the balance sheet.

 (vi) A short-term investment in a government bond will be included as a current asset.

Question 2

Although the two companies are said to be virtually identical, the advice from the two accountants offers very different approaches to the key areas identified. Accounting rules and regulations sometimes offer more than one approach to the same problem, and which is appropriate depends upon the circumstances at the time. To take each area in turn:

 (i) If Company B's accountant believes that the value of goodwill is uncertain, then he is right to be cautious regarding its valuation. Company A's accountant is obviously taking a more positive view of that company's goodwill, and as long as it is expected to have value over the twenty-year period, it is acceptable to write it off over that length of time.

 (ii) Again, Company B's accountant is taking a more cautious line. By writing off the development expenditure, Company B's profits would be reduced by £2 million, whereas Company A's intangible assets on its balance sheet would be increased by £2 million, and profits would be unaffected. For company A's accounting policy to be acceptable, it must follow the relevant accounting standard, which sets out detailed criteria for capitalizing the development expenditure. If it does not meet these criteria, it must be written off against profits.

 (iii) Again, Company B's accountant is more cautious than Company A's. Bearing in mind that an overriding aim of financial statements is to show a 'true and fair view', it could be argued that company A's policy shows a more realistic valuation. The fact that fixed assets are not bought for resale does not mean that their balance sheet value should be unrelated to circumstances prevailing at the balance sheet date. If the increase of £5m is considered to be permanent, then it is realistic to increase the value.

 (iv) Company A's accountant's advice is incorrect. One hundred per cent of the subsidiary's net assets must be included within the group balance sheet even if less than 100 per cent of the subsidiary's shares are owned by the parent company. In such circumstances, a calculation of the *minority interest's* value in the subsidiary is made, and is shown in the group balance sheet, to recognize that shareholders who are 'outside the group' have a stake in a group company.

 (v) Either stock valuation method is acceptable.

In all cases, the appropriate accounting policy which has been adopted must be stated in the notes to the accounts. When analysing information, due regard must be paid to the specific policies followed by each company, and appropriate adjustments made to ensure that the information is comparable between the two companies.

Question 3

(i) Stock should be valued at the lower of 'cost and net realizable value', therefore it would be valued at £20,000. This would have the effect of increasing the operating profit (as the 'cost of goods sold' is reduced), and increasing the current asset shown in the balance sheet.

(ii) If a project has been abandoned, the related development expenditure must be written off against profits. This will result in a reduction in the value of fixed assets, as well as a reduction in the year's operating profits.

(iii) Assuming that the additional £0.5m is considered a permanent increase in the valuation of the land and buildings, it can be added to the value of the tangible fixed assets, and also shown within an 'asset revaluation reserve'. The increased value of land and buildings will result in an increased annual depreciation charge, which will reduce the year's operating profit.

(iv) A bad debt must be written off against profits, and the current assets reduced. Only 'good' debts can be included within the balance sheet total. The year's operating profit will be reduced.

(v) Goodwill that has not been purchased cannot be included within the company's balance sheet, as it has not been tested by a market transaction and is therefore subjective. It has no effect on the year's operating profit.

Chapter 7

Question 1 (a)

Amended profit and loss account for the year ended 31 December 2003	
	£
Sales	520,000
Cost of sales (230,000 + 20,000)	(250,000)
Gross profit	270,000
Less expenses(115, 000 + 18,000)	(133,000)
Operating profit before taxation	137,000
Taxation (£35,000 1 £16,000)	(51,000)
Operating profit after taxation	86,000
Less proposed dividend (500,000 × 2p)	(10,000)
Retained profits for the year	76,000
Retained profits b/f	230,000
Retained profits c/f	306,000

Amended balance sheet as at 31 December 2003	£	£	£
Fixed assets (net book value):			327,000
Current assets:			
Stock (£162,000 − £20,000)		142,000	
Debtors		152,000	

Bank		24,000	
		318,000	
Less creditors due for payment within one year:			
Trade creditors	135,000		
Other creditors (directors' bonus)	18,000		
Proposed dividend	10,000		
Taxation	35,000		
		(198,000)	
Net current assets			120,000
			447,000
Provisions for liabilities and charges (deferred taxation)			(16,000)
Total net assets			431,000
Called-up share capital			
500,000 ordinary shares of 25p each			125,000
Reserves			
Retained earnings (P&L a/c)			306,000
			431,000
Note: Capital commitment			
Capital expenditure authorized but not yet contracted		£80,000	

(b) Suggestions can include:

- Explore reasons why the accounts were so inaccurate. Is the accounting system defective? What responsibility does the financial director bear?
- Were the accounts audited? Was the auditor's report qualified in any way? If not, the auditors should be replaced.
- Were draft accounts circulated and approved prior to audit?
- What were the grounds for rejection by the shareholders? Were they genuinely dissatisfied with the results or was it a more general attack against the directors?

Question 2

(i) 6 per cent Irredeemable unsecured loan stock

- the interest rate is 6 per cent per annum on the amount of the loan
- 'irredeemable' means that there is no set date for the loan to be repaid
- ' unsecured' means that the lender has no right to seize any of the company's assets in the event of the company being unable to pay the interest due.

(ii) 5 per cent convertible debentures 2014–18, secured by a floating charge

- the interest rate is 5 per cent per annum on the amount of the loan
- the loan can be converted into ordinary shares between the set dates, at the discretion of the lender
- the earliest date for conversion is in 2014, and the latest date is in 2018
- the lender has the right to seize any of the company's assets in the event of the company being unable to pay the interest due, or repay the loan itself if the conversion rights are not taken up.

(iii) 4 per cent Debentures 2008, secured by a fixed charge

- the interest rate is 4 per cent per annum on the amount of the loan
- the loan is repayable by the company in 2008
- the lender has the right to seize specific assets of the company in the event of the company being unable to pay the interest due, or repay the loan itself.

Question 3

(i) The error has been discovered in the post-balance sheet period, and is an adjusting post balance sheet event. This requires the stock valuation to be increased at 31 December 2003 by £80,000.

(ii) Again, this has happened in the post-balance sheet period, but it is a non-adjusting event, as it does not relate to conditions existing at the balance sheet date. A note giving the details of the takeover bid will be shown in the annual report.

(iii) This is a contingent liability that could be noted in the annual report. No provision is necessary, as there is uncertainty regarding the outcome of the case. However, if the auditors agree, the amount involved might be considered as immaterial in the context of the company as a whole, and may be omitted.

(iv) This is relevant to the 2003 financial statements, and the correct treatment would be to create a provision, and credit £100,000 to it each year for the next five years.

Chapter 8

Question 1

(a) The legal acceptability of each of the four alternatives is as follows:

1. A share premium account is a capital reserve, and therefore is not distributable to the shareholders by way of dividend. This suggestion would therefore be illegal.

2. A limited company must maintain its share capital and capital reserves, as this represents the core capital of the business invested by shareholders which is relied upon by lenders and creditors. If the suggestion were adopted, the company would be in the paradoxical position of having no shareholders and therefore no owners. Again this suggestion would be illegal.

3. Either type of reserve, capital or revenue, can be used to 'pay up' shares to be issued as bonus shares, free of charge, to shareholders. This suggestion, therefore, is legal. It has no effect whatsoever on the cash resources of the company, but does rearrange the balance sheet so that part of the profit and loss account (a 'distributable' revenue reserve) is transferred into share capital, which is non-distributable. Hence, it is reducing the amount potentially available to pay dividends, which might reduce pressure from shareholders.

4. Because the profit and loss account reserve is distributable, in theory, all or part of it can be used to pay a dividend. However, the availability of cash resources must be considered, and the company directors should only declare a dividend that the company can afford to pay.

(b) The relative advantages from the shareholders viewpoint of alternatives 3 and 4 are, first, that the bonus issue, whilst not giving shareholders any cash, does send a signal that the company has surplus profits available to make the issue. This is often interpreted as a positive sign by a stock market (assuming that the company's shares are listed on a stock market), and the share price may rise accordingly. Alternative 4 gives the obvious advantage to shareholders of receiving a cash dividend of £200,000.

(c) One key advantage to the company of alternative 3 is that a bonus issue is not a drain on the company's cash resources. Also, it reduces the total of distributable reserves, thus reducing the potential dividends which could be payable at a future date if the shareholders used their voting power to force the company to pay the maximum dividend possible.

Alternative 4, the payment of a cash dividend, may have the advantage of 'keeping the shareholders happy', as they would expect a profitable company to reward the providers of capital in this way. The amount proposed as a dividend is using just over a quarter of the reserves available, and, providing that there are sufficient cash resources available, this seems an appropriate amount—for further details of the company's financial situation would be needed before we could come to a definite conclusion.

(e)

	31 December 2003 £000	5 January 2004 £000	12 January 2004 £000
Called-up share capital (5p shares)	240	720	720
Share premium account	200	200	200
Profit and loss account	760	280	80
	1,200	1,200	1,000

Question 2

(a)

Pitchford plc Balance sheet as at 31 May 2004		
	£000	£000
Fixed assets: tangible		106,240
Fixed assets: intangible		32,000
		138,240
Current assets		
Stock	20,820	
Debtors	52,300	
Bank (26,200 − redeemed preference shares 16,000 + rights issue 85,000)	95,200	
	168,320	
Creditors due for payment within one year		
Creditors	41,260	
Proposed dividend (5p × 400,000)	20,000	
	61,260	
Net current assets		107,060
Total net assets		245,300
Issued share capital		
400,000 ordinary shares of 25p each, fully paid (W1)		100,000
Share premium account (b/f 35,000 − Bonus 35,000 + on rights issue 60,000)		60,000

Capital redemption reserve		16,000
Profit and loss account (b/f 105,300 − to capital redemption reserve 16,000 − Proposed dividend 20,000)		69,300
		245,300
W1		
Opening share capital £40,000 × £1 = 40,000 shares		
Converted to 25p nominal		160,000 shares
Bonus from share premium account £35,000 × 4		+140,000 shares
Rights issue		+100,000 shares
Total		400,000 shares

(b) If a company's share price has risen considerably, it may deter potential smaller investors, as relatively few shares can be bought for the amount invested. Splitting the share price from £1 to 25p quadruples the number of shares in issue, and will reduce the share price to one-quarter of what it was before the share split.

(c) Reasons for protecting a company's share capital and capital reserves include:

- The concept of a 'creditors' buffer' where capital is protected and must be maintained within the company.

- If capital was drained from the company, the risk borne by shareholders would be reduced whilst that of lenders and creditors would increase.

- Unscrupulous directors might repay capital selectively, leaving weaker shareholders to carry all the risks.

Question 3

(a)

(i) 'Non-cumulative' means that if sufficient profits are not available to pay preference dividends in one year, the 'missed' dividends are not accumulated to be paid out of future profits. Preference shares are 'cumulative' unless stated to be non-cumulative.

(ii) 'Redeemable' means that the company can repay the share capital to its shareholders. In the case quoted, the earliest redemption date is sometime in 2005, whilst the latest date is sometime in 2009.

(iii) 'Preference' refers to the priority which such shares have both in obtaining their dividends (i.e. preference over ordinary shareholders) and in the event of liquidation (they would be repaid capital in priority to ordinary shareholders).

(iv) 'Convertible' means that the debentures are convertible into a different form of loan or into share capital. For example, it may mean that debenture holders can convert into ordinary shares.

(v) The earliest date for conversion is 2005, whilst the latest date is 2009.

(b) A capital redemption reserve would have to be created, in order to preserve the total share capital and capital reserves at the same level before and after the redemption.

(c) Debenture interest is 'allowable' for tax purposes (i.e. is treated like most other overhead expenses), whereas dividends are not allowable. The reason is that dividends, being profit allocations, are deemed to come from profits *after* the taxation charge has been calculated. Interest, however, is not a profit allocation, but the *cost* of financing loans.

Chapter 9

Question 1

(£)	A	B	C	D
Net cash inflow from operating activities	15,800	**23,570**	19,400	50,660
Net interest paid	(5,800)	(2,900)	(6,000)	(2,950)
Tax	(7,200)	(4,500)	(7,100)	(24,880)
Capital expenditure	17,300	(2,970)	**(5,930)**	(6,520)
Changes in financing	800	(1,800)	14,680	(17,490)
Dividends	(9,820)	(4,200)	(3,300)	**(6,270)**
Increase/(decrease) in cash for the period	**11,080**	7,200	11,750	(7,450)

Question 2

Report to the shareholders of Barnacle plc

As can be seen from the table below, the major changes shown by the cash flow statement in 2004 concern the net cash inflow from operating activities, which decreased by 42 per cent the acquisition of a subsidiary (£2m), and the repayment of loans and purchase of own shares (£2.4 m). All the other categories (other than returns on investments and servicing of finance) changed to the detriment of the company's cash flow. However, active, expanding and profitable companies will invest heavily in acquiring assets and new businesses, whilst making loan repayments where necessary to keep down borrowing levels. Spending £1.2m on the purchase of the company's own shares makes sense only if they are needed to meet share options given to employees, or if there are no other viable investments that the company could make.

	2004 £000s	2003 £000s	% change
Net cash inflow from operating activities	7,011	12,506	−42
Returns on investments and servicing of finance			
Interest paid	(53)	(68)	−28
Interest received	1,035	945	+9.5
	982	877	+12
Taxation	(5,083)	(2,716)	+87
Capital expenditure			
Purchase of tangible fixed assets	(372)	(320)	+16
Sale of tangible fixed assets	22	16	+37.5
	(350)	(314)	+11.5
Acquisitions			
Purchase of subsidiary undertaking	(2,062)	—	—
Equity dividends paid	(1,092)	(930)	+17.4

Financing			
Repayment of loans	(1,185)	(210)	+464
Purchase of own shares	(1,230)	—	—
Issue of shares	391	97	+303
	(2,024)	(113)	+1,691
(Decrease)/Increase in cash	(2,618)	9,320	−128

Question 3

Nickleby plc: cash flow statement for the year ended 31 October 2004	
	£000
Net cash inflow from operating activities (note 1)	28,800
Interest paid	(1,200)
Tax	(4,000)
Net capital expenditure (£22m − £1.8m)	(20,200)
Changes in financing	(8,900)
Equity dividends	(2,000)
Business acquisitions/disposals	—
Decrease in cash for the year (note 2)	**(7,500)**
Note 1	
Reconciliation of operating profit to net cash	
inflow from operating activities	
Operating profit	25,900
Depreciation charges	6,000
Loss on sale of tangible fixed assets	3,200
Increase in stock	(1,000)
Increase in debtors	(1,500)
Decrease in creditors	(3,800)
Net cash inflow from operating activities	28,800
Note 2	
Analysis of changes in cash during the year	
Balance at 1 November 2003	4,800
Decrease in cash for the year	(7,500)
Balance at 31 October 2004	(2,700)

Chapter 10

Question 1

(i) Sometimes, when a company takes over another, investors holding a minority of shares do not wish to sell their shares in the acquired company, preferring to remain as 'minority' shareholders in that company. The group must acknowledge the financial interests of the minority shareholders within the group profit and loss account and balance sheet, by calculating, respectively, the minority's interest in the subsidiary's profits for the period, and its interest in the subsidiary's balance sheet value at the end of the period.

(ii)   A company would be regarded as an associate when another company holds between 20 per cent and 50 per cent of its voting share capital, and it is subject to 'significant influence' by the company making the investment. For this purpose, significant influence exists when the investor is actively involved in formulating the operating and financial policies of the company in which it has invested. Such involvement may take the form of participation in such policy decisions as the expansion or contraction of the business, changes in products, and determining the balance between what proportion of the profits should be declared as dividends and what should be reinvested within the company. A typical situation for such an investment would be where one company is a major customer or supplier to the other company, and decides to take a sufficiently large shareholding to enable it to appoint a director and influence company policy.

(iii)   Goodwill arising on consolidation is the difference between the purchase price given for the subsidiary's shares and the fair value of the net assets acquired. It must be calculated and treated in accordance with accounting standards.

Question 2

(i)   Goodwill arising on consolidation: £100,000 − (60% × £80,000) = £52,000

(ii)   The minority interest in Pablo Ltd. at 31 December 2004: 40% × (£80,000 + £40,000) = £48,000

(iii)   The amount of Pablo Ltd.'s reserves which can be added into the reserves of the group at 31 December 2004: 60% × £40,000 = £24,000 (only 'post-acquisition' reserves can be added)

Question 3

Frinton Plc Group balance sheet as at 30 April 2004		
		£
Tangible fixed assets		378,000
Intangible fixed assets (note ii)		4,400
		382,400
Current assets	49,000	
Creditors: amounts falling due within one year	(61,700)	
Proposed dividend	(10,000)	
		(22,700)
Total net assets		359,700
Share capital and reserves		
Called-up share capital		150,000
Profit and loss account (note iii)		167,820
		317,820
Minority interests (note iv)		41,880
		359,700

Workings:

	Frinton plc £	Groudale Ltd. £	For consolidated balance sheet
Fixed assets	163,000	215,000	378,000
56,000 shares in Groudale Ltd.	80,000		n/a
Loan to Groudale Ltd.	55,000		(cancelled)
Current assets	23,000	26,000	49,000
Less current liabilities	(15,300)	(46,400)	61,700
Proposed dividend	(10,000)		10,000
Loan from Frinton plc		(55,000)	(cancelled)
	295,700	139,600	
Share capital and reserves			
Called-up share capital (£1 shares)	150,000	80,000	150,000
Revenue reserves	145,700	59,600	see note iii
	295,700	139,600	

Notes:

(i)   Frinton plc owns 70% of Groudale Ltd (56,000 of 80,000 shares issued).

(ii) Goodwill on acquisition: cost £80,000 less value at acquisition date:
70% × (£80,000 + £28,000) = £80,000 − 75,600 = £4,400.

(iii) Subsidiary's reserves (Frinton plc's share of 'post acquisition' only) = 70% × (£59,600 − £28,000) =
70% × £31,600 = £22,120, plus Group's reserves £145,700 = Total £167,820.

(iv) Minority interests at 30 April 2004: 30% × £139,600 = £41,880.

Chapter 11

Question 1

(a) *The chairman's report.* The chairman's report contained within the annual report gives the chairman an opportunity to reflect in general terms on the company's progress in the past financial year, and to comment on current and future trading prospects. It is a general, reflective report which is not prepared to a set format, but will vary from company to company.

(b) *The directors' report.* In the UK, most of the information contained within the directors' report is required by statute—particularly the Companies Act 1985. Much of the information, for example the group profit for the year and the total dividend, can be found in other parts of the annual report. However, details such as the directors' shareholdings, significant shareholdings above 3 per cent of the issue capital, the company's policy regarding payment to suppliers, and payments to political parties and charities are usually only found within this part of the annual report. For public limited companies listed on a stock market, a further section on 'corporate governance' is required, which explains the way in which the board of directors operates, what its responsibilities are, and how the board maintains internal control to safeguard the company's assets.

(c) *The auditor's report.* The auditor who presents this report is an independent qualified accountant or firm of accountants, who reports to the shareholders as to whether or not the financial statements and related notes show a true and fair view of the company's state of affairs. The auditor also states whether the statements comply with relevant legislation and accounting standards.

(d) *The operating and financial review*. Many large companies, in addition to a chairman's report, publish an 'operating and financial review' (OFR), which gives a discussion of the company's operating results, a review of the group's financial needs and resources, and a commentary on shareholder's return and share value. The overriding purpose is to convey the 'real dynamics' of the business, including, where material, the company's relationships with stakeholders such as customers, employees, suppliers, and the community.

Question 2

The company must be viewed as a very high-risk investment until such a time as the financing problems have been resolved. The auditors are doing their duty in drawing attention to the company's going concern status, and how it is dependent on current borrowing facilities continuing, and refinancing being necessary. The consequences if the company was not regarded as a going concern are stated: asset values would be reduced to their 'recoverable amount' (i.e. what they would realize in a liquidation sale), causing additional depreciation to be charged in the profit and loss account. The point about contingent liabilities is pertinent, as guarantees regarding loans and other obligations would be activated in the event of the company ceasing to trade.

Question 3

The article does not give details of what form the small shareholders' 'platform' might take, but it is clear that Sir Richard is proposing something much less formal than the existing AGM. Small shareholders might argue that the existing arrangements are democratic, and serve to remind directors that they are acting on behalf of all shareholders, large and small. Realistically, the influence of shareholders is proportionate to their shareholdings, and so large institutional investors can exercise far greater power than small investors. The real purpose of the article is to wake the large investors from their slumber of inactivity, and get them to attend company meetings, question directors, and vote accordingly. As for any disruption caused by the one-share owning individuals, it could be argued that this is the price companies pay for operating in capitalist democracies!

Chapter 12

Question 1

(a)

GP Margin	$\frac{\text{Gross profit}}{\text{Turnover}} \times 100$	Aldridge plc's margin is much higher than average. Possible reasons include lack of competition, better buying policies, or errors in stock counts.
Net profit margin	$\frac{\text{Operating profit before interest and tax}}{\text{Turnover}} \times 100$	Aldridge plc's margin is higher than average. Possible reasons include greater control of expenses, more automation (lower wage costs).
ROCE	$\frac{\text{Operating profit before interest and tax}}{\text{Share capital} + \text{reserves} + \text{Long-term loans}} \times 100$	Aldridge plc's margin is higher than average. Possible reasons include greater efficiency overall, less competition.
Acid test	(Current assets − Stock) : Current liabilities	Aldridge plc's margin is lower than average. Possible reasons include increasing trade creditors due to payment cash flow difficulties, fewer credit sales than average resulting in fewer debtors.
Gearing	$\frac{\text{Long-term loans} - \text{Cash and blank balances}}{\text{Share capital} + \text{reserves}} \times 100$ (or alternatives outlined in chapter)	Aldridge plc's margin is much higher than average. Possible reasons include past expansion financed by borrowings, or borrowing in anticipation of future expansion.

(b) A current ratio of 5:1 might indicate too much stock being carried, poor control of debtors, or surplus bank balances not being reinvested into fixed assets. Alternatively, it may represent a temporary surplus of liquid funds, for example due to selling a property. It would be useful to know (for this and the other ratios listed) what the previous year's ratio were, in order for trend analysis to be assessed.

Question 2

(a)

Trend Analysis	2004	2003	2002
Dividend cover	Nil	67.6	100
PE ratio	Nil	94.7	100
Basic eps	−156	83.3	100
Diluted eps	−22.9	87.1	100
Dividend yield	428.6	292.8	100
Stock market price at end of year	61.1	88.9	100

(b) All the ratios show a downward trend, apart from the dividend yield. It is apparent from the decline in the eps calculations that the company was making a profit after interest and taxation in 2002 and 2003, but recorded a loss after interest and taxation in 2004. However, the fact that there was a positive dividend yield in 2004 means that the company continued to pay a dividend in that year out of reserves. To look at each statistic in turn:

1. Profit available to cover the dividend declined between 2002 and 2003, and in 2004 no profit was made.

2. PE ratio deteriorated slightly between 2002 and 2003. The fact that there were no earnings in 2004 meant that no PE ratio could be calculated.

3. The basic eps, which is the profit available for the ordinary dividend divided by the number of equity shares issued, declined between 2002 and 2003, and recorded a loss per share in 2004.

4. The diluted eps shows the potential effect of stock options and future conversions of loan stock. This would have the effect of spreading the loss over more shares, so the diluted eps shows a lower loss per share than the basic eps.

5. The dividend yield has increased due to the decline in the share price. An investor could buy a share at the end of 2004 for 110p, so the 6 per cent dividend yield meant that the company was declaring a dividend of 6.6p. The previous year, the closing stock market price was much higher (160p), the yield was 4.1 per cent, so the dividend in that year was also 6.6p. This shows that the company decided to send a positive signal to the stock market that it was prepared to maintain its 2003 dividend level even in the loss-making year of 2004.

6. The stock market price declined over three years, which would be expected in view of the reducing profit. The fact that the company had 'until relatively recently . . . an unbroken record of growth and profitability' indicates that it has substantial reserves which can cushion it during a short loss-making period. However, if losses continue, then the company's dividend policy will be under threat and the share price might collapse.

Question 3

Company A: Over-trading
If a company does not have enough working capital to support its level of sales and production, then it may be unable to meets its liabilities as they fall due. Young, aggressive companies often try to gain

market share by undercutting competitors' prices. Whilst this might achieve its objective in increased sales percentages, it may result in a strain on a company's resources if it requires additional fixed assets, stock handling facilities, high stock levels, and increased creditors and borrowings. If the increased sales cannot be quickly converted into cash inflows, unpaid creditors may grow impatient and force the company out of business.

Company B: High Gearing

A company with relatively high borrowings in relation to its equity shareholders' capital is called a 'high-geared' company. Management strategy may be to run a high-geared company, making use of a high proportion of borrowed funds to expand. However, the reason for the high borrowing may be simply 'survival', with the company borrowing to repay existing loans, borrowing to pay off creditors, borrowing to pay the employees' wages, etc. The finance director would need to make a more detailed analysis of Company B, to establish the reasons for that company's gearing policy.

Company C: High PE ratio, low return on capital employed.

A company with a high PE ratio is well regarded by the stock exchange, as its share price is trading at a higher multiple of its latest earnings per share than its competitors. The fact that the company has a low return on capital employed seems to indicate that there are other factors driving up the share price. The eps figure is historic, but the share price reflects *future* prospects. With the stock market price rising, investors might be anticipating increasing profits, new contracts, or possibly a takeover bid for the company.

Answers to mini case studies

Chapter 1

1. A business makes a profit if its income exceeds its expenditure. During the course of a financial period, sales of goods and services will be made and additional income may be generated from such transactions as selling assets at a profit or receiving interest on loans. The accruals concept requires that we ignore the dates on which cash is received or paid and instead include transactions when they occur. The income and expenditure totals therefore will include amounts that are unpaid at the end of the financial period. Profit is not the same as simply 'cash received less cash paid'.

2. Accountants must follow generally accepted accounting principles (GAAP). These are found within the laws of the countries in which a business operates, the rules laid down by the accounting profession itself, regulations specified by stock exchanges, and long-standing principles for recording financial transactions (the double-entry bookkeeping system). There is a growing trend for the internationalization of the regulatory framework, in particular the move to recognize International Accounting Standards.

3. The main objective of providing financial statements is to give information about the financial performance and financial position of an enterprise that is useful to a wide range of users for assessing the stewardship of management and for making economic decisions. Users include investors, lenders, suppliers, customers, employees, and governments.

Chapter 2

Cash book

	Receipts					Payments				
Date	Details	Total	Capital	Sales Ledger	Date	Details	Total	Equip	Travel	Expenses	Purchase Ledger
1 Jan.	M. von Mausen: capital	**20,000**	20,000		3 Jan.	Safari Supplies Ltd.	**380**	380			
5 Jan.	Great Rocky Zoo	**15,000**		15,000	3 Jan.	Aardvark Airlines	**500**		500		
		35,000			4 Jan.	Office Expenses	**400**			400	
					5 Jan.	Pachyderm plc	**8,000**				8,000
							9,280				

Sales journal

Date	Details	Invoice ref.	Total	Sales
2 Jan.	Great Rocky Zoo	S001	20,000	20,000

Purchase journal

Date	Details	Invoice ref.	Total	Trade purchases	Fixed assets
2 Jan.	Pachyderm plc	P001	16,000	16,000	
4 Jan.	Micro Machines	P002	850		850

Sales ledger

Great Rocky Zoo					
Date	Details	Invoice ref.	Debit	Credit	Balance
2 Jan.	Sales: 8 elephants	S001	20,000		20,000 Dr
5 Jan.	Bank			15,000	5,000 Dr

Purchase ledger

Micro Machines					
Date	Details	Invoice ref.	Debit	Credit	Balance
4 Jan.	Purchase: computer	S002		850	850 Cr

Pachyderm plc					
Date	Details	Invoice ref.	Debit	Credit	Balance
2 Jan.	Purchase: 8 elephants	P001		16,000	16,000 Cr
5 Jan.	Bank		8,000		8,000 Dr

General ledger

Capital				
Date	Details	Debit	Credit	Balance
1 Jan.	Cash book		20,000	20,000 Cr

Computer				
Date	Details	Debit	Credit	Balance
5 Jan.	Purchase journal	850		850 Dr

Office expenses				
Date	Details	Debit	Credit	Balance
4 Jan.	Cash book	400		400 Dr

Purchases				
Date	Details	Debit	Credit	Balance
5 Jan.	Purchase journal	16,000		16,000 Dr

Safari equipment				
Date	Details	Debit	Credit	Balance
3 Jan.	Cash book (Safari Supplies Ltd.)	380		380 Dr

Sales				
Date	Details	Debit	Credit	Balance
5 Jan.	Sales journal		20,000	20,000 Cr

Travel				
Date	Details	Debit	Credit	Balance
3 Jan.	Cash book (Aardvark Airways deposit)	500		500 Dr

Trial balance

MinnieBeasts trial balance as at 5 January 2003

Sales ledger	Debit	Credit
Great Rocky Zoo	5,000	
Purchase ledger		
Pachyderm plc		8,000
Micro Machines		850
General ledger		
Capital		20,000
Computer	850	
Office expenses	400	
Purchases	16,000	
Sales		20,000
Safari equipment	380	
Travel expenses	500	
Cash book		
Bank (35,000 − 9,280)	25,720	
Totals	**48,850**	**48,850**

Chapter 3

MinnieMax Limited Opening balance sheet

Fixed assets		20,680
Current assets		
Stock	2,000	
Debtors	3,600	
Bank (72,000 − 20,000)	52,000	
	57,600	
Less current liabilities		
Creditors	(6,280)	
Net current assets		51,320
Total net assets		72,000
Share capital (120,000 × 50p nominal value)		60,000
Share premium account (120,000 × 10p)		12,000
		72,000

Chapter 4

MinnieMax Limited (part) Profit and loss account for the year ended 30 September 2004

	£	£
Sales		486,000
Less cost of sales:		
Opening stock	2,000	
Expedition costs and other cost of sales	130,000	
	132,000	
Less closing stock	(5,000)	
		(127,000)
		359,000
Other operating income		11,000
		370,000
Distribution costs	46,000	
Administrative expenses	62,000	
Exceptional cost	40,000	
		(148,000)
Operating profit before interest and taxation		222,000

Chapter 5

MinnieMax Limited (part) Profit and loss account for the year ended 30 September 2004

	£	£
Operating profit before interest and taxation		222,000
Interest receivable	2,000	
Interest payable	(3,500)	
		(1,500)
Profit on ordinary activities before taxation		220,500
Taxation		(62,500)
Profit on ordinary activities after taxation		158,000
Dividends:		
Interim	(26,000)	
Proposed final	(50,000)	
		(76,000)
Retained profit for the year		82,000

Chapter 6

MinnieMax Limited (part of) Balance sheet as at 30 September 2004

Fixed assets (n. 1)		
Intangible fixed assets	26,600	
Tangible fixed assets	240,080	
		266,680
Current assets		
Stock	5,000	
Debtors and prepayments	27,200	
Investment (government bond)	50,000	
Bank	115,120	
	197,320	

Note 1

Intangible fixed assets

Brand name	28,000
Less amortization (1/20)	(1,400)
Net book value	26,600

Tangible fixed assets

	Freehold land	Motor vehicles	Equipment	Computers	Total
Cost	200,000	30,000	16,000	850	246,850
Depreciation[a]	—	(5,000)	(1,600)	(170)	(6,770)
Net book value	200,000	25,000	14,400	680	240,080

[a] Workings:
Motor vehicles: $25\% \times (30,000 - 10,000) = 5,000$
Equipment $10\% \times 16,000 = 1,600$
Computers $20\% \times 850 = 170$

Accounting policies

Intangible fixed assets are amortized over a twenty-year period.

Tangible fixed assets, other than freehold land, are depreciated as follows:

- Motor vehicles over four years by the straight line method.
- Equipment at 10 per cent per annum by the reducing balance method.
- Computers over five years by the straight line method.

Chapter 7

(a)

MinnieMax Limited (part of) Balance sheet as at 30 September 2004

Fixed assets*		
Intangible fixed assets	26,600	
Tangible fixed assets	240,080	
		266,680
Current assets*		
Stock	5,000	
Debtors	27,200	
Investment (government bond)	50,000	
Bank	115,120	
	197,320	
Creditors: amounts falling due within one year		
Creditors and accruals	42,500	
Finance lease creditors	3,000	
Taxation	62,500	
Proposed dividend	50,000	
	(158,000)	
Net current assets		39,320
Total assets less current liabilities		306,000
Creditors: amounts falling due after more than one year		
Finance lease creditors	12,000	
Loan (4% Debenture 2010–12)	140,000	
		(152,000)
Total net assets		154,000

*Details as shown in the answer to Chapter 6's case study (see p. 381).

(b) The amount claimed by the tribe represents a contingent liability of MinnieMax Ltd., and the fact that the case is in progress at 30 September 2004 indicates that the claim is not to be dismissed without due consideration. However, at the balance sheet date, as there is sufficient uncertainty about the probable outcome, there is no need to create a provision for potential damages. Instead, the following note outlining the circumstances of the contingency should be disclosed:

Contingent liability
The company is the subject of a legal action brought by the Peruvian Wherearewe tribe, which is seeking damages relating to the unfortunate capture and subsequent sale of the tribe's sacred Ibrox bird. The company has already compensated the tribe for this incident, but does not accept any further liability in this matter. Due to the remote possibility of the tribe's claim being successful, no provision has been made in these accounts.

Chapter 8

(a)

MinnieMax Limited Balance sheet as at 30 September 2004

Fixed assets		
Intangible fixed assets	26,600	
Tangible fixed assets	240,080	
		266,680
Current assets		
Stock	5,000	
Debtors	27,200	
Investment (government bond)	50,000	
Bank	115,120	
	197,320	
Creditors: amounts falling due within one year		
Creditors and accruals	42,500	
Finance lease creditors	3,000	
Taxation	62,500	
Proposed dividend	50,000	
	(158,000)	
Net current assets		39,320
Total assets less current liabilities		306,000
Creditors: amounts falling due after more than one year		
Finance lease creditors	12,000	
Loan (4% debenture 2010–12)	140,000	
		(152,000)
Total net assets*		154,000
Capital and reserves		
Called-up share capital (120,000 shares of 50p nominal value)	60,000	
Share premium account	12,000	
Profit and loss account	82,000	
		154,000

* Details as shown in Chapter 7's case study.

(b) A bonus issue is a free issue of shares given to existing shareholders pro rata to their current holdings. The issue does not affect the balance sheet value; all that happens is that some or all of the reserves are 'capitalized', i.e. transferred into the share capital of the company. For example, a company with 10,000 ordinary shares of £1 each and £120,000 accumulated in its profit and loss account may decide to make a bonus issue on a 5 for 1 basis in order to reduce the amount of the company's distributable reserves. After the bonus issue, the share capital will have increased by £50,000 to £60,000, and the balance on the profit and loss account will have reduced from £120,000 to £70,000. The balance sheet total remains unchanged at £130,000. There are a number of reasons why a company might make a bonus issue including:

- If the company wants to restrict potential dividend payouts, a bonus issue out of revenue reserves converts *distributable* reserves into *non-distributable* reserves. This reduces the pressure on directors from shareholders wanting increased dividends.

- A high stock market price may act as a deterrent to potential investors. As a bonus issue increases the number of shares traded, the price per share will decrease to a more realistic level.

- Stock exchanges tend to link bonus issues with 'good news' from profitable companies, leading to an increase in share prices.

- Over time, a company might accumulate many different reserves—distributable and non-distributable. A bonus issue serves as a convenient way of tidying up the balance sheet by transferring some or all of the reserves into share capital.

Chapter 9

(a)

MinnieMax Ltd. cash flow statement for the year ended 30 September 2004

		£
Net cash inflow from operating activities (n. 1)		240,470
Returns on investments and servicing of finance		
Interest received	2,000	
Interest paid	(3,500)	
		(1,500)
Taxation		
Corporation tax paid		—
Capital expenditure and financial investment		
Payments to acquire tangible fixed assets (274,850 − 15,000)		(259,850)
Management of liquid resources		
Purchase of government bond		(50,000)
Equity dividends paid		(26,000)
Net cash outflow before financing		(96,880)
Financing		
Issue of ordinary share capital	72,000	
New long-term loan	140,000	
		212,000
Increase in cash (n. 2)		115,120

Note 1

Operating profit	222,000
Depreciation and amortization	8,170
Increase in stocks	(5, 000)
Increase in debtors	(27,200)
Increase in creditors	42,500
Net cash inflow from operating activities	240,470

Note 2

Increase in bank balance for the year £115,120

Chapter 10

(i) If MinnieMax Ltd. buys all the shares of Wild Life Holidays Ltd., it takes total control of that company and assumes a parent–subsidiary relationship, with no minority interests. When preparing the group profit and loss account, it will include 100 per cent of the income and expenditure of its subsidiary, other than that which relates to intra-group trading. In the group balance sheet, all the subsidiary's assets and liabilities will be included, other than intra-group indebtedness, which is eliminated on consolidation. If the subsidiary was purchased for a price which was greater than the fair value of its total net assets, goodwill arises, and this must be treated as an intangible fixed asset in the group balance sheet. The company must then decide its amortization policy for the goodwill.

(ii) If MinnieMax Ltd. buys 70 per cent of the shares of Wild Life Holidays Ltd., the 30 per cent who are not selling their shares will remain as minority shareholders in the subsidiary. The accounting treatment for the group accounts is virtually identical to the 100 per cent purchase as described above. However, the value of the 'minority interests' must be calculated, and shown separately within both the group profit and loss account and group balance sheet. In the group profit and loss account, the minority interest will be valued at 30 per cent of the subsidiary's retained profit for the year. In the group balance sheet, the minority interest will be 30 per cent of the subsidiary's total net assets.

(iii) If MinnieMax Ltd. buys the net assets of Wild Life Holidays Ltd., it is not acquiring a subsidiary company. All that happens is that the individual assets and liabilities will be combined with the existing assets and liabilities of MinnieMax Ltd. at the values agreed on acquisition. No group accounts need to be prepared. Wild Life Holidays Ltd. might continue as a separate company, but has no group relationship with MinnieMax Ltd.

Chapter 11

The holder of 10 per cent of the issued equity share capital of a company has very little power to influence the way that the company is operated or managed. However, equity shares carry certain rights, including the right to attend, and vote at, general meetings.

The auditor's report shows an adverse opinion, declaring that the financial statements 'do not give a true and fair view'. This can have a damaging effect on a company, particularly if the financial statements are being sent to the company's bankers or other lenders. If the directors persist in ignoring the auditor's views, the company's credibility will suffer and there is also the possibility that creditors and lenders might see it as a bad risk.

Lottie should attend the AGM, and should both speak and vote against the resolution. If she can persuade the other shareholders to vote against the resolution, the accounts will have to be redrawn so that an unqualified audit report can be given.

In failing to provide for the legal settlement, the directors are ignoring the accrual concept, which states that *all* relevant information must be included within the financial statements, regardless of whether cash has been paid or received in respect of the transaction.

Chapter 12

Detailed numerical analysis of Wild Life Holidays Ltd.

(a) Horizontal and numerical analysis: profit and loss account

Wild Life Holidays Ltd.							
Profit and loss account			Horizontal	Vertical		Trend	
Year ended 31 August	**2004**	**2003**		2004	2003	2004	2003
	£000s	£000s	%	%	%		
Turnover	2,600	2,800	−7.14	100	100	93	100
Less cost of sales	−2,200	−2,250	−2.22	−84.62	−80.36	98	100
Gross profit	400	550	−27.27	15.38	19.64	73	100
Distribution costs	−10	−10	0.00	−0.38	−0.36	100	100
Administrative expenses	−95	−85	11.76	−3.65	−3.04	112	100
Other operating income and expenditure	−5	−15	−66.67	−0.19	−0.54	33	100
Profit on ordinary activities before interest and taxation	290	440	−34.09	11.15	15.71	66	100
Interest receivable	10	25	−60.00	0.38	0.89	40	100
Interest payable and similar charges	−50	−30	66.67	−1.92	−1.07	167	100
Profit on ordinary activities before taxation	250	435	−42.53	9.62	15.54	57	100
Taxation	−70	−120	−41.67	−2.69	−4.29	58	100
Profit for the financial year	180	315	−42.86	6.92	11.25	57	100
Dividends	−120	−120	0.00	−4.62	−4.29	100	100
Profit retained for the financial year	60	195	−69.23	2.31	6.96	31	100

(b) Horizontal and numerical analysis: balance sheet

Wild Life Holidays Ltd.			Horizontal	Vertical		Trend	
Balance sheet as at 31 August	**2004**	**2003**		2004	2003	2004	2003
	£000s	£000s	%	%	%		
Fixed assets							
Tangible assets	4,500	3,300	36.36	128.57	116.20	136	100
Current assets							
Stocks	4	4	0.00	0.11	0.14	100	100
Debtors due within one year	105	120	−12.50	3.00	4.23	88	100
Cash at bank and in hand	5	20	−75.00	0.14	0.70	25	100
	114	144	−20.83	3.26	5.07	79	100

Creditors due within one year	−414	−104	298.08	−11.83	−3.66	398	100
Net current liabilities (2003: assets)	−300	40	−850.00	−8.57	1.41	−750	100
Total assets less current liabilities	4,200	3,340	25.75	120.00	117.61	126	100
Creditors due after more than one year	−700	−500	40.00	−20.00	−17.61	140	100
Total net assets	3,500	2,840	23.24	100.00	100.00	123	100
Capital and reserves							
Called-up share capital	2,000	1,600	25.00	57.14	56.34	125	100
Share premium account	1,000	800	25.00	28.57	28.17	125	100
Profit and loss account	500	440	13.64	14.29	15.49	114	100
Equity shareholders' funds	3,500	2,840	23.24	100.00	100.00	123	100

(c) Horizontal and numerical analysis: cash flow statement

Wild Life Holidays Ltd.							
Cash flow statement	2004	2003	Horizontal	Vertical		Trend	
Year ended 31 August	£000s	£000s		2004	2003	2004	2003
			%	%	%		
Net cash inflow from operating activities	**403**	**72**	459.72	100	100	560	100
Returns on investments and servicing of finance							
Interest received	12	18	−33.33	2.98	25.00	67	100
Interest paid	−40	−25	60.00	−9.93	−34.72	160	100
	−28	**−7**	300.00	−6.95	−9.72	400	100
Taxation	**−120**	**−80**	50.00	−29.78	−111.11	150	100
Capital expenditure and financial investment							
Payments to acquire tangible fixed assets	−1,100	−140	685.71	−272.95	−194.44	786	100
Receipts from sales of fixed assets	150	20	650.00	37.22	27.78	750	100
	−950	**−120**	691.67	−235.73	−166.67	792	100
Equity dividends paid	**−120**	**−100**	20.00	−29.78	−138.89	120	100
Net cash outflow before financing	**−815**	**−235**	246.81	−202.23	−326.39	347	100
Financing							
Issue of ordinary share capital	600	100	500.00	148.88	138.89	600	100
New long-term loans	200	50	300.00	49.63	69.44	400	100
	800	**150**	433.33	198.51	208.33	533	100
Decrease in cash	**−15**	**−85**	−82.35	−3.72	−118.06	18	100

(d) Ratio analysis

Ratios		2004	2003
Profitability group			
ROCE (return on capital employed)	$\dfrac{\text{Operating profit before interest and tax}}{\text{Share capital} + \text{Reserves} + \text{Long-term loans}}$	$\dfrac{290}{4,200} = 6.90\%$	$\dfrac{440}{3,340} = 13.17\%$
Gross margin (or gross profit margin)	$\dfrac{\text{Gross profit}}{\text{Turnover}}$	$\dfrac{400}{2,600} = 15.38\%$	$\dfrac{550}{2,800} = 19.64\%$

Mark-up	$\dfrac{\text{Gross profit}}{\text{Cost of goods sold}}$	$\dfrac{400}{2,200} = 18.18\%$	$\dfrac{550}{2,250} = 24.44\%$
Net margin (or net profit margin)	$\dfrac{\text{Operating profit before interest and tax}}{\text{Turnover}}$	$\dfrac{290}{2,600} = 11.15\%$	$\dfrac{440}{2,800} = 15.71\%$
Efficiency group			
Fixed assets turnover	$\dfrac{\text{Turnover}}{\text{Fixed assets at net book value}}$	$\dfrac{2,600}{4,500} = 0.58$ times	$\dfrac{2,800}{3,300} = 0.85$ times
Stock turn	$\dfrac{\text{Closing stock}}{\text{Cost of goods sold}} \times 365$	$\dfrac{1,460}{2,200} = 0.66$ days	$\dfrac{1,460}{2,250} = 0.65$ days
Trade debtors' collection period	$\dfrac{\text{Trade debtors}}{\text{Credit sales}} \times 365$	$\dfrac{31,025}{2,600} = 11.93$ days	$\dfrac{36,500}{2,800} = 13.04$ days
Trade creditors' payment period	$\dfrac{\text{Trade creditors}}{\text{Credit purchases}} \times 365$	$\dfrac{7,300}{2,200} = 3.32$ days	$\dfrac{29,200}{2,250} = 12.98$ days
Short-term solvency and liquidity			
Current ratio (aka 'working capital' ratio)	Current assets : Current liabilities	$\dfrac{114}{414} = 0.28{:}1$	$\dfrac{144}{104} = 1.38{:}1$
Acid test (aka 'quick assets' test)	(Current assets − Stock) : Current liabilities	$\dfrac{110}{414} = 0.27{:}1$	$\dfrac{140}{104} = 1.35{:}1$
Long-term solvency and liquidity			
Gearing	$\dfrac{\text{Long- term loans − Cash and bank balances}}{\text{Share capital + reserves + (long- term loans − cash and bank balances)}}$	$\dfrac{695}{4,195} = 16.57\%$	$\dfrac{480}{3,320} = 14.46\%$
	(or)		
	$\dfrac{\text{Long- term loans − Cash and bank balances}}{\text{Share capital + reserves}}$	$\dfrac{695}{3,500} = 19.86\%$	$\dfrac{480}{2,840} = 14.46\%$
Interest cover	$\dfrac{\text{Profit before interest}}{\text{Interest payable}}$	$\dfrac{290}{50} = 5.80$ times	$\dfrac{440}{30} = 14.67$ times
Investment ratios			
Eps (earnings per share)[a]	$\dfrac{\text{Profit available for ordinary dividend}}{\text{No. of equity shares issued (000s)}}$	$\dfrac{180}{2,000} = 9.0$ p	$\dfrac{315}{1,600} = 19.7$ p
PE (price/earnings)	$\dfrac{\text{(Notional) stock market price}^{a}}{\text{Earnings per share}}$	$\dfrac{90}{9.0} = 10.0$ times	$\dfrac{250}{19.7} = 12.7$ times
Dividend cover	$\dfrac{\text{Profit available to pay dividend}}{\text{Dividends paid and proposed}}$	$\dfrac{180}{120} = 1.5$ times	$\dfrac{315}{120} = 2.6$ times
Dividend yield	$\dfrac{\text{Dividend per share}}{\text{(Notional) stock market price}^{a}}$	$\dfrac{6}{90} = 6.67\%$	$\dfrac{7.50}{250} = 3.00\%$

[a] As the company is not listed on a stock exchange, this is a theoretical price only.

(e) Summary and conclusions

Ratios		Change	Trend (immaterial changes ignored)
Profitability group			
ROCE (return on capital employed)	6.90%	13.17%	⇓
Gross margin (or gross profit margin)	15.38%	19.64%	⇓
Mark-up	18.18%	24.44%	⇓
Net margin (or net profit margin)	11.15%	15.71%	⇓

Efficiency group			
Fixed assets turnover	0.58 times	0.85 times	⇓
Stock turn	0.66 days	0.65 days	—
Trade debtors' collection period	11.93 days	13.04 days	—
Trade creditors' payment period	3.32 days	12.98 days	Faster payment to creditors
Short-term solvency and liquidity			
Current ratio (aka 'working capital' ratio)	0.28 : 1	1.38 : 1	⇓
Acid test (aka 'quick assets' test)	0.27 : 1	1.35 : 1	⇓
Long-term solvency and liquidity			
Gearing	16.57%	14.46%	⇑
Debt/equity	19.86%	16.9%	⇑
Interest cover	5.80 times	14.67 times	⇓
Investment ratios			
Eps (earnings per share)	9.0p	19.7p	⇓
PE (price/earnings)	10.0 times	12.7 times	⇓
Dividend cover	1.5 times	2.6 times	⇓
Dividend yield	6.67%	3.00%	⇑

Note: the companion website includes an Excel spreadsheet showing the above calculations.

Conclusions

By any standard, 2004 has been a poor year for the company. Although the company is still profitable, the horizontal analysis shows significant declines in percentage margins between the two years. In particular, gross profit margin has dropped by 27 per cent, and there has been a 34 per cent drop in profit on the ordinary activities before interest and taxation. Dividend levels have remained constant, which is a positive signal to shareholders, but this has led to a 69 per cent reduction in the profit retained for the financial year. The vertical analysis shows that cost of sales represents £84.60 per £100 sales in 2004 compared with only £80.36 in the previous year. Overall profit before taxation represents only £9.62 in 2004 compared with £15.54 in 2003. The trend analysis shows significant increases in administrative expenses and interest payable.

In the balance sheet, current assets have declined by nearly 21 per cent, but current liabilities have increased by nearly 300 per cent! Long-term creditors have also increased, by 40 per cent. The vertical analysis highlights the increase in tangible assets, but the deterioration in the working capital is also apparent. The trend analysis reveals the major changes in the short-term and long-term creditors, as well as reductions in the debtors.

The analysis of the cash flow statement shows some positive information, as the net cash inflow from operating activities increased by nearly 460 per cent. There had been a major increase in the cash outflow relating to tangible fixed assets during the year, but also the cash inflow relating to financing (issuing share capital and raising a new long-term loan) showed a 433 per cent increase compared with 2003. Overall, there was a relatively immaterial decrease in cash of £15,000 for the year.

All the profitability group ratios are a cause for concern, but there are no major changes in the efficiency ratios (the trade creditors' payment period has fallen considerably, but this may be the result of being offered cash discounts by suppliers). The short-term solvency and liquidity ratios show a major decline during 2004, to a point where the viability of the company must be queried. The acid test for 2004 shows that the company could raise only 27p of quick assets for every £1 of current liabilities, a significant drop from the 1.35 : 1 ratio in the previous year. The gearing has increased, but is still under 20 per cent. Interest cover has worsened. With the exception of dividend yield, the investment ratios for 2004 show a weaker position. As the share price has fallen dramatically, but the dividend levels have been maintained, the yield has more than doubled.

The conclusion is that the company is profitable, but there are major concerns regarding its short-term survival due to its very poor acid test ratio. However, its gearing ratio is quite low and there may be the prospect of further borrowings secured against the increased value of the tangible fixed assets. The directors of MinnieMax Ltd. could use the weak 2004 results as a bargaining tool to buy the shares of Wild Life Holidays Ltd. at a much reduced level when compared to the notional stock market price.

■ REVISION BRIEFINGS

If this book is your property, cut out these pages to help with pre-examination revision

Chapter 1

- Accounting is defined as: 'The process of identifying, measuring, and communicating economic information about an organization or other entity, in order to permit informed judgements by users of the information.'
- There are two main branches: financial accounting and management accounting. Financial accounting concentrates more on the recording and summarizing of financial information and compliance with GAAP and relevant legislation. Management accounting tends to concentrate on decision making, planning, and control.
- There is a 'Statement of Principles' for the preparation and presentation of financial statements.
- There are seven user groups defined in the Statement: investors; lenders; suppliers and other trade creditors; employees; customers; government and their agencies; the public.
- Qualitative characteristics of financial information are that it should be: material; relevant; reliable; comparable; understandable.
- Policies are needed which enable a true and fair view to be shown.
- Going concern and accruals concepts have a 'pervasive role' in selecting policies.
- Published accounts in the EU must follow defined formats.
- International accounting practices vary but there is great impetus towards harmonization.
- US accounting scandals have boosted the influence of international standards.

Chapter 2

- Businesses need to have a logical system to record financial transactions.
- The double-entry bookkeeping system is the basis of accounting information systems.
- Transactions are broken down into the effect they have on five key categories: Revenue Income, Revenue Expenditure, Assets, Liabilities, and Capital.
- Accounting formulae are used to establish overall profit or loss and the value of capital at a specific moment in time.
- Transactions are first recorded in books of prime entry.
- The double-entry is completed when information is entered in the general ledger.
- The trial balance checks whether the debit entries equal the credit entries. If they don't agree, then something must be wrong in the system.

Chapter 3

- A business's financial period can be of any length, but 'final accounts' usually cover a twelve-month period.

- The Statement of Principles requires that the accrual basis of accounting be used when producing a profit and loss account and balance sheet.
- Accruals, prepayments, provisions, and unsold stocks must be taken into account when preparing the profit and loss account and balance sheet.
- The trial balance is the starting point for preparing the profit and loss account and balance sheet.
- Partnerships and limited liability forms of business organization have various advantages and disadvantages when compared to sole traders.
- Partnerships and limited companies will require further information to be shown in the profit and loss account and balance sheet when compared to sole traders' final accounts.

Chapter 4

- Profit and loss account might also be called 'statement of income' or 'statement of operations'.
- Revenue should only be recognized once the company has a right to be paid.
- A *group* profit and loss account combines the results of a parent company and its subsidiaries.
- Profits or losses on long-term contracts can be recognized as the contract term progresses.
- Information relating to performance in the main classes of business and geographical areas must be disclosed in a segmental analysis.
- Gross profit is the difference between the value of the company's sales and its cost of sales.
- Operating costs are usually divided between distribution costs and administrative expenses.
- Operating profit is the profit left after operating costs have been deducted from the gross profit, plus any sundry income.
- The results of continuing, discontinued, and acquired business operations should be disclosed separately.
- Exceptional items can be disclosed separately, but are still included within the overall calculation of the operating profit or loss.
- Any profit or loss from associated undertakings or joint ventures must be disclosed separately on the face of the profit and loss account.
- Goodwill amortization is usually included as part of the operating costs, unless it relates to joint ventures, in which case it is adjusted against any profit or loss arising from that joint venture.

Chapter 5

- Interest payable includes the finance charges relating to leasing and hire purchase contracts.
- The taxation on the profits of sole traders and partnerships is a personal liability of the owners, but as a limited liability company has separate legal identity from its owners, the company itself is responsible for its taxation liability.
- The taxation charge shown in a company profit and loss account usually comprises two elements, the *current* tax charge and a *deferred* tax charge.
- Accounting profit is not usually the same as taxable profit.
- Any minority interests must be recognized within the profit and loss account.
- Dividend policy varies from company to company: directors in low-geared companies tend to have more flexibility in comparison with high-geared ones.

- Interim dividends are paid part-way through the financial period, but final dividends can only be paid after shareholders give their approval at the annual general meeting.
- Companies may provide a statement of total recognized gains and losses and a note of historical cost profits and losses in some situations.
- Earnings per share figures are used to calculate the PE ratio, which is a widely used indicator of a company's stock market performance. If there is the possibility of the company issuing more shares at a later date due to its having issued stock options or convertible loan stock then a diluted eps figure must also be calculated.

Chapter 6

- For a group of companies, two balance sheets are presented within its annual report: the consolidated (group) balance sheet and the parent company's own balance sheet.
- Debts between companies of the same group are eliminated when preparing the group balance sheet.
- In some countries, balance sheets are shown in a two-sided format, with assets on one side and capital and liabilities on the other.
- The balance sheet does not show the current value of the company—it shows the value in the company's own accounting records.
- Some assets might not be included in the balance sheet as they are incapable of object valuation. One example is goodwill generated *internally* by the company, the value of which has never been 'tested' by being sold.
- Balance sheet assets are divided between fixed (which might be either tangible or intangible) and current.
- The useful life of goodwill does not normally exceed twenty years and will be amortized. In the UK however, goodwill might have an *indefinite* useful life, in which case no amortization is needed but extensive information must be given.
- Fixed assets must be reviewed for impairment on a regular basis.
- Research and development costs are usually written off in the profit and loss account. In exceptional cases, development costs may be treated as a deferred asset on the balance sheet, with amortization starting when commercial production commences.
- Freehold land is the only type of tangible asset that is not normally depreciated.
- Some countries allow companies to revalue assets, in which case a revaluation reserve would be created, and the asset values (usually land and buildings) increased or decreased accordingly.
- Leases are divided into two classifications, operating and finance. A company leasing assets under an operating lease shows rental payments in the profit and loss account, but under a finance lease it would show the asset on the balance sheet together with the liability to the lessor. Future accounting standards are likely to require all leased assets to be included on the balance sheet.
- Current assets are likely to change in value within a year from the balance sheet date. In practice, their value might change many thousands of times during the course of the financial period.
- The amount of stocks and debtors held at the end of the financial period are key indicators of the efficiency of the company.
- 'Just in time' (JIT) stock supply systems are used increasingly by companies who want to keep their own stock to a minimum and put the responsibility for stock control onto their suppliers.

Chapter 7

- Liabilities are divided between those due within one year and those due after more than one year.
- The taxation charge shown in the profit and loss account is unlikely to be the same as the liability shown under current liabilities.
- The dividend owing at the balance sheet date is likely to be the final, proposed dividend.
- Loans might be secured on a fixed or floating charge against asset values.
- 'Net current assets' is also known as 'working capital'.
- Debentures are also known as *bonds* and usually carry a fixed interest rate.
- Closing provisions relating to depreciation or doubtful debts are deducted from the related assets, but other provisions, such as for deferred taxation or pension liabilities, will be shown separately.
- Pension schemes may be either *defined contribution schemes* or *defined benefit schemes*.
- Contingent liabilities and gains must be considered, and any material capital commitments shown.

Chapter 8

- Called-up share capital is the nominal value of all shares, equity and non-equity.
- Public companies can sell shares directly by an offer for sale, or indirectly through a placing.
- Non-equity shares might be redeemable or convertible into equity shares.
- The value of share capital might be increased by new share issues, rights issues, and stock conversions.
- The number of shares might also be increased by bonus issues and share splits.
- The value of share capital might be decreased by buy-backs or redemptions.
- The number of shares might also be decreased by share consolidations.
- Companies might give stock options as an incentive to directors and employees.
- Reserves might be non-distributable (capital reserves) or distributable (revenue reserves).
- Reserves can be reduced or eliminated by being used for bonus issues.

Chapter 9

- A cash flow statement summarizes cash inflows and outflows over the financial period.
- Profitable businesses may fail due to poor liquidity.
- Cash flows are organized under several key headings to make the statement more meaningful.
- Operating profit is converted into a cash flow figure by adjusting for the effects of depreciation, unsold stock, debtors, and creditors.
- Analysts must monitor the net cash flows over several accounting periods, particularly if net cash outflows are reported on a regular basis.

Chapter 10

- Parent–subsidiary group structures can be advantageous for companies as they enable separate boards of directors to be established and give some financial protection if a subsidiary company fails.

- There are various ways in which groups can be structured, and sometimes companies only take over the net assets of another business, without creating a subsidiary.

- Minority shareholdings will exist if less than 100 per cent of the subsidiary's shares are owned by the parent.

- The parent–subsidiary relationship depends upon either the proportion of shares owned (over 50 per cent) or whether the parent has a 'dominant influence' on the subsidiary.

- Acquisition accounting is used to consolidate the results of a parent and its subsidiaries: all the income, expenditure, assets, and liabilities are combined, subject to adjustments for intra-group trading, minority interests, and goodwill arising on consolidation. Pre-acquisition reserves are excluded from the total of group reserves.

- Associated companies are established where an investing company owns between 20 per cent and 50 per cent of shares in another company and is subject to 'significant influence'. The equity method of consolidation is used, where only the investor's share of the associate's results are included in the group profit and loss account, and its share of the net assets plus undistributed profits is shown on the group balance sheet.

- Joint ventures exist when two or more businesses jointly control a business enterprise. Similar accounting treatment to associates, but with additional disclosures.

- Shareholdings of up to 20 per cent without 'significant influence' are treated as simple investments. Dividend income is shown in the group profit and loss account, and the cost or valuation of the shares is shown as an asset on the group balance sheet.

- Related parties are those organizations or individuals who have some influence on the operating or financial policies of the business. In most cases, the consolidated financial statements reflect the transactions with related parties, but occasionally further transactions occur which must be revealed to users of the statements.

Chapter 11

- The annual report is the key communication that a limited company has with its shareholders. Interim reports are published either half-yearly or quarterly.

- Some parts of the annual report are required by statute, others by accounting or stock exchange regulations, and there may also be voluntary disclosure of information.

- Many companies publish an 'operating and financial review' which gives an objective commentary on the company's performance.

- Most large companies have an audit committee, whose primary responsibilities include monitoring the system of internal control, approving the company's accounting policies, and reviewing the interim and annual financial statements before their submission to the main board of directors.

- Independent, qualified accountants act as external auditors, reporting to the shareholders as to whether or not the financial statements show a true and fair view. The auditors' report might be either unqualified or qualified.

- Annual and extraordinary general meetings are held so that shareholders can vote on company resolutions. Examples of such resolutions include the approval of a dividend and the election or re-election of directors.

- Financial summaries showing the financial highlights of several years are often provided within the annual report, but they are unaudited and the company itself selects the information to be included.

Chapter 12

- There are three stages to the analysis of a company's results: preliminary research, horizontal, vertical, and trend analysis, and ratio analysis.
- Preliminary research investigates the company's background, including what it does, who manages it, and where it sells its products or services.
- Horizontal analysis is a percentage analysis showing the change between the current and previous year's figures.
- Vertical analysis is an analysis showing the percentage that each item comprises in each year, related to a key component of that statement.
- Trend analysis uses one year as the base year, and shows subsequent years in relation to that base year.
- Ratio analysis looks at five key areas for analysis: profitability, efficiency, long- and short-term liquidity and solvency, and investors' ratios.
- Information must be summarized, and a suitable overall conclusion drawn.
- Consideration must be given to concerns about the basic validity of the information contained within annual reports.
- Table of ratios:

Group	Name of ratio	Formula[a]	Expressed as:
Profitability	ROCE (return on capital employed)[a]	$\dfrac{\text{Operating profit before interest and tax}}{\text{Share capital} + \text{Reserves} + \text{Long-term loans}}$	%
	Gross margin (or gross profit margin)	$\dfrac{\text{Gross profit}}{\text{Turnover}}$	%
	Mark-up	$\dfrac{\text{Gross profit}}{\text{Cost of goods sold}}$	%
	Net margin (or net profit margin)	$\dfrac{\text{Operating profit before interest and tax}}{\text{Turnover}}$	%
Efficiency	Fixed assets turnover	$\dfrac{\text{Turnover}}{\text{Fixed assets at net book value}}$	multiple
	Stock turn	$\dfrac{\text{Stock (average or closing)}}{\text{Cost of goods sold}} \times 365$	days
	Trade debtors' collection period	$\dfrac{\text{Trade debtors (average or closing)}}{\text{Credit sales}} \times 365$	days
	Trade creditors' payment period	$\dfrac{\text{Trade creditors (average or closing)}}{\text{Credit purchases}} \times 365$	days
Short-term solvency and liquidity	Current ratio (aka 'working capital' ratio)	Current assets : Current liabilities	ratio
	Acid test (aka 'quick assets' test)	(Current assets − Stock) : Current liabilities	ratio
Long-term solvency and liquidity	Gearing[a]	$\dfrac{\text{Long-term loans} - \text{cash and bank balances}}{\text{Share capital} + \text{reserves} + (\text{long-term loans} - \text{cash and bank balances})}$	%
	Interest cover	$\dfrac{\text{Profit before interest}}{\text{Interest payable}}$	multiple
Investment ratios	Eps (earnings pence per per share)[a]	$\dfrac{\text{Profit available for ordinary dividend}}{\text{No. of equity shares issued}}$	share
	PE (price/earnings)	$\dfrac{\text{Stock market price}}{\text{Earnings per share}}$	multiple
	Dividend cover	$\dfrac{\text{Profit available to pay divdend}}{\text{Dividens paid and proposed}}$	multiple
	Dividend yield	$\dfrac{\text{Dividend per share}}{\text{Market price per share}}$	%

[a] There are alternative formulae which might be used in these cases, explained when discussing each ratio in the chapter.

■ INDEX